THE DAWNING OF WISDOM

Other Theosophy Trust Books

Wisdom in Action
Essays on the Spiritual Life
by Raghavan Iyer

Teachers of the Eternal Doctrine
From Tsong-Ka-Pa to Nostradamus
by Elton Hall

Symbols of the Eternal Doctrine
From Shamballa to Paradise
by Helen Valborg

The Key to Theosophy
An Exposition of the
Ethics, Science, and Philosophy
by H. P. Blavatsky

Evolution and Intelligent Design
in *The Secret Doctrine*
The Synthesis of Science, Religion and Philosophy
by H.P. Blavatsky
compiled by The Editorial Board of Theosophy Trust

THE DAWNING
OF WISDOM

ESSAYS ON WALKING THE PATH

BY

RAGHAVAN IYER

COMPILED BY
THE EDITORIAL BOARD OF THEOSOPHY TRUST

THEOSOPHY TRUST BOOKS
WASHINGTON, D.C.

The Dawning of Wisdom
Essays on Walking the Path

Copyright © March 10, 2007 by Theosophy Trust

All rights reserved. No part of this book may be used or reproduced by any means - graphic, electronic, or mechanical - including photocopying, recording, taping or by any information storage retrieval system without the written permission of the publisher, except in the case of brief quotations embodied in critical articles and reviews.

Theosophy Trust books may be ordered through BookSurge, Amazon.com, and other booksellers, or by visiting:

http://www.theosophytrust.org/online_books.php

ISBN 978-0-9793205-0-7
ISBN 0-9793205-0-X

Library of Congress Control Number 2007901071

Printed in the United States of America

Dedicated To
Spiritual Aspirants
All Over The Earth
That The Dawn Of Wisdom
May Arrive Swiftly

KRISHNA:

A man is said to be confirmed in spiritual knowledge when he forsaketh every desire which entereth into his heart, and of himself is happy and content in the Self through the Self. His mind is undisturbed in adversity; he is happy and contented in prosperity, and he is a stranger to anxiety, fear, and anger. Such a man is called a Muni. When in every condition he receives each event, whether favorable or unfavorable, with an equal mind which neither likes nor dislikes, his wisdom is established, and, having met good or evil, neither rejoiceth at the one nor is cast down by the other. He is confirmed in spiritual knowledge, when, like the tortoise, he can draw in all his senses and restrain them from their wonted purposes. The hungry man loseth sight of every other object but the gratification of his appetite, and when he is become acquainted with the Supreme, he loseth all taste for objects of whatever kind. The tumultuous senses and organs hurry away by force the heart even of the wise man who striveth after perfection. Let a man, restraining all these, remain in devotion at rest in me, his true self; for he who hath his senses and organs in control possesses spiritual knowledge.

The Bhagavad-Gita, Ch. II

CONTENTS

INTRODUCTION xi

EDITOR'S NOTE ON SANSKRIT TERMS xv

THE DAWNING OF WISDOM 1

THE PHILOSOPHY OF PERFECTION 10

AS ABOVE, SO BELOW 23

THE ALLEGORY OF THE CAVE 31

ANAMNESIS 38

SPIRITUAL ATTENTION 49

MENTAL POSTURE 55

THE JOY OF DEVOTION 62

THOUGHTFULNESS 71

SPIRITUAL PERCEPTION 78

THE HERO IN MAN 92

BETWEEN HEAVEN AND EARTH 104

EVOLUTION AND KARMA 119

KARMA AND DESTINY 133

INDIVIDUATION AND INITIATION 142

SELF-TRANSFORMATION 152

EVOLUTION AND CONSCIOUSNESS	164
THE COMMUNITY OF THE FUTURE	171
UNIVERSALITY AND SECTARIANISM	182
THE GOSPEL ACCORDING TO ST. JOHN	203
PURITY AND POLLUTION	218
THE HEALING OF SOULS	230
THE GANDHIAN BRIDGE BETWEEN HEAVEN AND EARTH	245
BUDDHI YOGA AND SVADHARMA	257
BUDDHA AND THE PATH TO ENLIGHTENMENT	270
CHOOSING THE TAO	280
THE ZERO PRINCIPLE	291
DRAWING THE LARGER CIRCLE	302
THEOSOPHICAL GLOSSARY IN BRIEF	311

INTRODUCTION

The spiritually penetrating essays in this volume were written for the expressed purpose of shedding the pristine light of universal Theosophy on the path of spiritual self-regeneration in the service of humanity. The Theosophical philosophy is predicated on the ageless truth that divine wisdom exists, and, most significantly, that wise beings exist who dynamically embody it in world history; that sages and seers still grace the globe and that they continually oversee the spiritual, mental and physical evolution of man and nature. The secret Society of Sages that guides human progress periodically sends forth one of their own to sound afresh the Divine Philosophy and exemplify the spiritual life in all its richness and mystery. Such an enlightened spiritual teacher articulates eternal but forgotten truths in ingenious ways, adopting modalities that inspire the mind, release soul perception, and cut through the froth of history and the miasma of an age. The wisdom-teachings of such a being are essentially "correctives in consciousness" aimed at redirecting our attention from the all-consuming mundane to the hidden, unconscious divinity that exists within but which is temporarily obscured by collective ignorance and chronic perversity. To those individuals who seek a deeper understanding of the problems and prospects of contemporary man, these sublime essays can become therapeutic remedies for the innumerable spiritual, moral, and psychological ills of our time.

These writings – radiant with a cool 'spiritual fire' – were originally talks given by Shri Raghavan Iyer at the United Lodge of Theosophists in Santa Barbara, California between 1969 and 1989. They are pellucid, mantramic expressions of *Theosophia* or divine wisdom – referred to frequently in the journal HERMES as *Brahma Vach*. They sparkle with deep *logoic* brilliance and reveal a consciousness attuned to the "great heart and mind of all mankind". These talks were not given simply for the benefit of a particular group or Lodge – however noble – nor were they presented for present humanity alone, but were sacrificially invoked for the humanities yet to come. Like any Promethean forerunner who deliberately enters into the unfolding historical drama, Shri Raghavan Iyer did more than awaken suffering humanity to the forgotten curatives of the soul and mind. He did more than anticipate the humanity of the future: through the magical power of spiritual sound, he helped to create it.

The wide-ranging articles in this volume span the spectrum of human thought from the metaphysical to the mystical, the ethical to the psychological, the spiritual to the material. They reveal the fundamental basis of religion, philosophy and science. The periodic study of these essays turns us back upon ourselves – in the highest sense – and releases that laser-like insight that allows us to increasingly discern the true, the good, and the beautiful in all known religious teachings, in all available philosophical musings, and in all ancient and modern scientific discoveries. When carefully meditated upon and skillfully applied to the realm of self-chosen duties, they purify the mind, cleanse the heart, and uplift the human condition.

Shri Raghavan Iyer, the transmitter of these marvelous and mysterious teachings, was himself a man of immense magnanimity and unparalleled spiritual genius. Born in Madras, India in 1930, he matriculated at the University of Bombay at the precocious age of fourteen and received his bachelor's degree in economics at age eighteen. Two years later he was selected as the Rhodes Scholar from India. While studying at Oxford University, he actively participated in a variety of august and intellectually engaging societies: the Oxford University Peace Association, the Voltaire Society, the Socratic Society, and the Buddhist Society. He was also the founder of the Plotinus Society and was elected President of the Oxford Union in his final undergraduate year. At age twenty-four he earned first-class honors in Philosophy, Politics and Economics and later was awarded his doctorate in Philosophy.

He was an outstanding teacher of philosophy and politics throughout his public life. He assumed the mantle of teaching at the age of eighteen when he was appointed Fellow and Lecturer at Elphinstone College,

University of Bombay. After completing his bachelor degree at Oxford, he was selected at age twenty-six to be an Oxford don (or tutor) in philosophy and politics. In addition to his tutorials at Oxford, he lectured throughout Europe and also in Africa. His profound insights, sparkling intellectual clarity, mastery of different conceptual languages, and his infectious enthusiasm inspired thousands of students and earned the deep respect of eminent thinkers and professors as diverse as Isaiah Berlin, James Joll, and Houston Smith. After accepting a professorship at the University of California, Santa Barbara in 1965, he taught classes and seminars in political philosophy until his retirement at the age of fifty-six. His introductory classes and graduate seminars were legendary for their philosophical depth, theoretical openness, and visionary richness. They were full of wit as well as wisdom, and they unfailingly inspired students with an abiding confidence in themselves as learners and as viable contributors to the emerging City of Man. His formal lectures as well as innumerable informal gatherings affected generations of students who later inhabited diverse fields of work, worship, and humanitarian service.

In addition to his vast and varied gifts as a teacher, Shri Raghavan Iyer was an eminent international author. His most prominent writings were *The Moral and Political Thought of Mahatma Gandhi* and *Parapolitics – Toward the City of Man*. Written in lucid and impeccable English, each of these remarkable works is accessible to both the profound thinker and the beginning inquirer, the erudite scholar and the dedicated student, the earnest seeker and the committed practitioner. He also edited an extraordinary collection of inspirational readings entitled *The Jewel in the Lotus*, aptly characterized by Professor K. Swaminathan as "a universal bible". In addition, he edited and wrote the introductions for numerous sacred texts, including Hindu, Buddhist, Jain, Jewish, Christian, and Sufi teachings.

Shri Raghavan Iyer became a Theosophist at age ten when his father first took him to the United Lodge of Theosophists in Bombay. There he encountered the profound writings of H.P. Blavatsky – the founder and teacher of the modern Theosophical Movement. Soon after entering the orbit of the Theosophical Movement, he made a sacred resolve to serve the Lodge of Mahatmas and increasingly assumed responsibility for forwarding the impulse of the world-wide Theosophical Cause of promoting universal brotherhood.

As repeatedly witnessed by close students, Shri Raghavan Iyer spoke at many different levels and freely interacted with each and all – regardless of race, creed, or condition. He exemplified – for the sake of the future – a multitude of Aquarian modalities and qualities. He was, in one sense, very Hindu: a true Brahmin – spiritual, cultured, brilliant, full of the graces that immediately remind one of ancient India and of golden ages long past. He was also very English: confident, highly educated, extremely literate and at ease with statesmen, scientists, educators, and royalty. He was also very American: a true and fearless rebel, innovative, resourceful, visionary, and the eternal friend of the common man. Beyond all this, he was in a much deeper sense the Universal Man, original, *sui generis*, and timeless. His sympathies were always compassionately inclusive and his repeated emphasis – from first to last – was to "draw the larger circle" in thought and in act. Shri Iyer died in Santa Barbara, California on June 20, 1995.

The selected essays in this volume – culled from the golden journal *HERMES* – represent the efflorescence of a life-time dedicated to the welfare of the human race, to the great cause of the Theosophical Movement: universal brotherhood. They were written for Everyman and will always benefit the ready and the receptive of whatever race, of whatever religion, and in whatever age.

>Dr. James E. Tepfer
>June 2006
>Santa Barbara, CA

EDITOR'S NOTE ON SANSKRIT TERMS

The observant reader will note in these 28 remarkable essays by Professor Raghavan Iyer the deployment of a vast wealth of intellectual resources drawn from the entire spiritual inheritance of Humanity. There will also be found in these essays an abundance of terms that will be unfamiliar to many readers; a quick count turns up over 300 Sanskrit words that are used frequently enough to be called "significant" to understanding the philosophy of Theosophy that forms the foundation of these writings (not to mention the various Greek terms: *logos, agathon,* etc. – and Hebrew terms: *Ain-Soph, Elohim,* etc.). One may perhaps wonder about the presence of so many Sanskrit words: why use Sanskrit words and not English words? Can these ideas be expressed in simple language, so that the "non-technical" reader can also understand?

The answer to the latter question is simply that the writings in this book, in the journal *HERMES*, as well as the rest of Theosophical literature, deal with a science -the science of spirituality -that, like any of the other modern sciences such as biology, has its own system of thought and a vocabulary that expresses that system. The vocabulary of this spiritual science is as extensive and employs the same level of precision as any modern science. Anyone who wishes to study and understand the science of cellular biology, for example, has to learn at least the basic conceptual vocabulary that describes the components of cells, terms like cytoplasm, mitochondrion, vacuole, organelle, vesicle, plasma membrane, etc., these words incorporate and are a reflection of the conceptual structure of that science. Grasping the core meaning of these concepts and learning their precise applications is an essential part of learning that science.

Similarly, if one wishes to study and understand the science of spirituality -which is as old as thinking man himself -one must become conversant with its terminology, many words of which are Sanskrit: *Atman, Buddhi, Manas, Kama, Linga sarira, Prana, Sthulala sarira,* just to name the terms which describe the components or "principles" of the human being. Each of these terms has a place in the philosophical scheme of the science, as well as a precise application: one does not use 'Atman', or Universal Spirit or Supreme Soul to describe 'Kama ', "Evil desire, lust, volition; the cleaving to existence" (*Theosophical Glossary*). There is a breathtaking wealth of terms in this science that describes everything in the visible and invisible universes, but as many a neophyte in this science has learned at great cost, simply learning the terminology of the science should not be mistaken for "spiritual knowledge". There are, indeed, beings in this world who are knowers of the Atman: they are called in the *Baghavad Gita* and many other places, *Atma-Jnanis*, Knowers of the World Soul, or Knowers of Soul in general. Simply knowing the word Atman and its definition or application obviously does not make one an *Atma-Jnani*. However, moving in the direction of such beings as *Atma-Jnanis* requires that we become aware of their existence, and knowledge of the terminology can help us to do that.

But why use Sanskrit words when many of the readers have never encountered them? There are several very good answers to this question, one of which is quite simple: Sanskrit, like the science of spirituality but unlike the English language, has been in existence for hundreds of thousands of years, and many of its terms are embedded in the myths and sacred writings of ancient peoples who had a remarkable level of knowledge of this science, which is now largely lost to the modern races. These myths and writings are the inheritance and birthright of all of Humanity, and they have been preserved and transmitted over the ages in a form which preserves some of their original meanings. Second, there is the issue of the nature of the Sanskrit language itself. Something of the nature of this language can be glimpsed from the meaning of the original word itself: 'sanskrita', the "well made, refined, or perfected language". In what way is Sanskrit the perfect language? It is said by some wise beings that the very sounds of the language that make up the words reflect the essential nature of the objects (or subjects) to which they refer. This is a subtle point to grasp in its fullness, as it presumes a complex theory of language, but the basic idea is that the words of Sanskrit are not merely arbitrary and conventional referents, but have a more fundamental and intimate connection with the nature of reality.

Third, there is a paucity of terms in the English language that describe the reality of spiritual worlds; this is due to the absence of much spiritual knowledge of the modern Western peoples. Our language reflects that absence. The plain truth is that English does not, in many cases, have equivalent terms for the Sanskrit. For example, the English 'soul' cannot convey the complex of meanings associated with the Sanskrit 'Atma' (Supreme Soul), 'Alaya' (Universal Soul), 'Buddhi' (Spiritual Soul), 'Antaskarana' (the Human Soul), 'Manas' (the Thinking Soul), 'Kama-Manas' (the Animal Soul), and 'Linga sarira' (the Astral Soul). However, the English language has a wonderful flexibility in absorbing new ideas and terms from other cultures; hence, words such as 'karma', 'guru', 'mantra', and 'yoga' have found their way into common usage in the West. In the meeting of English with the rest of the world's cultures, English is enriched and transformed, and along with the language, the spiritual lives of the peoples who use that language are similarly enriched and transformed. Much is to be gained spiritually from this cross-pollination now taking place all over the globe at a pace more rapid than at any previous time in history. One result is the emergence of what Professor Iyer calls, in the essay "Between Heaven and Earth", "Sanskritic English", words from our common language which have been ensouled by their connection with their Sanskrit counterparts.

Finally, it is well to remind ourselves that knowledge of any science worthy of the name is an arduous undertaking; the science of spirituality is no exception. According to *The Voice of the Silence*, the end result of mastery of that science will affect the whole of humanity in no less measure than the achievements of any of the exact materialistic sciences of the past four centuries. Both the end result and the intrinsic value of this work make it for many spiritual aspirants the only undertaking in their lives that really matters.

An abbreviated glossary of about 70 terms is appended to the end of this work; those who want a more comprehensive glossary of terms used in these essays and in Theosophical literature generally would do well to consult H.P. Blavatsky's *The Theosophical Glossary*, which is available on the Internet at http://www.theosophytrust.org/online_books.php (in a free downloadable PDF) and other locations.

Editorial Board
Theosophy Trust
http://www.theosophytrust.org/

THE DAWNING OF WISDOM

'What is it that ever is?' 'Space, the eternal Anupadaka.' 'What is it that ever was?' 'The Germ in the Root.' 'What is it that is ever coming and going?' 'The Great Breath.' 'Then, there are three Eternals?' 'No, the three are one. That which ever is is one, that which ever was is one, that which is ever being and becoming is also one: and this is Space.'

'Explain, oh Lanoo (disciple).' – 'The One is an unbroken Circle (ring) with no circumference, for it is nowhere and everywhere; the One is the boundless plane of the Circle, manifesting a diameter only during the manvantaric periods; the One is the indivisible point found nowhere, perceived everywhere during those periods; it is the Vertical and the Horizontal, the Father and the Mother, the summit and base of the Father, the two extremities of the Mother, reaching in reality nowhere, for the One is the Ring as also the rings that are within that Ring. Light in darkness and darkness in light: the "Breath which is eternal." It proceeds from without inwardly, when it is everywhere, and from within outwardly, when it is nowhere – (i.e., maya, one of the centres). It expands and contracts (exhalation and inhalation).'

The Secret Doctrine, i 11–12

The metaphysical connection between spiritual knowledge and material manifestation is conveyed in the Proem to *The Secret Doctrine* through illustrations from an archaic palm leaf manuscript, ancient beyond reckoning and impermeable to all the elements. On the first leaf of the manuscript there is an immaculate white disk within a dark background. On the second, the immaculate white disk remains on the dark background, but with a central point. The first diagram represents a state which is before the awakening of any universe. It is Cosmos in Eternity, the Ideal Cosmos which is veiled within Ideal Space and endures throughout Ideal Time, or Eternity. It is the Germ in the Root lying within *Anupadaka*, parentless, boundless Space. It is that which ever was, whilst the Great Breath is ever coming and going and Space ever exists. These three are all One in the dawn of differentiation. This pristine state is mirrored in the rising of Venus as Lucifer, the depth of silence which inaugurates each day, analogous to the dawn of a *manvantara*. The dawn of differentiation must be seen in relation to the one circle which is divine unity. The circumference, which is not a fixed line but a metaphysical, fluctuating boundary, is the All-Presence that sets limits upon an entire period of manifestation. The plane of that circle is the universal soul, the *Anima Mundi*, *Alaya*, the *Paramatman*, and every human being is an immortal ray of that ineffable Light.

Divine Wisdom is at the hidden core of all manifestation, and hence one cannot possibly understand nature without seeing it as intelligent, as innately a manifestation of divine Reason. Man as part of nature is richly endowed with creative faculties that are analogous on planes of consciousness with powers and forces in nature. Every human being is ensouled by individuated *Manas*, which affords, through the sum of states of consciousness, an initial representation of universal Mind, in which divine Thought is potentially ever-present. It is the sacred teaching of Krishna and Buddha, Pythagoras and Plato, Christ and Confucius and a galaxy of Teachers throughout history and before recorded history, that every human being is inwardly and inherently capable of spiritual vision. Each person may embrace the whole of manifestation, for the immortal soul is capable of standing outside time, transcending the boundaries of manifestation, reaching beyond the visible universe. Through contemplation, one can come to the very core of one's being and become attuned to the invisible ideal universe in the realm of divine Thought. This teaching implies that all possible knowledge available in principle to any human mind is enshrined in the totality of things. The totality may be compared to the face of the disk, set against the limitless background, symbolizing the fact that myriad universes in all periods of manifestation do not exhaust the potential of the realm of Be-ness or Non-Being.

Each world is an extraordinary mirror of the whole. It is vast, massive, but it is still a fragment, yet within that massive fragment each human being is like a microscopic drop within a cosmic ocean. Within every drop there is the same quintessential life, light and wisdom or energy found in the entire ocean. It is possible for the individual human being self-consciously to become united with the One that is secondless, and from a reflection of which emanates the entire universe during a *Mahamanvantara*. As the Mahatmas teach, "The whole of Nature lies before you, take what you can." Nature is the repository of far more knowledge than human beings are willing or ready to use. Fortunately, it is now widely recognized that human beings use only a minute fraction of the potential energy of the brain. They not only live well within their means, but also live far below their needs. When it comes to creative ideation, human beings are extremely bankrupt, or unduly thrifty.

If pioneering individuals could learn to partake of the generous teaching of *The Secret Doctrine*, making it the basis of their ideation, they would increase the proportion of their available mental energy. They could become more wide awake and more attentive to the secret Wisdom and the compassionate purposes of invisible Nature. By using the teaching they could grasp the hidden logic of the Logos in manifestation. They could come to see in every dawn meditation an archetypal sequence of states of consciousness partly corresponding to the subtle stages of differentiation of the noumenal light in darkness. The phases of dawn meditation correspond to the stages of the dawn of manifestation. Those who make meditation a regular practice come closer to those beings who eternally are awake, the Watchers in the Night of non-manifestation, the Self-Governed Sages, the Mahatmas and the Rishis, who are on a plane that is far removed from that of mundane concerns. The moment of choice has come for many individuals, who must either endure the atrophy of their faculties or become attentive to these immense possibilities. One can begin to use intuition to come closer to the concealed plan, not of every future cosmogony, but to the vast design that is deeply relevant to human evolution. Intuition rapidly soars above the tardy processes of ratiocinative thought. The quickest minds are too slow compared to the speed of the laser beam of the light of intuition, the light of Hermes. Hermes-Mercury takes the slowest minds and gives to them self-training through meditation, so that *Buddhi* may be activated from a germ and surely develop into that pure light of intuition which is the essential basis of all knowledge.

Any real awakening of the Buddhic light is inevitably connected with the breathing – spiritual, mental and heart breathing, as well as the physical breathing – of every human being. The profound Catechism in the Proem, in setting forth the cosmic nature of breath, distinguishes between two archetypal modes in all manifestation. The Great Breath either proceeds from without inwardly when it is everywhere, or from within outwardly when it is nowhere. This may be understood in relation to human nature by considering the cosmic origins of the quintessentially human faculty of *Manas*:

> Whatever the views of physical Science upon the subject, Occult Science has been teaching for ages that A'kasa – of which Ether is the grossest form – the fifth universal Cosmic Principle (to which corresponds and from which proceeds human Manas) is, cosmically, a radiant, cool, diathermanous plastic matter, creative in its physical nature, correlative in its grossest aspects and portions, immutable in its higher principles. In the former condition it is called the Sub-Root; and in conjunction with radiant heat, it recalls 'dead worlds to life.' In its higher aspect it is the Soul of the World; in its lower – the DESTROYER.
>
> *The Secret Doctrine, i 13*

If, while breathing, one thinks of the One Source of the One Light, this will alter the quality of breathing by taking the grosser exhalation and using it to destroy that which needs to be destroyed, simultaneously taking the subtler inhalation and using it to rejuvenate. What has become dormant or is dying in one's subtler thought-forms will be called back to life. This is just the initial step. Next, a pause, or retention, between inhalation and exhalation is introduced to make it a three-in-one, corresponding to the macrocosmic Breath:

> *Hiranyagarbha, Hari,* and *Sankara* – the three hypostases of the manifesting 'Spirit of the Supreme Spirit' (by which title Prithivi – the Earth – greets Vishnu in his first Avatar) – are the purely metaphysical abstract qualities of formation, preservation, and destruction, and are the three divine Avasthas (lit. hypostases) of that which 'does not perish with created things' (or Achyuta, a name of Vishnu).
>
> *The Secret Doctrine, i 18–19*

Of the three, inhalation, retention and exhalation, the middle would be the most crucial because it will enable one to slow down and suspend inhalation and exhalation, keeping them from becoming chaotic and spasmodic. When one has begun to do this, one will soon find that it cannot really be done on a continuous basis without working causally upon one's mental breathing. This means that when a thought is going out and before a thought rushes in, one must pause. This is a most precise and radical mode of "deliberation". It may be put in the form of a simple injunction: *Think before you speak*. If one really thinks before speaking, if one thinks before choosing a line of action, it will certainly steady the mental breathing and thereby steady the mind. This is truly helpful to others because, as one gains a measure of serenity or stillness, one can become a source of benediction to those who come into one's sphere of influence.

The implications of this ancient teaching for the distant future are suggested in a statement following the Catechism, indicating that there are seven cosmic elements. Four of them are physical, and the fifth, which may provisionally be called ether, is a semi-material aspect of *Akasa* corresponding to *Manas* and critical to the relationship of thought and breathing, as well as to the further incarnation of *Manas*. Those who have refined their sense-perceptions will show this by the way they handle all objects, through the manner in which they eat, breathe, listen and watch. During World War II, resisters like Sartre recognized that something they had always taken for granted, the privilege of thinking, became very precious because of the Gestapo. Solzhenitzen states in *The First Circle* that when prisoners find that everything has been taken away from them, they suddenly experience freedom, the sheer joy of thinking. Many people would rather not think but merely emote, cerebrate and react passively. Once one develops a taste for such mindless activity, deep thinking becomes painful. It is like having one's teeth ground, since it will break down the incrustations of half-chewed and half-dead ideas that have settled down like a crust. Thinking forces these to be broken up because they have got to be eliminated. How much this will have to be done will depend upon the degree of damage already done by the crust. The mind can be always revivified by turning to seminal ideas which, like the rain on parched soil, will quicken germs of living seeds of regenerative truths. The plant of *Manas* will begin to take root. Long before it becomes a tree, it will release the fire of creative thought, making it a thrill to create by the power of ideation. Those who begin to do this are going to find that they are also tapping a subtler realm of matter. One cannot separate thought from matter, subject from object. To really think is to tap subtler life-atoms in one's vestures, and that means also to become more receptive and attentive to subtler life-atoms in visible forms, prepared to design new structures. This is necessary for *Manas* to incarnate further.

H.P. Blavatsky said in the nineteenth century that the Aquarian Age will bring about a lot of psychological disturbances. These arise in the vestures because of the unwillingness to let go of what is dead or dying. Many human beings have a morbid love of decay and are threatened by the Ray, terrified of living seeds. They are so fond of the husk that they have forgotten what the germ is like. The husk of indigestible, decaying ideas prevents the living wheat germ of spiritual ideas from giving birth to new thought-forms. Individuals who cannot do this now will have to do it by the end of the Fourth Round, because the great moment of choice must come finally in the Fifth. This is far in the future, but even the highest two elements, the sixth and the seventh, which are now far beyond the range of human perception, will be sensed during the Sixth and Seventh Races of this Round, though they will not become known to all until the Sixth and Seventh Rounds. They will be aroused partially and by anticipation in the Sixth and Seventh Sub-Races of the Fifth Root Race. Those of the Fifth Sub-Race who are touched by the current of the Sixth Sub-Race with the help of Teachers using the seventh principle, the *Atman*, will be able to germinate living seeds of creative thought. This will enable them to serve in future civilizations in those arenas where the seed-bearers, the vanguard of human growth, will be vitally active. Those who cannot keep pace will incarnate in those portions of the earth where slower moving structures carry on the work of evolution. Evolution takes care of everyone. There is a joy and a thrill in activating *Manas*, the power of abstract ideation, with the help of seminal spiritual ideas and laying down fertile seeds of self-regenerating modes of thought and patterns of living.

The Third Root Race was characterized by an effortless sense of universal unity and brotherhood. The whole of humanity was of one lip, one language, one religion, one race and this was the Golden Age, though there have also been minor golden ages. For the mystic the golden age is ever present. The golden age for the whole of humanity would correspond to the dawn of differentiation, the descent of the gods and the awakening of the fire of self-consciousness.

> 'Fire and Flame destroy the body of an Arhat, their essence makes him immortal.' (*Bodhi-Mur*, Book II.) 'The knowledge of the absolute Spirit, like the effulgence of the sun, or like heat in fire, is naught else than the absolute Essence itself,' says Shankaracharya. IT – is 'the Spirit of the Fire,' not fire itself; therefore, 'the attributes of the latter, heat or flame, are not the attributes of the Spirit, but of that of which that Spirit is the unconscious cause'.
>
> *The Secret Doctrine*, i 6

The Spirit gave birth to self-consciousness in the Third Root Race in a paradisaic state characterized by Plato in the *Statesman* as the Age of Kronos. Since that was an epoch of human solidarity and universal brotherhood, it is hardly surprising that it was marked by effortless devotion.

Devotion is the highest of human qualities. Devotion sustains the universe through that mysterious and irresistible force of mother love, which no psychologist, no misanthrope, has yet been able to destroy. The human babe, unlike animal offspring, is very vulnerable; it will not survive without solicitude. The infant is vulnerable especially in that tender spot on the head which should not be touched. The protective power of mother love makes human evolution possible. It also provides proof, if proof were needed, that devotion is the most natural human quality. Those people who find mental prostration or devotion unnatural are themselves unnatural. Love of parents and of children, love of brothers and sisters, respect for elders, devotion to teachers: this is what is natural. Anything else is unnatural and will be wiped out because there is no room for it in human evolution. H.P. Blavatsky states in *The Secret Doctrine* that the Hindu heart is the most devoted, and also that the Hindu mind is the most metaphysical, readily able to visualize the abstract. To contemplate the abstract and also cherish the deepest feelings is indeed to approximate the paradigm of the Golden Age of the Third Root Race when the fire of self-consciousness was lit. These excellences are essential to the humanity of the future, the civilization of tomorrow. The Theosophical Movement, under the guidance of the Brotherhood of Bodhisattvas, offers every human being the golden opportunity to develop the devotional heart and to engage in the meditation of the abstract mind that is capable of lighting the fire of self-consciousness. The Bodhisattvas ceaselessly sacrifice so that every soul may make the effort to come out of the cold gloom of sick egotistic fear for its own salvation, become free from obsession with the shadow caused by self-hatred, and enter the light of the Spiritual Sun.

If the potency of the Third Root Race vibration were used in concert with *Manas*, the active power of the Fifth Root Race, and the latter became the servant of spiritual intuition, a very fruitful combination would result, whereby the Sixth corresponding to the Third through the Fifth is able to alchemize the Fourth. What is fundamental is what is beyond every series, the Self-existent, the Seventh, which gives life-energy to the First, the temple of the Divine, wherein lies the holy of holies. Deep reflection upon these themes can be enriched by meditation upon the basic symbols taken from the ancient palm leaf manuscript: the plain disk, the disk with the point, the disk with the diameter and the disk with the cross. The mundane cross marks the point where humanity reached the Third Root Race. In the Fourth Race it became the cross without the circle, although among the spiritually wise the loss of the Divine Eye implicit in this separation did not occur.

The Egyptian *Tau* cross, which later became the sign of Venus and also the swastika, Thor's hammer or the Hermetic cross, is a most profound symbol. Originally it was the Jaina cross, the swastika within a circle or Thor's hammer within a circle, called the *Tau*. In meditating upon these sacred glyphs, the third *Stanza* would be most helpful. The difference between the first *Stanza*, the state of the One All during non-manifestation, and the second – which is almost indistinguishable from the first except to the most intuitive – would be like the difference between the first and the second months of pregnancy. The third *Stanza* depicts the reawakening of the universe to life after *pralaya*. After each terrestrial dawn every morning, there is a reawakening of the universe, a new birth or micro-*manvantara*. Each night is like the night of non-manifestation, a micro-*pralaya*, to be inevitably followed by the reawakening to life of the universe of monads. The third *Stanza* refers to the emergence of monads from their state of absorption within the One. Analogically on earth, human monads would be absorbed within the One in *sushupti* during sleep. The first stage is analogous to the seventh, which is why the Self-Governed Sage is sometimes compared to a newborn babe. But whereas the babe utters the AUM and then forgets it, the Sage ever remains in the AUM.

The term 'monad' may apply equally to the vastest solar system or to the tiniest atom. The most self-conscious monads enjoy fellowship with the entire solar system, with all other monads as well as with the tiniest atoms. When the Sage is teaching disciples, he is not addressing them as personalities, but is adjusting their life-atoms and affecting their *sushupti*. He is not talking to the lower mind, but pushing it out, freeing the higher mind in its descent. He is awakening the *Buddhi*. The difference between the Third Root Race and the Fifth is that the former intuitively knew this to be true. In the Aquarian Age, which has entered its second degree, Fifth Race laggards can self-consciously re-enact what was intuitively known by all in the Third Root Race. Self-consciously they could come together and learn from the Teachings of Sages, thereby altering their modes of breathing and becoming a help rather than a hindrance, not only to each other, but also to all living beings on earth.

Hermes, February 1980

THE PHILOSOPHY OF PERFECTION

The philosophy of perfection centres upon a constellation of important ideas which can be clarified by distinguishing between three levels of reflection. First are those considerations that turn upon the relativity of perfection as a concept in the realm of time and in the world of the visible. Secondly, there are other factors which focus upon what may be called the engine or motivating power which actually makes perfection not just a concept, but a driving force in human life and evolution. The elements in this engine – imagination, illumination and devotion – all participate in the problems of relativity which arise in reference to the concept of perfection and require a philosophy or metaphysics to put in perspective. Thirdly, there are those transcendental virtues (*paramitas*) that refer to perfection in its deepest and highest aspect: perfection in spiritual wisdom. In *The Voice of the Silence* the Teacher speaks of "the great Perfections three". These are like three degrees in the attainment of spiritual wisdom.

To take the simplest level first, 'perfection' as a term is always relative. It is relative to a context, relative to standards set or recognized as relevant. It is also relative to expectations, and so to the dynamic and painful, contradictory and compelling, pattern of human relationships. A great deal of misdirected energy goes into perfecting other people, coupled with a refusal to learn anything at all, let alone to be told anything by anyone else. This involves something tricky and even treacherous, which has a lot to do with perfectionism, fussiness and sheer bloody-mindedness. Such perfectionism, indeed, has given the very notion of perfection a bad name, making it static and tyrannical, and making the notion of perfectibility seem at best a fantasy myth in politics. No wonder, then, it is the prevailing fashion among right-wing thinkers to turn their noses against perfectibility; though few Americans would have the courage to turn their noses directly against the Founding Fathers, they will readily turn their noses against their ideas – all in the name of being Americans. This has happened before. It happened in reference to Buddha. It happened in reference to Christ. It happened, to a lesser extent, in reference to earlier Teachers like Krishna and later Teachers like Pythagoras. It certainly happened a great deal in reference to Confucius, a fact central to the history of China.

If the word 'perfect' is used in a relative sense, it is most meaningful when talking about the perfection of a skill or a function. Everyone can understand a functional view of perfection: mastering a craft or a musical instrument, or else summoning a certain speed, smoothness or efficiency, as when one sits before a typewriter and aims at a certain standard of perfection. This idea, however, has been infected in the modern age with a spurious precision that arises entirely out of quantification. This approach is perfectly meaningful, though somewhat illusive, at the cosmic level, but when translated into machines it gives one a mechanistic view of robotic perfection. This can enormously oppress a whole nation, such as Japan, which has become the latest entrant in the appallingly perverse drift towards mechanization in the name of progress.

Such a mechanized and quantified notion of perfection, connected with the use of machines, may allow one to speak of perfectly smooth-running machines or perfect computers. But this notion has spread so far that some people have forgotten about the deeper organic meaning of perfection, as, for example, when it is applied to the human body. The human body is still a mystery, not only to medicine but also to modern man. If perfection has as much to do with resilience, resistance and abstention as with smoothness, if it involves not doing something as much as doing something, it becomes much more than a merely functional term. If the heart or any of the human organs ever overdoes something, that is a sure sign not only of imperfection but of disease and death. In the body, perfection consists in doing only what is needed. This applies to the brain, with its vast complex of mostly untapped centres of electricity. It is true in reference to the heart and the entire nervous system. It is crucially true in reference to the cerebellum and the sympathetic and autonomic systems and their relation to the cerebrum and the conscious process of selection. There is something about the way the process of selection works that is balanced by a sense of limit – one only selects as much as one can handle. These considerations alone yield a concept of perfection much richer than what one would find in a purely functional notion grafted onto a mechanistic picture of robots.

Nonetheless, at the root of this limited and limiting idea of perfection is an idea that anyone, even a child, can understand, and is relevant to the very highest levels of spiritual perfection. It is the idea of an art. It is the idea of judicious use. It is most readily understandable in music. One may listen to several distinctive but "perfect" renditions of a great piece of music. How can there be several different perfect versions of the same piece, each communicating something different, each transmitting something distinctively new? To understand this is to pay tribute to the inexhaustible depth of music and to the potential wealth of artistic genius. But it also refers to that complex relationship between human beings and instruments matured over a period of time which enables a person to use an instrument so as to hover trembling at the limits of what is audible, and, in pregnant moments of silence, to give a sense of the deeper unstated meaning of music.

This conception is much subtler than even the organic notion of perfectibility. It involves a rich conscious relationship between subject and object. This leads one to ask what is the metaphysical basis of a view of perfection which can accommodate myriad possible views, modes and instances – in function or form, in art or music, in a leaf or a flower – without limiting or exhausting the content of possibility. In short, perfection requires assumptions not only about what actually exists but also about what is possible. In other words, there is a dynamic relation between potential and actualization. To admit this capacity to actualize unknown potential necessarily inserts a subjective element into the notion of perfection. It is therefore totally absurd to say that a human being can ever settle for an objective external view of what is perfect. If ten imperfect men befriended a "perfect" woman, each would have to work out a very different relationship with her. Each would also have to revise and rethink the notion of what is perfect.

Whenever one considers a relational notion of perfection, which is to be experienced, assessed, tested, revised and rethought, one must acknowledge the element of subjectivity. To take a simple example, when one talks of a perfect meal, there is a good reason why nothing tastes quite like what one's mother cooked long ago, and nothing in turn tastes like what one's mother learnt from her mother. And so it goes, from the accumulated wisdom of cooking that is not transmissible through a recipe book. Cooking becomes esoteric and can never be revealed; cooking becomes exemplified. Here one is talking about one's own experience of examples in the past, one's own attempt to relate them to expectations and evolving standards, all of which affect one's notion of perfection.

This much being clear, one is beginning to stand at the threshold separating the empirical, the linguistic and the semantic from the metaphysical. What, then, is the metaphysical basis of perfection? An excellent example in modern thought is provided by Leibniz, for whom there is something intrinsic in every organism and therefore in every monadic atom in every being in all the visible kingdoms. There is, in the monad, an entelechy, an intrinsic propulsion towards realization and elaboration of all that is already programmed in everything that is already potential. Because the monad is not concrete, this has metaphysical implications. The monad is not limited by reference to external physical form, nor is it psychologically bounded in reference to inward experience. It is philosophically similar to the theological notion of the soul, which was tainted by dogmatism even in the time of Leibniz, but which implies something abstract, having to do with logical possibility, and therefore something that is theoretically prior to the empirically given.

At the same time, what makes this conception metaphysically compelling is the notion of necessity attached to that which is theoretically and ontologically prior to what exists. This is a philosophical way of saying that human beings, as immortal souls, have already within themselves something which is deeper than an image, profounder than a concept, and more lasting than even an urge to perfection – something rooted in the nature of consciousness itself. Metaphysically, it concerns the relationship of the infinite richness of consciousness to the infinite variety of possible form. It does not lie in either separately, but is hidden in the relationship of consciousness to form. If this is the metaphysical basis of such a notion of perfection, it is equally important in practice. Every human being is searching for a sense of distinction between the real and the unreal, the ever changing and the evanescent, the immortal and the mortal. Every human being is engaged in defining what is perfect and perfectible amidst conditions of limitation and imperfection.

This insight gains especial significance when seen in the light of a central metaphysical tenet of the philosophy of perfection in *Gupta Vidya*: namely, the proposition that all human beings are both perfect and imperfect, both immortal and mortal. Human beings are capable of a degree of creative vision and imagination in elaborating what is potentially possible. At the same time, the fullness of perfection far transcends the capacity of expression in words, in sketches or even in mathematical formulae. One can always draw a circle to circumscribe something in the mind, but there is much more that is implied in the blank space within and outside the circle. There is always a gap between what people are capable of conceiving and what people are actually capable of creating. There is a further gap between what they are capable of creating and what in fact they actually create. These two gaps are crucial to the philosophy of perfection.

Given the second gap in human life, much weight is given to intention. Where there is an intention to create for a noble and selfless purpose, a great deal can be overlooked in the realm of the created. Suppose that one person actually creates something better than another person, but in the first person the motivation is largely self-satisfaction, competition and self-indulgence, while in the second person the motive is charity, inspiration and gratitude. An objective observer looking at the two will notice a very real sense in which the more imperfect creation is actually a greater example of the richness of mental perfection. Ever since the last war, people have become used to having international exhibitions of children's paintings. Many people have come to see that in these often badly structured and crude paintings there shines a vitality, a dignity and a beauty that transcends many finished works of art. The trained eye sees in them an *eros* struggling to break through.

Chinese and Japanese artists often held that one should never attempt anything without including incompleteness and imperfection, an emptiness that leaves room for further growth. To do otherwise is an insult to the viewer, a failure to leave room for the imagination. In that sense, the greater part of any actual creation is what it intimates about the future. Put in a paradoxical way, the less perfected something is, the more perfect it is. That which is less perfected opens the door to greater perfection.

Metaphysically, if every human being is both perfect and imperfect, there is a clear need for a much deeper explanation of the relation between spirit and matter, consciousness and form, *purusha* and *prakriti*. If one is perfect in consciousness, whilst imperfect in form, what, then, is human perfection? Human perfection must refer to the relationship between that which is mortal and that which is immortal, that which is finite and that which is inexhaustible. Clearly, one cannot work out such a doctrine of perfection without a doctrine of planes of consciousness and states of matter, with correspondences and consubstantiality between each plane of ideation and each state of matter. Therefore, the entire notion of perfection involves a cosmology. It also involves a complex system of teachings about the interactions between the finitizing tendency in Nature and in human consciousness and the transcendent elements that work through matter.

Thus one reaches the critical conclusion that one cannot know from the outside, in the realm of the mortal and the imperfect, what is really going on inside human beings. One has very little clue to the degrees of growth made by souls. Yet by watching the way a person sits, the way a person moves, the way a person chooses, one can see something about the relation between inner and outer. A crucial starting point, which provides a criterion of the spiritual quality of different cultures and collective notions of progress, goes back to a contribution of Pico della Mirandola at the time of the Renaissance: *human beings are so constituted that what is paradigmatic about being human is the possibility of exercising the power of choice.* This goes much further than any Aristotelian emphasis on reason or any conception of man as a rational animal capable of seeking happiness. Yet it is also diametrically opposite to the conventional Christian notion of man as an original sinner created by an omnipotent god. Man is that being who, alone in the universe, has both the prerogative and the predicament of exercising free choice. The extent to which a human being matures, develops and perfects the power of choice governs the extent to which he or she is able to bring down perfection into the realm of time, while at the same time recognizing the limits of what is possible in time. One cannot perfect the power of choice if one's concern is with anything less than the universal good. This insight goes all the way back to Plato. It comes through in Leibniz and it is implicit in Pico. If one is choosing in relation to a universal standard or the universal good, it is important to choose well. But it is also important not to expect that what one chooses will be more than a limited actualization of what is possible.

Take an example of effective choice. The average person has forty or fifty years between youth and old age in which to hold a job. One may, at high school and in the early years of university life, be spoilt by being able to switch constantly from course to course, by dropping out and coming back. Nonetheless, a point comes at which one has to choose to make the most of one's life vocationally, in terms of perfecting a skill and offering something useful to society. One stays with the job until ready to retire. Whatever the limitations of one's job, one makes the most of it, lending it meaning from outside, and bringing to it a moral quality that goes beyond the technical job description. One must make an art of one's life, of the way one discharges duties, grows as a human being, and continues to read, think and learn. At the same time, one must learn from errors and make adjustments, not only in one's psyche, but also in one's expectations, and above all in one's relationships, so that one comes to value fidelity. One must not see others as expendable in terms of one's erratic notions of unlimited satisfaction, but must stick with them. The moment one chooses a specific vocation – what Buddha called right livelihood – one must limit oneself.

The moment one begins to see the subtleties in the notion of perfection, one must prepare for a shock. Every human being defines himself or herself at the moment of birth by the way he or she pronounces the AUM. Human beings delude themselves over a lifetime, because they have in fact defined themselves by the sound they uttered at the moment of birth. The way that sound is uttered, the quality of it, the degree of detachment it represents, marks the degree of honest recognition of the limitations built into physical incarnation. It is a cry of universality, of enthusiasm and of gratitude to the mother. If this is not shock enough, one must also see that the sound uttered by human beings at the moment of death has consequences equally devastating to complacency. How many human beings are able to die with the same sound they began with as babies? If all babies begin life with the AUM, how many can die with it on their lips, not uttered in the same way as before, but uttered with wisdom, detachment and compassion? If one sees this connection between the moment of birth and the moment of death, one will understand something about continuity in life.

How little, then, is known about human beings from the outside, and how little do people know about themselves. There is no basis whatsoever for making any external judgments about the status of human souls, because all such notions can only be made from the outside. No wonder, then, that people caught up in empiricism and perfectionism reduce their assessments of human stature to false ideas about tall and short. Often people are imprisoned in totally false and unnecessary myths. It is so sad to think of whole nations wasting their energy trying to be taller. There must be something more inspiring to human life. Yet this is what happens when people will not be agnostic and calm, will not look within and be honest with themselves. Anxious to settle for an external criterion, they will usually go for a crude measure that tells nothing at all about the human condition. This is only possible because today, as never before, people are willing to divorce notions of perfection from ethical considerations. All the notions of perfection that sustained excellence in classical cultures for a long time had ethical foundations. In the most ancient civilizations, this went far beyond any notions of heaven and hell, salvation and damnation.

Once one has genuinely faced one's ignorance of perfection, one is entitled to ask what it is that will actually provide consciousness a means of sifting and selecting. How can one not only get to know, but get to know better? How can one learn to do better and sustain an incentive to grow, to perfect oneself beyond specific skills and beyond limiting lists of moral virtue? To answer these questions, one will have to look at all the ingredients involved in this process. The most important are illumination and imagination. Illumination is very rare. Each human being may have moments of illumination in deep sleep, certainly in meditation, but illumination is not something one can command. Nor is it something one can contrive or fool oneself about: it is something for which one has to prepare oneself. Imagination, on the other hand, is something everyone can start working with. The first step involves a good spring-cleaning job, as one cleans out the imagination, empties out all the rubbish put into it for years by television, the media and the visual bombardment of sensation. One should remove all limiting concepts of a perfectionist nature in regard to either the moral or the mental life, let alone the spiritual. One should also completely eradicate any lingering notion about whether perfected men are either bearded or beardless. *Yogins* may look like beggars. They may come as kings. They may come in whatever form suits them, for part of their whole purpose is to come in a form in which they are invisible. They are certainly not going to fulfil the requirements and expectations of those who are looking from outside.

In deep sleep, the immaculate imagination may recover the forgotten language of the soul. This may take the form of geometrical signs or more elaborate glyphs and symbols, but it can also take the form of powerful ideation. Above all, there is no richer food for the imagination than the magnificent portraits of Sages given in the sacred texts. Every day in his *ashram* throughout his adult life, Gandhi used the last nineteen verses in the second chapter of the *Bhagavad Gita*, the great section on the Self-Governed Sage. That one passage gives a basis for meditating about the perfected man, not in terms of anything external, but in terms of internal essence. Like a master musician who is not concerned with performing on stage, the Sage has perfected within himself his relationship to the instrument, to the vestures. One may read these great portraits in the *Gita* and make them come alive, just as millions of people around Southeast Asia have made come alive something that is intangible behind the Buddha statue. Such statues are all too often the subject of humour in Western drawing rooms, but to the poor peasant in Thailand they are everything. God, humanity and all the Sages speak to him through the silence of that small stone statue. The gap in consciousness between this purity of imagination and the so-called sophistication of the polluted modern mind underscores the necessity of refining and redefining one's sense of imagination. When an island of pure thought is formed in waking meditation, it can link up with deep sleep, and the soul can become ready for illumination.

Full illumination requires complete mastery of the paradox of the manifest and the unmanifest, and supreme spiritual perfection requires effortless exemplification of the transcendental virtues "that transform the body into the Tree of Knowledge". Mystically, the three great Perfections are the three *kayas*, the three bodies of the perfected man. In Buddhist tradition they are the *dharmakaya*, the *sambhogakaya* and the *nirmanakaya*. Each represents a type of spiritual perfection. In the first case, spiritual perfection involves a long, deliberate and strenuous process of detachment through meditation upon emptiness, *shunyata*, and mastery of the ability to withdraw at will from one's astral form. At some point in some life, one attains absorption into the golden aura of the unmanifest Logos. This is a very high nirvanic state, equivalent to *moksha* or liberation in the Hindu tradition. It enables an individual to cut the chain of involuntary incarnations into a body in a world of suffering. But this emancipation is secured at the expense of cutting such beings off from any possibility of communication with ordinary suffering humanity. Those who take this *dharmakaya* vesture are absorbed into the most pristine state of matter that can be imagined. It is actually the state of matter that is the basis of the *Adibuddha*, the ultimate Buddha-nature. Essentially, it is the basis of all perfected beings, but there are crucial differences in the ways that different kinds of perfected beings make use of that light-substance, *shuddhasattva*. The *sambhogakaya* represents a second mode of spiritual perfection that is universally relevant to all manifested divine incarnations: Krishna is a paradigm of it. Wherever an exalted incarnation comes to give an indication of the divine graces and excellences possible for human beings, that is the *sambhogakaya*. Such a glorious being lives in the golden aura of the manifested Logos, whether he is called Christos,

Krishna or by any other name.

The third type of spiritual perfection, designated as the *nirmanakaya*, is the specific goal represented by Gautama Buddha and the continuing work of the Brotherhood of Bodhisattvas, the Mahatmas who breathe solely for the sake of universal enlightenment. The *nirmanakaya* is a distinctive and extremely difficult kind of perfection. It involves perfection of the capacity to create out of the subtler vestures an astral form which is devoid of qualities. This alchemically regenerated form enables one to move anywhere invisibly and to assist human beings unknown to them. It also enables one consciously to take whatever body is necessary or available for the purpose of extending the work of universal enlightenment. Most *nirmanakayas* are unseen, anonymous and disguised. One cannot discern them from outside, because they have chosen to come in ways in which they can perfect right livelihood and, at the same time, maximize the work they do in the realm of contemplation, ideation, true theurgy, healing and, above all, beneficent meditation.

The three types of spiritual perfection represented by the three *kayas* may be thought of in terms of different types of meditative discipline. The paradox is that going higher does not necessarily represent the attainment of a higher level of spiritual perfection. Going high and bringing down what one can for the sake of raising others is the highest perfection. Among the Mahatmas, therefore, there is no greater example of the perfect man than Gautama Buddha. Greatness among Mahatmas has to do with greatness in renunciation, greatness in control of temper, greatness in freedom from possessions, and greatness in total sacrifice for the sake of the least and the most tormented, so that they may re-enter the kingdom of divine selfhood. The whole challenge of the philosophy of perfection lies in one's potential, which is something less than one's conceivable perfection and more than one's actual perfection. It lies in the ratio of silence to speech, of patience to self-assertion, of surrender to imposition. The more one is non-violent, the more one is willing to yield to another. "Greater love hath no man than that he lay down his life for another" is one of the greatest *mantras* of all times. Here is the authentic accent of that particular kind of spiritual perfection which is the highest and holiest in human evolution. It is much harder than everything else because it involves overcoming the ego, while at the same time remaining in a world which, as depicted in the Allegory of the Cave, remains a dungeon whose language is egotism.

Spiritual perfection requires extraordinary courage and patience. Continuity of consciousness is, therefore, the most meaningful way of looking at perfectibility. How much can one maintain a vibration through day and night? Through the days of the week? Through a month? Through the seasons between the winter solstice and the spring equinox, between the spring equinox and the summer solstice – not just through one year, but through seven years? Can one even imagine what it means to maintain a spiritual vibration until the last breath? If so, can one then begin to imagine what it is like to be able to keep appointments across future lives, not in the realm of fantasy, but in the realm of painful fact?

An extraordinary story is told of Ananda, the disciple of Buddha, who once turned aside an attractive young lady because she was totally unready for renunciation. Before she could curse him, he said, "One day, when no one else wants you, I will be there." Decades later, when she was a dying, rotten carcass in the streets, Ananda heard her cry and left the company of Buddha. He went many miles to reach her, and then, practically unknown even to her, washed her body, tended it, and helped her enter the *Sangha* before she died. What a different criterion of greatness this is from anything in modern times. The present is an age in which people cannot even be true in the evening to a promise made in the morning. Yet this sad fact only reinforces the therapeutic importance of considering examples of beings so great that they can keep appointments over decades and across lives.

The one thing one must never do is sell short the ideal of human perfection. All human beings are perfected gods in chains. But all human beings also have to go through the same arduous process before they can attain to a high degree of spiritual wakefulness, fidelity and control. Where individuals can remain true to a vibration, they must do so, showing the moral courage of those, like Thoreau, who listen to the beat of another drummer. Those who hear and heed the music of the spheres can rarely share it with others, because most people are totally caught in the noise of the age. To be able to remain with and among all those people, who are like lotuses suffocating in the mire, while at the same time giving hope and instruction to those rare flowers that are struggling to rise to the surface, is indeed a high degree of continuity of consciousness.

Unless one establishes oneself in what is universal, on the side of all beings and the future, one will irreversibly fall behind. The stakes for humanity have become extremely high, and the ultimacy of choice represented by the words of Jesus, "Whom choose ye this day", has come to pass. It is truly the case that the Perfect Sage has no name and no form. He lives in the nameless, and he is formless. But the current of light-energy and good represented by such a being leaves one no choice except to be with it or to be tossed away by its force. Starting from small concepts and simple examples, one can see that the notion of perfectibility embraces something so much vaster than can ever be put into any categories. At the same time, it is a viable, living, relevant ideal for every human being, because each human being archetypally goes through the same stages, is involved in the same powers and faculties, and lives in a common field of space, time and energy. Every human being by day, and certainly in deep sleep at night, experiences something of the true meaning of the odyssey of the soul in its long and immemorial quest towards the perfecting of all humanity.

Hermes, March 1987

AS ABOVE, SO BELOW

> *Thus is repeated on Earth the mystery enacted, according to the Seers, on the divine plane. The 'Son' of the immaculate Celestial Virgin (or the undifferentiated cosmic protyle, Matter in its infinitude) is born again on Earth as the Son of the terrestrial Eve – our mother Earth, and becomes Humanity as a total – past, present, and future – for Jehovah or Jod-he-vau-he is androgyne, or both male and female. Above, the Son is the whole KOSMOS; below, he is MANKIND.*
>
> The Secret Doctrine, i 60

The mystery of immaculate conception is inherently inseparable from the magic of the Tetraktis, which, Pythagoras taught, is too sacred to be spoken of and should rather be the subject of profound meditation over a lifetime. "The triad or triangle becomes Tetraktis, the Sacred Pythagorean number, the perfect Square, and a 6-faced cube on Earth." The Tetraktis is incarnated by the enlightened being, the Initiate, who is more than *Atma-Buddhi-Manas*. If the Initiate were only *Atma-Buddhi-Manas*, he would be on so high a plane of universal consciousness that he would hardly be able to incarnate. The Initiate is *Atma-Buddhi-Manas* plus the visualized essence extracted from all the lower principles and planes so as to serve as a stable focus for the immortal Triad in space and time. The Initiate permanently synthesizes individuation and universalization. The universal principles are brought together through *Buddhi* in an individuated, perfected instrument, which exemplifies the Tetraktis. This exalted condition is founded upon the metaphysical axiom in all spiritual growth that the higher one ascends, the more one's sense of being is essentially a mode of participation in cosmic principles.

Atma-Buddhi-Manas cannot incarnate in personal consciousness as long as its dominant concerns are almost entirely bound up with pleasure and pain, fame and shame, gain and loss. These evanescent if hectic preoccupations bind together the *skandhas* and colour the composite vestures, producing an illusory panorama which people commonly call life, but which is viewed by the Adept as the night of nescience.

The only way one can activate the higher faculties is by a conscious and continuous attunement to universal principles. *Atman* is an unconditionally universal essence, while *Buddhi* is connected with *Mahabuddhi* and *Manas* derives from *Mahat*. The Mahatma is one whose mind has become "like a becalmed and boundless ocean" – the ocean of cosmic ideation – and whose heart has become the hebdomad, the Dhyan Chohanic heart that pulses at the core of all manifestation. The uninitiated cannot understand this owing to the tenacious sense of separateness that attaches to the personality but which is entirely inapplicable to the Adept. The Adept cannot be sundered from the whole of Nature, but is truly, as in Leonardo's diagram, the man within the man, the enlightened cosmic man that overbroods man as a unit and whose unity is mirrored in that unit. The *Atma-Buddhi-Manas* of the Adept is necessarily inseparable from the *Atma-Buddhi-Manas* of individual human beings. The Adept is verily the spiritual soul of all humanity.

Human beings represent varying degrees of self-consciousness in inverse proportion to their personal attachment to the limited modes of life available in the world of sensation. Like assertive adolescents, they are engrossed in the *Mahamaya*, partly because they wholly identify with name and form and pant with thirst for embodied life and an ever-present fear of pain and deprivation. Yet, while the human condition is characterized by *avidya*, all individuals are fundamentally light-rays from the same luminous source. They are most likely to experience their essential humanity in deep sleep, where even those who are demons by day become like little children. According to the Upanishadic teachings, all phenomenal distinctions disappear in deep sleep. There is no father and no mother; there is no husband and no wife, no brother and no sister, no enemy and no friend; there is neither young nor old, neither male nor female. The distinctions that people make entirely disappear in *sushupti*. During deep sleep the soul is able to speak its own language, what Erich Fromm called "the forgotten language", which was once known as the language of the gods. This is the language of unconditioned consciousness in which our pristine humanity comes into its own. Human beings are most assured when they are least deluded. The Mahatma is totally free from all delusion and can fathom the secret heart, the pulsing reverberation of the whole of humanity that gives its forward impulse to evolution.

When spiritual knowledge becomes conscious awareness, wisdom through use, *Gupta Vidya* becomes *Paramarthasatya*. *Paramartha* is the ultimate comprehension of *Satya*, the truth of all things, of *SAT*, pure being, the ideal universe. *Paramarthasatya* is consummate comprehension of the noumenal universe that does not manifest but is the Divine Ground spoken of by mystics, which is latent in *Hiranyagarbha*, the divine bosom, and animated by *Mahat*, divine thought. The mystery of immaculate conception has to do with the paradox that the most fully incarnated being is also the least incarnated. While this is too enigmatic to reduce to discursive logic, it is intuitively clear that the more complete the incarnation, the less is the being involved in incarnation in the sense of attachment to so-called living. The paradox is deeply enshrined in the mystery of the immaculate conception:

> The Primordial Substance had not yet passed out of its precosmic latency into differentiated objectivity, or even become the (to man, so far,) invisible Protyle of Science. But, as the hour strikes and it becomes receptive of the Fohatic impress of the Divine Thought (the Logos, or the male aspect of the Anima Mundi, Alaya) – its heart opens. It differentiates, and the THREE (Father, Mother, Son) are transformed into four. Herein lies the origin of the double mystery of the Trinity and the immaculate Conception.
>
> *The Secret Doctrine*, i 58

At the dawn of manifestation, *Mulaprakriti*, the Germ, which is the Father-Mother potentially and the point in every atom, is latent in cosmic substance. When the Germ is awakened by the descending ray, Divine Thought becomes the inseminating force which activates the sleeping energy within every life-atom. Then the three become the four through the transformation of the primordial Triad in a pure state of Parabrahmic latency into a creative Logos that lights up and makes

Mulaprakriti radiant. It thereby becomes *Daiviprakriti*. also known as *Brahma Vach*, Divine Wisdom, the Verbum, the Word, the Light of the Logos. This gives rise to the manifest universe. The same idea is found in Aryasanga's *Precepts for Yoga* in a metaphorical form, indicating that absolute Unity may not be comprehensible to the individual unless that absolute Unity is seen in relation to primordial, indestructible matter and also in relation to eternal duration:

> If thou wouldest believe in the Power which acts within the root of a plant, or imagine the root concealed under the soil, thou hast to think of its stalk or trunk and of its leaves and flowers. Thou canst not imagine that Power independently of these objects. Life can be known only by the Tree of Life.
>
> The Secret Doctrine, i 58

To visualize the invisible Root, it is easier to think as well of the massive trunk and its many branches. This is a cosmic analogue to something that can be actualized within the human constitution, as suggested by Bhavani Shankar in his Commentary on the *Gita*. It is veiled in the sacred teaching of the lotus, which is "the product of heat (fire) and water (vapour or Ether)". Lotus plants are phanerogamous, containing in their seeds complete representations, as prototypes, of the future plant. The lotus is a representation in the vegetable kingdom of a sacred macrocosmic mystery, which is why the spiritual centres in the human constitution have from the most ancient times been compared to lotuses. Bhavani Shankar speaks of the thousand-petalled lotus in the brain, which is also referred to in the *Bhagavad Gita* and which symbolizes the radiance and the richness of the energy-field that is latent in human beings. The Guru can activate the spiritual seed in the disciple who is ready. This would also have a bearing upon the mystery of the caduceus. When a disciple has reached a moment of ripeness in inward development, it is possible for active *Buddhi*, or what is called in *The Voice of the Silence*, *Kundalini*, that mysterious energy which flows through two alternating currents intertwined, to become a reality. Thus a creative fusion of consciousness can be attained wherein the Third Eye may open, the eye for which there is no past, present or future, the eye of spiritual vision, of universal wisdom and of inner enlightenment, the eye of Shiva, the eye of Dangma.

In metaphysical language it is possible, when cognizer, cognized and cognition are one, for absolute consciousness to become a pervasive reality in the life of a perfected human being through *Paramarthasatya*, through Divine Wisdom embodied and manifested. Such a man is called a sage, a *muni*, in whom there is such a vast expansion of individual self-consciousness that it has become universal self-consciousness. This is also expressed in terms of the noumenal realm of *Akasa*, which is connected with the subliminal astral light, sometimes called in mythic language the immaculate virgin mother. It is Sarasvati, the Light of the Logos, the goddess of wisdom, Sephira in the Kabbalah, the mother of the Sephiroth. These are different words for the divine sphere of universal consciousness that is the elixir of immortality, which may pour like rain into the receptacle of the clear mind undarkened by personality and raised to the realm of pure receptivity. Shankaracharya differed here from the Dvaita schools, which put strong emphasis upon devotion but in terms of the gap between God and man. Shankara taught that man is one with God, that *Atman is Brahman* and that devotion is simply a return to one's true nature. The simulacrum of devotion fostered by orthodox religion, which puts strong emphasis upon one's own insignificance and inability to do anything at all, is fundamentally different from that self-energizing devotion which is like breathing.

Real devotion is a return to one's true nature. All human souls in the Third Root Race were natural exemplars of humanity, and were joyously devoted. In the infancy of the human race, immortal souls did not know any way other than devotion and harmony, which is why devotion has often been compared to the child state. Any other mental posture was unnatural to them. To discover one's true nature through *jnana* is also to release that true devotion which may bring back the spiritual knowledge that was one's own in many former lives. True devotion is a fusion between the chela and the Guru, the mind and the heart of the disciple becoming totally attuned to the mind and the heart of the teacher. So great is the luminous beauty of this state of total attunement that it is a shining paradigm of the immemorial teaching of Divine Wisdom and the sacred process of initiation. Mystics have conveyed this in many ways because it is a state that is understandable at some level by every human being who has the hidden spark which helps to recognize the flame that intimates the fire. As there is a spark of true devotion in each human heart, so there is *Buddhi* in every human being, even though latent and reflected in *kama*. If *Buddhi* is the seed of the Buddha, the lighting up of *Buddhi*, the spark of devotion, in vast multitudes of human beings is the alchemical function of all spiritual Teachers. They come to awaken soul-memories in human beings who have forgotten and fallen from their pristine state, soul-memories of what they essentially are and what they self-consciously could become.

It is a metaphysical axiom of Eastern psychology that something can cease to exist and still be. The analogy is given of hydrogen and oxygen which exist independently as gases, but in water they seem to have disappeared, though they are still there. This is an apt analogy to what happens to the entire universe in *pralaya*, when it goes to sleep, ceases to be. Imagine a state of supreme stillness such as in the depths of the ocean or when it is well past midnight and one is meditating upon the midnight sun. One can also visualize the veiled full moon on the first day of the new moon. Such analogies suggest that one can generate a sense of reality which is not dependent upon Nature's photographs and the astral light, which is sometimes called Nature's infinite negative. Beyond these periodical manifestations there is the living, breathing stillness, the divine darkness, the absolute unconscious consciousness which is within the secret heart of Nature. During *pralaya* the universe seems to have gone to sleep. The archetypal noumenal matrices in thought that lie behind all manifest forms are reabsorbed into the supreme consciousness. If there is to be unbroken continuity between one *manvantara* and another and also through *pralaya*, analogous to self-conscious continuity between one incarnation and another through *Devachan*, there must be a sense in which this process is analogous to the rhythmic inhaling and the exhaling of breath.

Innumerable universes are like winks in the eye of Self-Existence, their appearance and disappearance resembling the twinkling of stars. If it is possible to make a meaningful analogy with the long periods between *manvantaras* and the intervals between incarnations as well as the silences between breaths, there must be some profound secret here which contains the clue to conscious immortality. Human beings get caught in the processes of emanation and involution, which is why they are obscured. Physiologically it is a losing race against clock-time, because they are dying faster than they are recharging themselves. This is the result on the physical plane of what takes place in consciousness. On the mental plane they are not absorbing ideas, that is, they are not meditating, not reflecting, and are receiving impressions in such a chaotic rush that the mind is like a worn-out record that is overused. They are making use of only a minute percentage of their potential brain-energy and even less of their heart-energy. They will remain spiritual paupers, living far below their capacity, until they restore a natural rhythm in the relation between what they receive and what they give out.

Krishna teaches in the *Gita* that both receiving and giving may be seen as sacrificial. If the idea of sacrifice is linked up to what is inhaled, which is a form of receiving from outside, then it is clear that one is continually benefiting from the sacrifice of Nature. Exhalation is also a mode of sacrifice because every time one breathes one is giving to the world. Much of this is erratic and involuntary since most people's minds are not cooperating with their lungs. The personal mind tends to ruin whatever knowledge it has by possessiveness. That is not true of breathing, which goes on all the time and, while it is sometimes disordered, it also has its recurring rhythms. The breath should become less hurried and short, deeper and more gentle, until it is non-violent and sacrificial. Through carelessness in speech, the greatest harm is done to breathing and to eating, but if one is alert and mindful, pausing with quiet gratitude periodically and rhythmically, then one moves away from a polarized activity towards a triune motion. Instead of taking in and throwing out, one takes in, holds, and then gives. As one's rhythms become triune in breathing, this becomes a conscious reflection of Brahma-Vishnu-Shiva, *Atma-Buddhi-Manas*. If one also keeps in mind the *Atma-Buddhi-Manas* of the life-atoms that one is dealing with, this will deepen continuity and ultimately transform and revolutionize the rhythm of one's life. These simple considerations are supremely practical examples of Buddhic analogy and correspondence between the cosmic and the human.

The authentic teachings of the *Gupta Vidya* are always intended to awaken slumbering intuition. Those who learn to profit from the gift begin to find that there is great Buddhic wisdom concealed therein as the inheritance of future races. By contact with what is Buddhic, one's own *Buddhi* is stirred. By concentrating on retention, which is connected with continuity of consciousness, there can be a strengthening of the *antaskarana* bridge between nous and psyche, the immortal and the mortal, the universal and the particular, the infinite and the finite, the transcendental and the temporal, eternal duration and present time. When the first steps are taken upon the Path, the disciple's heart will quicken to a sense of the joyous mystery of the immaculate incarnation of the Light of the Logos in Mankind.

Hermes, April 1980

THE ALLEGORY OF THE CAVE

Those having Lamps will pass them on to others.

Plato

In *The Secret Doctrine* we are told that Plato was not merely the greatest philosopher of Greece but also an Adept who belonged psychically, mentally and spiritually to the higher planes of evolution, a "Fifth-rounder" in the Fourth Round, immensely higher than is our present humanity. He imparted spiritual truths through myths and allegories as his aim was both to awaken the *Manas* and to arouse the *Buddhi* of his hearers. In the ratiocinative climate of our own age, his myths have been often dismissed as mere poetic fantasies, and some have even suggested that they were employed to cover up deficiencies in his chain of reasoning. As a result his system of philosophy and political thought has not been properly grasped by his critics.

One of Plato's most well known myths is the "quaint parable" with which the Seventh Book of the *Republic* opens. In this allegory of the cave, he intimated the teaching that there is a truth beyond sense, pertaining to the eternal noumena underlying earthly phenomena, a deeper realm of reality which cannot be adequately apprehended except by the philosopher who has been initiated into the Mysteries. Even to realize the distinction between the intuitive standpoint of the true seer and the shared delusions of most men is an important step forward from the region of *avidya*, ignorance, to the realm of truth. Our tragedy lies simply in our refusal to recognize that we live in a condition of perpetual imprisonment, clinging tenaciously to the sights and sounds of earthly life, mistaking slavery for freedom and shadows for realities.

The allegory begins with a graphic picture of the pathetic condition of the majority of mankind. We are like chained slaves living in an underground den, which has a mouth open towards the light and reaching all along the den. Here we have been from our childhood, unable to move or to see beyond, being prevented by the chains from turning round our heads. Above and behind us a fire is blazing at a distance, but between the fire and ourselves there is a low wall like the screen which marionette players have in front of them to foster the illusion necessary for a puppet-show. We are like the strange prisoners in this den who see only their own shadows or the shadows of one another, which the fire throws on the opposite wall of the cave. To them the truth would be literally nothing but the shadows of the images, and they cannot distinguish the voices of one another from the echoes emanating from the surrounding darkness.

Given this allegory, we might think that if only the prisoners were released from their chains by some external agency, they would cease to mistake shadows for realities and would be automatically disabused of their former errors. The allegory points out that no such simple deliverance from illusions is possible. At first, when any of the prisoners is liberated and compelled suddenly to stand up and turn his neck round and walk and look towards the light, he will suffer sharp pains. Further, the glare will disturb him and he will be unable to see the realities he formerly identified with their mere shadows. If he is now told that what he saw before was an illusion and that now he is approaching real existence and has a clearer vision, he will be perplexed. He will continue to fancy that the shadows he saw for so long were truer than the objects which are now shown to him. If he is compelled to look straight at the light, the pain in his eyes will induce him to turn away to take refuge in the objects of vision that have acquired a false but greater reality than the things which are now being shown to him. If he is dragged up a steep ascent and forced into the presence of the sun, his eyes will be dazzled and he will not be able to see anything at all.

The liberated prisoner will obviously require to grow accustomed to the sight of the upper world. He will first see the shadows best, then the reflections of men and objects in the water, and then the objects themselves; and then he will gaze upon the light of the moon and the stars by night. At last he will be able to see the sun. He will come to see that the sun is the guardian of all that is in the visible world and in a certain sense the cause of all that he and his fellows had been accustomed to behold. He would remember his old habitation and the delusions of his fellow prisoners, pity them and felicitate himself on the change in himself and in his position. He would no longer care for the honours conferred upon one another by the ignorant prisoners on the basis of who were the quickest to observe the passing shadows.

The first test that the liberated prisoner has to face is to get accustomed to his new condition and to forsake his long-cherished illusions. The second test is to see the unity of all things. The third is to show compassion towards his fellow prisoners and not merely revel in his own happiness. The fourth is to detach himself completely from the false valuations and hierarchical distinctions made by the men in the den. His fifth and much more difficult test comes if he is then made to re-enter the cave of darkness, for he would appear ridiculous to the prisoners who still cling to their former illusions centered on the shadows. They would say that he had become blind to realities since leaving the cave, that it is better not even to think of ascending, that they would be entitled to put to death anyone who tried to free another and lead him up to the light.

The allegory then explains that the prison-house is the world of sight, the light of the fire is the sun, and the journey upwards is the ascent of the soul into the intellectual world. In the world of knowledge the archetypal idea of Good appears last of all and is seen only with an effort. It is only then inferred to be the universal author of all things beautiful and right, the lord of light in this visible world and the immediate source of reason and truth in the intellectual world, the power upon which the eye must be fixed in private and public life in order to act rationally. It is not surprising, we are told, that those who attain to this beatific vision are unwilling to descend to human affairs; for their souls are ever hastening into the upper world where they desire to dwell. Those who do descend from divine contemplations to the underground den will not find it easy to deal with those who have never yet seen Absolute Good or Justice.

The bewilderments of the eyes, the bodily eye as well as the mind's eye, are of two kinds and arise either from coming out of the light or from going into the light. The plight of the soul as soon as it comes from darkness into the light is to be pitied, and there is no reason to laugh at the condition of the soul which has come out of the brighter life and is unable to see because unaccustomed to the dark. It is wrong to think that we can put sight into blind eyes or knowledge into the soul, which was not there before. The power and capacity of learning exist in the soul already, and just as the eye was unable to turn from darkness to light without the whole body, so too it is only by the movement of the whole soul that the instrument of knowledge can be turned from the world of Becoming into that of Being, and can learn by degrees to endure the sight of the good and the true. Whereas the other so-called virtues of the soul can be implanted by habit and exercise, the virtue of wisdom or of spiritual sight contains a divine element which is the identifying property or function of the soul. Sensual pleasures, like leaden weights, drag down the soul and turn its vision upon the things below, but if the soul is released from earthly impediments, the faculty of seeing the truth comes into full play.

Every detail of the allegory of the cave has been mentioned here because everything in it is significant. The entire allegory could be interpreted in several ways – mystically, psychologically or even politically. It was Plato's great genius that he could give us a parable, archetypal in meaning and full of occult truth that is rich in its symbolism and suggestive of several profitable interpretations. His method was to descend from universals to particulars, to use his insight into the process of Becoming or of cosmic evolution to derive lessons for personal and social life. He exemplified the ancient maxim: "As above, so below." Recent interpreters have concentrated on the political moral to be drawn from the parable and some have wrongly regarded it as a poetic rationalization of a particular political outlook designed to make the philosopher acceptable in a polis. Plato explicitly states that the founders of the State must compel the best minds to continue to ascend until they arrive at the highest truth or ultimate good and then to make them descend again into the den and partake of honours and labours for which they do not care. They must become the benefactors of the entire community. They are not obliged to share in the toils of politics, but if they were deliberately encouraged in their quest for truth, they must share the fruits of their vision with their fellow men. Being Just Men, they will comply with the demands made upon them. The State in which the rulers are most reluctant to govern is always the best.

The entire political moral of the parable has a close resemblance to the *Kumaras*, who refuse to create but are induced by cosmic necessity to complete divine Man by incarnating in him. The unwillingness of the sower in the field to heed the voice of his master involves the latter in unearned and unnecessary suffering, but he accepts this burden flowing from his decision to become involved in the process of evolution. The incarnation of the *Kumaras*, which makes cosmic evolution possible, is paralleled by the sacrifice of the *Nirmanakayas* who resolved, even before attaining perfection, to renounce its fruit and re-enter the world of human ignorance and suffering. Similarly, the *Avatar* who descends amidst humanity cheerfully accepts the risk of ridicule and rejection, so that at least a few may be called to the pursuit of spiritual truth and many more aroused out of their state of slavery and illusion. The probationer on the path of the spiritual life has to emulate the example of the *Avatars* and the *Nirmanakayas*. He has both to isolate himself from humanity in his all-absorbing pursuit of pure truth and to heed the voice of suffering humanity, ever ascending on the pathway of the soul and ever preparing himself for the perfect service of humanity.

The parable also contains the mystical truth that, as the soul is initiated into the higher realms of being, it experiences a sense of strangeness, a new birth, until it has become accustomed to the sights and sounds of its higher plane of consciousness and become wholly indifferent to the lower impulses of earthly life. In his ascent, the mystic comes to worship the spiritual Sun, which gives sustenance to the whole universe, and to perceive the unity of all life and being. At the same time, the mystic who has chosen the path of renunciation and not of liberation has to learn to preserve his vision of the unity of the unseen universe while moving among the shadows of earthly existence, to bring back the soul's memory of its inward ascent and spiritual faculties while also becoming able to cope with the limitations of incarnated existence in a phenomenal world. These truths pertain not merely to the mystic and the Initiate but also to the psychological evolution of our entire humanity. We are so overpowered by the shadowy attractions and images from the Astral Light that we shut ourselves from the archetypal ideas radiating from *Akasa*. Our earth – Plato's den – is only "the footstool of man in his ascension to higher regions; the vestibule" –

> ". . . to glorious mansions,
> Through which a moving crowd forever press."

"Kosmos – the NOUMENON – has nought to do with the causal relations of the phenomenal World" (*The Secret Doctrine*, i 3). We are told by Shankaracharya that the knowledge of the absolute Spirit, like the effulgence of the sun, or like the heat in the fire, is naught else than the absolute Essence itself. The Dhyan-Chohans do for the universe what Plato's guardians do for the *polis*. "They are the Intelligent Forces that give to and enact in Nature her "laws," while themselves acting according to laws imposed upon them in a similar manner by still higher Powers" (*The Secret Doctrine*, i 38). Where the normal eye sees only blackness, the average mystic sees a grey twilight and the spiritual eye of the Initiate sees absolute Light. The One Being is the noumenon of all the noumena which must underlie phenomena and give them whatever shadow of reality they possess, but which we have not the senses or the intellect to cognize at present.

The ascent of the soul is beautifully described in *The Secret Doctrine* and its descent into the world is referred to in *The Voice of the Silence*.

> The existences belonging to every plane of being, up to the highest Dhyan-Chohans, are, in degree, of the nature of shadows cast by a magic lantern on a colourless screen; but all things are relatively real, for the cognizer is also a reflection, and the things cognized are therefore as real to him as himself. Whatever reality things possess must be looked for in them before or after they have passed like a flash through the material world; but we cannot cognize any such existence directly, so long as we have sense-instruments which bring only material existence into the field of consciousness. Whatever plane our consciousness may be acting in, both we and the things belonging to that plane are, for the time being, our only realities. As we rise in the scale of development we perceive that during the stages through which we have passed we mistook shadows for realities, and

the upward progress of the Ego is a series of progressive awakenings, each advance bringing with it the idea that now, at last, we have reached 'reality'; but only when we shall have reached the absolute Consciousness, and blended our own with it, shall we be free from the delusions produced by Maya.

The Secret Doctrine, i 39–40

The Secret Doctrine, with its teaching about planes of reality and appropriate states of consciousness, generalizes at a metaphysical level the truth underlying the allegory of the cave. In *The Voice of the Silence* we are given the practical and ethical corollary of this metaphysical truth. We are made to realize the helpless condition of the hosts of souls who will not avail themselves of Alaya, and we are firmly told: "Give up thy life, if thou wouldst live."

Hermes, February 1975

ANAMNESIS

> *Since, then, the soul is immortal and has been born many times, since it has seen all things both in this world and in the other, there is nothing it has not learnt. No wonder, then, that it is able to recall to mind goodness and other things, for it knew them beforehand. For, as all reality is akin and the soul has learnt all things, there is nothing to prevent a man who has recalled – or, as people say, learnt' – only one thing from discovering all the rest for himself, if he will pursue the search with unwearying resolution. For on this showing all inquiry or learning is nothing but recollection.*
>
> Plato

Anamnesis is true soul-memory, intermittent access to the divine wisdom within every human being as an immortal Triad. All self-conscious monads have known over countless lifetimes a vast host of subjects and objects, modes and forms, in an ever-changing universe. Assuming a complex series of roles as an essential part of the endless process of learning, the soul becomes captive recurrently to myriad forms of *maya* and *moha*, illusion and delusion. At the same time, the soul has the innate and inward capacity to cognize that it is more than any and all of these masks. As every incarnated being manifests a poor, pale caricature of himself – a small, self-limiting and inverted reflection of one's inner and divine nature – the ancient doctrine of anamnesis is vital to comprehend human nature and its hidden possibilities. Given the fundamental truth that all human beings have lived many times, initiating diverse actions in intertwined chains of causation, it necessarily follows that everyone has the moral and material environment from birth to death which is needed for self-correction and self-education. But who is it that has this need? Not the shadowy self or false egoity which merely reacts to external stimuli. Rather, there is that eye of wisdom in every person which in deep sleep is fully awake and which has a translucent awareness of self-consciousness as pure primordial light. We witness intimations of immortality in the pristine light in the innocent eye of every baby, as well as in the wistful eye of every person near the moment of death. It seems that the individual senses that life on earth is largely an empty masquerade, full of sound and fury, signifying nothing. Nevertheless, there is a quiet joy in the recognition that one is fully capable of gaining some apprehension not only of the storied past but also of the shrouded future by a flashing perception of his unmodified, immutable divine essence. If one has earned this through a lifetime of meditation, one may attain at the moment of withdrawal from the body a healing awareness of the reality behind the dense proscenium of the earth's drama.

The esoteric doctrine of anamnesis presupposes the everlasting memory of the immortal soul. Soul-memory is essentially different from what is ordinarily called memory. Most of the time the mind is clouded by a chaotic association of images and ideas that impinge upon it from outside. Very few human beings, however, are in a position to make full use of the capacity for creative thinking. They simply cannot fathom what it is like to be a thinking being, to be able to deliberate calmly and to think intently on their own. Automatic cerebration is often mistaken for primary thinking. To understand this distinction, one must look at the fundamental relation between oneself as a knower and the universe as a field of knowledge. Many souls gain fleeting glimpses of the process of self-enquiry when they are stilled by the panoramic vistas of nature, silenced by the rhythmic ocean, or alone amidst towering mountains. Through the sudden impact of intense pain and profound suffering they may be thrown back upon themselves and be compelled to ask, "What is the meaning of all of this?" "Who am I?" "Why was I born?" "When will I die?" "Can I do that which will now lend a simple credence to my life, a minimal dignity to my death?" Pythagoras and Plato taught the Eastern doctrine of the spontaneous unfolding from within of the wisdom of the soul. Soul-wisdom transcends all formal properties and definable qualities, as suggested in the epistemology, ethics and science of action of the *Bhagavad Gita*. It is difficult for a person readily to generate and release an effortless balancing of the three dynamic qualities of nature – *sattva*, *rajas* and *tamas* – or to see the entire cosmos as a radiant garment of the divine Self. He needs to ponder calmly upon the subtle properties of the *gunas*, their permutations and combinations.

Sattvic knowledge helps the mind to meditate upon the primordial ocean of pure light, the bountiful sea of milk in the old Hindu myths. The entire universe is immersed in a single sweeping cosmic process. Even though we seem to see a moving panorama of configurations, colours and forms, sequentiality is illusory. Behind all passing forms there are innumerable constellations of minute, invisible and ultimately indivisible particles, whirling and revolving in harmonic modes of eternal circular motion. A person can learn to release anamnesis to make conscious and creative use of modes of motion governing the life-atoms that compose the variegated universe of his immortal and mortal vestures. The timeless doctrine of spiritual self-knowledge in the fourth chapter of the *Bhagavad Gita* suggests that human beings are not in the false position of having to choose between perfect omniscience and total nescience. Human beings participate in an immense hinterland of differentiation of the absolute light reflected within modes of motion of matter. To grow up is to grasp that one cannot merely oscillate between extremes. Human thought too often involves the violence of false negation – leaping from one kind of situation to the exact opposite rather than seeing life as a fertile field for indefinite growth. This philosophical perspective requires us to think fundamentally in terms of the necessary relation between the knower and the known. Differences in the modalities of the knowable are no more and no less important than divergences in the perceptions and standpoints of knowers. The universe may be seen for what it is – a constellation of self-conscious beings and also a vast array of elemental centres of energy – *devas* and *devatas* all of which participate in a ceaseless cosmic dance that makes possible the sacrificial process of life for each and every single human being. If one learns that there are degrees within degrees of reflected light, then one sees the compelling need to gain the faculty of divine discrimination (*viveka*). That is the secret heart of the sacred teaching of the *Bhagavad Gita*.

The *Gita* is a jewelled essay in *Buddhi Yoga*. *Yoga* derives from the root *yog*, "to unite", and centres upon the conscious union of the individual self and the universal Self. The trinity of Nature is the lock of magic, and the trinity of Man is the sole key, and hence the grace of the Guru. This divine union may be understood at early stages in different ways.

It could be approached by a true concern for *anasakti* – selfless action and joyous service, the precise performance of duties and a sacrificial involvement in the work of the world. It may also be attempted through the highest form of *bhakti* or devotion, in concentrating and purifying one's whole being so as to radiate an unconditional, constant and consistent truth, a pure, intense and selfless feeling of love. And it must also summon forth true knowledge through altruistic meditation. *Jnana* and *dhyana* do not refer to the feeble reflections of the finite and fickle mind upon the finite and shadowy objects of an ever-evolving world, but rather point to that enigmatic process of inward knowing wherein the knower and the known become one, fused in transcendent moments of compassionate revelation. The pungent but purifying commentary by Dnyaneshvari states in myriad simple metaphors the profoundest teaching of the *Gita*. In offering numerous examples from daily life, Dnyaneshvari wants to dissolve the idea that anything or any being can be known through *a priori* categories that cut up the universe into watertight compartments and thereby limit and confine consciousness. The process of true learning merges disparate elements separated only because of the looking-glass view of the inverted self which mediates between the world and ourselves in a muddled manner. The clearest perception of *sattva* involves pure ideation.

The *Gita* presents a magnificent portrait of the man of meditation who has all his senses and organs under complete control. Whatever he does, he remains seated like one unaffected and aloof (*kutastha*). He does not identify with any of the instruments musically necessary for the creative transformation of the cosmic process. The Religion of Responsibility is rooted in *Rta*, sattvic motion in unmanifested nature, and it makes sattvic consciousness (*dharma*) accessible to imperfect individuals. A human being who valiantly journeys in consciousness behind and beyond the visible process of Nature – like a ballerina in Stravinsky's "Rite of Spring" becoming Spring itself while remaining a single character in the concordant ballet – maintains a joyous and silent awareness of the whole process while coolly functioning at various levels with deft dexterity. All human beings, insofar as they can smoothly function at diverse levels of precise control and painless transcendence, can attain to firm fixity of mind and serene steadfastness of spirit – the sacred marks of initiation through sattvic ideation in the secret heart. Sattvic knowledge is the invisible common thread transcending all apparent differences. It gives support to rhythmic activity which is simultaneously precise, liberating and intrinsically self-validating, without the creeping shadow of inconstancy. The self of the individual who is sattvic is integrated with the Self which surveys the whole world with its congeries of forms and objects, whilst seeing all of these appearances in local time and visible space as evanescent parts of a continuous process of interconnected if conceptually discrete causes and consequences. This is like a mighty river that flows from a hidden stream issuing from a sacred source in the depths of the highest mountain ranges. Dnyaneshvari offers an apt analogy which applies both to anamnesis and to *Turiya-Sattva*. Just as when a stream becoming a river empties itself into the great ocean, so too will individual consciousness when it withdraws itself from its reflected sense of "I-ness" within the world of insupportable illusions. When the principle of self-consciousness initiates this inner withdrawal, it quietly empties itself into the great ocean of primordial light, *Daiviprakriti*, universal and self-luminous consciousness. Yet at the same time it remains active within *Hiranyagarbha*, the pristine golden egg of immortal individuality, cosmic and trans-human.

From the standpoint of the man of meditation, light and darkness are archetypal categories applicable at many levels. Philosophically and mystically, darkness at the level of inversion is chaos, and light as we understand it in nature is associated with the illumination of a field of consciousness. Psychologically, for many sad souls darkness is the deepening shadow of loneliness, and light shines as the resplendent vision of human brotherhood and the spiritual solidarity of all that lives. This can become a glorious vision of enduring hope, invulnerable faith and unwavering affirmation. Rodin's well-known simile in stone suggests that the pilgrim-soul and weary toiler is plunged in deep thought. All such persons are asking the oldest question – "Who am I?" Significant trends are emerging across the globe, and the crisis is aggravated by the breakdown of alternatives everywhere and especially in the North American continent. Light and darkness refer to every revivified conception of what is real, what is abstract and what concrete in the vast field of unilluminated objects and hazy memories, the negations and affirmations of consciousness resulting from the repeated negation of a false sense of "I" in a fast-changing world.

The Secret Doctrine offers the ancient analogy of the Sun to the individual emerging out of the cave of avidya in search of Universal Good (*SAT*). Though difficult to exemplify, a talismanic exercise in practical instruction is conveyed. Close your eyes, and from the depths of inmost consciousness travel outward to the extremest limits in every direction. You will find equal lines or rays of perception extending evenly in all directions, so that the utmost effort of ideation will terminate in the vault of a sphere. Think of yourself as within a numinous golden egg, a divine sphere. Close your eyes, draw within, behind and beyond your own shadowy conception of yourself, behind the superficial and self-limiting images of the mind's surface, cast there by the lunar activity of the world, and eclipse your own restless lunar self. As you withdraw behind your five senses, focus upon the place between your eyes and see that point as only a representation in the physical face of a field of consciousness where there are innumerable points, each of which is at the centre of a radiant sphere formed by a reflection of the fiery substance of the dark ocean of space. From the standpoint of your own self-conscious ray of light, try to think outward to the extreme limits of boundless space in every direction. You will find that equal lines or rays of perception will terminate in all directions in the invisible vault of a macrocosmic sphere. The limit of the sphere will be a great circle, and the direct rays of thought in any direction must be right-line radii from a common centre in an immaterial, homogeneous medium. This is the all-embracing human conception of the manifesting aspect of the ever-hidden *Ain-Soph*, which formulates itself in the geometrical figure of a circle with elements of continuous curvature, circumference and rectilinear radii. This geometrical shape is the first recognizable link between the *Ain-Soph* and the highest intelligence of man. The rule proclaimed at the portals of the Pythagorean School and the Platonic Academy limited entry to those who had deeply reflected upon divine geometry. At this stage of the Seventh Impulsion, the qualifications for initiation are naturally stringent.

According to Eastern esotericism, this great circle, which reduces to the point within the invisible boundless sphere, is *Avalokiteshwara*, the *Logos*. It is the manifested God, the *Verbum* of *The Gospel According to St. John*, unknown to man except through its manifested universe and the entirety of mankind. The One is intuitively known by the many, although the One is unthinkable by any mode of mere intellection. Reaching within consciousness means going behind and beyond every possible perception and conception, every possible colour and form. Form corresponds to knowledge on the lower reflected lunar plane; colour corresponds to the knower at the level of the reflected ray. The objects of knowledge are merely modifications of a single substance. These do not yield any simple triadic diagram, but involve a gradual ascent within consciousness, in a tranquil state of contemplation, towards the greatest parametric conception of the One. The Logos sleeps in the bosom of *Parabrahm* – in the Abstract Absolute – during *pralaya* or non-manifestation, just as our individual Ego is in latency during deep, dreamless sleep. We cannot cognize *Parabrahm* except as *Mulaprakriti*, the mighty expanse of undifferentiated cosmic matter. This is not merely a vesture in cosmic creation through which radiate the energy and wisdom of *Parabrahm*. It is the Divine Ground.

The Logos in its highest aspect takes no notice of history. The Logos is behind and beyond what appears important to human beings, but the Logos knows itself. That transcendent self-knowledge is the *fons et origo* of all the myriad rays of self-conscious, luminous intelligence focussed at a certain level of complexity in what we call the human being, rays which, at the same time, light up the infinitude of points in space-time. As the Logos is unknown to differentiated species, and as *Parabrahm* is unknown to *Prakriti*, Eastern esotericism and the Kabbalah alike have resolved the abstract synthesis in relatively concrete images in order to bring the Logos within the range of human conception. We have images, therefore, such as that of the sun and the light, but there is freedom through concentration, abstraction and expansion, while there is bondage through consolidation, concretization and desecration. The Logos is like the sun through which light and heat radiate, but whose energy and light exist in some unknown condition in space and are diffused throughout space as visible light. If one meditates at noon on the invisible midnight sun, which sages reflect upon in a calm state of ceaseless contemplation, and if one remains still and serene, one could exercise the privilege of using the divine gift of sound. The sun itself is only the agent of the Light in *The Voice of the Silence*. This is the first triadic hypostasis. The Tetraktys is emanated by concentrating the energizing light shed by the Logos, but it subsists by itself in the Divine Darkness. A tremendous light-energy flows from the deepest thought, wherein one continuously voids every conception of the reflected ray of egoity or the individual self, all objects and universes, everything in what we call space and time. Thus the individuating mind enters subtler dimensions, through which it can approach universal cognition in a resplendent realm of noumenal reality, opening onto a shared field of total awareness in *Mahat*, wherein the self-consciousness of divine wisdom (*Vach*) is eternally enacted by self-luminous Mahatmas, the Brotherhood of Light.

The true teaching of *Brahma Vach* is enshrined in the secret code language of nature. A new mode of initiation has already begun. Invisible beings in their *mayavi rupas* cherish the teaching, but no visible beings are entirely excluded. The quintessential teaching is conveyed in so many different ways that prepare for the sacred instructions in deep sleep, even for those struggling souls who seize their last chance in this life. The more any person can maintain during waking hours the self-conscious awareness of what is known deep within – even though one cannot formulate it – the more one can hold it and see it as blasphemous to speak thoughtlessly about it. Though such persons participate in all the fickle changes of the butterfly mind, the more attentively they can preserve and retain the seminal energy of thought with a conscious continuity, the more easily will every anxiety about themselves fade into a cool state of contentment. Like a shadow following the lost and stumbling seeker of the light, a true disciple will unexpectedly encounter the forgotten wisdom, the spiritual knowledge, springing up suddenly, spontaneously, within the very depths of his being. Then he may receive the crystalline waters of life-giving wisdom through the central conduit of light-energy, symbolized in the physical body by the spinal cord. One may walk in the world with deep gratitude for the sacred privilege of being a self-conscious *Manasaputra* within the divine temple of the universe for the sake of shedding light upon all that lives and breathes. In seeing, one can send out beneficent rays. In hearing, one can listen beyond the cacophony of the world. Whilst one is listening constantly to the music of the spheres echoing within one's head and heart, one is able to send forth thoughts and feelings that are benevolent and unconditional, extended towards all other human minds. These thoughts could become living talismans for the men and women of tomorrow in the fields of cognition wherein the war between light and darkness, the living and the dead, is now being waged.

The Philosophy of Perfection of Krishna, the Religion of Responsibility of the Buddha, and the Science of Spirituality of Shankara, constitute the Pythagorean teaching of the Aquarian Age of Universal Enlightenment. There are general and interstitial relationships between the idea of perfectibility, the idea of gaining control over the mind, and the exalted conception of knowledge set forth in the eighteenth chapter of the *Gita*. To begin to apprehend these connections, one must first heed the mantramic injunction from *The Voice of the Silence*: "Strive with thy thoughts unclean before they overpower thee." Astonishingly, there was a moment in the sixties when millions became obsessed with instant enlightenment; fortunately, this is not true at present. Few people now seriously believe that they are going to die as perfected beings in this lifetime. This does not mean that the secret doctrines of the 1975 cycle are irrelevant to the ordinary man who, without false expectations, merely wants to finish his life with a modicum of fulfilment. All such seekers can benefit immensely from calmly meditating upon the *Sthitaprajna*, the Self-Governed Sage, the Buddhas of Perfection. This is the crux of Krishna's medicinal method in the *Gita*. He presents Arjuna with the highest ideal, simultaneously shows his difficulties and offers intensive therapy and compassionate counsel. This therapeutic mode continues until the ninth chapter, where Krishna says, "Unto thee who findeth no fault I will now make known this most mysterious knowledge, coupled with a realization of it, which having known thou shalt be delivered from evil." In the eighteenth chapter he conveys the great incommunicable secret – so-called because even when communicated it resides within the code language of Buddhic consciousness. The authors of all the great spiritual teachings like the *Gita*, *The Voice of the*

Silence and *The Crest Jewel of Wisdom* knew that there is a deep mythic sense in which the golden verses can furnish only as much as a person's state of consciousness is ready to receive.

H.P. Blavatsky dedicated *The Voice of the Silence* to the few, to those who seek to become *lanoos*, true neophytes on the Path. Like Krishna, she gave a shining portrait of the man of meditation, the Teacher of Mankind. In chosen fragments from the *Book of the Golden Precepts*, the merciful warning is sounded at the very beginning: "These instructions are for those ignorant of the dangers of the lower IDDHI." In this age the consequences of misuse of psychic powers over many lives by millions of individuals have produced a holocaust – the harvest of terrible effects. Rigid justice rules the universe. Many human beings have gaping astral wounds and fear that there is only a tenuous connecting thread between their personal consciousness and the light of the higher nature. Human beings have long misused *Kriyasakti*, the power of visualization, and *Itchasakti*, the power of desire. Above all, they have misused the antipodal powers of knowledge, *Jnanasakti*, so that there is an awful abyss between men of so-called knowledge and men of so-called power. What is common to both is that their pretensions have already gone for naught, and therefore many have begun to some extent to sense the sacred orbit of the Brotherhood of Bodhisattvas. On the global plane we also witness today the tragic phenomenon of which *The Voice of the Silence* speaks. Many human beings did not strive with their unclean hobgoblin images of a cold war. The more they feared the hobgoblin, the more they became frozen in their conception of hope. Human beings can collectively engender a gigantic, oppressive elemental, like the idea of a personal God, or the Leviathan of the State, which is kept in motion by reinforcement through fear, becoming a kind of reality and producing a paralysis of the will on the global plane.

Today, for the first time in recent decades, we live at that fortunate moment when psychopathology and sociopathology have alike become boring, throwing the individual back upon his intuitions, dreams and secret intimations. Individuals cannot suddenly create refined vestures for the highest spiritual thought-energy, but they can at least desist from self-degradation. No protection a human being can devise is more potent or powerful than the arc of light around every human form. Any individual with unwavering faith in the divine is firmly linked with the ray descending into the hollow of the heart. One can totally reduce the shadowy self to a zero. The cipher may become a circle of sweetness and a sphere of light. It is imperative to keep faith with oneself in silence and secrecy, as every telling weakens the force that is generated. Krishna says, "In whatever way men approach me, in that way do I assist them." This is offered unconditionally to all. Near the end of his instruction he says, "Act as seemeth best unto thee."

Basic honesty will go far to clean out the cobwebs of delusion and confusion so that the seeds of spiritual regeneration may be salvaged. Patience is needed together with enduring trust in the healing and nurturing processes of Nature that protect the seeds silently germinating in the soil. They cannot be pulled up and scrutinized again and again, but must be allowed to sprout in the soft light of the dawn, enriched by the radiant magnetism of universal love which maintains the whole cosmos in motion. Even a little soul-memory shows that there is no need to blame history or nature, much less the universe, for the universe is on the side of every sincere impulse. Even the most wicked and depraved man may have some hope. Even a little daily practice delivereth a man from great risk. Even a minute grain of soul-wisdom, when patiently assimilated with a proper mental posture in relation to the sacred teachings and the sacrificial Teachers, will act as a beneficent influence and an unfailing guide to the true servant of the Masters of the Verbum. This incommunicable secret of Krishna is the sweetest and most potent gift of the divine Logos of the cosmos to the awakened humanity of today and the global civilization of tomorrow.

Hermes, October 1978

SPIRITUAL ATTENTION

Sit evenly, erect, at ease, with palms folded on the lap, with eyes fixed on the nose: cleanse your lungs by taking a deep breath, holding it in and then discharging it, raise in your heart the OM sounding like the tolling of a bell, and in the lotus of your heart, contemplate My form as encircled by light.

The path of knowledge is for those who are weary of life; those who still have desires should pursue the path of sublimation through works: and to those who are not completely indifferent nor too much attached the devotional path bears fruit.

Perform your actions for Me and with thoughts fixed on Me: untainted like the sky, see yourself within your self; consider all beings as Myself and adore them; bow to everybody, high or low, great or small, kind or cruel; by seeing Me constantly in all, rid yourself of jealousy, intolerance, violence and egoism. Casting aside your pride, prestige, and sense of shame, fall prostrate in humility before all, down to the dog and ass. This is the knowledge of the learned, the wisdom of the wise – that man attains the Real with the unreal and the Immortal with the mortal.

Krishna to Uddhava

The universe is mostly unmanifest, and every human being is a microcosmic reflection of the entire egg-like cosmos. Each individual is a vast but largely hidden force field, but all are manifesting with varying degrees of knowledge, deliberation and discrimination. These diversities are the product of a long history of use, overuse and misuse of the sheaths and vestures in which immortal monads have been embodied in myriad environments over eighteen million years. Given this far-reaching perspective, how can any person use this potent teaching in order to become a better human being? How can an individual become more attentive and discriminating in using the sacred gift of creative imagination, training the mind as an instrument for concentrated thought, directed with a benevolent feeling towards goals compatible with the purposes of all living beings, towards universal good? Strange as it may seem, everyone can discover indispensable clues for answering this question in the simple fact that he or she is a certain kind of human being. The whole story is recorded from head to toe: the way a person walks and talks; the way a person holds himself or herself; the way a person thinks, feels and acts; the way a person relates to other beings; but, above all, the way a person lives through waking and sleeping from day to day, passing through the three halls of consciousness – *jagrat*, *swapna* and *sushupti* – connecting moments in childhood through the seasons of human life, growing, maturing and mellowing with intermittent glimpses of wisdom.

Every person can test motives and methods in the daily attempts to translate thought and intention into outer modes of expression. If someone gets a chance to work upon certain details of some part of a larger work in which the levels of motivation markedly vary, that person can learn through what karma brings to him or her. If, by mistake, one became involved in more than one can manage, this would be known within a short time because one would get burnt. To be unready is to have a shrunken sense of self and therefore a force field that is very congested with blurred, contradictory and weak currents liable to short circuits and shocks. As long as there is the opportunity to learn and to correct, it is always possible to make a difference because all human beings are capable in their finest moments of the highest possible motivation. There is hardly a person who has not had moments of pure love of the human race. There are few who have gone through the whole of life without even once having looked at the stars and sky and wondered at the magnitude of the universe. Nature cannot support a human being who cannot ever negate the suffocation of confinement within shallow perspectives of mind and heart. As long as there is the beneficence of sleep, every human being has abundant opportunities to renew the larger Self, the greater motive, the fuller perspective. The problem then is not that a human being is without spiritual resources, but rather how to make those resources tapped during deep dreamless sleep relevant when one is out in the field of duty, *Kurukshetra*. Wakeful deployment of resources will require sufficient noetic detachment to avert captivity to compulsive activity, and thereby avoid being cut off from the greater Self. When the only correction available is sleep, it is too inefficient to rely upon automatically because the daily passage through confused dream states vitiates the healing effects of deeper dreamless states.

Meditation is the source of noetic understanding, but this depends upon an initial humbling of the false self that otherwise undermines every effort. Learning without unlearning is not only useless, but, like eating without elimination, it can be fatal. Bad habits must be unlearnt while learning new ways of doing things that come from new ways of thinking, and in this continuous process one has to be courageous in assessing one's spiritual strivings. By seeing where one is going wrong and why, it is possible to make significant connections between causes and consequences and then see where a real difference can be made. It is always possible to make a difference, but only on the basis of self-examination that leaves one more determined and relaxed – more relaxed because of seeing oneself in relation to the whole of humanity. Without running away from the facts, it is possible to take an honest inventory, and if this is done, one will soon begin to discover that it is not that one's motive is entirely bad or that one is altogether no good. It is rather that one is not very good at learning because of having created blockages in the self through pride, blockages in the mind through prejudice, blockages in the heart through partiality, blockages in the will through perversity. These blockages precipitate very quickly in the presence of great resolves, and if they are not faced, it is difficult to avoid walking backwards. But if this realization brings a sense of defeat, that means one never really understood the teaching of Karma. The Self that has to make the effort of understanding is that ray of the immortal soul which is put in charge of the kingdom in which the different parts of one's being must be dynamically balanced. When there is a greater harmony within, it is possible to contribute more to harmony without. This is what each is meant to do. The general accounting can be left to Karma. By altering radically one's attitude to work, to motive and method, and one's way of balancing them, there is the opportunity for growth on the basis of a larger and a firmer recognition of the invisible forces, realities and laws constantly at work in Nature and in oneself.

One must use with care those living messengers called words, and this reference to messengers has to do with different classes of elementals, all the myriad invisible centres of energy that permeate the diverse departments of Nature. To be full of the fire of devotion and to do the best work one can, one must have the right basis in thinking. The immortal soul is capable of immortal love, of immortal longings that may summon the life-essence that permeates this globe, the omnipresent spirit that is dateless and deathless. Everyone is inherently capable of an unending, unconditional love and courage and endurance, ready "to suffer woes hope thinks infinite". The depth of devotion depends upon the level of being. Those who are unafraid of death, who see themselves neither in terms of the body nor in terms of the mind, but as immortal monads, can generate and sustain devotion to the greater hearts and minds of the Bodhisattvas. This constant devotion is in the context of universal mind or *Mahat*, and the hebdomadal heart of the cosmos. They come under the protection of supreme compassion, the universal umbrella of Dharma. When devotion thus becomes a sovereign talisman, it is continually enriched by *yajna* and *tapas*, sacrificial meditation. The wise are those who, starting from small drops of genuine devotion, humility and wisdom, make them grow. They are wise because they grow the way Nature grows. They will, of course, make mistakes, but as long as they maintain their original recognition of the utter simplicity, the transparency and truth of devotion, they can strengthen the current of resolve and regeneration. Magic is possible where there is authenticity, continuity and a sense of proportion, where there is sacrifice, care and a willingness to learn, as well as a capacity to merge the little self in the greater Self.

The path of spiritual attention is not easy, although anyone can make a beginning by trying to understand. Those who still have desires should pursue the path of sublimation through sacrificial works. To those who are neither completely indifferent nor too much attached, the devotional path bears fruit. One is not expected to be perfectly indifferent to everything nor suddenly to show effortless mastery in the practice of devotion. Devotees have their many limitations, but they are expected to moderate their attachment to the fruits of results. Then the path of devotion will bear fruit at the moment of death or in other lives. The mathematics of the universe is exact; one merely does the best one can and leaves the rest to the Law. It is necessary to elevate what is mortal and unreal with the help of a mental posture which involves true obeisance. To remember properly the original moment is to gain glimpses into the future. The divisions of time into night and day, clock time and calendars, engender an illusory sense of past and present and future. It may be that in a certain year upon a certain day one had a spiritual awakening because one came into the presence of spiritual wisdom. If so, to be true to that means to keep going back again and again to the original moment, because the more one can do that, the more one will come closer to the Teachers of Wisdom. If on any issue one understood the original moment, then one would see that the whole story is compressed in that original moment. In that is already determined and defined the future outcome of everything that is connected with that original moment.

One cannot awaken the powers of spiritual attention if one is preoccupied with externals. One cannot be spiritually awake and attentive if one has forgotten that one is an immortal soul. Even if at some level one knew it and then forgot it, that is going to have an effect upon the power of attention. Understanding means making connections. When one truly enjoys thinking about what one is trying to recall, then one can summon other ideas connected with the same line of thinking. Correlations begin to emerge and connections can be made. With calm and detachment and true love of something larger than oneself, there can be access to a vaster perspective. The reason why people forget and why they fantasize is that they do not really know in the present. The reason they do not know in the present is that they are not fully attentive as immortal souls. They are misled by the sensorium, by the shadowy screen of prejudice, by the film of false anticipation and by the burden of failure, shame and regret. Therefore, they have neither lightness nor freedom nor joy, neither do they have any fullness of receptivity and devotion. The path of spiritual reminiscence has to be summoned, and the future is obscure to those who desperately want clues or cues from the outside.

Human beings define themselves during the day by how they relate to deep sleep, and during their lifetime by how they relate to their golden moments. They could know their karma if only they would have the courage to look at their vows, at their highest moments and the extent of their fidelity to them. If they can say that they have at some level made an effort to be true but failed, then they should go on and say that they are willing for Karma to work. They must be honest with themselves if they would gain the strength they need through rekindling a golden moment. This could again become real for them in the present. Then they do not have to see their future only in terms of failures, betrayals, forgetfulness and loss of vision. They could see it in terms of a renewal of vision and a rekindling of strength.

To work with Karma is to learn why one is what one is at any given time on any plane, to look at one's strengths and with the help of this awareness to recognize the seeds of former resolve. One always has the opportunity to be grateful to those who made it possible, to have the courage to look at one's weaknesses and understand calmly how they arose, and be determined to counteract them. Then one has a sense of actually shaping the future on the basis of true knowledge, not on the basis of mere chance or the whim of a capricious god. This is true spiritual knowledge based upon a courageous correction of one's own relationship to the divine spirit within, the indwelling *Ishwara*. Great teachers work under a law where every genuine striving is noticed, but all human beings throughout the world come under the same law. Those who can see the past, the present and the future simultaneously will only let their gaze fall where it is merited, because where it falls there is a tremendous quickening of opportunities for growth, but also an enormous increase of the hazards of neglect. In a dynamic universe of thought and of consciousness, a great difference can be made in one's understanding of causality and of energy through one's concept of time which is determined by one's concept of selfhood and being. This is truly a function of how one thinks at this moment today, how one sleeps tonight and how one wakes up tomorrow, in a cycle of progressive awakenings through meditation and ethical practice, not for the sake of oneself but for the sake of all living beings in the visible and invisible cosmos.

Hermes, May 1979

MENTAL POSTURE

Seek this wisdom by doing service, by strong search, by questions, and by humility; the wise who see the truth will communicate it unto thee . . .

Sri Krishna

Lord Krishna strings the sacred teachings of the *Bhagavad Gita* on the golden thread of mental posture, the relation between the spiritual seeker and the Divine Wisdom embodied as the Light of the Logos in lustrous beings. Mental posture refers primarily to an attitude of mind, and constitutes the sacred trust between *chela* and Guru. Those who wish to become sincere and true servants of all mankind with its immense suffering, and of the Great Masters of Wisdom with their inexhaustible light, must prepare themselves by a process of purgation whereby they negate the false conceptions of themselves derived from the world into which they are born, from their heredity, upbringing, environment and education. This is done by a method of intense self-questioning. Platonic thought is essentially a dialogue with oneself. When people really begin to ask questions of themselves, and also attempt to apply the principles involved in formulating questions in a multiplicity of contexts, then they gradually begin to glimpse the dynamic, albeit mysterious, relation between manifest and unmanifest.

We could compare wisdom to light – the ineffable light of the Invisible Sun. Is this light obscured in a solar eclipse? Actually, it is then even more accessible to men of meditation. Is this light inaccessible during an eclipse of the moon? Not to men of meditation. But, alas, most human beings are not men of meditation. They have never really thought seriously, hungered sufficiently, wanted with enough intensity of one-pointed devotion, the great Teaching in relation to the immortality of the soul. Divine Wisdom can come alive through the *Manas-Taijasi*, the thinking principle irradiated by the Buddhic fire of the divine dialectic. Before *Buddhi* can become one with *Manas*, before Truth and Love can be brought together in a mystic marriage, there is a preliminary betrothal. The thinking principle sunders its false allegiance to the shadowy self or the astral body, and then draws towards the hidden light of the sun, the light of *Buddhi* which is fully lit in a Buddha.

If wisdom may be compared to light, method may be compared to a lens. We have different lenses for a microscope and a telescope. We need one lens for looking at that which is so invisibly small as to become visible only through a powerful magnifier. When looking closer at the stars, we need a lens suitable to a telescope, with specific refractive powers and made of particular kinds of glass. In all searching instruments, through which we wish to focus light for the sake of understanding and making discoveries in relation to the mysteries of matter at all levels, we also need to know something about the angle at which the refraction of light may affect the intensity, clarity, purity and stability of the images formed.

All human beings, every day of their lives, are involved unconsciously in the quest for wisdom. When they become postulants or neophytes, they are put on a preliminary probation and can be received as disciples only after they have completed preliminary qualifications. All of these involve a re-orientation of their life outlook in relation to who they are, why they were born, their attitude to the moment of death, where they are going, the nature of their every relationship, and above all whether they are ready to pledge themselves *irreversibly* towards that which they find irresistible – the great thrill that accompanies the light of daring lit up in the heart, the thrill of compassionate service to the whole of suffering humanity.

At the very beginning of the fourth chapter of the *Bhagavad Gita* there is an extraordinary statement. Having first established the inexhaustible nature of this yoga, Krishna states that the Secret Doctrine was first communicated to *Vivasvat* – the primordial manifestation of the divine Wisdom within the vast cosmic depths, understood in the *Kabbalah* as "the ancient of Days", and in the New Testament as "That which was in the beginning". It is eternal and yet a reflection of itself is the first light in every great period of manifestation. It was transmitted through *Vaivasvata Manu*, the essential root-type of the mankind in existence for at least a million years. Then it was communicated to *Ikshvaku*, the mighty Brotherhood of Mahatmas. Their compassion is boundless and their concern is profound for the primary needs of every epoch. They make allowances for the errors of thought that became magnified over the last two thousand years and more. They recognize the mathematical accuracy of the law of cycles under which there may be permitted from age to age – for the preservation of the just, the destruction of the demoniac and the establishment of righteousness – the timely promulgation of divine wisdom by the Avatars who come as the Great Teachers of Humanity.

Any human being in any part of the world who retires at night with a true feeling of responsiveness to the travails of suffering humanity, receives help in deep sleep, if his inmost self turns towards *Ishwara*. The intensity of desire, the propriety of motive, and the devotion of the heart will necessarily determine the infallible beneficent response that comes from within deep sleep, and also enables one to tap the pristine vibrations brought down by earnest sacrificial meditations from the peaks of universal ideation into the surrounding magnetosphere of the globe. Therefore, after Krishna says that the sacred teaching was communicated to Vivasvat and to Manu and also to *Ikshvaku*, and then to the Raja Rishis, the royal sages behind the chief dynasties of all the ancient kingdoms which witnessed the forgotten renaissances of antiquity, he says to Arjuna, "All of this I now make known to you." Why? Because "Thou art my devotee and my friend."

Mental posture is critical and crucial, and everyone can at any time alter his or her standpoint. One way to do it at all levels is to emulate the wise Rishis of the *Rig Veda*. Having given the great *Hymn of Creation*, raising questions about why, when, how it all began, they said, "Who knows?" The gods, the sages? Perhaps not even they. When people gain the thrill of true agnosticism, then they liberate themselves from the thraldom of strain and from self-concern in its negative, destructive, wasteful sense. They begin to release the living power of the continuity of the divine spirit within the temple and the tenement of the reflected ray, so that the solar light activates all latent centres and cells within the body. Therefore, they know at each step the preparation needed for the next. Each step shows the way, as in mountain climbing. A point is eventually reached where, out of enormous compassion for the multitudes in the plains, a stout fearlessness amidst the raging storms, with a steady, sure-footed stance, carrying a lantern that sheds the light hidden in the divine darkness, a person suffuses his pilgrimage with purity, strength, and immense joy. He recognizes that the universe is vast, boundless and beautiful, and is constantly willing to release beneficent thought-streams for the good of all, thereby deserving the grace of the Guru.

Recognition of the light and rectification of mental posture begin in the ability to ask real questions. A real question must itself be rooted in one's life. We have magnificent examples of this among little children, who initially find the universe so wonderful that they are constantly raising real questions. Why is it human beings lose child-like trust and cease to show the pure joy of questioning? The twentieth century will one day come to be known not only for concentration camps, not only for the horrors of all the killings in the world, but also for the massacre of minds under an educational system where children are treated as objects. Children are labelled and graded, and encouraged to pretend they know instead of honestly saying, "I don't know." The strain is too much. If one receives such instruction, one tends to be instantly threatened wherever there is real knowledge. After a point it starts to have its effect on the face, on lacklustre eyes which become either self-destructive or replete with the "jealous *Lhamayin* of endless space."

Could all these people start all over again? They can – because the *Gita* teaches that unknown to themselves, they are making sacrifices. Some make sacrifices to the god of work; others make sacrifices to the god of self-worship; still others make sacrifices to what they think to be knowledge. Consider the whole of humanity and those souls that did not like making sacrifices in previous lives. Where will they be reborn? Those who wanted opportunities life after life – complaining in villages, "If only I had education"; rebelling against arranged marriages, "If only I could choose freely"; restlessly looking for excitement, "The countryside is boring. I want to go to the big town" – such people generated a line of life's meditation. All of these are the world's discontented from all classes.

To sense this is to ask questions about meaning, rooted in experience. But questions about meaning become real only when they are rooted in experience of pain. Where one's experience of pain is inserted into the pain of humanity, there is universality in the quality of the suffering, in the myriad dimensions of experience, and in the hunger for meaning. Thus it is that Krishna endorses indifference to the multitude of differences abounding in the world. The offerings are the Supreme Spirit. The sacrificial butter is the Supreme Spirit. All is the Supreme Spirit. All comes back into the One, but in coming back into the One, the great choice for man is in relation to the whole or the part, the living or the dying, the future or the past; That which is unchanging or that which is ever changing; That which is indestructible, though invisible, or that which is both perishable and visible. One may choose That which is the eternal witness, the inmost sanctuary, the protective power within the immortal soul of every man. This soul-power can be released by any human being, despite all the confusions, muddles, mistakes, self-deceptions, rationalizations and wanderings in the dark. Somewhere the wonderings in relation to the light persist and all else drifts away as autumnal leaves.

What is hidden in the root systems of the trees that are so many human beings? It is the Real. As long as the waters of life below are mingled with the waters of wisdom above, then everyone is able, out of the moisture of the suffering of the heart and the sincerity of persistent attempts, to become rooted within the great hidden underground. It is possible to take a proper mental posture in relation to That which is spaceless and timeless, dateless and deathless, That which existed before birth and That which will exist after the moment of death. To do this within oneself is to find that the whole universe is a magnificent unbound encyclopedia of answers, and that the whole of life is a series of questions. One starts to walk in the world with the light of questioning in one's eyes. When one starts to move in the world with questioning in the heart; when one starts to see all others in terms of those fundamental and enduring questions that concern all human beings; and where the questioning becomes a quest, then life is a single question that cannot be answered without meditation upon birth, death, decay, sickness, but above all, upon error. When one meditates on all of these, in time one's life is not only a quest, but a beatific, ceaseless contemplation. Then a person comes closer to the great mystery of the fourth chapter of the *Gita*, which teaches: "That man who sees inaction in action and action in inaction is wise among men." There is action during deep sleep. There is inaction amidst the daily round and the common task, the milling crowds, lost and confined, cribbed and cabined, within the cast-iron cage of their shadowy selves and vociferating on behalf, not of the universal good, but of their own little selves.

Behind this masquerade there is the Soundless Sound. The *Mandukya Upanishad* says that eventually we truly come to recognize, to revere, and to renounce everything for the sake of the One – OM TAT SAT – That which is beyond all colours and forms, all limitations, all labels, all distinctions, all beginnings, changes and endings. We see beyond all conditions and conditionality itself when we feel that the unconditional is not distant but closer to us than our own heart. We become that which all beings are, at different degrees of knowledge and forgetfulness, but which we can self-consciously embody. Though there are many things we remember and also many that we forget, we are that which could never be remembered and could never be forgotten because it is beyond and behind memory. It is beyond and behind the limbos and the Lethe of delusive forgetfulness. It is that primordial pulse that precedes all manifestation and what we call recorded history. It is older than billions of years and is vaster than outer space. Behind and beyond all the labels which humanity hugs there is a boundless ocean and an eternal river. Like Hesse's Siddhartha, we may learn from the ferryman the great secret. All those who come to the river ask all kinds of questions, but most are questions about money or time, questions about all the other people who come, questions on behalf of themselves. But he who has watched it all, this Vasudeva, knows that there are great sounds of every kind in the river. Because he has seen behind and beyond all the ripples on the surface of the river, he has seen a tremendous compassion in the very depths of the waters.

When a man senses the living reality of the energy of the compassion of wisdom, then he begins to become a free man. For him the answer of the ancients is the start of his life. The Many come from the One because compassion first arose in It. That same compassion ensures the return of each and every one of the Many back into the One. When this teaching has been learnt, has been burnt into the brain and into the very heart and soul, then, as the *Mandukya* urges, we abandon all other questions. We cleave unto the truth of the Soundless Sound. When one comes to that point, then life is a question mark and each of us is the answer.

All questions are rafts that can transport a person part of the way and no further. In the end, the passenger plunges off the raft; this must be done again and again. No one can swim in mid-ocean without taking a small canoe or a small raft to the waters. When watching ships on the ocean, we may see that all of these are like human beings on a boundless voyage. We experience that transcendental feeling common to all. It could be lit and re-lit, purifying our motives, redeeming us from our own small-minded thoughts and self-defeating patterns, freeing us from our bondage to our limited conception of this world. We could move with the glory and the dignity of those who know that within every human heart is the possibility of sensing the immortal spirit.

The beginnings of all are protected by the Law. Wisdom, method and practice are fused in a dialectical inter-relationship. At the start, wisdom could be put at the apex of a triangle, and method at the midpoint of the base. At a later stage, the points could be varied. Then a time comes when one sees that the very separation between the knower, the known and the knowing is only a conventional one, and that the three are a union within the universe and a union within every man. In the end we always return to the same point. Man can gain self-knowledge only if he makes his soul-gaze centre on "the One Pure Light, the Light that is free from affection." Then and only then can he use the Golden Key of method to unlock and throw open the radiant portals of Wisdom.

Hermes, May 1977

THE JOY OF DEVOTION

The waters of immersion purify a man only if he is wholly immersed.

Hasidic Saying

True devotion is neither involuntary emotion nor gratuitous feeling, but an innate and indestructible soul-power. There is a vital difference between the surging depths of feeling and the oscillations of volatile emotion. Emotion is often compelling, but its seeming intensity is as short-lived as the cyclonic wind which howls and vanishes. Feeling is much more durable, corresponding to the unmoved silent depths of the ocean, a measureless expanse of water with a potential strength far greater than manifest energy. Every human being risks, through faulty upbringing or through grievous neglect of finer feelings – especially when the libido is awakened between fourteen and twenty-one – being scarred for life by becoming caught in one of two extremes. Either there is wasteful expenditure of emotion – excess of excitement with its inevitable shadow of disappointment, deficiency and gloom, or there is stern external control over emotion that induces an inability to convey authentic feeling in one's relationship to a child, in one's encounter with a stranger, or even in greeting a friend with the eyes of trust.

The term 'devotion' remains one of the more beautiful words in the language, its suggestive and sacred etymology harking back to the taking of a vow. At the popular level this may be seen in frenzied devotion to a secular cause such as that of a political party. There can be total commitment without any streak of scepticism. There is neither wavering nor weakening of such commitment, but it is focussed upon an abstract idea attached to some tangible form. Few human beings, however, can contain the vast energy of unconditional commitment within the vessel of any external organization. Attempts to do so in messianic politics merely re-enact what happened in earlier history in relation to dogmatic religion. Owing to the limitations of sectarian ideologies and organizational structures, and especially due to the difficulty of distinguishing between the impersonal, immortal individuality and the changing personal mask, ardent votaries fall prey to self-righteousness, an outburst of exaggerated emotion mistaken for deep feeling. No wonder Socrates challenged Euthyphro's claims to knowledge of piety or holiness – the relation between gods and humans – the most exalted, elusive and mysterious of subjects, wherein one's credential is the uncommon recognition that one does not really know. What was true in his day is even more evident in our own time. Many people are running away from past symbols of piety, from various forms of totalism and tokenism in churches, and from every kind of trivialized, degraded and vulgarized ritual and sacrament. But in rushing to the opposite extreme, pretending to be nihilists, they are often trapped in the tragic nihilism of having no faith in themselves, not even enough to carry on from day to day. Muddled thinking and negative emotions reinforce each other, corrupting the psyche.

Devotion is much more than wanting to be devoted. It is far more than having a euphoric feeling, however holy this may seem at the time. Devotion is a different order of consciousness from that involved in the expenditure of emotion. Its sovereign power can only flow freely from the *Atman*, the perpetual motion of transcendental light that shines upon every human soul. It is invoked through an inward prostration of the mind within the sanctuary of the heart, towards the Light of the Logos. To ask how one can prostrate before that which one does not comprehend is to ask how to be humble before the great mystery of nature, the vastitude of life, or the saga of humanity. To be humble in this sense is not merely to say to oneself that one does not know, but also means that one can thrill with the thought of the *mysterium tremendum*. Even though one does not know its destiny or destination, one may feel reverence for the whole of humanity; though one cannot fathom the breadth or depth of nature, one rejoices in one's kinship with nature; though one has no final answer to the basic questions of life, one remains open towards the life-process. Such simple devotion generates the proper mental posture, which Krishna depicts in the *Bhagavad Gita*. It is neither too high nor too low, neither so abject that one cannot generate any enthusiasm nor so lofty that one is isolated within an ivory tower of self-delusion.

True devotion comes to birth through the firm recognition of the unity of all life and the universality of the highest ideals and ideas conceived, transcending the human capacity to formulate and transmit them. When devotion continues undiminished through the trials that it necessarily brings – just as light increases the shadow – it renews itself. It must be put to the test, and it surely will be. The moment one approaches the presence of a spiritual Teacher and professes one's devotion, the jealous Lhamayin of endless space rush to taint and rupture the current of total commitment. That is always the way, illustrated in the fairy stories and myths of all peoples. One has to encounter the abyss; one has to be tried and tempted. Jesus had three great temptations, of which a beautifully perceptive account is given by Dostoevsky in the story of the Grand Inquisitor. All Initiates go through trials, and they do this deliberately because, although those who are perfected before birth really need no tests, they compassionately re-enact the archetypal story for the sake of the human race. Any person can, from small beginnings, tap the immense potential power in a vow to give birth to lasting devotion. This cannot be done even with an authentic start and a self-sustaining rhythm unless it is fortified by the fearlessness and courage that are rooted in the invulnerable truth of one's devotion. We can discover many analogies in daily life. Individuals may recognize that however much they muddied their relations with their parents, they need not be hostile toward those who gave them human bodies. Persons can look back and see that although they were dreadful in their behaviour towards their teachers, they can still cherish the feeling of gratitude to those who taught them the alphabet. Without retrospective veneration of parents and teachers, one has no right to speak or put words on paper or to enjoy the privilege of articulation. All of this is part of the universal code of human decency.

When a person is willing to put right his elementary obligations, then the more difficult problems in one's relationship to one's spouse or children, to friends, strangers, critics and so-called enemies can also be brought into the arena of rigorous self-examination. There is essentially one paramount choice for every person. Either one self-consciously tests oneself and cooperates with the process of testing by nature, or one is dragged unwillingly to life's examinations. Much as one may be afraid of failing every question, still, the only way one can calmly face the moment of death is by seeing that there is something yet to be learnt. No one can complete the probation of a lifetime without having learnt some critical lesson to be derived from each incarnation. In every age and all over the world, noble souls have taken birth for whom none of this is new. They have known from early childhood that their lives have a single sacred purpose, the golden karma of devoted service to the Brotherhood of Bodhisattvas. They faithfully nurtured the fire of devotion even before they found the sole object to which it could be fully directed. Therefore, as surely as day follows night – the long night of awakening which may seem very long indeed while it lasts – they infallibly enter the orbit of the Mahatmas who are ever at work in the world and who are compassionately concerned to extend every opportunity for the whole of humanity to benefit from the sacred circle of chelas. Disciples pledged and put through probationary trials and training become one-pointed in mind, single-hearted, and of one will in their heroic capacity to release a power stronger than the sum of its parts and truly a magnet for the highest forces in nature.

Devotion is rather like the harnessing of electrical energy. In order to be properly channelled to some end, the resistance or responsiveness of the conductor is crucial. Just as a river cannot rise above its source, the power of devotion is as great as the height upon which it is focussed. Devotion is also affected by the clarity of the mental picture of the ideal, even though that evolving picture may fall short of the ideal which, when fully realized, becomes so all-encompassing that it is beyond the possibility of formulation in words or of any expression in particular modes. As Shelley knew,

> Rome's azure sky,
> Flowers, ruins, statues, music, words, are weak
> The glory they transfuse with fitting truth to speak.

Human beings can come to learn that devotion fundamentally alters the relation and ratio between the unmanifest and the manifest: what is not said is more important than what is said; what is not shown or seen is more suggestive than what is shown and seen. Francis Thompson exclaimed –

> O world invisible, we view thee,
> O world intangible, we touch thee,
> O world unknowable, we know thee,
> Inapprehensible, we clutch thee!

This celebrates the passage from the region of maya to the realm of *SAT*. One of the oldest invocations in the Upanishads is: "Lead me from the unreal to the Real. Lead me from darkness to Light. Lead me from death to Immortality."

The relation between the manifest and the unmanifest is analogous to the relations between *chela* and guru, between *Manas* and the Manasas, and between man and mankind. Every human being is a necessary limb in the whole of humanity, a fact symbolized in the ancient and profound Jewish conception of humanity as the manifestation of Adam Kadmon, one great collective person. The same idea is found under different forms in the Renaissance, for example in Leonardo da Vinci's suggestive painting of a man within a man. Every human being is a microcosm of the macrocosm. Each is as a child in reference to the whole of humanity, a *chela* in reference to the sacred and mystical collective Host. But humanity is more than existing human beings. Though a difficult conception for a small minority of the world today, this is as obvious as $2 + 2 = 4$ to the vast majority. Humanity is always greater than the number of people incarnated at any given time. E. F. Schumacher pointed out that the earth could be seen as underpopulated. From the universal standpoint of global welfare, the resources of the earth are capable of supporting a larger number of people than the present population. When human beings fail in their plans – based upon false, half-true or short-term assumptions – they begin to mock Mother Nature. Nature in all her abundance and affluence has never failed the entire human race in recorded history nor earlier, and will not fail the human race in any time to come. Human beings bring upon themselves their own karma, collectively in groups and as individuals, and thereby they experience the holocaust, mentally or physically.

All human beings are fallen gods. As a thinking being with a highly complex brain that no animal possesses, with the sacred gift of speech, each human being already has the highest faculties. Each one has the sovereign powers of choice and of imagination – the king-faculty – which are both essential to the guru-*chela* relationship. Suppose a person suddenly awakens and affirms that to be a human being is a tremendous privilege. Even though it may be, as Thoreau said, that only one out of a thousand is a real individual with courage and strength, none the less anyone can gain access to the entire human heritage. If one is willing to rediscover what it means to be human, this brings one into the radius of the divine. One is at least on the threshold of the recognition that there are powers and principalities throughout the whole of nature, and that so far from being a blind and inanimate world moved mechanistically by collocations of atoms in random statistical patterns, this is indeed an intelligent universe with innumerable conscious centres of cosmic ideation and energy. If a person begins to see nature in this way, then it is possible to recover the richness of one's divine inheritance. Man is descended from those whom Pythagoras called the Fathers of the human race, whom the Hindus called the *Agnishwatha Pitris*, the givers of the solar light of self-consciousness to humanity. These spiritual ancestors were reverenced by the Chinese and the ancient Egyptians, just as the heroes of old were honoured by the Greeks and the Romans. The whole of the human story is a magnificent and mostly unrecorded saga replete with immense resources that are still accessible to individuals. By self-election and self-determination, each person must lay claim to the universal treasure of wisdom.

Mahatmas are primarily concerned with humanity as a whole, not with separate units in themselves. Their constant focus is upon universal good, and their wise efforts are directed to the humanity of tomorrow. How can a person with a restricted range of consciousness become a *chela* to Mahatmas, who are attuned to *Mahat* or cosmic ideation and whose compassion flows towards the entire human race, born and unborn? Although the vast gulf in awareness cannot be easily spanned by the prospective *chela*, it is bridgeable through true devotion. Inversion of standpoint begins with looking and judging from below above. It is like standing on a little footstool in a crowded room and formulating an exact conception of the Himalayas or of the galaxies moving through boundless space. This is futile and even perverse. Generally, the mental posture of diverse individuals towards mankind or the Mahatmas is not the same all over the world, and therefore none can really gauge the destinies of souls. How, then, may aspirants who from their own altitude cannot fathom the empyrean come any closer to the Mahatmas by devotion, determination and total dedication? This is possible only because the enlightened are generous in their shower of light and wisdom, like the rains which render the earth fragrant and fertile. One should rise mentally as far above as possible towards the most exalted conception of humanity, of Mahatmas and *chelas*, and then with eyes open, see everything mirrored below. Thus one can heal, correct and cure oneself.

One can become capable of showing expansiveness, generosity, magnanimity and gratitude and, above all, reverence, because without reverence one is less than human. Where there is reverence, there is growth. It is nurtured in the silence in which, from humble beginnings unseen below the soil, a plant may grow and in time become a tree that can take its place in secluded forests of towering sentinels. Primeval forests mirror something vastly more overwhelming in relation to the Mahatmas, who have been compared to the sturdy limbs of a mighty banyan tree with its roots above the firmament and its branches below on earth. The heavenly tree of wisdom has been known as *Brahma Vach*, *Bodhi Dharma*, gnosis and by many other names. The Vedas depict the Rishis and seers as of one mind, one heart, one will and one voice. It is the Voice of "the Ancient of Days", transcending all known frontiers and concepts of human history and evolution. With the vast perspective of the accumulated wisdom of the ages, the disciple must rejoice rather than despair in the realization that he is zero. The power of the zero in mathematics depends upon where it is placed. Zero before a number has no value. If zero is the numerator of a fraction, the value is nought; if it is the denominator, the value is infinite. If zero is put after a number, its power is significant. Everything depends on where the zero is inserted. The three-dimensional sphere filled with empty space can accommodate tetrahedrons and the dodecahedron. If a human being did not have analogous empty spaces within the brain and the chambers of the heart, there would be no room for the *Akashic* fires or the *Anahata* vibration.

True joy is far from a frenetic attempt to convince oneself that one is enjoying oneself. When one continually needs convincing, nothing adequately convinces. *Ananda* has nothing to do with ephemeral pleasures or private self-satisfaction. True joy or *ananda* springs up in the heart and mind like artesian wells, and though it may overflow in appropriate words and gestures, it is always greater than the power and possibility of expression. The highest joy lights a fire that can never be put out. If the level of joy reached is unstable, it may be no more than a compensatory form of consolation. It will be temporary and intermittent. It cannot mirror the *ananda* of the Mahatmas, whose every affirmation has the accent of transcendental truth and is verifiable through self-realization. Once deep joy is aroused, it is consistent and capable of self-maintenance. It is similar to the quiet cheerfulness of mountaineers carrying little lanterns across dark, iridescent slopes, patiently climbing steep ascents, crossing abysses and caverns while heedful of the great rumblings of nature. Theirs is the peaceful joy of knowing that even if they cannot climb any further now, they could start again, that even if each is alone and without friends in a solitary spot, yet somehow something may happen and timely help may come. And if indeed it is one's lot to die then and there, death comes as a deliverer and a friend. Human beings must seek out the meaning of life and death, asking the question, "Suppose I die tonight? What reason is there for me to be joyous?" If one can find it today, then one can live differently from tonight and tomorrow. There is always joy around us, and the hidden joy suffuses the manifest gloom.

The worst of times is also the best of times. Joy sees beyond the chaotic city that has to go. It is not clinging but courageous, willing to greet the unknown and the uncertain, fearlessly and with maturity. It is capable of drawing the larger circle and enclosing myriads of unknown human beings, never confining oneself within a small circle of confused allegiance. The ancient teaching of India declared: He who loves lives; he who loves himself lives in hell (the hell of loneliness and gloom); he who loves another lives on earth; he who loves others lives in heaven; but he who silently adores and loves the Self of all creatures lives in that Self – and that is eternal peace. The level of love determines the measure of joy. Joy flowing from the degree of love one is initially capable of generating acts as a stimulus to larger loves and greater joys that eventually will dissolve into the cosmic dance of Shiva, wherein all the elements are involved. This is enigmatic because it involves the mathematics of the soul and of the universe, the Karma of nations and the whole of humanity. The moment one reaches out beyond one's own shadow, turning towards the light that lighteth every man that cometh into the world, then there is joy flowing from the immortal soul in the realm of illimitable light. There is joy in the sure knowledge that though there is life and death, there is also immortality, which does not participate in what is called life and what is feared as death, but is greater than all the small cycles and little circles of time and space. There is joy in the awareness that there is limitlessness in the realm of cosmic ideation, eternal duration and boundless space.

This is the timeless teaching of divine wisdom, and it has always had urgency for the individual, as in the days of Jesus, when he asked, "Whom choose ye this day?" A critical, ultimate, irreversible choice is involved. Now, when the opportunities are great for the whole of the human race, something has begun which will become in time a mighty stream that will nourish the earth. It will reflect the hidden fire of the Mysteries, known to those who have travelled far on the secret Path that leads to the invisible summits of enlightenment. At the first portal of the Path, there is the fateful inscription: "Abandon hope all who enter here." Abandon hope for the petty personality, abandon hope for ambition, pride and selfish desire. Abandon hope, above all, for one's own salvation if one would enter the Path, which leads to a galaxy of Gurus, mighty men of meditation and lovers of all humanity who are wholly dedicated to the sacred goal of universal enlightenment. They have said: "If you wish to know us, study our philosophy. If you wish to serve us, serve our humanity. If you take one step in our direction, we will take one step in yours."

Hermes, February 1978

THOUGHTFULNESS

> *Man is the sole being in the natural order who is not compelled to pursue the same road invariably.*
>
> Claude de St. Martin

The *Mundaka Upanishad* provides the archetypal image of the spiritual archer. His is the unremitting quest for divine wisdom, seeking complete unison with *Brahman*, the ultimate Reality. In this quest there must be no thoughtlessness. Lack of thought is a serious impediment to the cultivation of skill in the art of creative action. At the same time, *The Voice of the Silence* enjoins disciples to free themselves from all particular thoughts and be attuned to All-Thought.

> Thou hast to reach that fixity of mind in which no breeze, however strong, can waft an earthly thought within. Thus purified, the shrine must of all action, sound, or earthly light be void; e'en as the butterfly, o'ertaken by the frost, falls lifeless at the threshold – so must all earthly thoughts fall dead before the fane.

Wherein lies the difference between thoughtlessness and that state of transcendence which is rooted in a serene identification with the Divine Mind?

There are myriad paradoxes in relation to the spiritual path, as everyone knows who makes a strenuous attempt to incarnate in daily life the immeasurable wisdom of Brahma Vach. These paradoxes are pertinent for anyone who is in earnest, who is not merely ready to plunge into the stream, but who has already entered the stream as a *srotapatti* and laved in its rushing waters. There are those who delay this crucial step for lifetimes, even after the privilege of contacting the presence of great Teachers from the Lodge of Mahatmas. They are afraid to take the first step into the stream. But those who have soaked in the struggle know that the recurring paradoxes are far from being instantly resolved, especially by the ratiocinative mind with its obsessive craving for certitude. Mystical paradoxes deepen as veil upon veil lifts and one finds veil upon veil behind. This must be so, for otherwise we would live in a static universe and Mahatmas would be but icons to be worshipped, like the discarded archangels of the past, periodically placated out of fear or the wish for favours. There is none of this in the vast philosophical cosmogony of *The Secret Doctrine*. It postulates one universal stream of consciousness which, at its source, is unconditioned and beyond all forms, qualities, colours and representations, beyond every finite locus in space-time. But equally, within this immense stream of encompassing and transcending consciousness, everything counts. Every being is significant and every single error has its consequence. It is difficult to accommodate so awesome a conception within one's mind and to insert one's own odyssey into the vaster odyssey of all. There is nothing in our upbringing, nothing in the limiting language of common conversation and trivial talk, that can sufficiently prepare one for the grandeur of the enterprise, so that one may feel the authentic joy of comradeship with the mightiest men of meditation. They are the immortal embodiments of universal *Mahat* who can, with a casual, relaxed and joyful sense of proportionality, hit the mark amidst the limitations of collective Karma. This means, paradoxically, that they cannot hit the mark every single time either, and this too is involved in hitting the mark.

The root of these paradoxes in relation to thoughtfulness and transcendence lies in the insuperable problem of formulating the aim. The aim cannot be anything less than *Brahman*. That is the eternal hope. Every single act can have that aim because each act focusses upon a specific target in time and space which is *Brahman*. That is, at one level, the joy and the absurdity of it. In every act of manifestation – bathing, walking, mailing a message – the Logos is present. There is a sense in which the aim – the transcendental *Brahman* – is present in each moment of time as well as in every act at each point of space and in every thought. What, then, obscures the aim of a manifold human being of becoming totally one and remaining constantly attuned to *Brahman*? Why does a person need the sacred OM as the bow and to be continually tuning all one's instruments? Can one ever receive in a world of shadowy knowledge any real teaching concerning the inward meaning of the Soundless Sound? Who will teach the true intonation of the OM and everything to which it corresponds in thought, motive, act and feeling? As the mystery deepens, one must come to recognize that even in the largest perspectives of life, one can discern something that is false and which obscures still greater realities.

The correction that needs to be made in the lesser perspective is archetypally related to the correction needed in the larger perspective. Whenever one has a sense of self-encouraging exaggeration – not only verbally or in terms of external expression, but in the feeling-content and motivational coloration of particular thoughts – there is falsity and distortion. *Brahman* could not be in everything if each single thing does not appropriately mirror *Brahman* and, in an ever-changing universe, recede into non-being. There is an intrinsic illusoriness in the shadowy self that emerges like a smoky haze. In Platonic language, this temporary excess necessarily implies temporal deficiency and therefore imbalance. This may become obsessional – like infatuation – and all cognate thoughts are thereby tainted. The condition is even worse for a person lacking in mental steadiness. One discovers this speedily when one really wants to concentrate on something and even more painfully when one sits down to meditation. The moment one tries to meditate on that which is above and beyond and includes all, one confronts limitations in one's conception of selfhood. There is no way even to ponder the profoundest of vows, the holiest motive of the Bodhisattvas, in relation to the ceaseless quest for the sake of every sentient being. One will encounter a multitude of hindrances. Most thoughts are premature, feeble and abortive. One is not truly awake, but is rather in a dizzy phantasmagoria in which distorted shadows flit. Through an illusory sense of self, one is attached to a misshapen bundle of memories and identified with a form, an image and a name. Persisting thoughtlessness means that one has fallen into a state of fragmented consciousness, and this is not only owing to the imperfections shared with all other human beings, but also through an irreverent attitude to the vestures brought over from previous lives. Such are the scars of failures from former times of opportunity to strengthen and perfect the spiritual will for the sake of universal good. Myriad are the ways in which many souls have frequently failed over an immense period of evolution.

Thoughtlessness is indeed the foremost obstacle. In a philosophical sense and in relation to the enormous manasic capacity of the highest beings, even the well-meant thoughts of most people reflect some sort of thoughtlessness, a large measure of unconscious inconsiderateness. When one considers the most elaborate schemes of reform, the astute strategies of clever planners, one comes to see that even those models and scenarios which are the product of great ingenuity and attempt to take so much into account, still leave out a lot which is evident to persons with common sense. In every case, they also leave out whatever is hard to reckon, especially the good of the unborn and of all beings on invisible planes. As long as one does not think about such considerations, they will recede from the horizon of human concern. Even if one thinks about them, it is difficult to discern how they are immediately relevant to any particular decision, however crucial. There is a deep philosophical sense in which what is tolerated at the beginning as unavoidable thoughtlessness is painfully costly in the long run. A Master wrote with characteristic casualness to one of his disciples that an Adept, when distracted, is fallible. Adepts put themselves on the same plane as vulnerable people. They want their pupils to understand the laws at work and the logic behind their acts, and not become prisoners of false assumptions or facile expectations. One can never fully fathom the spiritual archer, perfected in the capacity to control all vestures, to move freely from plane to plane, and to draw forth dialectically from the cosmic empyrean the laser beam of the Buddhic ray into the here and now. This precludes any attachment to perfection in the realm of time. Especially pertinent in Kali Yuga, it is always true as long as Mahatmas must take into account all imperfect beings in a universe of law. Hence the compassionate casualness and wise detachment of the sages, exemplified by the way in which Buddha in the *Diamond Sutra* dialectically negated the teachings of a lifetime. There is a symmetry and roundedness to the exalted vision of spiritual Teachers for which there is no substitute in any systematized teachings.

Unless one engages in repeated exercises in the effort to learn spiritual archery through meditation, it is impossible to comprehend the injunction: *"Thou hast to feel thyself ALL-THOUGHT, and yet exile all thoughts from out thy Soul."* To be one with All-Thought is not at all like a hypnotic or drug-induced euphoria. Nor is it like the fleeting sense of self-transcendence experienced through the lesser mysteries on the plane of physical *eros* or ordinary love. It is not even captured in that beatific union of a babe in the arms of its mother. These are incomplete and even deceptive intimations. There is something incommensurable in the joys of higher meditation, wherein one discovers an effortless emancipation from boundaries, not only of space and time but of ordinary language and conventional distinctions of aim, activity and result. There is a complete exemption from all dichotomies and also an assured knowledge of ontological plenty on the plane of profound meditation. Any person who picks up Patanjali's *Yoga Sutras* and reads that the sage, just by meditating on this or that, can do amazing things, may view this as metaphorical or miraculous. Noetic magic is extremely difficult for the mundane mind to comprehend. It may be partly understood, however, through one's efforts to loosen the hold of particular thoughts, what Patanjali called self-reproductive chains of thought. Thought-images recur repeatedly, and even though one may seem to be choosing one of several thoughts, one is rapidly drawn into a determinate series of thoughts enmeshed in unconscious likes and dislikes, memories and fears, other people's opinions and prejudices – indeed in everything floating in the astral light and numberless borrowed notions. There is also a sense in which one ceases to choose thoughts even when attempting to select a train of thought.

   Evidently there is no easy way of getting rid of inconsideration and thoughtlessness, much less of gaining an understanding of what *The Voice of the Silence* means by becoming one with All-Thought. To become one with All-Thought implies the capacity to see all possible worlds, to see one's own world simply as one of many, and furthermore, to sense the reality of coexisting worlds. The idea of Be-ness has nothing to do with existence on the physical plane in the realm of form. How, then, can a person truly accommodate what it means for a human being to have many possible conceptions of the good for one's family, for one's community and for the whole of humanity? Each manasic being is so rich in the potential capacity for seeing possible good that, upon descending from the plane of ideation into the realm of action and pursuing the best possible way to move oneself and others towards the larger good in a given karmic context, one must be extremely flexible. The richness of the realm of pure ideation is virtually incommunicable. Therefore, it is hard for a person even to conceive what it would be like to be a Mahatma, a radiant mirror of *Mahat*, and to see the galaxies and the solar system in visible space as manifested representations that hide many real though invisible existences. Although this is difficult, every attempt can be meaningful. The critical point is how honest one is prepared to be in making discoveries of one's limitations in one's daily efforts in the direction of meditation and spiritual archery. If a person is trying to learn *T'ai chi* or dancing and finds after a few months that he or she is not tough enough to take a teacher's honest report, someone else might see that this person is never going to learn *T'ai chi* or dancing.

In the spiritual life no one truly wise is going to be a censor or a judge. Nonetheless, a true guru, with knowledge of a person's strength and limitations, may show the delicate art of adjusting the *chela*. In doing that it would be impossible for him to break the laws governing the processes of spiritual growth by telling somebody in advance about his prospects. A person has to discern this for himself. He has to make his own critical progress report upon himself, and the more tough he is, the more he will see the need to relax, because he discovers so much that is painful. He either must escape, bluff or cheat or, if he can see that this is all part of what he is trying to be honest about, he must relax and resolve to move steadily and never give up. When a person vows never to give up and at the same time is clear-sighted in regard to difficulties, then that person is truly in earnest. Each sincere effort will be sacred. It will be witnessed by those mighty beings of compassion who, unknown to the aspirant, are on his side and see him as a friend. The Theosophical Movement exists in the world to show human beings that if they can make that critical breakthrough, take the first crucial step, then they will infallibly receive help, not as a favour, but because in trying to be on the side of the universe, the universe will be on their side. By rooting themselves in eternity, they could come to know, in a para-historical sense, that time is on their side. It is not on the side of any one person or of any one class, but of all. They could be assured that the future will triumph over the past, and that the circle will become ever larger. One may even come to understand why one's higher life has some sort of underpinning in the bedrock of the universe. Such assurances cannot be translated into the pseudo-certainties of the wandering mind with its daily thoughtlessness, but they arise in the consciousness of those who have touched the tranquil waters of All-Thought.

Hermes, June 1978

SPIRITUAL PERCEPTION

> *The possession of a physical third eye . . . was enjoyed by the men of the Third Root-Race down to nearly the middle period of the Third SUB-race of the Fourth Root-Race, when the consolidation and perfection of the human frame made it disappear from the outward anatomy of man. Psychically and spiritually, however, its mental and visual perceptions lasted till nearly the end of the Fourth Race, when its functions, owing to the materiality and depraved condition of mankind, died out altogether before the submersion of the bulk of the Atlantean continent.*
>
> The Secret Doctrine, ii 306

The ancient atrophy of the Third Eye, together with the possibility of its reawakening, is integral to the Teachings of *Gupta Vidya*. The elusive nature of that eye lies veiled in many myths and legends about the idyllic childhood of humanity and its paradisaic innocence. This lost and largely forgotten Elysium was not some sheltered sanctuary, but rather a pervasive state of consciousness. Within a triple scheme of human evolution, comprising spiritual, intellectual and physiological modes of development, the whole of humanity, at the dawn of evolution, enjoyed a foretaste of the glorious fullness of human potential, to be unfolded towards the close of the Seventh Round. During the enormous cycles of human evolution upon earth, there has been an alternation of longer and shorter periods of relative obscuration of the spiritual faculties of humanity. Some of these phases were intensified by human errors and avoidable tragedies. These became overlapping factors in succeeding cycles of obscuration and clarity in the human vestures, resulting from the centrifugal and centripetal forces behind evolution. The actual condition and constitution of human vestures in any epoch is the product of complex causes.

Mature wisdom calls for a strong sense of moral responsibility for the collective consequences of past conduct as well as active cooperation with the inexorable cycles of Nature. These include the familiar cycle of birth and death, the slow succession of the Golden, Silver, Bronze and Iron Ages, the emergence and disappearance of continents and also the myriad vicissitudes in the alteration and refinement of human vestures. The original awakening, subsequent atrophy and future recovery of the Third Eye are a moral saga illustrating the interweaving of cyclic necessity and moral responsibility. Even conscientious students of *Gupta Vidya* find it very difficult to preserve a proper balance in relation to the poignant theme of the atrophy of the Third Eye. It is upsetting to think of the vast majority of human beings as spiritually marred by the appalling consequences of the flagrant misuse of the higher faculties during earlier races. The inherent inability of most people even to consider the hidden Third Eye as the active organ of spiritual vision is the karmic heirloom of all humanity. And yet, the need to arouse the latent power of spiritual vision poses a profound and inescapable challenge to all aspirants on the path of spiritual enlightenment. We need to ask what was natural and what was unnatural about the early evolution and eventual petrification of the Third Eye.

Myths, legends and folklore indicate that, in archaic periods of prehistory, human beings were gigantic in stature and possessed a "Cyclopean" eye located in the forehead. *Gupta Vidya* assigns these distant epochs to the Third and early Fourth Root Races. According to arcane wisdom, the placement of this eye in the forehead is a poetic licence: the true locus was at the back of the head. What we now call the Third Eye was then the dominant organ of vision. To understand this, one must appreciate the primacy of the astral and inner vestures in relation to the organs of action and sensory faculties of the physical body.

> The First Race is shown in Occult sciences as spiritual within and ethereal without; the second, psycho-spiritual mentally, and etherophysical bodily; the third, still bereft of intellect in its beginning, is astro-physical in its body, and lives an inner life, in which the psycho-spiritual element is in no way interfered with as yet by the hardly nascent physiological senses. Its two front eyes look before them without seeing either past or future. But the 'third eye' 'embraces ETERNITY'.
>
> *The Secret Doctrine*, ii 298–299

As an organ, the "Cyclopean" eye belongs to the subtler vestures which antedate the emergence of the physical form with its familiar organs. The physical body, together with its complex and delicate physiological structure, constitutes a "coat of skin" which evolved from within outward, covering the astral vesture. This development took place at that point in cyclic evolution when there was a maximum involvement of Spirit in matter, correlative with the maximum differentiation of objective substance. The complete involvement of human souls in physical matter took place simultaneously with the infusion of the self-conscious Manasic ray into a set of developing human vestures. Once Manas was awakened, the Third Eye – which in reality is the *first eye* – served as the organ of spiritual sight, untrammelled in its activity by the nascent physiological vesture. Its mirror in the physical body is the pineal gland, intuitively identified by Descartes as the seat of the soul. In the animal kingdom, whose vestures were formed from the residues of human evolution, a similar physiological structure served as the organ of vision.

> Therefore, while the 'Cyclopean' eye was, and still is, in man the organ of *spiritual* sight, in the animal it was that of objective vision. And this eye, having performed its function, was replaced, in the course of physical evolution from the simple to the complex, by two eyes, and thus was stored and laid aside by nature for further use in Aeons to come. This explains why the pineal gland reached its highest development proportionately with the lowest physical development. It is the vertebrata in which it is the most prominent and objective and in man it is most carefully hidden and inaccessible, except to the anatomist.
>
> *The Secret Doctrine*, ii 299–300

These developments, encompassing millions of years and vast cycles of racial evolution, are all part of what may be called the programme of Nature. They marked the momentous intersection of the activity of the *Barhishad* or Lunar Pitris and the *Agnishwatha* or Solar Pitris. These two groups of ancestors endowed humanity with, respectively, its differentiated material vestures on several planes and its inward spiritual principles, especially *Manas* or self-conscious moral intelligence. The natural exercise of spiritual vision guided by self-conscious intelligence constituted the foundation of the Golden Age at the dawn of humanity. As the inevitable tide of physiological evolution gradually caused the "Cyclopean" eye to recede, human beings experienced a painful sense of loss. With much greater dependence upon the two front eyes during the early Fourth Root Race or Atlantean civilization, there were desperate physiological attempts to recover what had been lost. Many Atlanteans could not comprehend that their loss had to do with consciousness and with form. They became enormously preoccupied with forms and externals, and thereby brought about a diminution in the power and scope of consciousness itself at its most autonomous level. None of the repeated efforts to tinker with the physiological organs or to create substitutes by whatever means could quicken or reawaken the spiritual function of the Third Eye. Atlanteans became increasingly involved in something fundamentally unnatural which could only produce a consolidated concretization of consciousness. Eventually, quite apart from the loss of the Third Eye in the physical organism, there was an obscuration of spiritual perception associated with the Third Eye. This became a tremendous handicap to human evolution.

It was not necessary then, nor is it now, that all human beings remain spiritually blind, regardless of physiological evolution or the widespread atrophy of the pineal gland. The deliberate awakening of spiritual vision is integral to the exacting discipline of initiation into the Mysteries. Such preparatory training is based upon a truly philosophic understanding of human nature and incarnation, and upon a systematic ethical and psychological development which excludes short-cuts and adventitious aids. Mahatmas and Initiates who have guided and guarded the spiritual progress of humanity for over eighteen million years have continually made accessible the time-honoured path that leads to inward enlightenment. The *Commentaries* on the *Stanzas of Dzyan* convey the need for magnetic purity and proper guidance:

> There were four-armed human creatures in those early days of the male-females (hermaphrodites); with one head, yet three eyes. They could see before them and behind them. A KALPA later (after the separation of the sexes) men having fallen into matter, their spiritual vision became dim; and coordinately the third eye commenced to lose its power.... When the Fourth (Race) arrived at its middle age, the inner vision had to be awakened, and

> *acquired by artificial stimuli.... The third eye, likewise, getting gradually* PETRIFIED, *soon disappeared. The double-faced became the one-faced, and the eye was drawn deep into the head and is now buried under the hair. During the activity of the inner man* (during trances and spiritual visions) *the eye swells and expands. The Arhat sees and feels it, and regulates his action accordingly.... The undefiled Lanoo* (disciple, chela) *need fear no danger; he who keeps himself not in purity* (who is not chaste) *will receive no help from the 'deva eye'.*
>
> The Secret Doctrine, ii 294–295

During the descent of Spirit into matter, the spiritual and physiological processes are strictly coordinate. For example, if there is a loss in the inward power of seeing, the organ of sight is also commensurately weakened. This is equally true of all human faculties and their physical centres. Various atrophied organs survive in the human constitution, and these are hardly understood by contemporary physiology or medicine. They are virtually irrelevant to the vast majority of human beings. Sages of old knew that the disciplines which can truly help to reawaken inner vision are radically different from the artificial stimuli avidly sought during the latter Atlantean age. Yet, the appeal of these poor substitutes points to the pervasiveness and inevitability of the eclipse of the inner senses by overdeveloped outer senses. Most human beings shared in this psycho-physical heredity that was caused by the gross abuse of faculties and powers during the Atlantean period.

If there is an excessive development of the physiological eyes at the expense of the Third Eye during a particular phase of evolution, and if all human beings are involuntary participants in this process, then as later phases of evolution are reached human beings could awaken flashes of that original interior perception. As the balance of evolution shifts from the phase of involution of Spirit into matter to the evolution of Spirit out of matter, there is a corresponding lightening of the vestures and a quickening of the veiled organs of inner vision. Human beings could have flashes of perception, even though they might not be able to recover that perception fully, let alone quickly. In meditation they might experience a certain swelling and expansion, an agitation or heating up, connected with the intensity of activity in the pineal gland. No known physiological function may be assigned to the pineal gland,

and however much medical practitioners study the human corpse, they will never discover its real importance during life. Some do recognize that the pineal gland indirectly regulates hormone-producing glands, and it is now known that in animals it is sensitive to light. In fact, human beings can during deep contemplation or during some states of ecstatic trance have flashes of the expansion and contraction that affect the pineal gland and pituitary body. These in turn affect their perception of images and sounds. Even though there was an inescapable element in the loss of its original function, the Third Eye itself was not wholly lost. It is still dormant and remains intact in the subtle vestures. The problem for present humanity is the proper coordination between the functioning of the Third Eye in the subtle vestures and the physical body with its two eyes and the atrophied pineal organ.

If the natural veiling of spiritual sight through the inordinate development of the physiological vesture was the whole story, then humanity would not have melancholy recollections of the Golden Age, nor such a strong propensity towards gloom and doom, externalization and salvationism. In fact, the persisting dominance of entire theologies based upon guilt and sin at this particular point in human evolution is itself indicative of the perfidious moral history connected with the loss of the Third Eye. No matter how much contrasting theories of guilt and sin claim to account for the present human predicament, they can only gain credence through vulnerabilities in the human *psyche*. These revolve around a morbid sense of failure, pretence and pride, which are the unnatural result of past misuse of spiritual powers. Human beings may identify evil with violence and separativeness, with everything that is inimical and arises out of blindness and greed, stupidity and self-deception. Nonetheless, all these represent secondary effects. At the causal level, evil pertains to the perverse misuse of the very highest spiritual gifts. Such misuse induced religions to fall victim to priestcraft and lose touch with the Mysteries. Spiritual evil made human beings, who innately have extraordinary powers such as *Kriyashakti* and *Itchashakti*, lose all of them. Spiritual evil and deliberate misuse were a violation of the evolutionary programme of Nature.

> When spirituality and all the divine powers and attributes of the deva-man of the Third had been made the hand-maidens of the

newly-awakened physiological and psychic passions of the physical man, instead of the reverse, the eye lost its powers. But such was the law of Evolution, and it was, in strict accuracy, no FALL. The sin was not in using those newly-developed powers, but in misusing them; in making of the tabernacle, designed to contain a god, the fane of every *spiritual* iniquity.

The Secret Doctrine, ii 302

The deleterious consequences of this profanation cannot be blamed upon the logic of descent of Spirit into matter. They are the terrible karma of those who, far from merely becoming enslaved by carnal desire and sensory indulgence, in fact became proficient in treachery, blasphemy, profanation and betrayal of the sacred, especially in sacrificing the welfare of others for the sake of self. This has nothing to do with any passing weakness owing to a natural obscuration of faculties. Whatever the "ills" that mortal flesh may be heir to, the physical body is not the source of spiritual iniquity. As H.P. Blavatsky indicated,

> The reader who would feel perplexed at the use of the term 'spiritual' instead of 'physical' iniquity, is reminded of the fact that there can be no physical iniquity. The body is simply the irresponsible organ, the tool of the *psychic*, if not of the 'Spiritual man'. While in the case of the Atlanteans, it was precisely the Spiritual being which sinned, the Spirit element being still the 'Master' principle in man in those days. Thus it is in those days that the heaviest Karma of the Fifth Race was generated by our Monads.

The Secret Doctrine, ii 302

One must calmly contemplate how this spiritual sin arose and how it engendered enormous ruthlessness and extreme selfishness as well as an overpowering obsession with external dominance and a deeply entrenched resistance to admitting any fault, acknowledging any responsibility or making any amends. Through the perverse misuse of the highest powers with which they were entrusted, vast numbers of sick souls were trapped in a tragic condition wherein they were unable and unwilling to come to terms with their own karma and virtually incapable of finding or even seeking their proper place in the moral order of the cosmos and of society. Owing to this diseased perversion and compulsive inversion, an appalling corruption of consciousness resulted, which cannot be suddenly remedied at some future point in evolution, even when the interconnection between the subtle centres and physiological organs is radically altered. It is indeed imperative for the spiritually corrupt to begin now to reverse the karma of past misuse if they would at all reawaken spiritual vision and continue to participate in self-conscious human evolution in future races.

Certainly, it would be of great help to seek, and show true humility, amidst the company of stronger souls whose karma is untainted by ingratitude and perfidy in former lives. It is always salutary for everyone to admire and emulate freedom from a sense of separativeness wherever one sees it in others. This is ever preferable to the contagion of abject selfishness, stark ingratitude, rancour and envy. Anyone can attempt to make real for oneself the latent spiritual goodness, purity and innocence that one can *re-cognize* in any others around. Authentic admiration and emulation can be powerful purifiers for any human being, let alone for those who come into the magnetic orbit of a spiritual Teacher. It can bring one in closer touch with one's own spiritual heritage from the Third Root Race, which is even now recapitulated in childhood and infancy. Nonetheless, the root causes of spiritual and moral blindness must be faced. Until they are confronted, the, proper awakening of spiritual vision is impossible. This brings up the ultimate question of authentically accommodating the idea of universal compassion and enlightenment.

Can one develop sufficient self-transcendence and such a profound concern for the spiritual welfare of all human souls that one's entire conception of desire is revolutionized? When this becomes possible, one can be so creative and so saturated with universal compassion that one simply does not have any craving, let alone a compulsive need, to consider any other human being as a mere object for one's own sensuous gratification. There is a radical change in one's level of consciousness, and this has a decisive effect on the tropism and texture of elements and life-atoms in the subtle vestures and in the physical body. The flow of energy within the spinal cord is transformed, affecting the interaction between the pineal gland and the pituitary body, together with the medulla oblongata and the multiple centres of the brain.

It is only if one apprehends the necessity of these fundamental transformations in human nature that one can recognize that the essential logic of human evolution did not envisage such damage to spiritual vision. To grasp this is to be ready to engage in an examination of one's motives, one's potentials, one's capacities and the hindrances that obstruct one's consciousness. Through *tapas* and daily meditation one may appreciate the feasibility of increasing continuity of consciousness between waking and sleeping, between life and death, bridging all the pairs of opposites and transcending the succession of time. One may then come to comprehend that the Third Eye has retreated from without inwardly because an earlier phase of the logic of evolution extruded it from within without. The withdrawal inward of the organ of the Third Eye corresponds to a greater withdrawal of consciousness from concretization, which is indeed crucial in the current phase of human growth and maturation. Concretization of consciousness does not refer only to the amount of stimuli on the physical or sensory plane; it also takes place through limiting concepts and mental ossification, through craving for certainty, through harsh judgementalism and an addiction to self-pity and even nihilism. The inability to restore the fluidity of ideation on metaphysical abstractions, spiritual ideas and moral ideals is the sad consequence of concretization and externalization.

Whatever corruption of consciousness originally occurred has been compounded many times over through repeated failures to come to terms with the propensity to prolong spiritual iniquity and accelerate self-destruction. This cannot be put right instantly, and to imagine otherwise is only a symptom of the basic problem. One must resolve to try, to try and try again. In order to strengthen this resolve, the Teachers of *Gupta Vidya* have sought to share relevant portions of arcane knowledge about the history of the Third and Fourth Root Races. Some understanding of past evolution is essential if one seeks to grasp the logic and significance of systematic self-training and self-testing. In order to rejoin the forward movement of humanity, one must realize that all human beings are fallen gods, disinherited from their divine estate through the loss of the eye of wisdom. As a result, they have become almost exclusively dependent upon sensory perception. And yet, the actual range of the physical sense-organs has become narrower and narrower over time. Since the energy of spiritual life is independent of physical form and matter, the more preoccupied one is with the physical form and with sense perceptions, the more one is alienated from the true source of strength, volition and self-direction.

When individuals initially confront this problem, they run the risk of entangling themselves in what might be called a meta-problem. Contacting the Teachings of *Gupta Vidya* and reading about the earlier races of humanity, the karma of Atlantis and the loss of the Third Eye release latent forces within one's nature. The processes which originally held one back can repeat themselves in one's apprehension and use of arcane wisdom. If one's basic loyalty is to the world and to one's self-image on the personal plane, then whatever vows and resolves one adopts can only operate and have force on that plane. One may maintain a sanctimonious charade reminiscent of hypocritical religion and monkish facades. One may even manage to conceal the persistent play-acting from oneself for a long time. Inevitably, the time comes when one recoils from the sham with self-loathing and a mixture of indignation and despair. This is a tragic and pitiable condition for any human soul. The danger of becoming trapped in this meta-problem must be coolly confronted, since the restoration of spiritual vision cannot occur without unleashing the very tendencies that originally led to spiritual blindness.

Typically, this problem shows itself in a grasping attitude towards the Teachings of *Gupta Vidya*. Instead of putting oneself in the position of a postulant who is wide awake, who absorbs through osmosis and calmly assimilates the Teachings, seeking to apply them to daily duties and encounters, one becomes addicted to over-analysis and judgementalism. Through one's continuing contact with the Teachings, there is a powerful quickening of the energies available to the restless lower mind and the attendant risk that these energies will be appropriated by the ahankaric and acquisitive self. When the individual receives more spiritual food than he or she is able to assimilate on a higher plane, then *kama manas* becomes hyperactive, destructive and harsh. Fascinated with its own weaknesses and faults, it ceaselessly looks for vulnerabilities in others and even becomes adroit in self-serving rationalizations and endless excuses. As a result there arises a powerful blockage to the release of intuitive insight.

It is through the power of Buddhic intuition that individuals are initially drawn to the Teachings of *Gupta Vidya*. In learning a language, one must try to speak, making mistakes, correcting them, and thereby gradually gaining facility. If this is true of ordinary language, it is much more so with the language of the soul. Spiritual intuition is like fire. It is only through the use of real fire that fuel can be kindled, and wherever real fire is used, there is the risk that it will be misused. This is paradigmatically true with regard to the Promethean fire of mind given to humanity over eighteen million years ago. Every neophyte who would approach the Mystery-fires must be prepared to assume full responsibility for the right use of the fire of knowledge. The more one has the proper qualifications to become a *chela*, the more one is able to assimilate and reflect deeply and patiently upon the Teachings, endowing them with vivid relevance to daily life. The fire of *Buddhi* can become quickened through the study, contemplation and practice of *Gupta Vidya*. As Krishna affirmed in the *Bhagavad Gita*, in the course of time spiritual knowledge will spring up spontaneously within oneself.

In order to release soul-memory and activate one's higher faculties, one must be fortunate enough to have come consciously and voluntarily to the spiritual life, not out of any compensatory motives but out of love and reverence for Divine Wisdom and with a deep longing to benefit humanity. Only those who live and breathe benevolently can avoid the awful consequences of misappropriating the higher energies in the service of the lower, thereby forfeiting the great opportunity gained under karma of coming closer to the immemorial Teachings and to authentic spiritual Teachers. For such seekers who are suffused with a profound humility and a deep desire for learning for the sake of others, there will be a natural protection. True *shravakas* or learners will be able to use the archetypal method from the first, proceeding from above below and from within without and emphasizing at each stage the steady assimilation of mental and spiritual food through moral practice. There need be no partiality and imbalance, no one-sidedness or bias, in the apprehension and application of *Gupta Vidya*. As Mahatma M. pointed out,

> In our doctrine you will find necessary the synthetic method; you will have to embrace the whole – that is to say to blend the macrocosm and microcosm together – before you are enabled to study the parts separately or analyze them with profit to your understanding. Cosmology is the physiology of the universe spiritualized, for there is but one Law.

In order to embrace the whole, one must grasp the fundamental continuity of cosmic and human evolution, establishing one's consciousness in a current of Buddhic compassion and unconditional love for all that lives. One must learn to move back and forth continuously between the macrocosmic and the microcosmic. One must strive to see the relevance of universal ideation to specific contexts. One must ever seek to bridge the universal and the particular in waking consciousness, maximizing the good even in highly imperfect situations. Tremendous aid can come through the Buddhic stream of Hermetic wisdom pouring forth from the Brotherhood of Bodhisattvas. With a mind moistened by wisdom and compassion, one may return again and again in meditation and self-study to seek appropriate connections and correspondences between the macrocosm and the microcosm. Drawing upon the rich resources of *Gupta Vidya*, one must grasp its universal synthesis before attempting to study the parts separately or analytically. This means that one must engage in daily *tapas* or mental asceticism. In the Aquarian Age, we need to relinquish the entrenched modes of the inductive and analytic mind, replacing them by cultivated skill in deep concentration, creative imagination and calm receptivity towards universal ideation. In this way one will come to comprehend the connections between the most primordial and abstract and the most dense and differentiated levels of manifestation of consciousness and matter. The continuity of consciousness which one seeks is, in fact, a mode of mirroring the metaphysical integrity of cosmic unity.

If one can learn to let go of the rationalizing pseudo-intelligence of the personality, then one can begin to draw upon the natural strength of *Manas*. One must learn to take the simplest ideas and apply them universally. Action based upon spiritual insight has a moral simplicity that neither can be understood nor imitated by the lower mind. For a long time in the life of any disciple, it is wise to consider the spiritual vision of the Third Eye as equivalent to moral discrimination. This is eloquently illustrated in the life of Mohandas Gandhi, who was skilful in finding potent analogies between the circulation of blood and global economics or psychological health. Anyone who arouses *Buddhi* can take seriously the integrity of the cosmos and deduce practical wisdom. One can learn to perceive vital connections between the mental and spiritual health of individuals and society as a whole, and apply these perceptions to oneself.

If one gains some proficiency in this daily use of Buddhic intuition, one will soon find that it becomes meaningful to use the myths and symbols of *Gupta Vidya* as a basis for meditation upon the structure and function of the human form. One must learn to contemplate the cosmic dimension of human existence and become capable of deriving from such contemplation a vital sense of sanctity, plasticity and potentiality in relation to the physical body. Great philosophers and mystics have done this, seeing in the human form the paradigmatic metaphor for all growth. They have used the analogy of sight when speaking of soul-knowledge and spiritual wisdom, referring to the eye of the soul and the mind's eye. But even to appreciate this analogy, one must to some degree awaken *Buddhi*. Just as one can hardly convey the operation of sight and vision to a person born blind, one cannot readily communicate the nature of spiritual vision to those in whom it is totally blocked. Similarly, one could hardly convey the thrills and challenges of mental perception to persons with undeveloped mental sight.

As the ability to apprehend analogies is itself an essential element in soul-vision and also conducive to the awakening of the inward capacity for noetic insight, it is always wise to recognize and acknowledge the limits and levels of human experience. Without actually developing spiritual and mental insight and tasting the ineffable bliss of authentic mystical vision, one cannot comprehend or even appreciate the scope and range of possible peak experiences. Owing to the pervasive principle of continuity in the cosmic order and in human nature, there is the ever-present possibility of transcending the limits of known and shared experience. By using analogies and correspondences to move from the familiar and the bounded to the unfamiliar and the unbounded, one may gain sufficient skill in the dialectical art to subdue the mind and absorb it into the pulsating consciousness of the spiritual heart. In a mystical sense, one can make the mind whole, and enlist it into the service of the heart, while at the same time making the heart intelligent and strong.

In order to attain a state of heightened spiritual awareness and effortless vigilance, compassion and receptivity, it is essential to recognize and remove persisting discontinuities in consciousness. The familiar gaps between sleeping and waking, between dreaming and deep sleep, between ephemeral fantasies and enduring commitments, are connected with lesions in the subtle vestures which induce a fragmentation and distortion of spiritual insights. One must patiently identify these deficiencies, seek out their root causes, and initiate an appropriate course of corrective exercises. In the meantime, it is meaningful to establish and strengthen a continuous current of deep ideation upon the highest conceivable ideals, principles and goals relevant to the future of humanity. The mind and heart may be fused through an ardent devotion to Bodhisattvic exemplars of continuity of consciousness in the ceaseless service of all humanity. Through this very attempt, even the sick may slowly heal themselves and seek *satsang*, the company of the wise, who can help to nurture the seed of *bodhichitta*, the potent resolve to awaken the Wisdom Eye for the sake of universal welfare.

Hermes, October 1984

THE HERO IN MAN

The air is full of souls.

Philo Judaeus

The homeless tribe of mystics, the fraternity of spiritual exiles, inherit the ancient title *mystikos*, from *mystes* – those whose eyes and lips are closed, who have entered into the Mysteries. Its sacred verities can neither be fully articulated nor wholly validated in any language. The unmanifest may be suggested and shrouded by the manifest, and the mystic experiences this through his endeavours to translate his insights from the region of things felt to the region of things understood. The mystic's eyes are necessarily closed to the mundane world in as much as they intently and inwardly gaze upon the hidden realm of supersensuous realities. The mystic's lips are sealed – even in eloquent speech – because of the unutterable beauty of beatific experience and the transcendent glow of transfiguring insight. Authentic mystical awareness is markedly different from the varied forms of fantasy and reverie. Mystical experience is essentially noetic, rooted in the cognitive capacity for enlarged comprehension of noumenal truths, rather than the rush of emotion or the randomness of memory. Though the mystic path is etched across the awesome vault of infinite duration, each mystical experience is an event in time, transient, limited by a fragile beginning and a frustrating end. The experience is also episodic in that the temporal and captive consciousness of the individual cannot control it. In the enigmatic language of the Upanishads, the *Atman* – the universal overbrooding Spirit – shows itself to whom it will. Daydreams and fantasy, though they share the wayward charm of evanescent but joyous wonder, do not convey the ethical consequences of a deep mystic experience. In the presence of the magnanimous sweep of the mystic vision, a natural self-effacement fuses with a profound sense of self-completion. One becomes a selfless participant in the silent sacrifice of invisible and visible nature, in which each part has clarity and significance in relation to every other part, all sharing the diffused light of an architectonic unity.

The mystic senses the priceless privilege of being alive and the sacredness of breathing; awareness of this sanctified continuity of all life affects every thought and act, at least during peak experiences. The fragmentation and discontinuity in consciousness of the vast majority of mankind – gaps between thought and feeling, idea and image, sensibility and sense, belief and knowledge – are integrated in the mystic's self-awareness. Sensing a fundamental continuity within himself, the mystic witnesses an equally vibrant solidarity between individuals. What is possible for one person to discover is possible for another, however adverse conditions may appear. The intense flashes of awareness that the mystic is privileged to enjoy are stepping stones on the path of awakening, most of which are trod in silence.

Within the historical tradition of sages, saints and seers, a few, like St. John of the Cross, St. Teresa, Bernard of Clairvaux, as well as the author of the *Cloud of Unknowing*, speak of actual experiences encountered upon the mystical way. Other sources, such as the writings of A.E., *The Voice of the Silence* and *Light on the Path*, characterize the phases of the mystic path without attention to details of particular experiences. Still other influential thinkers – Plato and Plotinus, Shankara and Eckhart – elaborated the metaphysical framework and philosophical underpinnings of the path itself. A.E. presents an account of his haunting visions both directly, in works like *The Candle of Vision*, and metaphorically in stories and poems like "A Strange Awakening" and "A Priestess of the Woods", interwoven with thoughts on the nature of the universe and man's relation to it. He affirms that anyone who wills it can awaken spiritual insight within himself.

> So the lover of Earth obtains his reward, and little by little the veil is lifted of an inexhaustible beauty and majesty. It may be he will be tranced in some spiritual communion, or will find his being overflowing into the being of the elements, or become aware that they are breathing their life into his own. Or Earth may become on an instant, all faery to him, and earth and air resound with the music of its invisible people. Or the trees and rocks may waver before his eyes and become transparent, revealing what creatures were hidden from

him by the curtain, and he will know as the ancients did of dryad and hamadryad, of genii of wood and mountain. Or earth may suddenly blaze about him with supernatural light in some lonely spot amid the hills, and he will find he stands as the prophet in a place that is holy ground, and he may breathe the intoxicating exhalations as did the sibyls of old. Or his love may hurry him away in dream to share in deeper mysteries, and he may see the palace chambers of nature where the wise ones dwell in secret, looking out over the nations, breathing power into this man's heart or that man's brain, on any who appear to their vision to wear the colour of truth. So gradually the earth lover realises the golden world is all about him in imperishable beauty, and he may pass from the vision to the profounder beauty of being, and know an eternal love is within and around him, pressing upon him and sustaining with infinite tenderness his body, his soul and his spirit.

The Candle of Vision

A.E.'s mysticism emphasizes understanding through love, and he embroiders mystical naturalism with suggestions of the rich void beyond and throughout nature. He emphasizes man's identity with all nature because he sees the soul in nature and in humanity. "The great heart of the earth is full of laughter", one of his characters says, "do not put yourselves apart from its joy, for its soul is your soul and its joy is your true being." As the veil of visible nature is dissolved before the mystic's sight, time itself is seen as an illusion from a metaphysical standpoint. Consciousness is expanded or constricted by its apprehension of time. The mystic senses a vibration prior to visible nature, though insofar as it is expressible, it too has a beginning and an end. Mystical experience is timeless though located in time, and the mystic is hard pressed to describe the crossings between the unmanifest and the manifest. Speaking of the hour of twilight as a metaphor for that time when "the Mystic shall be at home", A.E. calls it "the hour for memory".

> . . . wherever it is spent, whether in the dusky room or walking home through the blue evening, all things grow strangely softened and united; the magic of the old world reappears. The commonplace streets take on something of the grandeur and solemnity of starlit avenues of Egyptian temples; the public squares in the mingled glow and gloom grow beautiful as the Indian grove where Sakuntala wandered with her maidens; the children chase each other through

the dusky shrubberies, as they flee past they look at us with long remembered glances: lulled by the silence, we forget a little while the hard edges of the material and remember that we are *spirits*.

When the horizon set by one's awareness of time is foreshortened, memory is reduced to recent particulars redolent with echoes of childhood remembrance. As that horizon is expanded through a sense of eternity, recollection arises with a profound awareness of mythic time, and the soul gazes within the archaic history of humanity. Soul-memory exhibits natural affinities to strange dreams, insignificant in detail yet suggesting a cosmic drama in which each creature plays an appropriate role. Soul-memory also portrays to waking consciousness what would otherwise be witnessed only in *sushupti* or Devachan. If most individuals see nature as a static created world comprising myriad separate entities, the mystic beholds *natura naturans*, a dynamic process constantly unleashing creative energies. The mystical experience is grounded in the commonality of human life.

> For this in truth it seems to me to mean: all knowledge is a revelation of the self to the self, and our deepest comprehension of the seemingly apart divine is also our furthest inroad to self-knowledge; Prometheus, Christ, are in every heart; the story of one is the story of all; the Titan and the Crucified are humanity.
>
> *The Hero in Man*

Precisely because Christ is incarnate in all humanity, every human being has golden moments and mystical glimpses, yet because Prometheus is bound for ever within us, such moments and glimpses are obliterated in waking life through indulgence, egotism, obsession with results and the concern for salvation. And if these barriers to deeper unity are bypassed without genuine self-transcendence, they become still stronger obstacles: passivity, aggression, fantasy and malign interference in the lives of others. To thread passing moments into a continuous current in life, one must hold firmly to a selfless line of thought and motivation.

> . . . these moods, though lit up by intuitions of the true, are too partial, they belong too much to the twilight of the heart, they have too dreamy a temper to serve us well in life. We should wish rather for

our thoughts a directness such as to the messengers of the gods, swift, beautiful, flashing presences bent on purposes well understood.

The Hero in Man

One's mind must be prepared and alert. One needs to identify with the whole of nature so as to become inconspicuous as a persona, yet ever vigilant and willing to follow the injunction given in *The Voice of the Silence* – "Thy Soul has to become as the ripe mango fruit: as soft and sweet as its bright golden pulp for others' woes, as hard as that fruit's stone for thine own throes and sorrows." Although this lies far ahead of contemporary humanity, there is a fundamental continuity between the mystic's unwavering vision of the Hero in man and everyday experience, through the idea of sacrifice on behalf of the wretched of the earth.

> Now if the aim of the mystic be to fuse into one all moods made separate by time, would not the daily harvesting of wisdom render unnecessary the long Devachanic years? No second harvest could be reaped from fields where the sheaves are already garnered. Thus disregarding the fruits of action, we could work like those who have made the Great Sacrifice, for whom even Nirvana is no resting place. Worlds may awaken in nebulous glory, pass through their phases of self-conscious existence and sink again to sleep, but these tireless workers continue their age-long task of help. Their motive we do not know, but in some secret depth of our being we feel that there could be nothing nobler, and thinking this we have devoted the twilight hour to the understanding of their nature.

The Hour of Twilight

When the Ever-Unknowable reflects itself in the process of manifestation, the root substance-principle – the absolute Archaeus – unfolds itself as the invisible and visible cosmos in three hypostases. The first may be called Spirit, transcendent and overbrooding; the second, matter, the immanent side of nature; while the third, connecting these two at every point, might be likened materially to electricity and spiritually to mind. This third term is the impersonal intelligence of number and ratio, geometric form and arithmetic progression. The basic triad is present at every level of being, for Spirit expresses itself through matter – like the partially revealed dancer in the Dance of the Seven Veils – while matter lives and is transformed only under the vivifying impulse of Spirit. Both join in innumerable permutations and elaborations of the initial threefold Word, fused in cosmic intelligence (*Mahat*) which is also cosmic law (*Rta*). In the sphere of self-consciousness, this triad can be qualitatively defined as Wisdom (*Prajna*), Compassion (*Karuna*) and Intelligence (*Buddhi*). Each depends upon the others for its own level of purity, clarity and activity. The elaboration of the primal Word is the movement from homogeneity to heterogeneity, from subtle to gross, from potential to actual, and from subjective to objective. The creative energy enshrined in the Word is pure *eros*, and its every expression reveals as well as masks its more fundamental nature. Hence every level of being finds light and darkness, the greater and the lesser, knowledge and relative ignorance, in ceaseless contraction. The urge to manifest is the urge to objectify, to take form, to exist in time, rather than to abide in eternity. At the spiritual level, this impulsion is towards individuation, but at the natal level it is the desire to live as an ego; psychophysically it is the thirst for life.

The mystic retraces this gestation of consciousness and returns, self-consciously and spiritually awake, to its source. He experiences, understands and controls the avenues leading from personal and individual existence to cosmic and universal consciousness. Self-transformation requires self-knowledge at every stage, a path fraught with dangers. The mystic recognizes that "knowledge is power" but also knows that power corrupts the unwary. He must make compassion his own. Only then will persistent effort and unremitting vigilance lead to supreme wisdom. A.E. depicted the quest as lying

> . . . between the darkness of earth and the light of spiritual self-consciousness, that the Master in each of us draws in and absorbs the rarest and best of experiences, love, self-forgetfulness, aspiration, and out of these distils the subtle essence of wisdom, so that he who struggles in pain for his fellows, when he wakens again on earth is endowed with the tradition of that which we call self sacrifice, but which is in reality the proclamation of our own universal nature.
>
> *The Hour of Twilight*

This passage is similar to that from the rich silence of dreamless sleep, where all personal consciousness is dissolved, through the veneer of chaotic images in the transition from dreams to the waking state. But self-created enemies lie along the uncharted paths waiting to mislead and destroy the pilgrim who glimpses the golden summit in the distance but ignores the steep ravines and rocky ledges between himself and that glorious height. Ethereal sights may be mistaken for divine intimations, misleading the erratic seer. In the archetypal story "A Priestess of the Woods", the daughter of a magician learns about the elemental intelligences of nature.

> She saw deeper things also; as a little child, wrapped up in her bearskin, she watched with awe her father engaged in mystic rites; when around him the airy legions gathered from the populous elements, the Spirits he ruled and the Spirits he bowed down before; fleeting nebulous things white as foam coming forth from the great deep who fled away at the waving of his hand; and rarer the great sons of fire.

But her father died before she learned about more than superficial signs and appearances. Her knowledge of the spirits of the earth was sufficient to make her priestess, but she knew nothing of the formless orders and divine principles. In the course of time, her message was reduced to the repeated warning of the dangers of becoming linked to gnomes, sylphs, salamanders and undines. She saw how men utterly enslave themselves to elemental intelligences through seeking worldly delights, and how they bargain away their lives for momentary gain. There is law in nature, and to violate its orders is necessarily to call forth recompense. Yet she could teach nothing that confers a greater vision, a larger perspective, a fuller hope.

When a young man passing through the forest heard her compelling discourse to the woodland fold, he took up his lyre and sang:

> I never heed by waste or wood
>   The cry of fay or faery thing
> Who tell of their own solitude;
>   Above them all my soul is king.

Though angered by the intrusion, the eyes of the youth dazzled the young priestess with the secrecy of joy. Fearlessly he told her: "Your priestess speaks but half truths, her eyes have seen but her heart does not know. . . The great heart of earth is full of laughter; do not put yourselves apart from its joy, for its soul is your soul and its joy is your true being." She could not counter his confident affirmation, so she bowed down before it, telling her people, "His wisdom may be truer; it is more beautiful than the knowledge we inherit."

Though she maintained her vigils and cleaved to her knowledge, her heart dwelt upon a deeper mystery. Her dominion over nature spirits ebbed, and with it her life. Life is structured by a lesser mystery, and her awakening was accompanied by a release from incarnate life itself. The young priestess, despite her ignorant elemental worship, was pure, and so her heart was touched. Those more travelled on the spiritual path may not find awakening to a deeper life so easy, for their images of the goal may involve conditional aspiration, residual desires for unearthly sensations and incomplete knowledge. The gods have many names and titles, each signifying some level and form of manifestation. The celestial Aphrodite points beyond herself to *Alaya*, compassion absolute, which, like boundless space, encompasses all things arising in it but favours none. She also appears as the terrestrial Venus of Plato's *Symposium*, who satisfies every desire without quenching the endless thirst of desire itself.

In "A Tragedy in the Temple" Asur entered the service of the Temple of Isthar wherein a friend blew to flames the mystic fire which already smouldered within him, but became attracted to her sidereal form.

> 'Brother,' he said, 'I am haunted by a vision, by a child of the stars as lovely as Isthar's self; she visits my dreaming hours, she dazzles me with strange graces, she bewilders with unspeakable longing. Sometimes I know, I must go to her, though I perish. When I see her I forget all else and I have will to resist no longer. The vast and lonely inspiration of the desert departs from my thought, she and the jewel-light she lives in blot it out.'

The tendencies and habits of lifetimes do not easily melt away under the heat of religious fervour. As the pilgrim-soul approaches the gateway to the arduous spiritual path, all which must perish in the divine fire precipitates the conflict between the aspirant's will to merge in the universal light and all temporal traits. This fierce struggle has been portrayed as the great battle in the *Bhagavad Gita*, shown in the Buddha's final contest with Mara before his Enlightenment, and depicted in the Psalms as the valley of the shadow of death. Mara-Lilith waits at the entrance to the mystic path to fascinate and terrify the lonely wayfarer. "At the portal of the 'assembling', the King of the Maras, the *Maha Mara*, stands trying to blind the candidate by the radiance of his 'Jewel' " (*The Voice of the Silence*).

Asur's friend could not help him, not understanding how the jewel of Mara is formed from all the lurking passions which agitate the dark recesses of worldly consciousness. But in a dream he saw the dreadful prospect:

> The form of Asur moved towards a light streaming from a grotto, I could see within it burning gigantic flowers. On one, as on a throne, a figure of weird and wonderful beauty was seated. I was thrilled with a dreadful horror, I thought of the race of Liliths, and some long-forgotten and tragic legends rose up in my memory of these beings whose soul is but a single and terrible passion; whose love too fierce for feebler lives to endure, brings death or madness to men. . . . I saw her in all her terrible beauty. From her head a radiance of feathered flame spread out like the plume of a peacock, it was spotted with gold and green and citron dyes, she raised her arms upward, her robe, semi-transparent, purple and starred over with a jewel lustre, fell in vaporous folds to her feet like the drift of a waterfall.

For anyone not unconditionally devoted to the diamond light of formless Spirit, this opalescent glamour exercises a fatal fascination. When his friend next saw Asur, "his face was as white as the moon, his eyes only reflected the light".

The dominion of Mara-Lilith is limited to the weaknesses of human beings. In A.E.'s "The Cave of Lilith" the temptress tells a sage:

> I, here in my caves between the valley and the height, blind the eyes of all who would pass. Those who by chance go forth to you, come back to me again, and but one in ten thousand passes on. My illusions

are sweeter to them than truth. I offer every soul its own shadow. I pay them their own price. I have grown rich, though the simple shepherds of old gave me birth. Men have made me; the mortals have made me immortal. I rose up like a vapour from their first dreams, and every sign since then and every laugh remains with me. I am made of hopes and fears. The subtle princes lay out their plans of conquest in my caves, and there the hero dreams, and there the lovers of all time write in flames their history. I am wise, holding all experience, to tempt, to blind, to terrify. None shall pass by.

The sage knows that desire attaches itself to objects which must decay and perish, and that much sorrow ensues. When suffering becomes so intense that it touches the inmost depths, the soul searches for a profounder joy. "When desire dies the swift and invisible will awakens", the sage replies. Those who have entered the cave of Lilith emerge again, never to go back.

"The Secret of Power" depicts the war within and without the individual over his destiny. Light and darkness are qualities embodied by beings. In a universe where magic is possible – where Nature's secret operations may be learnt – both good and evil magicians exist, and both exert their magnetism on the soul.

> Two figures awful in their power opposed each other; the frail being wavering between them both, It alone wavered, for they were silent, resolute and knit in the conflict of the will; they stirred not a hand nor a foot; there was only a still quivering now and then as of intense effort, but they made no other movement. . . . Here were the culminations of the human, towering images of the good and evil man may aspire to. I looked at the face of the evil adept. His bright red-brown eyes burned with a strange radiance of power; I felt an answering emotion of pride, of personal intoxication, of psychic richness rise up within me gazing upon him. His face was archetypal; the abstract passion which eluded men in the features of many people I knew, was here declared, exultant, defiant, giantesque; it seemed to leap like fire, to be free. . . . I withdrew my gaze from this face and turned it on the other. An aura of pale soft blue was around this figure through which gleamed an underlight as of universal gold. . . . I caught a glimpse of a face godlike in its calm, terrible in the beauty of a life we know only in dreams, with strength which is the end of the hero's toil, which belongs to the many times martyred soul; yet not far away nor in the past was its power, it was the might of life which exists eternally.

All desire is an aspect of love. In "A Talk by the Euphrates" Merodach the priest explains:

> There are two kinds of love men know of. There is one which begins with a sudden sharp delight – it dies away into infinite tones of sorrow. There is a love which wakes up amid dead things: it is chill at first, but it takes root, it warms, it expands, it lays hold of universal joys. So the man loves: so the God loves. Those who know this divine love are wise indeed. They love not one or another: they are love itself.

Universal love is the philosopher's stone, reducing all things to their essence because it is consubstantial with *prima materia*, the core of the cosmos. Personal love may warm but it is partial, while the greater love identifies with and affects every condition. In "The Meditation of Ananda" the monk comes to feel this love for all creatures flowing through him.

> From his heart he went out to them. Love, a fierce and tender flame, arose; pity, a breath from the vast; sympathy, born of unity. This triple fire sent forth its rays; they surrounded those dark souls; they pervaded them; they beat down oppression.

The divine magic of universal love invisibly affects beings everywhere. Kind acts by others may be sparked by Ananda's love, though unknown to the doers or to him. Magic is a force of nature directed by self-conscious intelligence, and its exercise affects all nature for better or for ill. As a science, magic involves exact knowledge, but as an art, it must be either wisdom or sorcery. In time this becomes an ultimate question for the soul. Will its sorrows be merged with the sorrows of humanity, as in "A Strange Awakening", so that the gloom of the world is dispelled by the pristine light of the Spiritual Sun, or will suffering only drive the soul to a ferocious, demonic pride, leading it to join the company of Dostoevsky's Grand Inquisitor? A.E. saw that one dare not experience joy and hear the whole world cry in pain, that the quest is completed successfully only when one helps to lead others to its goal. "The Midnight Blossom" expresses this great affirmation:

> 'Brother,' said Varunna, 'here is the hope of the world. Though many seek only for the eternal joy, yet the cry you heard has been heard by

great ones who have turned backwards, called by these beseeching voices. The small old path stretching far away leads through many wonderful beings to the place of Brahma. There is the first fountain, the world of beautiful silence, the light which has been undimmed since the beginning of time. But turning backwards from the gate the small old path winds away into the world of men, and it enters every sorrowful heart. This is the way the great ones go.

Hermes, July 1979

BETWEEN HEAVEN AND EARTH

The great antique heart, how like a child's in its simplicity, like a man's in its earnest solemnity and depth! Heaven lies over him wheresoever he goes or stands on the earth, making all the earth a mystic temple to him, the earth's business all a kind of worship. Glimpses of bright creatures flash in the common sunlight; angels yet hover, doing God's messages among men.... A great law of duty, high as these two infinitudes (heaven and hell), dwarfing all else, annihilating all else – it was a reality, and it is one: the garment only of it is dead; the essence of it lives through all times and all eternity!

The essence of our being, the mystery in us that calls itself 'I', – what words have we for such things? – it is a breath of Heaven, the highest Being reveals himself in man. This body, these faculties, this life of ours, is it not all as a vesture for the UNNAMED?

Thomas Carlyle

Rounds and Races are integral to cosmic and human evolution. This septenary teaching is of crucial significance to the conceptual framework of the *Gupta Vidya*. Metaphysics and ethics are fused in one unbroken series of instinctual and intuitive states of unfolding monadic consciousness in slowly evolving material vestures. Of the seven planes of Kosmic consciousness, the lower four *rupa* planes provide the seemingly objective matrix for the seven globes of the Earth Chain. The upper three *arupa* planes are almost incomprehensible by the uninitiated and are closely connected with the ineffable mystery of Mahatic self-consciousness, at once the source and support of universal progress upon the seven globes of human evolution.

> These seven *planes* correspond to the seven *states* of consciousness in man. It remains with him to attune the three higher states in himself to the three higher planes in Kosmos. But before he can attempt to attune, he must awaken the three 'seats' to life and activity.
>
> *The Secret Doctrine*, i 199

Any human being who is truly serious about activating these dormant spiritual centres and selflessly attuning them to the three higher planes of Kosmic consciousness must think away entirely from the enveloping vestures and move upon the "waters of Space", the empyrean of "airy nothings", the *Akashic* void within the Hebdomadic Heart, the Kingdom of Heaven on Earth. In the alchemical process of progressive self-attenuation the enlightened person makes fruitful discoveries about the limits and possibilities, the tendencies and tropisms, of all the varying classes of elementals in the illusory vestures. If any seeker of truth is *Buddhic* regarding the broad scheme of evolution, which is triple in function and sevenfold in the great circlings of globes by the Monadic Host, then the voluntary assumption of incarnation by Divine Self-consciousness at a certain critical stage of global evolution yields a richer view of the true stature of being human, God *in actu*.

If any sensitive person fully thought out what it means to be a self-conscious being, making meaningful connections in reference to all aspects of life and death, then one would verily become capable of cooperating with the evolutionary scheme by staying in line with those gods and sages who are the unthanked Teachers of Humanity. No such fundamental revolution in consciousness is possible without becoming intensely aware of both motive and method. Motive has to do with morality in the metaphysical sense, the rate of vibration of one's spiritual volition. Is the individual soul consciously seeking to help, heal and elevate every single life-atom? Or, owing to fear, ignorance, suspicion and doubt, is the fugitive soul trapped in a mechanical repetition of moribund hostilities inimical to those whom it irrationally and unintentionally injures? Through unremitting attention to such internal obstructions, one could rise above the lower or lunar planes of consciousness, seeing compulsive tendencies for what they are, and thus introduce by renewed acts of noetic will a strong current of spiritual benevolence. This would be the basis of Bodhisattvic ethics, a joyous mode of relaxed breathing. In pursuing this Aquarian lifestyle, one is certain to encounter various difficulties in the realm of the mind in regard to one's permeability to astral forces, one's personal vulnerability to reversals, perversion and pride, and also a strange susceptibility to distortions and awkwardnesses that come between what is spontaneously felt at the core of one's being and its deliberate enactment in the chaotic context of social intercourse. One would have to become mathematically objective about the fluctuating patterns of mental deposits and tendencies that have cut deep grooves in the volatile vestures of personal existence. One would have to see all this in relation to human evolution as a whole, asking relevant questions about the uncouth Fourth Race as well as concerning what one really learnt in the first sub-race of the Fifth Race of original thinkers and theophilanthropists who were effortlessly capable of creative ideation and concentrated endeavour. In asking such questions one has to lift ethical sensitivity beyond the level of the individual monad, through active concern with all humanity, to cosmic planes of cognition. In so doing, one could gradually come to make fundamental readjustments in the elusive relationship between one's lower and higher centres of perception, volition and empathy.

Although such a prospect of self-sovereignty may seem to be an enormous evolutionary advance, in retrospect, once it is attained, it will be seen as no more than a self-conscious restoration of the primeval modes of moral awareness of the Third Root Race. Soon after the descent of the gods, the pristine Sons of Wisdom who incarnated into the Third Race, they engendered through *Kriyashakti* the sacred progeny of the truly twice-born, the fabled Sons of Ad, the mythic "Sons of the Fire-Mist", the immaculate Sons of Will and Yoga. What they emanated in unison was a wondrous collective being (Bodhisattvic Golden Egg), a mysterious Bodhi-Tree and deathless fountainhead, the Tree of Noetic Knowledge, from which arose all the initiated Adepts and god-men, gurus and sages of the human race in subsequent epochs of evolution. The arcane teachings affirm that Dakshinamurti, the Initiator of Initiates, was the original *Jagadguru* (*Amitabha*), Rishi Narayan or Shri Krishna, the Ancient of Days who stood as Shiva (*Avalokiteshwara*) behind Buddha, Shankara, Pythagoras and Plato, Confucius and Lao Tzu, Christ and Paul, Count St. Germain and Claude St. Martin, Cagliostro and Mesmer, H.P. Blavatsky and W.Q. Judge. There have always existed on earth the secret mystery-temples in which the whole life of the neophyte through a series of preparatory initiations must eventually lead to grateful prostration before the Great Sacrifice (*Adhiyajna*) and a

Host of Hierophants, the Buddhas of Contemplation, silently sustaining the whole world, the Wheel of *Samsara*, the Great Chain of Being. It was H.P. Blavatsky's accredited privilege to transmit this ancient and sacred teaching in a memorable hymnody in *The Secret Doctrine*, from which every *Lanoo* may derive inspiration and strength in reawakening the mighty power of sacrifice, the invocation of *Adhiyajna* through *Agniyoga* by the grace of *Adi Sanat*, the Mahat-Atman.

> The 'BEING' just referred to, which has to remain nameless, is the Tree from which, in subsequent ages, all the great historically known Sages and Hierophants, such as the Rishi Kapila, Hermes, Enoch, Orpheus, etc., etc., have branched off. As objective *man*, he is the mysterious (to the profane – the ever invisible) yet ever present Personage about whom legends are rife in the East, especially among the Occultists and the students of the Sacred Science. It is he who changes form, yet remains ever the same. And it is he again who holds spiritual sway over the *initiated* Adepts throughout the whole world. He is, as said, the 'Nameless One' who has so many names, and yet whose names and whose very nature are unknown. He is *the* 'Initiator,' called the 'GREAT SACRIFICE.' For, sitting at the threshold of LIGHT, he looks into it from within the circle of Darkness, which he will not cross; nor will he quit his post till the last day of this life-cycle. Why does the solitary Watcher remain at his self-chosen post? Why does he sit by the fountain of primeval Wisdom, of which he drinks no longer, as he has naught to learn which he does not know – aye, neither on this Earth, nor in its heaven? Because the lonely, sore-footed pilgrims on their way back to their *home* are never sure to the last moment of not losing their way in this limitless desert of illusion and matter called Earth-Life. Because he would fain show the way to that region of freedom and light, from which he is a voluntary exile himself, to every prisoner who has succeeded in liberating himself from the bonds of flesh and illusion. Because, in short, he has sacrificed himself for the sake of mankind, though but a few Elect may profit by the GREAT SACRIFICE.
>
> It is under the direct, silent guidance of this MAHA – (great) – GURU that all the other less divine Teachers and instructors of mankind became, from the first awakening of human consciousness, the guides of early Humanity. It is through these 'Sons of God' that infant humanity got its first notions of all the arts and sciences as

well as of spiritual knowledge; and it is they who have laid the first foundation-stone of those ancient civilizations that puzzle so sorely our modern generation of students and scholars.

The Secret Doctrine, i 207–208

This sublime portrait must speak to the imperishable spiritual intuition in the inmost heart of every human being who seeks to cross the threshold. It is truly a theme for reflection, and if used as the basis of deep and daily meditation, it should act upon the sovereign spiritual will. It should lend hidden strength to the capacity to marshal and concentrate in one's divine sphere all sacrificial thoughts, feelings, energies, words and acts. It should also give the indestructible strength to remain like the solitary watcher totally bound to his self-chosen post. The very idea of any shadow of turning or variation from one's sacred commitment would be deeply repugnant to one's nature. The esoteric teaching given above was always whispered but only enacted within the *sanctum sanctorum* of the Mystery Schools. It is a theurgic teaching meant to fire a human being through *Agniyoga* and arouse soul-memories (*anamnesis*) from pre-manvantaric aeons in cosmic evolution. To be able to incarnate such a therapeutic teaching is to light up the rising flame of resolve such as will never be extinguished in the mighty task of universal enlightenment.

Many seekers have genuinely attempted such an authentic and generous discipline but have still been unable to extricate themselves from their own inane servitude to their shadow, their envy and suspicion, their compulsive expansion of that shadow of inherent inferiority through fear and doubt, through obsessional thinking and delusional feeling, and the overwhelming chaos of undeliberate, undiscriminating responses to the worlds of form. This is not only fatal but also like a terminal case of cancer in a human being who has used the priceless boon of truth for blocking the door to the humanity of the future. Regardless, however, of the mistakes and failures of most neophytes, there must come a decisive moment of choice when one is prepared to combine solemnity and simplicity in a joyous acceptance of one's own spiritual mission as a pilgrim-soul, as a true disciple upon the Path, as a vigilant listener to the utterance of Divine Wisdom, as a Happy Warrior in the Army of the Voice, and as a creative restorer of the natural order of spontaneous fellow-feeling towards the whole of humanity. One must cherish constantly the light of daring, the moral courage to take the Kwan Yin pledge – an irrevocable decision that confers true dignity, spiritual wakefulness and the resonance of responsibility. For such a sacred resolve to be an exemplar of spiritual strength, all of one's being must be involved, without withholding any asset or evading any obligation. Nature is by no means ungenerous in affording seasonal opportunities for honest rededication to self-renewal and service. The fortnight commencing with the winter solstice and culminating on the fourth of January, consecrated to Hermes-Buddha, marks the potent seed-time for the coming year. Soren Kierkegaard once observed that "Life can only be understood backwards, but it must be lived forwards." It is important that a sensitive person should prepare for the future by taking a firm, all-inclusive, unconditional position gestated out of deep reflection. One should set apart abundant time for that noble purpose to be truly able to generate the permanent basis of alchemical resolution and spiritual will. Then as one comes down from that exalted state of *samadhi*, enriched by constant meditation and manvantaric sleep, one could renew and resume this profound preparation in the dawn and the dusk, using all the precious time available to "get ready for *Dubjed*". If this is done between the ages of fourteen and thirty-five, then the time between the solstice and fourth of January could be used annually to light the fires in all souls of the irrevocable and effortlessly selfless commitment to the whole of life and to all the solar and lunar ancestors. If anyone truly performed this *yajna* in the sacred name of the Guru of Gurus, the Hierophant of Hierophants, the Initiator of Initiates, one would receive untold benefits from the service of Krishna, the *Purna Avatar*, the Logos in the Cosmos and the God in man.

Those who wish to enjoy this sanctification might well look back calmly at the lost years and wasted lives, not in self-serving images in elaborate detail but philosophically in terms of ingrained tendencies and fear-ridden preoccupations. Even through looking back over one year, one could make many discoveries about human vulnerabilities, excuses and rationalizations. One may also see in one's pseudo-Promethean struggles the neglected hooking-points that support one's better self in surviving the *pralaya* of a disintegrating bimillennial epoch and in widely sharing all one's truest perceptions and finest perspectives. While venturing upon this meditative retrospection, one must recognize that one is only seeking the sacred tribe of those who have effortlessly renewed their Bodhisattvic pledges in recurring cycles of descent and incarnations of ascent for the sake of all. One is imbibing strength from those to whom this is as natural as breathing, as effortless as meditating upon the mantrams of *Lanoos* and Arhats. Having assimilated the sacred teaching of *Jnana Yajna*, one must deeply desire (*Itchasakti*) to insert one's own labours of love and acts of devotion into the Great Sacrifice (*Maha Yajna*). People are both cursed and blessed by being told these things, because if they listen to Krishna's secret teaching and do nothing about it, then their karma is needlessly burdensome. There is always a risk assumed in intoning *Brahma Vach*. In general, Gandhi's axiom is fundamental: human nature is such that it must either soar or sink, and whether one goes forward or backward is determined by the benevolent use of modern knowledge and ancient Wisdom.

When spiritual knowledge is made the enduring basis of deep reflection, where it is moistened by the liquid fire of devotion to Universal Good and by the concentrated current of aspiration, then it becomes a breakthrough into inner space. With noetic insight, one can burn out at the core all those defeatist devices of thinking, feeling, speaking and acting which continually toss the initiative back to the illusory self, thereby making spiritual life seem a wearisome, defensive and cheerless struggle, with tension and tightness, and little sweetness or light. In fact, the taking of a Vow during a rising cycle of immense promise for mankind means the restoration of the reins of kingship to the Sovereign Self, and the firm refusal to allow the initiative to be smothered in the ashes of vain hopes and burnt-out ideals. This requires a period of intense *tapas*, a time of mental and physical fasting, self-renewal through silence, abstention and calmness: otherwise, one remains compulsively caught up in muddy streams of sterile emanations and the accompanying flotsam of fuzzy elementals that crowd in and clog the nerve-currents of noetic will. At the root of this dismal predicament is the false idea of who one is and a delusive image of oneself as the egocentric pivot of a world upon which one may make myriad claims. The sacrificial, humane, adult, mellow and mature outlook is the exact opposite. Dag Hammarskjold once wrote that human life involves a bringing together of oil and air, and then there is a spark. The moment one thinks of rights, there is no spark; the oil and air will never come together. Sadly, human beings repeatedly abort, murder or damage their own chances as souls because they cannot get rid of this fundamentally false idea of a separate self, and even more sadly, in the light of divine teaching, they sometimes cling to it with melodramatic versatility. This is such piteous karma that it is all too poignant to contemplate – on behalf of a single human soul. Therefore one should, for the sake of all, awake, arise and seek the Great Sacrifice, and seek a pellucid reflection in the waters of wisdom. Thus the soil of the brain-mind is stirred, washed and prepared to receive the hidden seed of moral resolution, releasing the spiritual will in silence and secrecy, strengthened by inner humility and true courage during the seed-time of the golden harvest that will feed the hungry.

Those who are dedicated to serve Krishna should meditate upon the hymnody to the Great Sacrifice, or the rhapsody of the Self-Governed Sage in the second chapter of the *Bhagavad Gita*, or on any one of the magnificent portraits of Avatars (Magus-Teachers) in any sacred text, each of which is a great gift which *Rishis* (Sages) are ceaselessly beatified to hear and chant. If this is the endearing characteristic of all Mahatmas and Bodhisattvas, surely the least any human being can do who has the golden opportunity to use such a text is to become somewhat worthy of the sacred privilege. It is now time to awake from preparatory slumber and truly meditate upon those mantramic texts (in Sanskritic English or German and Russian) and taking even a few sentences, think deeply about their meaning and use. All sacred texts will suggest to their ardent devotees the different stages in reference to mind control, the method of collecting the mind, and the infallible means for removing the delusion and commotion of worldly concern. Having learnt how to settle the mind in a state of calm so that it is like the still lagoon or swan lake, one can let it expand like the blue vault of the sky when enshrined in that serene state. In time, one will come to see the golden sphere of cosmic light within the hollow of the heart in the expanding universe of the *Hiranyagarbha*, the Egg of Brahma. This will reverse the polarities in the *laya* centres for those who persist in the discipline of selflessness. This secret teaching is jewelled in the hidden heart of every authentic tradition, is always given for the sake of all humanity to those who silently serve the City of Man. Since *samsara* is merely a mirage of the mind, the disciple must examine and expunge all thoughts that pollute the holy avenues of expression. To do this, one has to meditate upon mighty spiritual conceptions, readily forgetting oneself and thrilling with a feeling of universal gratitude and individual responsibility, reverence and renunciation. From within the spiritual heart, one must evoke the cool courage to look at one's faults with the unerring eye of *Buddhic* discernment.

It is always crucial to growth that the positive meditations shall be far greater than the negative sacrifices, and that one should really savour the sheer joy of mental procreation and self-cancellation. One should lose one's morbid taste for self-righteous condemnation and image-crippling which is rooted in the paralysing fear of failure and sprouts into the cankerous weeds of an *asuric* and demonic way of life. Thinking in terms of votive offerings rather than death sentences could vitalize that vacuum in the brain and the heart where lies hidden the elixir of decisiveness and definiteness, a crispness and magnanimity which authenticate the true signature of selfhood. Too many human beings have repeatedly subverted their lives owing to their obsession with their own repulsiveness instead of learning the lesson that they must confront the lie in the soul which conceals the virginal beauty within the antediluvian monster. They have hugely enjoyed meditating upon themselves as total failures, thereby insulting the integrity of the Mahatmas and also doing immeasurable harm because they would have been able to do much good with even a little of this mental prostration to Krishna. One has to recover an exquisite sense of the sacred, the numinous and the unmanifest. One has to reach out repeatedly to that light of the Logos which is above the cerebrum, that which is without any limits or reservations, that divine lustre which can never be mirrored except through *Buddhi* in *Manas*. This is the pristine ray of *Mahat-Atman*, the Universal Self of the Maha Yogin serenely seated upon Mount *Kailas* while dancing amidst the ghouls of the graveyard, releasing them from self-torture and their unending cruelty to gnomes and undines, sylphs and salamanders. *Buddhi* is latent in every atom, and yet as *Buddhi* mirrors Atman, there is an infallible result, a humbling decisiveness and sovereign assurance which comes from nowhere else than the transcendental Buddhas of Compassion. *Nishchaya* in Sanskrit means "without any shadow". When a true yogi, from the depths of his or her meditation upon human suffering and the need for Divine Wisdom, vitalizes that immaculate light of the Atman in the inmost brain, perfectly mirrored in the cells of the occipital lobe, there arises an ancient assurance and selfless certainty which is concealed and can never be erased. It can never be shown to the blasphemous even though it remains as a hidden lamp behind the borrowed mask. The light of true conviction engenders an irreversible current through *Sachakriya*, a sacred affirmation of the truth of a lifetime. Even though a fallen disciple has languished for long with wasted words, harsh sounds, violent speech, empty offerings, even though enormous karma has been generated by the Atlantean *rakshasa* (monster), all of which will have to be rendered in full account in future lives, nevertheless if he invokes the grace of Krishna-Christos through penitential meditations upon the Soundless Sound, he can place the demonic dwarf beneath the feet of the Divine Dancer and rescue from the debris of shipwreck the white dove of peace, the olive branch of humility, and the self-cancelled pledge of true service.

All who take advantage of this matchless means of true self-renewal can inaugurate a fundamental change in the polluted *Manas* through *Agniyoga*, the sacred science of baptism through the fires of self-purgation. *Kama manas*, the inverted reflection of *Manas*, becomes constricted through the cohesion of the delusive image of personal identity bound up with intellectual autoeroticism, physical sensations, sights and sounds, deceptive externalities, and the knots of perversion tightening the myriad cords of foreshortened conceptions of space-time. *Kama manas* is the externalizing and rationalizing mind that needlessly negates others as well as oneself. It is the mediocre miseducated insecure mind that cuts up everything and dismisses the divine with faint praise and the sneer of guilty derision! *Kama manas* is discontinuous and it creates a monotonous movement from one extreme to the opposite so that it cannot come to rest, but is constantly enslaved by restless caution and is constitutionally incapable of transcending its own meanness and spiritual sterility. All of this is the unnatural legacy of the Fourth Race of graceless giants. Whilst, in the economy of Nature, even such tendencies to grossness represent the tortured descent of the light of consciousness to the lesser hierarchies and lower emanations, the excess of humbug with which this self-assassination is perpetrated through cowardly speech is indeed abnormal. This is the origin of obsessive guilt and compulsive fear, arising from the degradation of the Holy of Holies, the desecration of the sacred tabernacle, the massacre of innocents, the endlessly evasive abdication of responsibility through pride in hypocrisy, self-torment, and the dressing up of moral blindness in the cloak of false modesty. On the other hand, all human beings of every race and tribe, every creed and nihilistic sect, innately enjoy a residual sense of decency, a feeling for tenderness, forgiveness and magnanimity towards the unloved. This is innate in all human beings because it was the great gift of the gods to the Third Race of Innocents. Without a spark of empathy there would be no *conatus*, no basis for a rational self-preservation except in the case of those soulless beings who behave like machines and robots. Knowing all this at some level, one can invoke the blessing of the Avatars to fan the faint spark of *Buddhi* buried within the burnt-out charcoal of a self-throttled *Manas*. Krishna hinted in the *Uttara Gita* that even the elongated shadow of self-betrayal could be slowly shrunk by self-attenuation through sacred speech and abstention from harm to the helpless life-atoms.

Each and all must restore what is natural to the whole of humanity and was exemplified *par excellence* by the authentically initiated Brahmins of antiquity who had little to do with the India of recent millennia, but were true transmitters of the oral traditions of theurgic utterance until the time of betrayal of the Buddha except in cloistered sanctuaries of *yogins* and *sannyasins*.

> When, moved by the law of Evolution, the Lords of Wisdom infused into him the spark of consciousness, the first feeling it awoke to life and activity was a sense of solidarity, of one-ness with his spiritual creators. As the child's first feeling is for its mother and nurse, so the first aspirations of the awakening consciousness in primitive man

were for those whose element he felt within himself, and who yet were outside, and independent of him. DEVOTION arose out of that feeling, and became the first and foremost motor in his nature; for it is the only one which is natural in our heart, which is innate in us. . . .

It lives undeniably, and has settled in all its ineradicable strength and power in the Asiatic Aryan heart from the Third Race direct through its first 'mind-born' sons, – the fruits of Kriyasakti. As time rolled on the holy caste of Initiates produced but rarely, and from age to age, such perfect creatures: beings apart, inwardly, though the same as those who produced them, outwardly.

The Secret Doctrine, i 210–211

The Initiates of the deathless Race scattered the seeds of primordial wisdom among all the races of men and the Mystery Schools in cloistered gardens, caves and sanctuaries around the globe. The innate feeling of devotion throbbed in the sacred chamber of every human heart, but to be able to exemplify it naturally and instantly has become the lost art of magnanimity in the age of *Varna Shankar* or the Tower of Babel. The gift of graciousness cannot be bequeathed by external structures or physical heredity in *Kali Yuga*, the Age of Iron. The class of souls which delayed incarnation – owing to pride in purity, cowardly caution, fear of involvement in the mire of human fallibility, and a stubbornly selfish refusal to move into more differentiated realms – paradoxically became those very beings who, once they had incarnated, were captive to carnality, weakness of will, and fear-ridden worship of the printed word. The iron of self-contempt and false toughness, image-crippling and spiritual circumcision, entered into their souls, their blood and brain-cells. In the legends and myths of antiquity, the original fear of incarnation, owing to deficiency in active meditation upon the entire scale of ascent and descent, resulted in the perverse or compulsive pollution of the powers of thought, imagination and reverence for life. The resulting corruption of consciousness and simian imitativeness became the karmic burden of the *Pratyeka* Buddhas of spiritual selfishness. The atoms of matter were tainted by the double sin of the mindless and miscegenation. As a result, many gluttonous men and women are constantly caught up in those material particles, or become mediumistic through foul thoughts and fear of invasion. Among the sorcerers, traducers and traitors the power of the AUM was lost. The Third Eye closed, with a consequent suffocation of spiritual intuitions in the moral dwarfs of humanity.

The therapeutic restoration of the porosity of the brain-mind to the light of *Atma-Buddhi* is possible. It depends upon the progressive exemplification of five criteria of what is natural to human self-consciousness. *First* is the irrepressible feeling of reverence for the unbroken line of descent of the Great Sacrifice of the Hierophantic Host under the eternal Initiator of Initiates, the Evergreen Trees of Knowledge, Enlightenment and Immortality. Honouring others is innate to the human heart: it would show as a true reverence for Nature, for the Spiritual Sun and its myriad rays among all humanity, for all the constellations and the seven kingdoms and the Illustrious Predecessors, Light-Bringers and Pathfinders, reverence that is natural. Anything less is unnatural and abnormal, a moral monstrosity. *Secondly*, there is a longing for the ideal forms and archetypes, a great joy in withdrawing from the pressure of concern with the concrete to the empyrean of invisible potentials, a pure love of Truth, Beauty and Goodness in all forms, selfless ideation on metaphysical paradigms, parapolitical ideals and Universal Good – the *Agathon*. *Thirdly*, and this is certainly a very decisive test, an innate, instructive and ineradicable conviction (regardless of culture) that the sexual act is sacred, that the Lesser Mysteries of Eros must mirror the pristine Light of the Logos invoked through Sound and Silence in the Greater Mysteries. Anything else runs the risk of ever-increasing desecration of the dignity of human beings, the sanctity of the Holy of Holies, as well as the fecundity of human potentials. *Fourthly*, there is devotion, the only feeling natural to the hearts of men and women of all races, common to the human babe and the young of animals. Devotion, understood rightly, shows in the Rishis and Sages as well as in a child's simplicity which co-exists with authentic solemnity and inner depth. Inherent in the human heart is the ever-present sense of the sacred and the feeling that everything in human worship of the Divine is worthy of minimal respect. This is magically shown in that which corresponds to *Manas* among all the senses, the synthesizing sense of touch. The *fifth* criterion of culture is a recognition of the human body as a temple, not a tomb, of the pilgrim-soul in every person.

> There is but one temple in the universe, and that is the body of man. Nothing is holier than that high form. . . . We touch heaven when we lay our hand on a human body! . . . If well meditated it will turn out to be a scientific fact; the expression . . . of the actual truth of the thing. We are the miracle of miracles, – the great inscrutable Mystery.
>
> *The Secret Doctrine*, i 212

The pervasive sense of the sacred and universal respect for freedom of thought and choice have become obscured in many victims of modernity owing to a hypnotic fascination with corruption and evil, forgetfulness of the divine mission of the immortal Soul, alienation from others and oneself, especially through fear of failure, estrangement through loneliness, distrust of oneself, and possible misuse in former lives due to cowardice and false ideas connected with evasion of the laws of Nature. Corruption of consciousness must be healed, and what is natural must be restored through the Golden Rule of reciprocity. Already, since 1963, many souls have taken birth in diverse cultures who have a recognition of the need to restore the ethical foundation of human society. This transcends the claims of all cultures to preeminence. Such souls will increase in number until a time comes when there will be so many for whom this is so natural that any encouragement given them will help the regeneration of the human race. This will be a distinctly different class of souls from those who came mauled and tormented by the degradation of two world wars, which helped to make popular the works of the corrupt. The attempt to make normal what was abnormal has failed, so far. It was tried in every way, but once the alternatives are known, then what is abnormal had to become more and more desperate and self-destructive because it could not any more pretend to be normal.

The twilight hour of sadists and masochists has now struck, and myriads of pilgrim-souls seek the Midnight Sun and the sacred constellation of the Aquarian Age, which began soon after the *fin de siecle*. The invisible dawn of the cosmopolis is summoned by the flute of the divine cowherd, beckoning home the matured innocents that dared to dream of a Golden Age. Meanwhile, Nataraja of *Kailas* and

Kala-Hamsa enacts the *Tandava* Dance over the heads of epicurean giants, stoical dwarfs and cynical eunuchs. The age of sectarian religions, technocratic politics and cultural envy is dead. *Kama manas* has been dethroned by *Buddhi-Taijasi*, the Light of the Logos. The age of humanistic science, authentic spirituality and mini-communes has just begun, foreshadowing the end of the twentieth century and the emergence of the City of Man. The inevitable return of initiative to the scattered supporters of what is innate, universal and spiritual, merely suggests that no special pleading is needed for true gratitude and an authentic sense of the sacred. Despite the failures of so many, the philosophy of perfectibility, the religion of responsibility and the science of spirituality will spread far and wide, like the myriad branches of the *Ashwatha* tree, with its roots in heaven.

The collective self-consciousness that has been perverted must be released through love and wit. If one sees clearly the sacredness of the indestructible teaching of antiquity, one can recognize the *kama manasic* self-interest of Arjuna as a necessary tool in the service of Krishna in the Great War between *psyche* and *nous*, the Tower of Babel and the New Jerusalem, the head and the heart of every human being on earth. The true spark of universal brotherhood, reverence for teachers, gratitude to the good earth, and reticent sanctity may, even from a spark, be fanned into the fires of creativity in the service of the civilization of the future. This is the great hope which hides the golden promise. If even a few theophilanthropists would now serve the Bodhi-Tree and the City of Man, the Isle of the Blessed would be grateful beyond measure. Every such sincere effort is assuredly of help in relieving the pain of the human heart, which is widespread today, and also in laying down the universal cornerstones of the academies and *ashrams* of the future. All cultures need to rediscover what it means to be truly humane. Builders of bridges between Heaven and Earth are few and far between, and always have been; they may be readily recognized by their unswerving fidelity to pledges on behalf of mankind. Citizens of the cosmopolis will unite when they have nothing to lose but their masks of misanthropy – or their fugitive souls, on earth as in heaven.

Hermes, December 1980

EVOLUTION AND KARMA

> *It now becomes plain that there exists in Nature a triple evolutionary scheme, for the formation of the three periodical Upadhis; or rather three separate schemes of evolution, which in our system are inextricably interwoven and interblended at every point. These are the Monadic (or spiritual), the intellectual, and the physical evolutions. These three are the finite aspects or the reflections on the field of Cosmic Illusion of ATMA, the seventh, the ONE REALITY. . . . Each of these three systems has its own laws, and is ruled and guided by the different sets of the highest Dhyanis or 'Logoi.' Each is represented in the constitution of man, the Microcosm of the great Macrocosm; and it is the union of these three streams in him which makes him the complex being he now is.*
>
> The Secret Doctrine, i 181

Man and nature, *Atman* and *Brahman*, are One in their transcendental origin, but threefold in their manvantaric manifestations through interlocking planes of consciousness and form. The mystery of the Three-in-One is mirrored in the archetypal mode of instruction exemplified by Gautama Buddha, who shed the nirvanic light of Bodhisattvic Wisdom upon the span of all three worlds, teaching *devas*, men and gods. The complex riddle of human nature inscribed in the sevenfold vestures of man and nature can only be deciphered through a progressive comprehension of all its interconnected links ranging from the homogeneous planes of *arupa* ideation to the most material planes of differentiated form. The complete union of *karuna* and *prajna*, of compassion and self-knowledge, depends upon the all-inclusive integration of every element and atom participating in the cyclic sweep of cosmic evolution.

Under the supreme decree of eternal harmony, all that lives form a single community and brotherhood, bound together and governed by the law of Karma. Within that vast programme, each evolving unit is joined to every other by laws of collective and distributive action, and it is upon the correct understanding of these coordinate links, inherent in the interrelationships of the embodied vestures, that the further spiritual growth of humanity depends. In practice, and in time, this requires the seeker self-consciously to differentiate and comprehend the origin, functions and virtues of each of the principles in man. To acquire skill in action, the logic of the programme of evolution must first be seen in terms of its triadic nature, and then applied, with moral discrimination, according to the laws of analogy and correspondence, within each of the seven kingdoms of nature. Through *tapas* and ascetic striving, guided by devotion to the Mahatmas and rooted in a vision of the Bodhisattvic ideal, each pilgrim-soul can discover and unlock the mysteries hidden within the microcosmic world of the visible and largely invisible vestures.

Examined from the standpoint of individual effort, this task may be seen as a progressive and painful, though extremely rewarding, process of inserting personal existence into universal human history and ultimately into cosmic evolution. For the student of *Theosophia* privileged to use *The Secret Doctrine*, this may be put in terms of the fusion of cosmogenesis with anthropogenesis through entry into the path of *The Voice of the Silence*. Acquisition of a dialectical understanding of the operation of Karma, in its triple operation in the spiritual, intellectual and physical fields, arises from an awareness of eternity in time which yields that timeliness in conduct spoken of by Krishna as renunciation in action and by the Buddha as skilful means.

As a starting-point, one must come to see that the diverse rules and laws applying to the different kingdoms of nature and their coordinate schemes of evolution are inseparable expressions of one universal law of growth. Whether put in terms of the relationship between the Unmanifest Logos and the diverse *Logoi* operating on different planes, or in terms of the differentiations of Spirit and Matter out of one homogeneous Substance-Principle, the complex structures and varied modes of growth participated in by human beings represent a single triadic process. In the language of the Commentaries upon the *Book of Dzyan*, this central principle is put in terms of the magnetic attraction exercised by the model of the Heavenly Man over every spark of sentient life evolving throughout the infinitudes of space.

> 1. *Every form on earth, and every speck (atom) in Space strives in its efforts towards self-formation to follow the model placed for it in the* 'HEAVENLY MAN.' . . . *Its (the atom's involution and evolution, its external and internal growth and development, have all one and the same object – man, as the highest physical and ultimate form on this earth; the* MONAD, *in its absolute totality and awakened condition – as the culmination of the divine incarnations on Earth.*
>
> The Secret Doctrine, i 183

This is a general law applicable to the whole of life, from the tiniest atom to the most massive form, all of which evolve from *Akashic* prototypes that are like seeds within the Cosmic Egg of Brahma, the container of the Heavenly Man. As in the awesome metaphor of the *Ashwatha* tree, with its roots in heaven and its branches and leaves below on the planes of manifestation, life proceeds from formlessness into form and ever seeks to return through the circulation of its essences and elixirs to its transcendental source.

For all human beings in the present period of evolution, spiritual growth consists in awakening noetic awareness of formless spiritual essences, a process of Manasic maturation which requires precise apprehension of the different sets of Dhyanis and ancestors involved in the complex karmic heredity of humanity. The ascent to Monadic awakening culminating in self-conscious divinity proceeds *pari passu* with an increasing participation in the sacrificial descent of the Light of the Logos into the human temple. Humanity is the beneficiary of vast processes of evolution that were completed on preceding globes both in the present earth chain and in the previous chain of globes known to us as the moon chain. Like dwarfs seated upon the shoulders of giants, men and women of the present enjoy the privilege of self-conscious existence and survey the grand prospects of future evolution only because of the sacrifice of Avatars, Mahatmas and Dhyanis throughout ages without number. Metaphysically, there is neither a beginning nor an end to the series of vast epochs of manifestation, and the significance of reaching the man-stage of evolution lies in the prerogative and potential of becoming a co-worker with Nature, with *Amitabha*, the Boundless Age.

Terrestrial evolution may be conceptually divided into three streams, corresponding to the Monadic, the intellectual and the physical components set forth in the *Gupta Vidya*. The phrase 'Monadic evolution' points to the emergence of successively higher phases of spiritual activity of the metaphysically indivisible unit called the Monad, or the *Atma-Buddhi*. In reality, that Monad is not subject to change or alteration, but is the constantly presiding divine presence at the heart of the sphere of *mayavic* and *samsaric* existence. In its highest sense, the MONAD is single and impartite, and the conception of a plurality of Monads is merely a terminological convenience within the veil of illusion. Pythagoras taught that the MONAD, having radiated Divine Light, retires into the Divine Dark.

Although Monadic evolution is spoken of as equivalent to spiritual evolution, both Spirit and Matter, with all their differentiations, are ultimately One, inseparable from meta-Spirit or Atman. Nonetheless, within the planes of differentiated existence and consciousness, it is helpful to distinguish the realized degrees of universality and individuation of consciousness attributable to the evolving sparks of the One Life. Hence, in the metaphysics of *The Secret Doctrine* there is a fundamental distinction between the hosts of solar and lunar Monads, the *Agnishwatha* and *Barhishad Pitris*. Within the stream of intellectual evolution, and associated with the Solar or *Manasa Dhyanis*, are to be found the exalted bestowers of self-conscious intelligence upon incipient humanity. Within the stream of physical evolution and associated with the building of the mortal vestures of man are to be found the hosts of the lunar *Pitris*. Whilst it is possible to distinguish the ancestry and attributes of the various principles of sevenfold man, ultimately there is only One Principle – the *Atman*.

The development of humanity in the present series of globes began at a point like the intersection of cosmogenesis and anthropogenesis. As the sevenfold theatre of evolution known as the earth emerged from *pralaya*, and the *Fohatic* life-wave began to quicken the sleeping centres, those Monads from the moon chain which had attained the highest degree of physical evolution on the old chain commenced their activity in the first of the new worlds. Restricted in their degree of Monadic activity to the fourth plane, these builders of form were capable of recapitulating evolutionary development only up to the incipient human-germ stage. Progressively, over the first three and one-half Rounds of the development of the earth chain, these lunar Dhyanis unfolded, through the power of instinctual intelligence, the *rupas* that constitute the lower kingdoms of nature.

Viewed from the Monadic standpoint, this process is equivalent to a descent or involution of Spirit into Matter, of consciousness into form. Viewed from the standpoint of *Prakriti*, it is a process of elevation of the undifferentiated life-essence characterizing the elemental kingdoms through stages and degrees of refinement, corresponding to a progressive permeability to the Atmic light. By the mid-point of the present or Fourth Round, this process of the working up of substance into incipient human form reached its culmination. It was at this juncture that the preferred forms became the vehicles of already self-conscious Monads associated with the intellectual stream of evolution. This point is depicted thus in the Commentaries upon the *Stanzas of Dzyan*:

> 2. *The Dhyanis (Pitris) are those who have evolved their* BHUTA *(doubles) from themselves, which* RUPA *(form) has become the vehicle of monads (seventh and sixth principles) that had completed their cycle of transmigration in the three preceding Kalpas (Rounds). Then, they (the astral doubles) became the men of the first Human Race of the Round. But they were not complete, and were senseless.*
>
> The Secret Doctrine, i 183

After this long period of gestation, the prepared *rupas* became the vehicles of Solar Monads through the lighting up of *Manas*, which occurred over eighteen million years ago. To understand this awakening of consciousness, one must clearly distinguish between the evolution of intelligence and the development of form. Although, for the sake of our comprehension, it is helpful to speak of lunar Monads reaching the human germ stage in earlier Rounds, and to speak of incipient human Monads throughout the early phases of the Fourth Round, it must be understood that these references are to beings which are human in form though not in consciousness. Further, the emanation of the fires of Manasic awareness into these incipient forms should not be understood as the entry of Monads into forms which are already occupied by other Monads. It is like the successive passage of two rays of light through the same aperture – the ray has become intensified, rather than multiplied. Referring to this mystery, Jesus said: "I and my Father in heaven are One." True human existence presupposes the inherent possession of the higher *arupa* fires of Manasic awareness.

Amongst the *Agnishwatha* custodians of the sacred fire, distinctions may be drawn between those who had attained full enlightenment in prior periods of manifestation and those who had not yet completed the task of intellectual human self-evolution during the Rounds of the moon chain. There is a further distinction between those differentiations of the Monadic essence which only reached the incipient human stage in the middle of the Fourth Round of the present globe and which only entered upon the stage of human existence on that globe, and the former two classes of human beings. It is upon the correct understanding of the karmic status of each of these three classes of human beings that a proper understanding of justice and injustice in human life depends.

Much contemporary confusion between the spiritual and the intellectual, between the intellectual and the physical, is due to the unwarranted degree to which human consciousness is presently limited by attachment to the outward plane of sensory existence. As a result, wandering into the astral regions is often mistaken for awakening to spiritual consciousness, whilst intellectual life is reduced to an inductive enumeration of empirical particulars. *The Secret Doctrine* devotes considerable attention to the development by the lunar *Dhyanis* of the ethereal vestures underlying physical evolution. The student of *Theosophia* must understand that the region of outward sensation is a reflection of the lowest, or seventh, component of the astral; the realm of the lunar Pitris comprises the entirety of the lower four planes of existence. Hence, the ethereal lunar *Dhyanis* evolved out of themselves astral doubles. This process of subtle development proceeded from within without throughout the entirety of the first three Rounds, beginning with the most developed lunar Monads and eventually including all those less developed Monads which would enter the human kingdom on the present globe.

By the beginning of the Fourth Round, incipient humanity was essentially complete as an astral type, though as yet lacking in self-consciousness. During the Fourth Round, with each successive Race and Sub-Race, up until the beginning of the Fifth Race, there has been a progressive consolidation of the external form surrounding the astral double, the *linga sarira*. Corresponding to this process, and running parallel with it simultaneously, was a progressive adaptation of the physical form and structure of the fauna of the earth as the latter passed through its stages of geologic formation. Altogether, there was a tremendous consolidation of matter which produced a connection between the astral and the physical that has an important bearing on the porosity of the evolving brain to the Light of the *Atman*.

Given this broad understanding of the development of human form through the activity of the lunar *Pitris*, most of the inheritance of humanity from the early Rounds, and indeed the early Races of the present Round, lies hidden within the casement of the physical form. Existing on subtler planes of matter and consciousness, the evolving humanity of the early Rounds was largely ethereal. Subsequent to the incarnation of the *Manasa Dhyanis* into the waiting forms in the Third Root Race, at what is called the balance point in a series of Races and Rounds, the development of the inner astral man has proceeded along different lines. Yet, owing to the tremendous debasement of human consciousness during the Fourth Root Race, both the nature of the transformations affecting the ethereal vestures, and even the very existence of those vestures, have become obscured to human awareness. Hence, the deeper meaning of these interior processes and their vital relevance to the intellectual evolution of humanity are virtually *terra incognita* to present humanity. Recognizing the blindness of contemporary awareness, the Commentaries go on to explain:

> 3. *The inner, now concealed, man, was then (in the beginnings) the external man. The progeny of the Dhyanis (Pitris), he was 'the son like unto his father.' Like the lotus, whose external shape assumes gradually the form of the model within itself, so did the form of man in the beginning evolve from within*

> *without. After the cycle in which man began to procreate his species after the fashion of the present animal kingdom, it became the reverse. The human foetus follows now in its transformations all the forms that the physical frame of man had assumed throughout the three Kalpas (Rounds) during the tentative efforts at plastic formation around the monad by senseless, because imperfect, matter, in her blind wanderings. In the present age, the physical embryo is a plant, a reptile, an animal, before it finally becomes man, evolving within himself his own ethereal counterpart, in his turn. In the beginning it was that counterpart (astral man) which, being senseless, got entangled in the meshes of matter.*
>
> The Secret Doctrine, i 184

This passage points to the underlying karmic continuity within the entire scheme of evolution and also to the crucial significance of the difference between its physical and intellectual components. Whilst the development of the inner astral man was the result of the sacrifice of the lunar *Dhyanis* through the early Rounds, the development of self-conscious individuality was the result of the Great Sacrifice of the *Manasa Dhyanis*, who lit up in every incipient human Monad the power of choice, the potency of intelligent conscious reflection in the human mind of the Universal Mind. Humanity, in the great height of its Golden Age over eighteen million years ago, was in a state of mystic meditation attuned to the universal host of Creative Fires which had come down as a single, beneficent initiatory Presence. This glorious truth and lost light has come down in every myth and tradition of all the tribes of humanity, including those who, alas, concretized and misused the sacred Teachings at terrible karmic cost to themselves. The principle that humanity is the progeny of the *Dhyanis*, "the son like unto his father", grown lotus-like from a seed within, has a dual and a triple meaning. In relation to the early Rounds, it refers to the process of formation and consolidation of the astral around the *sishta* or seeds of future human form borne by the lunar *Dhyanis*. Commencing with the descent of the *Manasa Dhyanis* in the Third Root Race, it refers to the flowering of the self-conscious powers of intellection around the bright ray of the descending *Manasa*.

Fundamentally, unfoldment *from within without* is the archetypal mode of growth on the spiritual plane. Both the ascent of the astral form and the descent of the higher principles are interrelated aspects of a single process of equilibration between the poles of Spirit and Matter. The lotus plant, each seed of which contains a complete blueprint of the full flower, provides through its phanerogamic growth a perfect model of the spiritual mode. In every spiritual system, therefore, the lotus is venerated, and various spiritual centres in man, as well as the cosmic centres of life-giving and death-dealing forces, have been compared to lotuses.

During the eighteen million years since the awakening of *Manas*, the modes of creativity and birth have shifted from the androgyne state of the earlier human races to the present separation of the sexes. The earlier Races of humanity, likened symbolically to dragons and to eggs, reproduced themselves by those agencies and means which are now somewhat familiar to students of biology through the study of various non-human species. With this shift, there was a reversal in the mode of development of form. Under the current scheme, embryogenesis recapitulates the entire series of forms assumed by the evolving astral form of man during the early Rounds. Here, however, it is important to recall the *mantram* – *Nature unaided fails*. Despite the marvellous complexity and variety of forms evolved by the lunar Pitris in the stream of physical evolution, it is simply impossible for these material agencies to produce a human being. It is for this reason, incidentally, that no amount of genetic manipulation can produce anything other than a Frankenstein's monster. To produce a human being, something more is needed than is contained in the karmic and genetic programme of material evolution.

The attainment of human consciousness can only come about through the descent of self-conscious beings perfected in prior periods of evolution. Hence, there is universal awe and reverence for the entire host of these beings, all of whom gathered around their Chief, Dakshinamurti, the Initiator of Initiates, and came down into the forming worlds of the earth chain. Fully perfected in previous *manvantaras*, their presence in these worlds is solely for the sake of presiding over the programme of intelligent human evolution. Reverence for the *Manasas* is the hallmark of the degree of human evolution of the soul; the more highly evolved an individual human being, the more readily does it display a spontaneous devotion towards Mahatmas and Gurus. Such is the natural tropism of human consciousness.

During this early Golden Age of humanity, when all alike felt the luminous presence of the *Agnishwathas* within, human beings at the same time enjoyed the use of the ethereal vestures, with their marvellous powers, evolved from the lower kingdoms. That these powers and faculties are now atrophied, and virtually unknown to present humanity, is the karmic consequence of the misuse of knowledge in the Lemuro-Atlantean and especially in the later Atlantean Fourth Root Race. Whilst the involvement of Spirit into Matter in the first three Rounds and in the early Races of the Fourth Round was a necessary aspect of the karmic programme of evolution, the self-conscious degradation of Manasic intelligence, through identification with the lunar forms, was not. The enormous liability of human beings to recurrent types of psychic and physical disease, as compared to the inhabitants of the animal kingdoms, is a direct consequence of this needless fall into matter. Grave though these susceptibilities may seem, however, they are of little import when compared to the spiritual consequences of the Fall – the closing of the Third Eye and the loss of awareness of the *Agnishwatha Pitris*.

Given the self-imposed burden of spiritual as well as psychic blindness, it is not surprising, though still tragic, that humanity is scarcely aware of, much less able to respond to, the challenge of the transformations being wrought by cyclic law within its mental and material vestures. In order to regain initiative as a Manasic being, one must grasp the deeper significance of the fact that, prior to the descent of the *Manasas* and prior to the separation of the sexes, the entire programme of human development was *from within without*, and that after this point, human development began with the recapitulation of the entire physical scheme of evolution within the mother's womb. Thus, on the physical plane, ontogeny recapitulates phylogeny, but only up to the point attained by mindless lunar evolution eighteen million years ago. Therefore, for the past eighteen million years, through the power of self-evolution, human beings have had to gestate out of their astral bodies, by a process of separation and self-training, the embryo of that which will become, over many lives in the future, an Adept.

H.P. Blavatsky took trouble to explain in a veiled way the secret and complex Teachings of threefold evolution to modern man for the sake of those who did not have access to Sanskrit, Chaldean or other ancient languages and texts, and those who could not use the arcane symbol systems to benefit from the wisdom of the enlightened. This Teaching is essentially different from any seventeenth century idea of human rationality or eighteenth century doctrine of human progress or Victorian doctrine of complacent optimism. This ancient Teaching is directed towards millions of years in the future and millions of years in the past, and its principal lesson, which should be more comprehensible in an age of computers, is that in this cosmic programme, the minutest difference that is made every moment has tremendous bearing upon what happens through exponential curves over millions of years.

Once one truly understands human evolution, as distinct from the instinctual and involuntary evolution of the lower kingdoms, one can also grasp the warning implicit in the esoteric Teaching that the cycle of metempsychosis for human Monads is closed at this point of the Fourth Round and the Fifth Root Race. It is technically impossible for human beings who totally fail to be human to take bodies in the animal kingdom. Hence, the tragic prospect awaiting those who cannot make full and proper use of the Manasic principle is eventual annihilation. Thus, one can also come to appreciate the enormous compassion of the Teachers in the nineteenth century when, since 1848, the muddy torrents of *kamaloka* broke loose. Owing to nefarious practices of mediumship in seances and elsewhere, and through an obsessive and excessive concern with lunar ancestors, there was at that time a vast outpouring of *bhuts* and elementaries from the dregs of the astral plane. This same year, termed by some historians as "that wonderful year", witnessed a great variety of outbreaks and upheavals throughout all the countries of Europe. Because of the appalling karma of 1848, great compassion was shown in the partial transmission of Teachings which had always been locked in the secret sanctuaries, and this in itself heightened the karma of human beings.

If one now looks back to the Victorian Age, it is evident that events did not work out as many people had hoped. Indeed, even in the last ten years of the last century, a death-blow was given to the Victorian Age. By the First World War the Victorian order, which had been so much taken for granted, had collapsed. In the Second World War, the entire old European order collapsed. Now we are witnessing the ending of the ancient Karma of Israel. All of this is part of the programme of Karma which is no respecter of personal emotions, likes or dislikes, or the sectarian predilections of human beings through excessive attachment to external forms.

There is a tremendous logic to the precipitation of karma in the programme of cyclic evolution. That logic is on the side of every immortal soul. It is not on the side of the ratiocinative mind. It is not on the side of *kama manas*. It is unequivocally on the side of *Buddhi-Manas*. Therefore, every human being's urge to transcend the boundaries of the personal self, and every human being's deep desire (which is expressed every night in *sushupti*, and which may be strengthened through daily meditation) to come closer to the One Flame, to the Light of the Logos in the heart, is truly blessed. But if one wanders in the opposite direction, one risks much and it would be the height of unwisdom. The Avatar quickens life amongst those who are responsive, but the Avatar also quickens the doom of those who are unwilling to avail themselves of the Light. This is evident to the intuition of growing numbers of souls throughout the world who wish to remain in the forward current of human evolution which gives birth, and not be caught up in that reverse current which propels into the vortex whatever is inconsistent with the humanity of the future.

This implies a decisive moment of choice for humanity; the power of choice is the hallmark of Manasic existence, and its intelligent exercise gives true self-respect. To meet the trials of the future, it is helpful to have some conception of the excellences inherent in humanity. The *lakshanas* displayed by the early Races can and will become the norms of the future Races. Each human being has participated in the spiritual civilization of the Third Root Race when

> . . . in the beginning, mankind were morally and physically the types and prototypes of our present Race, and of our human dignity, by their beauty of form, regularity of feature, cranial development, nobility of sentiments, heroic impulses, and grandeur of ideal conception.
>
> *The Secret Doctrine*, i 185

These are the marks of human potential and perfectibility of which every human being has been capable for the past eighteen million years. Over that span, alas, a small minority of mankind has become involved in psycho-physical inversion and

> . . . the gradual debasement and degradation of man, morally and physically, can be readily traced throughout the ethnological transformation down to our time.
>
> *The Secret Doctrine*, i 185

Even where this process of degradation leads to the permanent withdrawal of the soul from the human tenement, the withdrawal of the ray back into its parent source and the consequent need for the One Flame to emanate a new ray totally disconnected from the prior series of incarnations, there is no wastage. Even so unspiritual and materialistic a lunar form would be made use of in the programme of Karma, serving as a vesture for those Monads delayed in their entry into the human kingdom until the Fifth Round through the ancient sin of the mindless. Such is the karmic economy in nature that the astral vestures vacated by failed human beings will form the karmic compensation of those Monads held back from human life and imprisoned in anthropoid forms, owing to the omissions and delays of selfish egos in the Third Root Race. As the anthropoids die out during the latter part of the Fifth Root Race, their Monads will pass into the astral forms of the Sixth and Seventh Races of this Round. Then, in the Fifth Round, these Monads will enter directly the stream of Manasic intellectual evolution and be welcomed into the human family.

Distant though this age millions of years away may seem to ordinary mortals, in the eye of the Initiate it is like tomorrow. Strange and arcane as these Teachings may seem to an intelligence caught in the dark folds of matter, they are inevitable consequences of the universal decree of harmony and justice governing the sweep of cyclic evolution. Yet, for those courageous pilgrim-souls who want to take seriously the Pledge of Kwan Yin – the Bodhisattvic vow to aid every sentient being caught in the bonds of *samsaric* existence – the intricate and elegant complexities of Monadic, intellectual and physical evolution must be understood and mastered in their applications throughout the three worlds. For the aspirant to godlike Wisdom and Divine Compassion, everything turns upon the conception of space, time and consciousness. If one would rise above the ocean of *samsara*, above the fourth plane, and choose the path of renunciation, one must enter the boundless void and eternal motion of the *Atman*, and become the willing servant of the One Law of Compassion and Sacrifice, *mahakaruna* and *mahayagna*. OM MANI PADME HUM.

Hermes, May 1982

KARMA AND DESTINY

> *It is the Spiritual evolution of the inner, immortal man that forms the fundamental tenet in the Occult Sciences. To realize even distantly such a process, the student has to believe (a) in the ONE Universal Life, independent of matter (or what Science regards as matter); and (b) in the individual intelligences that animate the various manifestations of this Principle . . . .*
>
> *The ONE LIFE is closely related to the one law which governs the World of Being – KARMA. Exoterically, this is simply and literally 'action,' or rather an 'effect-producing cause.' Esoterically, it is quite a different thing in its far-fetching moral effects. It is the unerring LAW OF RETRIBUTION.*
>
> The Secret Doctrine, i 634

Karma is the universal law of the One Life in all its myriad manifestations from the cosmic to the atomic, spanning eternity and present in each moment. Every evolving intelligence encapsulated in matter is unerringly subject to the ceaseless effects of Karma and must conform itself, at first unconsciously and then freely, to its inexorable decree of universal harmony. The doctrine of Karma unveils the metaphysical key to the mysteries of authentic human choice, free will and divine destiny, but it can be comprehended only when applied with Buddhic insight to the large experiences and small events of life on earth. To discern the karmic meanings of the complex details of daily life, whilst experiencing the elusive mystery of incarnation, one must begin with the vibratory rates of the simplest thoughts and feelings, words and deeds, linking them to levels of motivation, states of consciousness, fixity of mind and fidelity of heart. Each thoughtful or thoughtless impulse of the inner nature magnetizes one's environment through the activity of the organs of the outer vestures, invoking exact compensation and ethical retribution. There is nothing mechanical in the karmic adjustment of magnetic differentials; it is an inward and moral process, an integral aspect of a continual choice between spiritualization and materialization. The distinction between distributive and collective

Karma, like the difference between the raindrop and the storm, exists within a larger process of essential unity. Humanity and its units, its races, nations, tribes and individuals, embody a vital energy and share a common destiny which none may resist or repel. The eternally patient and compassionate teacher of mankind, Karma sternly instructs each and all in the supreme lesson that there is no individual enlightenment or welfare apart from sacrificial service to every sentient being, collectively constituting the One Life.

This pivotal principle, the substratum of free will and destiny, may be understood in terms of the choice between the manvantaric star of one's individuality and the personal star of a single lifetime. Throughout all possible variations in personal destiny over myriad lifetimes, this choice must be made again and again. The clarity and direction of one's choices in previous lives shape the fabric of circumstances in which one chooses in this life and future lives. That fabric might be a refined tapestry in which may be etched the mystic emblems of the pilgrimage of the soul, or a coarsely knotted cloth of confused dreams and missed opportunities. Psychologically, there is the wayward choice between two voices: one is the voice of illusion and delusion, of the senses and *kama manas*, of the separative personal consciousness which cannot embrace a holistic perspective encompassing many lives; the other is the voice of Krishna-Christos, the voice of God in man which speaks in the universal language of the soul. There is a direct relation between one's recurrent choices in regard to these voices, and one's readiness, in the realm of action, to ally oneself with Krishna, standing luminously alone, or his innumerable adversaries. In the Mahabharatan war fought on *Kurukshetra*, the field of external encounters, individuals are constantly making, mostly unconsciously or with partial self-consciousness, fateful choices between Krishna and his armies. This archetypal choice was offered by Krishna to the depraved Duryodhana, who rejected Krishna in favour of the armies trained by him, reflecting the short-sighted empiricism of *kama manas*. When Arjuna, representing *Manas* bereft of such external supports, was offered the privilege of having Krishna as his charioteer, he happily and willingly chose Krishna, even though he did not fully fathom the invisible stature of Krishna, let alone his cosmic splendour.

Philosophically, the Mahabharatan war is emblematic of the inevitable ethical and spiritual struggle to which every human soul is irreversibly committed by the fact of Manasic awareness, traceable to the sacrificial descent and benediction of the solar ancestors over eighteen million years ago. Each chooses, Krishna teaches, according to his lights, whatever seems best. Thereby the subtle threads of one's self-devised destiny are fused, and one must pass below the throne of Necessity without looking back, like the pilgrims in the Myth of Er, to live out and learn from the karmic results of one's choice. Recorded by the Lipikas, engraved in one's vestures and reflected in surrounding circumstances, this destiny rises up to meet the soul at every turn in life. Yet, though it is "written in the stars", destiny does not preclude the risks and possibilities of further choice.

> Only, the closer the union between the mortal reflection MAN and his celestial PROTOTYPE, the less dangerous the external conditions and subsequent reincarnations – which neither Buddhas nor Christs can escape. This is not superstition, least of all is it *Fatalism*. The latter implies a blind course of some still blinder power, and man is a free agent during his stay on earth. He cannot escape his *ruling* Destiny, but he has the choice of two paths that lead him in that direction, and he can reach the goal of misery – if such is decreed to him, either in the snowy white robes of the Martyr, or in the soiled garments of a volunteer in the iniquitous course; for, there are *external and internal conditions* which affect the determination of our will upon our actions, and it is in our power to follow either of the two.
>
> The Secret Doctrine, i 639

Even if through past actions one is destined to suffer miseries at the hands of various agencies, the power of choice remains. It is a constant factor throughout all the vagaries of karmic precipitation. As Plato taught, the gods are blameless for the inward condition of the soul in every situation, and each sufferer must choose between either preserving purity of consciousness or becoming stained by the iniquities of unthinking reaction, mental violence and a refusal to take responsibility.

Choices are not random. Collectively, they show a tonality and texture which traces the line of life's meditation, the dominant choice over a lifetime. This choice depends upon the degree of discernment of the different types of external and internal conditions surrounding the soul. Externally, there are myriads upon myriads of elemental centres of intelligence already imprinted by the thoughts, feelings and acts of individuals, past and present, embodied and disembodied. They are drawn to each person and respond to the rationalized desires of the lower self, thus giving seeming substantiality to the entrenched delusion of personal existence based upon likes and dislikes. Those who are extremely weak-willed from the standpoint of the soul and excessively self-willed in the eyes of others have fostered the deceptive notion that they are forging their own path in the world, whereas in truth they are only acquiescing through compulsive reaction in their lunar destiny. Alternatively, there are internal conditions which include the solar potency of pure ideation of the Monad, the immortal *Buddhi-Manas* which is capable of sustaining a strong current of selfless meditation. The range and richness, continuity and depth, of such meditation depend upon mental calm, unconditional compassion and spiritual fearlessness. On the noumenal plane, thought, motivation and volition are indeed inseparable. Authentic mystical states arise from the fusion of the deepest aspirations, the finest feelings and the strongest affirmations of meditation within the solemn stillness of the sanctuary of the soul. Daily renewed in deep sleep, consecrated at dawn and dusk, and invoked with humility before sleep, the inward vision of universal good may be made into a continuous current through the potency of a Vow. In time one can silence the lower mind at will, altering the polarity of the nervous system, and ponder the karmic meanings and lessons inherent in the events and opportunities of each day. Thus reaching beyond any limited sense of identity and in the oceanic calm of one's true selfhood, one may listen to the voice of God within the heart, the daimon honoured by Socrates and Gandhi. For a trained mystic who has learnt to give Nature time to speak, the inner voice can become the ever-present *Chitkala*, the benediction of Kwan Yin as a constant guardian.

For the average person, whose highest vestures are veiled by the samskaric residues of past actions and present vacillation, the inner voice cannot be heard and the pre-birth vision of the soul is forgotten. Yet, they may be mirrored dimly in the muddled personal mind as vague and chaotic recollections, as feeble and faltering notions of some essential reform to be made in life, or some sacrificial act of goodness to be offered in the service of others. Through inconstant flickerings along the invisible spinal cord, there may be sporadic resolves to renew the most precious moment one can recall from early childhood or from fleeting contact with the benevolent current of past teachers. In a variety of ways, even if only fitfully and imperfectly, every person can receive help from internal conditions which can release the spiritual will. The greater the fidelity, the selflessness and self-assurance with which one cleaves to these inner promptings of the immortal soul, the more instantaneously they light up the immediate task at hand. Above all, the more they are heeded, the less the effort needed to sustain continuity. With the same certitude, the opposite consequences follow for those who foolishly ignore or flaunt this inner guidance for the sake of enhancing the delusive sense of personal self-importance. But even the most spiritually impoverished human beings are sheltered by the invisible protection of the Divine Prototype, and therefore even amidst the muddle and froth of psychic fantasy there is a concealed thread of truth. Wise and loving friends might be able to recognize and strengthen it. A true spiritual teacher could help to sift the wheat from the chaff, quicken the inward process of alchemical transmutation, and show the pathway to Divine Wisdom.

As the One Law of spiritual evolution, Karma is more generous to each and every human soul in need of help than the niggardly thinking of the nihilistic can envisage. It is neither a doctrine that is so abstruse and remote that it cannot be related to the present moment, nor is it nearly as inflexible and hostile as claimed by those who have gratuitously declared a vote of no-confidence in themselves and in the human race. Far from precluding the idea that each human being has a unique and inherently significant mission on this earth, the law of Karma actually ordains that every single person has a divine *dharma* which he or she alone can and must fulfil. There is an authentic dignity and beauty, a profound meaning, to the uniqueness of the divine presence in and around every human soul. The sacredness of individual choice was affirmed as the basis of human solidarity by the inspired forerunners of the Aquarian Age, those luminaries who initiated the Renaissance and the Enlightenment in Europe. If the prospect has not yet smiled upon all, this is because too many have laboured under the deadweight of traditional theology and secular fatalism. Where there is the quickening of *dharma*, there is also the precipitation of past and present *adharma*.

> Those who believe in *Karma* have to believe in *destiny*, which, from birth to death, every man is weaving thread by thread around himself, as a spider does his cobweb; and this destiny is guided either by the heavenly voice of the invisible *prototype* outside of us, or by our more intimate astral, or inner man, who is but too often the evil genius of the embodied entity called man.
>
> *The Secret Doctrine*, i 639

The heavenly voice of the invisible Prototype is heard and felt, without any external tokens of empirical certitude. In the life of a good and simple person, who makes a mental image of Christ or Buddha, Shiva or Krishna, that voice may seem to come in a form engendered by the ecstatic devotion of the individual who has purity of heart. Many thousands of people all over the world belong to the invisible fraternity of fortunate souls who, having made a fearless and compassionate invocation on behalf of a friend or relative in distress, suddenly heard a vibrant voice of authoritative assurance and sensed an aureole of light soon after. This voice may appear to come from outside oneself, and, paradoxically, that other voice, the voice of the intimate astral, all too often the evil genius of man, seems to originate within. When it speaks, it aggravates the confusions of the compulsive persona, urging the hapless listener to rush into mindless activity. When the heavenly voice speaks to the depths of one's soul, it has a calming influence and allays the anxieties of *kama manas*. There is a natural soul-reticence to tell others about the heavenly voice, and a grateful concern to treasure its words in silence. However well-intentioned, anything that is allowed to pass through the matrix of the psychic nature risks distortion and generates a smoky obscuration that acts as a barrier to further guidance and profounder help from the Divine Prototype. What begins as unthinking indiscretion soon becomes delusive, and unless promptly checked, culminates in abject servitude to the astral shadow. Then, deceived by this simulacrum, the shadow of oneself outside the path of Dharma, one is drawn in a direction that may be contrary to one's true destiny. This abdication from the soul's self-chosen task in the course of evolution may initially be imperceptible, but the choice of destinies remains as long as the two voices can be heard.

> Both these lead on the outward man, but one of them must prevail; and from the very beginning of the invisible affray the stern and implacable *law of compensation* steps in and takes its course, faithfully following the fluctuations. When the last strand is woven, and man is seemingly enwrapped in the net-work of his own doing, then he finds himself completely under the empire of this *self-made* destiny. It then either fixes him like the inert shell against the immovable rock, or carries him away like a feather in a whirlwind raised by his own actions, and this is – KARMA.
>
> *The Secret Doctrine*, i 639

One cannot continue to listen to the voice of delusion until one finds oneself trapped in the self-woven meshes of despair, and then hope to be suddenly and vicariously saved. Recognition of the futility of seeking vicarious salvation is no reason for inertia or fatalism. One should never underestimate the potency of *tapas* and true repentance. Sages alone are in a position to judge the karmic ratios and curves of any person, and they never dismiss the hope of self-redemption for a single human being. They understand the practical import of the Bodhisattva vow, which is rooted not in wishful thinking but in the essential nature of the soul. Even if only at the moment of death, when the Divine Prototype assists in the separation of the principles, inner guidance is available in recognizing the true meaning of one's life. Long before the transition called death, there are precious opportunities in times of cool reflection, and during the nightly passage into *sushupti*, to strengthen the bond with the Higher Self. But these opportunities must be used wisely if one is to take hold of the plank of salvation – the Monad – and not be carried off by the whirlwind of worldly distractions.

By bringing Buddhic intuition to bear upon the necessary relations of past causes and present effects in particular situations, it is possible to extract karmic lessons from a ceaseless process of becoming which would otherwise appear random, chaotic or even trivial. Whilst it may seem easier to apply a general principle to a specific situation than to derive higher meanings from lower phenomena, it is important though difficult to show relevance, integrity and proper timing in bringing the abstract to bear upon concrete contexts. These interrelated aspects of Buddhic understanding, intimately connected with the Platonic teaching about the upward and downward dialectic, are mirrorings of Karma operating on the mental plane through cyclic time. Both the seemingly subjective processes of thought and the apparently objective features of its activity are instantiations of the One Law. Metaphysically, it is the inseparability of spirit from matter that accounts for the immutability of law in nature and the correspondence of modes of action between different planes of substance or matter. Nevertheless, there is a fundamental distinction between noumena and phenomena, between spiritual factors and physical forces, and this is connected with the crucial difference between the Akashic Divine Prototype and the astral form, the manvantaric star and personal constellation of each incarnated individual.

The entire teaching of Karma is an elaboration of the truth of "absolute Harmony in the world of matter as in the world of Spirit". We need to see the similitude of all things and the signature of the Divine in all the works of Nature. Anyone can appreciate the beauty of the sunrise and sunset or look at the night sky and sense the harmony of the heavens. But in the West, since the days of Pythagoras and Plato, it was already known, and commented upon by Cicero and Philo, that few could connect what they saw in the firmament with what was taking place around them on earth. For too many people spend too much time in idle gazing, without looking from above below and from below above, bridging the gap between heaven and earth. The benevolent and protective feeling towards the whole of humanity experienced by astronauts privileged to view the good earth from outer space is a poignant pointer to the future. But it is not necessary to journey into outer space to gain a feeling for global welfare. Strong and mature men and women of universal culture can serve as witnesses to the human significance of the harmony of the heavens, and become attuned to the music of the spheres. Sensing in their own hearts the majestic harmony of the metaphysical world of spirit, they may recognize its mirrorings in the world of matter.

Karma either comes as an avenging "fury or a rewarding angel". The distinction has nothing to do with externals, but rather with the inward spiritual impulse of one's actions, which by their benevolent or selfish motivation, draw back upon the doer the blessings or curses of unerring destiny.

> Yea –
> Wise are they who worship Nemesis,
>
> – as the *chorus* tells Prometheus. And as unwise they, who believe that the goddess may be propitiated by whatever sacrifices and prayers, or have her wheel diverted from the path it has once taken. 'The triform Fates and ever mindful Furies' are her attributes only on earth, and begotten by ourselves. There is no return from the paths she cycles over; yet those paths are of our own making, for it is we, collectively or individually, who prepare them.
> *The Secret Doctrine*, i 642–643

The only prayer that is consistent with the religion of karmic responsibility is the sacrificial invocation of the Higher Self on behalf of all humanity. Through growing gratitude for the gifts already received from parents and teachers, one may gain the courage and honesty to correct one's freely chosen course. In time one can learn to insert oneself into the universal giving and receiving of that which is the heartbeat of sacrificial Karma. With greater intelligence and maturity, with more wisdom and discrimination, but above all, with a profounder benevolence for all living beings, one will enter into a richer sense of the citizenship of the world. Nourished in the silence and solitude of meditation upon the One Light, one can exemplify a detached precision and effortless transcendence as a compassionate participant in the visible cosmos of beings who are sharers in collective Karma. In time one may sense the awesome stature of the manvantaric star of each individual abiding behind and beyond the panoramic changes induced by the personal constellations which provide opportunities to participate in the samsaric stream of individual and collective self-consciousness.

Hermes, July 1981

INDIVIDUATION AND INITIATION

> *The* Daimones *are...the guardian spirits of the human race; 'those who dwell in the neighbourhood of the immortals, and thence watch over human affairs,' as Hermes has it. In Esoteric parlance, they are called* Chitkala, *some of which are those who have furnished man with his fourth and fifth Principles from their own essence; and others the Pitris so-called.... The root of the name is* Chiti, *'that by which the effects and consequences of actions and kinds of knowledge are selected for the use of the soul,' or conscience, the inner Voice in man. With the Yogis, the* chiti *is a synonym of* Mahat, *the first and divine intellect; but in Esoteric philosophy* Mahat *is the root of* Chiti, *its germ; and* Chiti *is a quality of* Manas *in conjunction with* Buddhi, *a quality that attracts to itself by spiritual affinity a* chitkala *when it develops sufficiently in man. This is why it is said that* Chiti *is a voice acquiring mystic life and becoming Kwan-Yin.*
>
> The Secret Doctrine, i 288

The integral relationship between initiation and individuation can be grasped through the essential logic of the entire process of evolution. From the standpoint of matter, the logic of transformation involves increasing heterogeneity, differentiation and complexity. At the same time, there is *pari passu* a commensurate withdrawal of subjective and spiritual faculties which cannot function freely through limited projections or distorted reflections. The degree of spiritual volition depends upon the texture of the reflecting medium. In the collective thrust of evolution every single life-atom in all the seven kingdoms of nature is touched by the same primal universal impulse towards self-consciousness. Within the broad perspective and purpose of evolution as a whole, the possibilities of initiation are enriched by individuation at a high level of self-consciousness. Initiation, in its most hallowed meaning, must always involve the merging of minds of Guru and chela into a state of oneness with the ineffable Source of Divine Wisdom. This mystical and magical relation of *Manas* and *Mahat* was comprehended and transmitted in secret sanctuaries. It was intimated in the enigmatic etymology of the word *upanishad*, "to come and sit close", so that there could be direct communion of minds and hearts. Sacred teachings are conveyed and communicated through the eyes and not merely through words, although mantramic sounds have a sacred and vital function. In the *Bhagavad Gita* Arjuna's earnest enquiries and Krishna's cosmic affirmations and psychological adjustments bring to birth within the mind of the *chela* the seed of *chiti*, a level of consciousness which negates, transcends, and also heightens individuality. Initiation is the highest mode of individual communication, and it necessarily involves a mystic rapport between one who has gone before and one who is to come after, rather like the magnetic transference between mother and child. Such a relation is inherent in the logic of evolution because, as a result of an extremely long period of evolution, it is impossible to find any mechanical sameness between all human beings. They are identical in their inmost essence but so markedly different in the internal relations of their vestures that there cannot be complete equivalence between any two persons. Hence experience and reflection reveal both the mystery of each individual human being and the commonality of what it is to be human.

At one level of communication *The Secret Doctrine* is a metaphysical treatise on cosmic and human evolution. But at another level, for those who are Buddhic, it is not merely a book, but the initiatory presence of the compelling voice of the Verbum or *Brahma Vach*, reverberating in the society of sages, the Rishis who are of one mind and one lip. For the ardent seeker of Divine Wisdom, *The Secret Doctrine* is a series of stepping-stones, as the Upanishads and the great scriptures of all times have been, towards initiations into the mysteries of Selfhood. Through ever-renewed contact with the teaching, the chela begins to enact self-consciously and by degrees the realities which ordinary individuals sporadically experience at some level through deep sleep. This process comes alive through prolonged meditation for the sake of universal compassion, making one's breathing more benevolent for the purpose of elevating all beings in all the kingdoms of nature. When a person begins to do this, it is the awakening of *Bodhichitta*, the seed of enlightenment. It is the first step in translating knowledge into wisdom, words into realities, and resolves into actions. Having turned the key of compassion in the lock of the heart, the disciple will come to realize, through inward communication with the Teacher, the fuller meaning of the Upanishads:

> *Upa-ni-shad* being a compound word meaning 'the conquest of ignorance by the revelation of *secret, spiritual* knowledge'...They speak of the origin of the Universe, the nature of Deity, and of Spirit and Soul, as also of the metaphysical connection of mind and matter. In a few words: They CONTAIN *the beginning and the end of all human knowledge* . . .
>
> *The Secret Doctrine*, i 269–270

The practical import of the metaphysical teaching of *The Secret Doctrine* lies in the fact that the highest spiritual powers are partly used by each human being every day but without fully knowing it. Light is universal, but it makes all the difference whether one has a blurred sense of perception and merely consumes light, or whether one can take a magnifying glass and concentrate light. There are also those who are like the laser beam which can direct a concentrated shaft of light to destroy cancerous cells and produce a range of extraordinary effects upon the physical plane. There is something of *Kundalini* at work in every human being. Electricity and magnetism are sevenfold and work at the highest cosmic level of *Akasa*, but they also work at the most heterogeneous and diffusive level because everything is electrical and magnetic, from the occult standpoint. The aspirant must grasp, even at a preliminary level, the moral and psychological implications of this metaphysical "power or Force which moves in a curved path" in man and nature.

> It is the Universal life-Principle manifesting everywhere in nature. This force includes the two great forces of attraction and repulsion. Electricity and magnetism are but manifestations of it. This is the power which brings about that 'continuous adjustment of *internal relations to external relations*' which is the essence of life according to Herbert Spencer, and that '*continuous adjustment of external relations to internal relations*' which is the basis of transmigration of souls...
>
> *The Secret Doctrine*, i 293

The two aspects of this omnipresent power mentioned here have to be totally mastered by the initiated yogi in all their possible manifestations. Long before this stage is reached, the disciple must begin to learn to govern these internal and external relations through *Buddhi Yoga* in order to fulfil the prerequisite conditions of magnetic rapport with a true Teacher of Wisdom.

The universal process of adjustment of the external to the internal, which leads to involuntary reincarnation for human beings, must be understood in terms of karma. At the most primary level, whenever human beings entertain and succumb to emotional reactions, they establish mental deposits and astral grooves which require many lives for proper adjustment. That is why over eighteen million years so many people approach the Path again and again but stumble and lose their track just as often. They cannot make a fundamental breakthrough even when in the presence of great teaching. For those who have made the teaching an internal living power in their consciousness, this is comprehensible as essential, just as the world seems clear to a child when its eyes are directed to the light of the sun. Whilst this is true for all human souls, the philosophical recognition of how this works is important. Every emotion registers an appropriate record in the astral vesture. It is wear and tear on the *linga sharira* and is at the expense of something or someone else. Thus selfishness is increased. This is true even if the emotion is benevolent for emotion itself is a form of passivity. Emotion is quite different from deep feeling which is unmodified by cyclic change or external event and is totally independent of outward demonstration. Emotion is like cashing a check: whilst it makes money available, it depletes the account. It is a way of demanding proof. As a form of external indulgence it is a passive fantasy which weighs heavily upon the astral vesture. To that extent it obscures one's inmost feelings which are detached and compassionate. All the higher feelings are ontologically powerful and at the same time they constitute a pure negation psychologically. Though only an initial understanding of the problem, this is sufficient to explain why merely sitting down to postures and trying to control the external breath by *hatha yoga* exercises cannot make a significant difference to the inevitable adjustment of internal and external relations inherent in life itself. There is no substitute for facing oneself, asking what one is truly living for, how one is affected by likes and dislikes, and how one's temper – or *sophrosyne* – is unbalanced through various irritations.

In the ancient schools one would not be allowed to begin serious study of yoga until one had mastered one's temper. In the school of Pythagoras candidates were tested from the first day in regard to their personal vulnerability. That was the stringent standard of all schools preparing for the Mysteries of initiation. The laws have not changed even though the external rules may seem to have been modified. It remains an inescapable fact of nature and karma that if one loses one's temper even after a lifetime of spiritual development, one's progress is destroyed in a single mood. Like a city or a work of art, the time to construct is long, but destruction can be swift. One has to think out one's true internal and external state of being, even if one goes to the Tolstoyan extreme of seeing every kind of fault in oneself. Tolstoy did not do this out of pride but rather because he was so thoroughly honest that he simply could not think of a single fault in anyone else which he could not see present in himself. This sense of commonality, rooted in ethical self-awareness, leaves no room for judging anyone else or for running away from anyone because one sees that the whole army of human foibles is in oneself, and that every elemental is connected with internal propensities in one's astral form. To think this out Manasically is crucial in the Aquarian Age. The wise disciple will recognize that thoroughness, urgency and earnestness are quite different from fatuous haste and impulsiveness. Even if it takes months and years to think out and learn to apply the elementary axioms of the Science of Spirituality, it is necessary to be patient and persistent, rather than revel in fantasies that leave residues in successive lives. When something so obvious which one can test and comprehend is taught, this is an opportunity for growth which demands honesty in thought and intelligence in response. To receive the timeless teaching in this way enables the self to be the true friend of the Self. Not to do this is one of the myriad ways in which the self becomes the enemy of the Self because it is afraid of facing the facts and the laws of nature connected with relations and patterns in the vestures. Self-regeneration is a precise science and it is possible to test oneself in a manner that fosters *sophrosyne*.

This spiritual intelligence test is not a matter of making some sweeping moral judgement about oneself, because that will have no meaning for the immortal soul. It would simply not be commensurate with eighteen million years of self-conscious existence. It is really a waste of time to say, "I'm no good, I'm this kind of person, I'm bound to do this." Such exclamations are absurd because they do not account for the internal complexity and psychological richness of sevenfold man, let alone the immensity of the human pilgrimage. It is more important to understand and recognize critical incipient causes, to see how the karmic process takes place, and to arrest the downward slide into fragmented consciousness. To do this firmly with compassion at the root, one has to meditate upon some fundamental idea. One might benefit from the golden example set by disciples who practise the precept: "All the time everything that comes to me I not only deserve but I desire." This form of mental asceticism is the reverse of psychic passivity and self-indulgent fatalism. It is a clear and crisp recognition that there is karmic meaning to every single event, that nothing is unnecessary, even though one may not yet know what its meaning is. Ignorance of the process of adjustment of internal and external relations is merely a reflection of the limitation of one's own growth at the level of lower mind. To accept totally one's karma is like a swimmer recognizing the necessity of accepting the tidal currents of the ocean. A swimmer is not doing a favour to the ocean by accepting its sway. Deliberate and intelligent acceptance of oceanic currents is the difference between drowning and surviving.

When it comes to karma on the causal plane with reference to human consciousness and invisible forces, the same principle applies. That is why the Buddha said, "Ye who suffer, know ye suffer from yourselves." Though the teaching seems obvious when stated, it must really be thought through at the core of one's being if one is going to alter the karmic tendencies of the forces at work. One must ask whether the whole of one's being is cooperating with the totality of one's karma. Unless one engages in this meditation and willingly accepts all karma even though one does not understand most of it, no regrets or resolves will make any difference. The constant task of learning, which is a matter of activating and sensitizing all the centres of perception, has an intimate bearing upon diminishing the range and reach of the irrational in one's responses to life. There is a direct connection between the *Kundalini* force of adjustment of internal and external relations, which moves in a curved path, and the karmic predominance of the various elemental powers in the human constitution. In the words of Hermes Trismegistus:

> All these Genii *preside over mundane affairs*, they shake and overthrow the constitution of States and of individuals; they *imprint their likeness on our Souls*, they are present in our nerves, our marrow, our veins, our arteries, and *our very brain-substance*...at the moment when each of us receives life and being, he is taken in charge by the genii (Elementals) who preside over births, and who are classed beneath the astral powers (Superhuman astral Spirits). They change perpetually, not always identically, but revolving in circles.
>
> *The Secret Doctrine*, i 294

Throughout the cyclic development of each soul, the proportional composition of the vestures out of the five elements is continually being adjusted. Through the attraction and repulsion of their coessence to the vestures, certain elements become the dominant ruling factors in one's life. Unless one engages in noetic mental asceticism, one will invariably remain passive to the psychic sway of these irrational forces. Without ratio, harmony and proportion, one cannot employ the vestures as channels for the benevolent transmutation of life-atoms: rather one will needlessly compound the karma of selfishness. The compassionate projection of the spiritual energies of the soul requires that the genii be made subordinate to the awakened Buddhi-Manasic reason. The genii

> ... permeate by the body two parts of the Soul, that it may receive from each the impress of his own energy. But the reasonable part of the Soul is not subject to the genii; it is designed for the reception of (the) God, who enlightens it with a sunny ray. Those who are thus illumined are few in number, and from them the genii abstain: for neither genii nor Gods have any power in the presence of a single ray of God.
>
> *The Secret Doctrine*, i 294–295

By the "few in number" is meant those Initiates and Adepts for whom there is no "God" but the one universal and unconditioned Deity in boundless space and eternal duration.

The truly reasonable part of the soul is extremely important in the Aquarian Age. To think clearly, logically and incisively must be the true purpose of education. To unfold the immense powers of pure thought, the reasonable part of the soul must be given every opportunity to develop so that the irrational side is reduced. Its false coherence must be broken by seeing it causally. One must begin with a willingness to acknowledge it readily, and see that there is no gain in merely pushing it aside. The development of the reasonable part of the soul, which is not subject to the genii, culminates in the reception of the god who enlightens it with a sunny ray, the *Chitkala* that is attracted by contemplation. Clear, pure reason characterizes the immortal ray which is connected with the star that has its genii, good and evil by nature. The use of reason and clarity of perception in the spiritual and metaphysical sense involves the heart as well as the mind because they cooperate in seeing and thinking clearly. Once this is grasped, one can make a decisive difference to the amount of unnecessary karma involved in one's irrational emanations and wasteful emotions. One can begin to let go of all that and calmly cultivate the deepest feelings.

At a certain point it will become natural for the mind to move spontaneously to spiritual teachings and universal ideas whenever it has an opportunity. It would not have to be told, nor would one have to make rules, because that would be what it would enjoy. When it becomes more developed in the art of solitary contemplation, it will always see everything from the higher standpoint whilst performing duties in the lower realm, thus transforming one's whole way of living. This will make a profound difference to the conservation of energy and the clarification of one's karma. It will also strengthen the power of progressive detachment whereby one can understand what it means to say that the Sage, the *Jivanmukta*, the perfected *Yogin*, is characterized by the golden talisman of doing only what is truly necessary. He only thinks what is necessary. He only feels what is necessary. There is so powerful a sense of what is necessary in the small, but from the standpoint of the whole, that there is no other way of life that is conceivable or imaginable. This internal Buddhic logic can never be understood by reference to external rules and characteristics because one has to come to it from a high plane of meditation and total detachment from the realm of external expression.

When the disciple is sufficiently self-evolved from within without, then the further individuation of the soul through self-conscious initiations may proceed. Prepared by testing and by trials, the reasonable part of the soul may receive a sunny ray, communicated by its spiritual ancestors, themselves inseparable from the disciple's own seventh principle. The parentless progenitors of spiritual intelligence or consciousness are known at one level as Bodhisattvas, at another level as Dhyani Buddhas, at still another level as Manushi Buddhas. All of these are spiritual ancestors of what is called *Buddhi* – individually one's own intuitive principle, but in a strict philosophical sense the pure vehicle of one universal light. *Buddhi* as a principle is its emanation, a gift from a Dhyani Buddha or spiritual progenitor. Seen in this way, all the higher principles are pure emanations from spiritual instructors and parents, in the same way that until the age of seven a terrestrial parent is the spiritual and mental progenitor of the thinking of a child. The child's own intelligence is involved, and children vary in their responses because of accumulated karma. So too with the *chela* on the Path. The language that parents use, the ideas that they evoke, and their mode of consciousness colour the child's psyche during the day, giving a certain tone to the environment. Though most parents hardly think deliberately about what is at stake, owing to their lack of knowledge and insight, nonetheless they have the inimitable opportunity of initiating the child into the wise use of its latent powers. This is only an imperfect analogy on the lower plane of differentiated consciousness and everyday relationships between highly vulnerable personalities. It can scarcely intimate the magical privilege of communicating with Adepts and Initiates, and of participating in the compassionate ideation that permeates the magnetic field in which the *chela* grows. As an immortal soul, each individual is potentially an inheritor of the whole field of human consciousness over eighteen million years; as an initiated *chela* each may freely assume this sacred birthright as a spiritual inheritor of the parentless *Anupadaka*.

The Bodhisattva Path of self-regeneration and of initiation into the mysteries of the higher principles begins and ends with the quickening of the reverential feeling of devotion and gratitude for every single being who ever did anything for oneself. Those who are fortunate enough to perfect that power of endless, boundless gratitude and spontaneous reverence to every teacher they ever learnt from are in a better position to understand how to invoke the highest gift of self-consciousness from the greatest spiritual progenitors. In a fearless way but also in a proper posture of true devotion and reverence, one can invoke the Dhyani Buddhas in dawn meditation, during the day, in the evening and at night, whenever and how often one reaches out in consciousness to them. Before this can be done effectively, one must learn to cleanse the lunar vesture, calm the mind and purify the heart. Every thought or feeling directed against another being makes that heart unworthy to feel the hebdomadal vibration of the Dhyani Buddhas. Self-concern pollutes rather than protects. Self-purification and self-correction strengthen the capacity to liberate oneself from the karmic accretions of lives of ignorance and foolish participation in the collective dross. Such are the laws of spiritual evolution that this purification can only proceed through the sacrificial invocation of the whole of one's karma. Then one can begin to become truly self-conscious in one's interior relationship to the Dhyani Buddhas, the Daimon, the Genius which can speak to one through the Kwan Yin, the *Chitkala*, the Inner Voice. Just as a vast portion of the world's sublimest music is only theoretically available to the average person, the finest vibrations of *Akasa-Alaya* must remain of little avail to most mortals until they fit themselves to come and sit close to the Teachers of *Brahma Vach*. "To live to benefit mankind is the first step."

Hermes, June 1981

SELF-TRANSFORMATION

> 'The worlds, to the profane', says a Commentary, 'are built up of the known Elements. To the conception of an Arhat, these Elements are themselves collectively a divine Life; distributively, on the plane of manifestations, the numberless and countless crores of lives. Fire alone is ONE, on the plane of the One Reality: on that of manifested, hence illusive, being, its particles are fiery lives which live and have their being at the expense of every other life that they consume. Therefore they are named the "DEVOURERS."'... 'Every visible thing in this Universe was built by such LIVES, from conscious and divine primordial man down to the unconscious agents that construct matter.'... 'From the ONE LIFE formless and Uncreate, proceeds the Universe of lives. First was manifested from the Deep (Chaos) cold luminous fire (gaseous light ?) which formed the curds in Space.'
>
> The Secret Doctrine, i 249–250

Matter distributed in Space manifests a series of dimensions or characteristics correlated with the different Rounds of cosmic and human evolution on earth. Just as shared perceptions of extension, colour, motion, taste and smell have developed through the persistent use of five familiar sense-organs, so too emerging humanity will experience through the sixth sense of normal clairvoyance the corresponding characteristic of matter which has been called permeability. The three so-called dimensions of length, breadth and thickness are merely the triple aspects of extension, marked out by measurements made through customary devices. To restrict the common conception of Space, as Locke did, to what is simply a single characteristic of Matter is severely to limit perception, to confine and condition it by a perspective that is not even fully three-dimensional. In order to free everyday consciousness from this narrow focus, one must sense a new dimension of depth, which is related to suffering rather than to length, breadth and thickness. Depth, which is sometimes termed height, in mystical parlance, is crucial to a person who is truly skilled in regular meditations, withdrawing the wayward mind to a still centre while visualizing an ever-extending circumference around that motionless point. Through conscientious practice this regenerative activity of consciousness can purify, elevate and intensify one's interior life. Lateral expansion can fuse with depth of concentration to generate the vibrant awareness of the vault of the luminous sphere of mystic meditation. A profounder sense of non-being can enrich the quality and range of all astral perceptions in the course of time. One becomes a modest master of one's own orchestra.

In general, a person largely sees what one expects to see, owing to an enormous routinization in sensory responses. This has been fully confirmed in contemporary experiments. Any person who perceives an unfamiliar object is apt to experience a proportionally greater variation in the retinal image than when watching a familiar object as it is removed and receding into the distance. The human organism is always adapting, through its sense-organs, all pre-existing sensations and memories of stimuli, to what is recurrent and what is unfamiliar and unexpected. Hence, physical pain and mental suffering often come through the compassion of *Maya*, which induces fleeting shocks to the sensory apparatus lest out of a false sense of familiarity, the mechanical observer takes too much for granted, thus making the creative faculties atrophy and the brain-centres sluggish. When suddenly one is confronted with what is strangely unfamiliar, one is compelled to think and contemplate. The immortal Triad overbrooding every human being is aware, like a Pythagorean spectator, that its reflected ray is continually tempted to abdicate its responsibility as a thinker and chooser. It becomes like a mindless robot mired in automatic responses. The more these compulsive reactions are moralized in terms of good habits and the spurious semblance of virtue, the more subtle and insidious they become, enmeshing noetic consciousness, substituting passivity for plasticity, and destroying flexibility in discriminative response to the flux of events. When restless beings encounter individuals with a very different pace of life, or who live in greater closeness to the good earth, they are forced to recognize a richer way of life, a greater awareness of depth. In modern society, there is a constant risk of awareness being reduced to a mechanical series of automatic responses which preclude true thinking and inhibit self-examination. When reflex responses in chaotic cerebration are reinforced through familiar clusters of tawdry images and shallow emotions, perverse thoughts invade one's sphere. This is a pervasive problem in our time of accelerated change and decisive sifting. Consider a person who attempts to become attentive while reading a text but who is not used to it and whose consciousness is shackled to the wandering mind, weak sensory responses and a general lack of attention and order in daily life. Such hapless persons cannot really read exactly what is in the text and cannot focus on it, let alone see around it and probe into profound suggestions buried within and between the lines of the text. To be able to shake the system out of this false familiarity, breeding a banal contempt for the supposedly stable world outside, the greatest teacher is suffering.

In the Aquarian Age in which many see the life-process as the continually enacted and essentially hidden interplay of harmony and disharmony, suffering always comes as a benevolent teacher of wisdom. Pain serves as a shock to one's sense of identity, illusory self-image and acquired or ancestral habits. It challenges one's pride and perversity. It compels one to pause for thought and radically reappraise the meaning of life, obligations, and potentials in oneself and others. When suffering comes, it plumbs below the surface of the psyche, touching depths of untrammelled consciousness. Noumenal and noetic awareness enters into everyday experience, and is saluted by myriad constellations of poets, singers and seers. Incidents of life once taken for granted suddenly look very different, because one's sensibility has been sharpened. Were this not so, there would be little meaning to the mere succession of events and the mere recurrence of mechanical responses to the sensory stream of consciousness. There is constant learning, and there is the ever-present possibility of deepening the cognitive basis of awareness, the operative level of self-actualization. This is part of the evolutionary and unending process of etherealization and refinement of life in the cycle of rapid descent and painful ascent. This is an exceedingly slow and subtle process – there is nothing automatic about it – but it is ubiquitous. Such a process of refinement must involve first of all an altered mode of awareness, which for most human beings means the conscious adoption of a radically different perspective on human life and cosmic evolution. But it must also transform the range and reach of one's sense-perceptions, through a better and finer use of the sensory powers of touch, taste, smell, sight and hearing. Further, this process of etherealization and refinement must proceed through a harmonious commingling of centres in the brain-mind and spiritual heart, through inward surrender to the Sovereign Self and the silent invocation of the Light of the Logos.

One may imagine the immortal Triad as overbrooding the head, though incompletely incarnated because its reflected intelligence must consciously ascend towards the level of proper harmonization. This could be expressed in terms of metaphysical truths about consciousness which operates under laws of expansion and contraction, implying continuous creation, preservation and regeneration through destruction. These archetypal modes have been traditionally symbolized in the Hindu pantheon by Nara-Nari, Agni, Varuna and Surya, and also by Brahmā, Vishnu and Shiva. This sacred teaching about cosmic and human consciousness could also be conveyed from the standpoint of matter. The essential axiom of the *Gupta Vidya* is the affirmation that Spirit and Matter are really two facets of one and the same Substance-Principle. Objectivity and subjectivity are wholly relative to centres of perception, to degrees of differentiation, and to the coadunition and consubstantiality of objects with subjects upon overlapping planes of substance. Put entirely in terms of matter, this would imply that a person whose consciousness is deepened would experience a richer awareness of the invisible aspects and mathematical points of visible matter. There would be a heightened sensitivity to the gamut of invisible relations between life-atoms, corresponding to subtle colours and rarefied sounds. One would also be replacing an angular view by a rounded view: the greater the depth, the greater the roundedness. The price people pay for the settled three-dimensionality of their conception of the world of phenomena is that the brain-mind becomes captive to angular views. If people are not truly self-conscious, they become extremely obtuse or are hopelessly caught within narrow angles and restricted orbits of perception. Whereas a person who can intensify the depth of perception and feeling, through private pain and unspoken suffering merged in effortless awareness of the vast suffering of all humanity, gains greater depth as a human being. This is continuously enriched by meditative experience of the Silence that surrounds the mystery of *SAT* and *Asat*, Being and Non-Being. The more this becomes a way of life, the more it is possible to have a profoundly balanced view of the world and a well-rounded conception of selfhood, alchemizing and elevating personal awareness and individual sensibility to the height and breadth of universal self-consciousness and the depths of boundless space, eternal motion and endless duration.

This process of self-transformation may be illustrated by an initially shadowy circle, a very narrow segment of which seems to be lit up. There is a seemingly central focus, but it is only central to that visible segment, whilst the centre of the whole circle, most of which is obscured, remains hidden. This is analogous to the relationship between the personal ego and the individual Self. A human being with a narrow sense of identity is living only segmentally, existing only at one sensory level with reference to an unduly restricted horizon of human experience. Such a person is not properly centering, not really trying to get as full and rounded a view of himself and the world as possible. Out of this roundedness he could begin to sense a sphere of light surrounding himself in which he lives, moves and has his being. This will loosen a great deal of the fixity of categories of thought and emotional responses which, if seen clairvoyantly, reveal a sad mutilated shadow of the true Self of a human being. Herein lies the rationale for recovery through meditation of that pristine and rounded conception of the Self which is more in harmony with the music of the spheres and the Golden Egg of Brahmā in the ocean of SPACE. This transformation is indeed the psychological equivalent to the Copernican revolution, in which the sun of the *Atman* is central to the solar system. For the *Atman* to become the centre of a luminous sphere of selfhood would require a firm displacement of the false centering of consciousness, through *kama manas*, within a distorting segment of separative identity which is trapped in a fragmented view of space, time and secondary causation. The dwarfing of one's true selfhood is the crucifixion of Christos, the obscuration of the light, the plenitude, the potential and the richness within every human being on earth.

To convey this as a criterion of human stature, the greater the depth of one's inwardness, the broader, the vaster, the wider the range of one's sympathies, and the more one is able to appreciate a wider variety of experiences, situations, contexts and human beings. The more secure one's depth of consciousness, the more one is able to exercise the synthesizing gift of the Monad, capable of seeing in terms of any of the specific sub-colours, and also able to penetrate to the very centre of the white light, seeing beyond it, and benevolently using the entire range of the spectrum. What is true of colours applies equally to sounds, and ultimately to consciousness itself. This is the sacred prerogative of a human being. It is because human beings fall, owing to shared and inherited limitations, but also owing to self-created limitations, they forfeit or forget altogether this sovereign prerogative and fail to mend themselves through meditation and self-study. Hence, the healing and restorative property of sleep which Shakespeare so suggestively describes as Nature's second feast, man's great restorer. The average human being deprived of the benefit of *sushupti* or sleep would simply not survive for long. Sleep and death are Nature's modes of restoration of balance. In order to take full advantage of sleep, the seeker must initially experience the pain of forcing the mind to return to a point on which it is placed, to a chosen idea, bringing the heart back to the deepest, purest and most pristine feeling of devotion, warmth and love. If one did this again and again, then certainly one would not only become more deep in response to life but one would also become more of a spiritual benefactor to the human race, drawing freely from the infinite resources of Divine Thought and the Light of the Logos, *Brahma Vach*.

> Just as milliards of bright sparks dance on the waters of an ocean above which one and the same moon is shining, so our evanescent personalities – the illusive envelopes of the immortal MONAD-EGO – twinkle and dance on the waves of Maya. They last and appear, as the thousands of sparks produced by the moon-beams, only so long as the Queen of the Night radiates her lustre on the running waters of life: the period of a Manvantara; and then they disappear, the beams – symbols of our eternal Spiritual Egos – alone surviving, re-merged in, and being, as they were before, one with the Mother-Source.
>
> *The Secret Doctrine*, i 237

The Monad-Ego is the three-tongued flame, the *Atma-Buddhi-Manas* which overbroods throughout the *manvantara* myriads upon myriads of personalities, instruments and vehicles through which the great work of evolution proceeds. This is made possible by the fact that the three-tongued flame of the four wicks is connected with the myriads of sparks. Although in each life these sparks seemingly become entangled through the four derivative principles into a shallow sense of separative identity as a personal man or woman in that life, this is really an illusion. All the elements in all the personal lives throughout the *manvantara* represent the diffused intelligence which is here ascribed to a single source – the Queen of the Night – radiating her lustre on the running waters of life. Between the hidden source of the flames throughout evolution – the Central Spiritual Sun – and the manifest source of all the myriad sparks involved in the evanescent phenomena witnessed by personal consciousness in incarnated existence, there would be a causal relationship. One is like a necessary reflection of the other. This is true cosmically. It is also true of every single human being. The astral form is like a lunar reflection of a solar light-energy that belongs to the *Atma-Buddhi-Manas*, which is like the sun overbrooding every single human temple. The profoundly mysterious relation between the two is intimated by the symbol of the thread of *Fohat*. A very fine thread connects the solar activity of the higher principles and the lunar activity involving the reflected and parasitic intelligence of personal consciousness. Everything can be seen, as in the Platonic scheme, as a reflection of what is higher on a more homogeneous plane. The relative reality of every single entity and event in life is a shadowy reality that presupposes something more primordial and more homogeneous. In this way, all life would trace back to the one single field of homogeneous ideation, homogeneous substance. If this is what makes the universe a cosmos – a single system – then the solemn task of the human being is to integrate life consciously and cheerfully; to do this, one must first negate the false sense of identity that belongs on the lunar plane. One must perceive in depth all the elements of being that contribute to the seeming continuity of consciousness in and through the astral form, and then reach further inwards through deep meditation to the sacred source of all consciousness and life. This alchemical work is represented in many myths as the separation of what is food for the soul from what is not, before and during after-death states. This sifting takes place through all nature and is the deliberate undertaking of those who are pledged to self-regeneration in the service of humanity. " 'Great Sifter' is the name of the 'Heart Doctrine', O Disciple."

The subtlety of this alchemical art arises from the fact that the pseudo-identity of the lunar plane involves not only the flux of fleeting emotional states but also a bewildering array of ghostly mental constructions. At a fundamental level of conceptualization, we have the tangled roots of the Ashwatha tree of Samsaric illusion. This endemic tendency to hypostatize the emanations of cosmic mind was ably diagnosed by Professor Bain.

> The giving reality to abstractions is the error of Realism. Space and Time are frequently viewed as separated from all the concrete experiences of the mind, instead of being generalizations of these in certain aspects.
>
> *The Secret Doctrine*, i 251

Here Bain is referring to a long-standing tendency to reification, the cardinal error of classical realism which eventually produced a welter of conflicting interpretations of what were designated as 'universals'. These universals were abstract entities and were wholly sundered from the wealth of particulars in the world of phenomena. This generated insuperable theoretical difficulties. When the universals are applied to Space and Time, independent of all concrete experiences of the mind, they give rise to the false impression that the archetypes are remote from and unconnected with the activity of *kama manas* in the everyday world of subjects and objects. Strictly, one should recognize that at any point of time, relative to the succession of states of consciousness, there is simultaneously a non-linear clustering of conceptual frameworks that presuppose a spatio-temporal field. Bain is stating at a simple level what is crucial to the macrocosmic process at its pregenetic level. Space and Time are suffused and conceptually bound up with cosmic and human consciousness. We cannot truly separate anything from conscious life. Every single point in space is animated by intelligence and the indwelling light of living awareness. There is nothing inanimate, nothing inert, nothing dead in the entire universe of matter and motion in Space and Time. In seeking through a series of philosophical negations to blank out all psychological concretions, and then embark upon mystic meditation in the Divine Dark, the great Night, one will view it not as an inane void but rather as intense absolute light which is also absolute darkness. All limited and limiting concepts of the contraries are derived from everyday experience of heterogeneity, in terms of which therefore, when one enters into the realm of the homogeneous, one becomes hypnotized by the contrast between the homogeneous and the heterogeneous. There is, however, a further stage of enlightenment wherein one begins to enjoy so strong, continuous and intense an awareness of the homogeneous that one cognizes the homogeneous in the heterogeneous, sees infinity in a grain of sand, eternity in an hour, the large in the small. This is the hidden message of the *Bhagavad Gita*: The cosmos is in the atom and the whole of the cosmos is like an atom. Commenting upon the mysterious Fohatic thread connecting all of life, H.P. Blavatsky states:

> This relates to the greatest problem of philosophy – the physical and substantial nature of life, the independent nature of which is denied by modern science because that science is unable to comprehend it. The reincarnationists and believers in Karma alone dimly perceive that the whole secret of Life is in the unbroken series of its manifestations: whether in, or apart from, the physical body. Because if –
>
> *Life, like a dome of many-coloured glass,*
> *Stains the white radiance of Eternity –*
>
> yet it is itself part and parcel of that Eternity; for life alone can understand life.
>
> *The Secret Doctrine*, i 238

When one is willing to gain a dynamic perception of the macrocosmic depth within microcosmic life, then one may develop a radically new mode of apprehending the world. In connection with restoring this vital continuity between all the aspects and phases of life, one must take up the difficult but important exercise of treating each day as an incarnation. It is hardly easy to grasp what this means at first. To understand truly, one can initially take four broad divisions, thus seeing a day in terms of the archetypal *process* of childhood, adolescence, adulthood and old age. One can make further and finer distinctions, once one has gained insight into the fourfold division of human life, thus transcending lumpy categories which ineffectually mediate between the atomic and the cosmic. One can gain a more mobile sense of reality, capable of reaching to the infinitesimal in consciousness, capable of rising to the transfinite. As this process becomes continuous, it inevitably affects all one's centres of perception, altering the flows of energy within the nervous system. This is why meditation must at some point give rise to a whole new set of sensory responses to the world and prepare one also for that level of cosmic consciousness where one becomes vividly conscious of the magical power of concentrated thought. When idea, image and intent are all fused in a noetic, dynamic energy which ignites the spiritual will, one gains precision and control, and can ultimately become a self-conscious agent in the transmutation of matter, the alchemical transformation of the vestures through the *tapas* and *yajna* of self-regeneration. Through calm reflection, one can begin to give a sense of reality to what are otherwise like metaphorical or vapidly abstract instances of universal consciousness, far removed from the prison-house of personal consciousness. But when one begins to enter into the activity of *Lila* itself, one can gain great strength, steadiness and spiritual sustenance, drawing apart from all forms, and gathering oneself into the mysterious interior intelligent centre of one's original spiritual consciousness.

> It is a MYSTERY, truly, but only to him who is prepared to reject the existence of intellectual and conscious spiritual Beings in the Universe, limiting full Consciousness to man alone, and that only as a 'function of the Brain.' Many are those among the Spiritual Entities, who have incarnated bodily in man, since the beginning of his appearance, and who, for all that, still exist as independently as they did before, in the infinitudes of Space.
>
> *The Secret Doctrine,* i 233

One must relocate oneself within the depths of this vast general perspective of a host of Dhyani Buddhas and Bodhisattvas, exalted beings of different degrees of consciousness ranging from the most universal consciousness that even transcends the solar system to very high consciousness in this solar world and in lunar bodies. This boundless and beatific panorama is presented in many different ways in all the great mystical texts, and given *par excellence* in the universal vision of the eleventh chapter of the *Bhagavad Gita*. Through it, one may begin to see that the world as ordinarily known is but a surface revealing only pale reflections in an immense shadow-play. One can begin to apprehend the initially discomforting, but ultimately revolutionary, thought that what is going on in oneself is not even guessed by one's lower mind. Many of the problems of human beings arise because the inefficient, insecure and fear-ridden lower mind – lamed in childhood and competitive hot-houses – claims to reveal all, although it is only a small part of the whole. In truth, most of what is really going on inside a human being occurs during deep sleep, or scattered moments of awareness in waking life, which do not register at all in *kama manas*. They cannot be recorded, still less reported. Hence, the paradox known to many mystics arises – what is called life is a form of death from the standpoint of the immortal soul. As Krishna says in the *Gita*, to the spiritually wise what men call day is the night of ignorance. It is a mere shadow-play of elemental interaction imperfectly edited by a lower mind which is naturally a helpless prisoner of its own particular perceptions, expectations and memories. This "tale told by an idiot" is independent of the true life of the immortal soul, which is well characterized as silent (since the immortal soul cannot find in the languages that belong to the heterogeneous realm any vocabulary for its own spiritual knowledge and cognition). It can, however, be reflected in the proper use of the sacred power of speech and the mystical potency of sound. The invisible entity may be bodily present on earth without abandoning its status and functions in supersensuous regions. If the overbrooding Spirit were not connected, like a daimon or indwelling tutelary genius, with personal consciousness, there would be no possibility of awareness and of learning for the soul with all its misfirings and mistakes. Even then, that learning itself is partial because what is truly happening within the real Self, the invisible entity and the immortal daimon, cannot really be summoned by the uninitiated without bringing the instruments in line with the spiritual will of the *Atma-Buddhi-Manas*.

What happens involuntarily and naturally in deep sleep must be done consciously in waking life through philosophical negation, deep meditation, calm reflection and Pythagorean self-examination. If done daily, in time it will be possible to bring closer the astral vesture and the true divine Self that otherwise is only partially involved or only inadequately incarnated. Taking this as a general truth about humanity, it connects with the complex doctrines of Rounds, Globes and Races and the eventual development that will take place in the Rounds far in the future. There will be much fuller incarnation possible, because of the radical change that would have taken place in the plasticity and resilience of the material vestures. Matter will be so markedly different that it can readily reflect Spirit with a pristine purity which is virtually independent of the entire stream of monadic and material evolution. To move self-consciously in this direction of depth perception is the willing contribution of the true pilgrim who enters the Path and takes vows for lives, vows that involve the ceaseless process of self-transformation for the sake of universal enlightenment. True disciples will consecrate each day to Hermes-Budha, to the Manasaputras, the descending luminous beings that make human self-consciousness possible. All Lanoos will strengthen the centre of silence within themselves until it can be used for the calm release of a new current of energy, a new line of life's meditation, which fuses thought, will and feeling in daily life for the sake of the larger whole. Wise men and women will take full advantage of this teaching to bring forth the greatest strength and sacrifice that can be released in their own lives for the sake of Universal Good, the Agathon on earth as in Heaven (*Akasa*), the *summum bonum* which flows from *Satguna Brahman* but is gestated within the bosom of *Nirguna Brahman*, boundless Space in eternal Duration. OM MANI PADME HUM. OM TAT SAT. TAT TVAM ASI. SOHAM. HARI AUM. NAMOSIVAVAM. OM.

Hermes, January 1981

EVOLUTION AND CONSCIOUSNESS

> *We see a flower slowly developing from a bud, and the bud from its seed. But whence the latter, with all its predetermined programme of physical transformation, and its invisible, therefore spiritual forces which gradually develop its form, colour, and odour? The word evolution speaks for itself. The germ of the present human race must have preexisted in the parent of this race, as the seed, in which lies hidden the flower of next summer, was developed in the capsule of its parent flower.*
>
> The Secret Doctrine, ii xvi

The twelve *Stanzas of Dzyan* on anthropogenesis, like the seven *Stanzas* on cosmogenesis, are accompanied by interwoven Commentary and supplemented by elaborate elucidations of myth and symbol, of science and philosophy. To gain a clear comprehension of the overall framework is difficult partially because it was meant to be difficult. There are numerous blinds, overlapping statements and various interlocking classifications which use terms differently in distinct contexts. There is a code language in *The Secret Doctrine* which is meant to arouse Buddhic intuition and to nullify the tendency of lower *Manas* to consolidate categories, classifications and even concepts. As an initial aid in gaining a broad picture of human evolution, H.P. Blavatsky gives at the beginning a brief account of the five continents which more or less roughly correspond with the five Root Races through which humanity has passed on this globe in reaching its present stage. If one sees the entirety of involution and evolution in the form of a circle, humanity as a whole has come down over half the circle and has begun to ascend back to its pristine source. This critical stage is represented by the Fifth Sub-Race of the Fifth Root Race in the Fourth Round. The purpose of understanding this entire scheme is to see more clearly the varied ways in which every human being today is bound up with all other human beings who ever lived or will live in the future.

It is not enough to do this vaguely in terms of some fuzzy proposition about what Feuerbach called the species nature of humanity. Rather, it must be done in terms that are significant from the standpoint of sentient beings, human souls that have lived and struggled, learnt and forgotten, erred, picked up the thread again, expanded consciousness, assumed contraction of consciousness involuntarily and voluntarily, by mutual impact in a multitude of conditions and contexts. In order to convey a vast gamut of possible relations between externality and internal states of consciousness, H.P. Blavatsky sets out the broad scheme of Continents and Races, beginning with the Imperishable Sacred Isle of the Blessed:

> This 'Sacred Land' . . . is stated never to have shared the fate of the other continents; because it is the only one whose destiny it is to last from the beginning to the end of the Manvantara throughout each Round. It is the cradle of the first man and the dwelling of the last *divine* mortal, chosen as a *Sishta* for the future seed of humanity. Of this mysterious and sacred land very little can be said, except, perhaps, according to a poetical expression in one of the Commentaries, that the 'pole-star has its watchful eye upon it, from the dawn to the close of the twilight of "a day" of the GREAT BREATH.'
>
> *The Secret Doctrine*, ii 6

The proper study of mankind is Man, declared the poet Pope. This is a mighty venture into the range and reach of human consciousness. The intuitive individual who turns inward, giving reality to the secret wisdom within the sanctuary of immortal consciousness, will necessarily turn back far beyond the confines of recorded and unrecorded history, beyond manifested events and finite memory. One must thus return to the primal fount of one's deepest kinship with enlightened beings on the Imperishable Sacred Land who were the divine guardians that nursed and protected the First Root Race. No poetical description, philosophical account or scientific scheme could do justice to that primordial state of collective consciousness. It is not to be located in the mists of antiquity, but lies in a realm transcending ordinary conceptions of past, present and future, perpetually present during the vast epoch of a *manvantara*. This is the noumenal basis for all theological or poetical conceptions of paradisaic consciousness.

In the para-temporal sequence of human evolution we are then told of the legendary home of the Second Race:

> The 'HYPERBOREAN' will be the name chosen for the Second Continent, the land which stretched out its promontories southward and westward from the North Pole to receive the Second Race, and comprised the whole of what is now known as Northern Asia. Such was the name given by the oldest Greeks to the far-off and mysterious region, whither their tradition made Apollo the 'Hyperborean' travel every year. *Astronomically*, Apollo is of course the Sun...
>
> But *historically*, or better, perhaps, ethnologically and geologically, the meaning is different. The land of the Hyperboreans, the country that extended beyond Boreas, the frozen-hearted god of snows and hurricanes, who loved to slumber heavily on the chain of Mount Riphaeus, was neither an ideal country, as surmised by the mythologists, nor yet a land in the neighbourhood of Scythia and the Danube. It was a real Continent, a *bona-fide* land which knew no winter in those early days, nor have its sorry remains more than one night and day during the year, even now. The nocturnal shadows never fall upon it, said the Greeks; for it is the *land of the Gods*, the favourite abode of Apollo, the god of light, and its inhabitants are his beloved priests and servants.
>
> *The Secret Doctrine*, ii 7

Then we have the Third Continent in which the Third Root Race came to experience the first stirrings of self-conscious awakening. It is designated as 'Lemuria', a name invented in the 1850's by P.L. Sclater, who held on zoological grounds that there was once a continent which extended from Madagascar to Ceylon and Sumatra, including some portions of what is now Africa. This gigantic continent stretching from the Indian Ocean to Australia and beyond has almost entirely disappeared, leaving only some of its highest points as scattered islands.

Next we have the Fourth Continent, now called Atlantis, the first "historical" land, which together with the Fourth Race, passed through markedly different phases. Following the era of the Fourth Root Race, a period as long as five million years, the Fifth Root Race, to which present humanity belongs, began a million years ago with its First Sub-Race in ancient India. Atlantis was originally much vaster than the last large fragment which disappeared about 850,000 years ago. Geologically, the Fifth Continent should be America, but H.P. Blavatsky says, "As it is situated at the Antipodes, it is Europe and Asia Minor, almost coeval with it, which are generally referred to by the Indo-Aryan Occultists as the fifth." The classification of the Continents follows the order of evolution of the Races, not the geological appearance of the Continents. Nor do the present configurations of land masses indicate the past relations of Races.

> There was a time when the delta of Egypt and Northern Africa belonged to Europe, before the formation of the Straits of Gibraltar, and a further upheaval of the continent, changed entirely the face of the map of Europe. The last serious change occurred some 12,000 years ago, and was followed by the submersion of Plato's little Atlantic island, which he calls Atlantis after its parent continent.
>
> *The Secret Doctrine*, ii 8–9

Any accurate appreciation of philosophical anthropogenesis and its spiritual implications must be consonant with cosmogenesis. One must work back from the fourth globe, our own earth, to its earliest inheritances which connect with the entire solar system. This is not only true on the physical plane, but also simultaneously on the invisible planes. This is difficult to understand but it is crucial if one is to make sense of the cosmic scale on which interact internal and external evolution. The nineteenth century conception of material evolution represented a considerable improvement upon the fragmented and arbitrary conceptions of creation which persisted among the credulous and the bigoted. This advance was accompanied by resuscitated cultural theories harking back to classical notions that were pre-Socratic, Platonic and Aristotelian. Nonetheless, it externalized, on the basis of a restrictive view of evidence, the fundamental concepts of mutation, change and chance, and organic growth. In order to accommodate a richer view of evolution even in the external world, and a much more formidable programme of internal evolution in consciousness, thoughtful individuals have to see beyond the orthodoxies of science and of religion. They need to draw freely upon their own subjective experiences in seeking and gaining self-knowledge. The process must be conceived as open-textured, admitting of fructification from the realm of ideation to the region of event. This demands the deliberate extension of the horizon of growth and the potentials in all human beings. The study of human nature must be undertaken in a disciplined manner that is both logical and also intuitively corresponds to that which is integral to cosmic evolution. The metaphysical power to abstract and to visualize has to be aroused if one seriously intends to make sense of human evolution in a universe of infinite unmanifest potentiality.

The methodology of the *Gupta Vidya* is linked to the process of self-regeneration. It focusses upon the purification and perfection of the vestures of the aspirant *pari passu* with the unfolding of perceptual mysteries. It is, therefore, inseparable from the actual course of human evolution itself. It is, in fact, evolution made self-conscious. In its conceptual framework, it mirrors the living matrix of both cosmos and man, and in practice it teaches the macrocosmic and microcosmic application of the different keys of interpretation to myths and symbols. These often offer hints about the vibrations connecting different parts of the universe and different parts of the human constitution. Anyone who begins to appreciate the richer classifications of the ancient world, especially in Sanskrit but also in Greek, will refuse to be bound by any simplistic cardboard categories such as 'mind' and 'body', 'irrational' and 'rational'. These are of little help in understanding the complex interaction between the cosmic and the atomic. Every human being has the same evolutionary task as every other human being who ever lived, lives now or will live in the future. In this pilgrimage there are ancient guidelines in cutting through the clutter of detail and getting to the core of noetic consciousness.

Owing to centuries of mutilation of the higher faculties by dogmatic religion and materialistic science, many people do not have metaphysical imagination. In mass society many find it difficult to generate abstract ideas or to sustain constructive thought. All too often persons get threatened if confronted by any idea that has no immediate concrete reference to their personal self-image. This sad condition demonstrates the inherited damage to consciousness which is transmitted, and even aggravated, by contemporary media. To correct this will require tremendous courage and compassion, and also great wisdom in altering the plasticity of the human mind. Eventually this subtle transformation will require that every human being make some effort to think metaphysically. After a point, what is initially difficult becomes easier, and suddenly a whole group of people who were once completely bewildered by metaphysical abstractions awaken a dormant aptitude for creative imagination. The metaphysical must connect with the mystical. Those who truly seek to prepare themselves for discipleship must choose a mode of life which can help to maintain an increasing continuity of consciousness. Using the method of analogy and correspondence, one will find that *The Secret Doctrine* is really giving instruction concerning meditation and self-study, about how to understand other human beings, and how to make a constructive difference to the collective karma of the human race. Each human being, every day and night, has microcosmic choices and opportunities which, if calmly understood from the perspective of the macrocosmic, enables an honest seeker to be truly helpful to the Brotherhood of Bodhisattvas. In the early stages this would be mostly unconscious to the lower mind but entirely clear to the immortal soul. Even small differences wrought in the moral choices one makes by night and day can unlock doors for vast numbers of human beings and open pathways which will be relevant to the Races to come and the Aquarian civilization of the future. Aspiring disciples will find that sometimes just by taking a phrase or a sentence and writing it out, reflecting upon it and sincerely attempting to apply it to themselves, trying to use it at dawn, midday, the twilight hour or late at night, but always so that one may become the better able to help and serve the whole of the human race, they will tap the inexhaustible resources of *Akasha*.

It is certainly possible to establish a strong nucleus of spiritual seekers who can imbibe the elixir of Divine Wisdom. One is automatically unable to glimpse the secrets of Nature if one is not of the right frame of mind, does not have the proper motivation or does not have the proper mental posture of a disciple. But if one does have even a modicum of these, one will receive intimations from unseen helpers as to how to make Hermetic wisdom come alive and become an alchemical, ambrosial source for self-transmutation. Speaking of winged Mercury as the perpetual companion of the Sun of Wisdom, H.P. Blavatsky pointed to the profound mysteries in human consciousness which are vitally relevant to *sushupti, dhyana* and *turiya*:

> He was the leader of and the evocator of Souls, the 'great Magician' and the Hierophant. Virgil depicts him as taking 'his wand to evoke from Orcus the souls plunged therein'... He is the golden-coloured Mercury, the χρυσοπηανεσ whom the Hierophants forbade to name. He is symbolised in Grecian mythology by one of the *dogs* (vigilance), which watch over the celestial flock (occult wisdom), or Hermes Anubis, or again Agathodaemon. He is the Argus watching over the Earth, and which the latter mistakes for the Sun itself. It is through the intercession of Mercury that the Emperor Julian prayed to the Occult Sun every night; for, as says Vossius: 'All the theologians agree to say that *Mercury and the Sun are one*. . . . He was the most eloquent and the most wise of all the gods, which is not to be wondered at, since *Mercury is in such close proximity to the Wisdom and the Word of God* (the Sun) . . .'

The Secret Doctrine, ii 28

Through daily meditation upon the Spiritual Sun, *Buddhi* is aroused and sheds its light upon the noumenal meaning of experience, the internal relations in human consciousness which are connected with the external conditions of material evolution. Hermetic wisdom bridges the gap between ideation, image and form, between universal Spirit and differentiated matter, between the cosmic and the human, between the abstract and the concrete. Meaningful correlations between noumenal causes and disconnected events are sensed in *sushupti*, dreamless sleep. *Dhyana* or meditation dissolves the boundaries of the separative self and prepares the awakened individual to attain unbroken continuity of consciousness. The process of evolution is reversed, the illusory succession of events is shattered by insight, and spiritual wakefulness (*turiya*) is eventually experienced. When this becomes an unbroken state of ceaseless contemplation, enlightenment is possible and all life may be experienced with therapeutic skill, the firmness of the caduceus, the fire of compassion.

Hermes, April 1981

THE COMMUNITY OF THE FUTURE

In a time of confusion, constant change, and continual crises, we are ever tempted to elevate our tentative half-judgments to the status of finalities, closing the door to the future, limiting the possibilities of growth in others and in ourselves. The therapist, Carl Rogers, emphasizes the importance of unconditionality in human relationships and is willing to see beyond the apparent constants of human nature and into that mysterious underground in which the origins of the fundamental capacity to change are found. Can these germs, hidden within the depths of human beings, for change in themselves and in their lives, be the basis of communities, communes, conceptions of community, at several levels and in concentric circles, in a new and more intentional sense than any known in recorded history?

A community is any collection of human beings, diverse but more or less united, who share in common an unconditional and continuing commitment to ends, to values, to beliefs, or maybe only to procedures, but to such an extent that they can rely upon each other to render voluntary compliance with accepted obligations, and show that they are at least minimally capable of self-correction, self-expression and self-transcendence. Put in this large and exacting way, a community is as utopian as the ideal man or the ideal relationship. But to the extent to which every human being is constantly involved in some kind of correction from outside, in his environment, he engages in criticism of others which is often only his own way of criticizing and defining himself. To the extent to which everyone sees through formal laws and coercive sanctions and recognizes some alternative among friendships or an easier, more natural, trustful context in which he can free himself and grow, to that extent human life is larger than social structures, and man is vaster than all the classifications of man. There is a deep sense in which the large definition of the community is close to some element in every one of us – an element which cannot be abolished, cannot be annulled, does not owe anything either to laws or institutions or constitutions, which sees beyond our parents and teachers and our environment, which includes lonely moments of bewilderment before the vastitude and versatility of nature. There is something in every human being which makes him want, seemingly, to get to the top of some professional scale but deep down only represents a desire to get to the top of a mountain, his own inward journey to some invisible summit from where he can see his life – if not steadily, at least less unsteadily than at other times; if not as a whole, at least sufficiently as a whole to make sense to himself and have self-respect as he recognizes and approaches the moment of death.

What we are witnessing today is a fragmentation of consciousness, more clearly seen in the structure of our society, towards which the whole world is tending: an excessive increase of roles, complexities, rules, pressures of every sort, such that human beings even with enormous social mobility cannot meet the challenge from outside because of inadequate psychological mobility. The contemporary revolution is elusive partly because of its insistent stress on flexibility against the rigidity of educational institutions, religious institutions, and political institutions. On the other hand, while we wish to be flexible, open-ended, willing to change, the very pace of change makes us want to do more than merely adapt. We are looking for a basis of continuity amidst the flux. Human beings, when their fragmentation of consciousness becomes insupportable, seek either through meditation or through music, through silence and solitude, if not through traditional forms of worship and prayer, through self-created rituals and rites of the sacred, to find a way by which they can dig into the very depths of their potential being. They thereby hope to tap latent energy so that they can have a tangible, ever existing sense of the unlimited at the very time when limitations are pressing.

The whole of American history, over two hundred years, has been not merely some sort of homogenized search for a national community. There was much more to the American Dream, which was understood not only by the so-called successes but perhaps even more poignantly by the failures – all the many immigrants who came to set up communes and communities, which no doubt eventually died, but who still somewhere felt that what these efforts represented was something real with a possible meaning for other human beings. There were over a hundred communes involving about a hundred thousand people. Of these, very few, like the communities of the Shakers, lasted for over a hundred years. The Rappites continued for almost a hundred years; the Icarians lasted for fifty years; but there were many, many more which were transient, dying almost within a few months after they were born. In all of these there was an assertion of an impulse which might have been premature, in certain respects, might have been misconceived and mistaken in the narrowness of the basis of allegiance or the degree of reinforcement through controls. But nonetheless they represented a kind of daring, a defiant and sometimes desperate assertion of freedom that is part of the American Dream.

If we look at all of these social experiments not only in terms of what went wrong, but also for what we could learn from them, there are certain lessons that could be drawn. These are not merely abstract lessons but rather concrete lessons that are now again being learnt by those who over the last ten years have attempted every kind of communal, semi-communal and mere transient, nomadic form of existence. One of the lessons, said Arthur Morgan, looking at these communities, was the fact that they were exclusive, that they were not universal. There are, of course, very few people anywhere on the globe who can rise to that ultimate affirmation of the American Dream represented by Buckminster Fuller. At a time when doomsday sayers talk in quasi-racialist language, reinforcing the same age-old fear of the whole and of diversity, Fuller insists that no utopia will ever be real or valid unless it is for all, unless it is for the hundred percent of human beings who live on the globe. He adds that the resources of the world today are used on behalf of about forty-four percent, but unless and until they can be used for all, there will be no Kingdom of Heaven on earth. Does this mean that any one community, any one communal experiment, must take on the burden of all? Does this mean that there must be a once-and-for-all, total change in the social structure? This was a natural thought for many pioneers of communes who felt that they would show the way to others, but they ignored their predecessors and their successors. When they came to America, they forgot timeless truths concerning the continuity of human history and of individual life – that birth and growth are inseparable from suffering and death; that the whole of life must accommodate a preparation for the moment of death and also welcome the moment of birth of other human beings; and that there is not merely togetherness in space but also a community over time. And there are many orders of time. At one level time is merely the succession of events; at another level it marks the transmission of ideas that cuts across purely temporal divisions or the historical delimitations of epochs.

If we try to draw lessons from the old communes, we might say that they were attempting something very real on a local plane. They wanted to be universal, but because of the intensity of isolation from the rest of the community – which was more possible in America than in Europe – in time these communes became unself-critical. There was no principle of negation built into the very structure of the community, so indeed people were prey to the very same desire which we find everywhere in modern society – the concern to settle down and find bourgeois stability and respectability.

Now, what was distinctive to California? As early as the late nineteenth century Josiah Royce could see California essentially in terms of social irresponsibility and sloth, indolence in a sunny climate and the impossibility of getting people to be truly cultivated, to do anything which required concentration. This was the sybaritic, hedonistic image of California which one still gets, of course, in other sectors of the United States. But there were also other voices. There were those who felt that California was not merely to be assimilated into some Mediterranean mythology; that there was something else involved here, which was a richer mixture and a greater ferment than elsewhere; and that it was a logical culmination of the American Dream. After pioneers had reached the limit of physical settlement, there was another kind of pioneering involved in another kind of journey. Whitman put this in his characteristic way, very broadly and boldly. He said that when he came to California he asked the question, "What is it that I started a long time ago and how can I get back to that?" It is a venture into the interior realms of consciousness, digging into the very depths of one's being, going beyond ancestral ties, racial affinities, cultural and social conditioning. It is the asking of deeper questions. Others saw this in terms of a mix of North and South, Latin and Anglo Saxon, East and West – much more evident in our own time – and a mix of many other kinds; also of Europe and America.

The history of California, even more perhaps than the history of the United States as a whole, is a history of lost opportunities, of misfired innovations. It is a history of intellectual and spiritual abortions in a state where in some years there are more physical abortions than births, more divorces than marriages. How then, in such a California, can we get excited and be credible to each other even in talking about the community of the future? Here let us invoke Plato who, when he spoke of *Koinonia*, said that a community involves a sharing of pleasures and pains. When Californians are sharing pleasures, for what they are worth, they are quite forgetful of communities. But when they share pains, they experience an immense void. When they experience post-coital sadness, when they experience the pain after every new wave of gush and excitement, when they experience that deep discontent – which may not always be divine and may sometimes indeed be demoniac – they know that there is something more.

This is reminiscent of what was said by a Sufi sage when one of his students asked him, "Why is it, O Master, that when people come to you for discourses, for teaching, for lectures, saying they really want enlightenment, you merely get them to become engaged in some activity?" The Master replied, "Very few of those who think they want enlightenment want anything but a new form of engagement. And very few of those who will get engaged will get engaged to the point where they can see through the activities, because they will get so totally consumed that they will have no opportunity to see beyond. But those few who are confident in their engagements know that they do not need to put themselves totally into them and can see limitations. They will say there is something beyond. They do not know what that something beyond is, but they are certain that there is something beyond. And when they are ready to maintain in consciousness that conception of something beyond, then they are ready for those processes of training that might lead to enlightenment."

California too is to be characterized not only by successes but also by its failures, and these failures prepare it for that ultimate hubris which is still the privilege of the American – to think big, to cherish the impossible dream, to ask whether even in the provincial town of Santa Barbara something profound can emerge. Whittier may have been extravagant rather than wholly wrong when he said that here could be the second founding. But this could be a very different kind of "founding" from what can be historically dated or blazoned forth by the national media. This is perhaps the most important lesson we might learn from the failures of the past decade. A few understood at the very beginning of the Hippie movement that the moment it was bombarded with publicity it could be killed even before it really got going. The early flower children were instinctively right in regard to the logic of inversion. Society had reached a point of such absurdity that one had to invert everything. Teachers were no longer teachers; parents were not really parents; scholars were usually not scholars. One had to allow each one to have his own ego games, while at the same time insisting that no one was taken in by any kind of phoniness. Many were desperately concerned to find some authentic meaning which could be sustained through trust, openness and love shown concretely in everyday relations. The innocents were right in their perception of the logic of inversion, but, of course, they could not stay apart from all the institutions, all the efforts to capture and formulate what they were doing. Above all, there was the insoluble problem of new entrants, which was also the problem of the old communes in America and in California. What can be done about new entrants? Either one closes the community to all new entrants, in which case we get a boring uniformity of belief and practice as well as intense mutual bitchiness, or we open the community to new entrants and every fresh wave will produce a dilution of what was there in the beginning.

This is a problem of every society, but also a problem that is peculiarly American because of the logic of assimilation, the logic of homogenization. The constant inflow of new entrants is part of the meaning of America. In that sense, it must always aim at the sky – at universality – despite all the tired old attempts to limit America to some narrow view of a Judaeo-Christian succession to the Roman

Empire. Historically and philosophically, America is that country in which every man can define himself and take what he needs from the world's heritage. It is that country in which each man can make his own authentic selection out of the entire inheritance of humanity. If he is not helped by his schools or his parents to exercise his privilege of individuation, he must self-consciously negate the conformist culture of Middle America. The first step for many today is to come loose, to try to shake off the hypnotic hold of an up-tight structure of transmitted prejudice. This is irreversible and is increasing every year. Even people who are apparently cosy in their middle aged, middle class existence are getting affected through their children by this determination to come loose. This is a painful step, a necessary break with the recent past. Of course it has produced a great deal of chaos, but that is no worse than the visible muddle of institutions that proliferate rules but are inefficient and no longer work fairly or properly. Truly we could say that the whole formal structure today makes America curiously less efficient than many other countries of the Old World.

In this context, and with the hindsight of some lessons learnt from two hundred years of American history, as well as a few from the last ten years, we might well ask about the community of the future. The community of the future would require a rethinking of fundamentals – the allocation of space, the allocation of time, the allocation of energy in the lives of human beings. It will have a macro-perspective and at the same time a micro-application. It may tie up with old and new institutions, but essentially those who enter into such communities will see beyond institutions. Some may drop out, others may cop out, and there will be those who are psychologically at a critical distance from their jobs, schools, and the entire system – psychologically outside even though for the sake of livelihood they may be inside them. There would also be those who have the imagination and the determination to create, with a minimum means, sometimes merely by throwing away excess or by juxtaposing skills that otherwise do not come together, experiments in new kinds of informal institutions.

It will take a very long time before we can really arrive at self-regenerating institutions. No society had a secret in regard to self-regenerating institutions, but there were other cultures which knew something about longevity. America knows many things, but it has still to learn the secret of institutional longevity. It took much effort from Plato to prepare the foundation for an Academy which lasted nine hundred years. In the thirteenth century groups of individuals in England set up houses, monasteries and small colleges which became the University of Oxford, which has lasted for so many centuries with some fidelity to what was there from the beginning. Americans are not unaware of the significance of such facts. Today when everything is so fragile and transient, and when they are willing, unlike earlier generations, to ponder the fact of death, they are also willing to discuss immortality on philosophical and not merely religious terms. They are now ready to find ways in which they could self-consciously thread together moments, days, weeks, months and years in their lives, and they are searching. The search is intense and poignant because there are so many mistakes, so many misfirings. And at every point, there is a re-enactment, a repetition of the same problems which are embedded in the existing structure.

One way of considering how new allocations of space, time and energy will eventually emerge is by seeing all institutions, the whole structure, in terms of a series of concentric circles. There is the inner circle of those who take decisions. We may call it the Establishment, though fortunately there is no real establishment in America which believes in itself. There is still the core constituted by those who control power and take decisions, and this is true at many levels. Outside that ring there is a large number of followers, people who are often apathetic, who seem blindly to go along, and some who will even think it unpatriotic to question decisions taken by central agencies. In the outer circle beyond the second, there are the negators and the critics. We might call them radicals and they may see themselves as revolutionaries, but essentially they are people who are more concerned with talk and analysis than with action and example. They are also the victims of the same social structure which they seek to negate and reject. These negators are nonetheless important and they certainly have played an indispensable role in the last ten years.

But beyond the negators there is still another ring in which are those who are willing to be quiet for a while, who are willing to move away from the limelight and to be engaged, to be fully occupied and even fulfilled at some level, in pioneering new ways of living, new ways of sharing. This could range from communal householders who simply learn to beat inflation by sharing their uses of time, space and money, to those who explore new avenues for the constructive concentration of energy. In this sphere we might also include people who merely get together to listen to music or to meditate. There are also those who are concerned with bolder and more ambitious experiments on a larger scale on vast farms and estates. In all of these circles the problem will persist which exists in every kind of structure. How is it possible to ensure an unconditional commitment to shared values and also to persons as sacred, an allegiance to the forms and not to the formalities?

How can we ensure that people will gain confidence in using rules so precisely that they will also have rule scepticism built into them, because they know that no general rule could ever fit a unique situation? People can conceivably gain so much confidence in the fulfilment of particular roles that they can also afford to show role flexibility and even to exemplify role transcendence. To take a simple example, we might find a man in the county administration or in a permit office who knows all the tortuous intricacies of legislation, but reciprocates an attitude of trust and is ready to show a layman how to cut corners. He knows the rules well enough to be confident that he is not violating them, but he also sees that they can be subserved and still leave room for legitimate manoeuvre, for freedom of action. To some extent this has always gone on in every society. Human beings don't have to be told to be informal. Human beings don't have to be told to see beyond laws and rules, because otherwise they could not fill up the large areas of human life which are unstructured. But where human beings become self-conscious – and this is a function of confidence in one's ability to operate the structure – they can combine precision with flexibility, mastery with transcendence.

Strange as it may seem, the most crucial factor of all in individuation is actually the immanence of death and the readiness to see through the incessant talk of catastrophe to the constant reminder of suffering that is inescapable from life. This is crucial to the present and future maturation of the American mind, but it does not involve anything that would sacrifice what is quintessential to the American Dream. Indeed, it is a kind of growing up which may for the first time make the vision of the Founding Fathers meaningful and relevant, outside the formal apparatus of rules and institutions, to creating not islands of instant Brotherhood but new areas of initiative with unprecedented avenues of commonality hospitable to the making of discoveries and the enrichment of the imagination. This demands, above all, a breaking away altogether from the very obsession with success and failure which is so corrosive to human consciousness, the obsession with external status.

Santayana, who was not an American by birth or at the time of death, thought a great deal about the American experiment and continued to ponder when he came to California. Basically he saw America as a contest between the aggressive man and the genteel woman. This sounds strange today, but it is historically very important and is relevant even now. Again and again men emerged who, though aggressive, were the purveyors of the creativity that is at the core of the American impulse. There were also women, from maiden aunts to wives, who naturally sought security, but also wished to become sophisticated, to become what they thought Americans were not. In this kind of tension between the male adventurer and the bourgeois lady, there was a constant peril to the creative impulse. A Marxist-Leninist would put this in a different way, and speak of "the bourgeoisification of the proletariat." Here came the world's proletariat, but as they became bourgeoisified, they forgot the deeper impulse behind America – which has nothing to do with class or status or structure, which has to do with the wanderer, the nomad, the free man. The original impulse became obscured, perverted into a false nationalist sentiment, a substitute for true feeling, a flight from real experience of the wide open spaces and their equivalents in the human mind.

Santayana thought that California, for the very reasons that others criticized it – its lack of gentility, its crudity, its slothfulness – would not permit maiden aunts and stylish women to set the pace. It was impossible in California for gentility to come up on top and eliminate the creative impulse. He also thought that, whereas elsewhere in America people came to exchange the strong Transcendentalism of the early years for a wishy-washy admiration of nature, here in California when people went to the Sierras they felt something deeper, a negation of argument, a negation of logic, a sense of the vanity of human life and the absurdity of so many of our structures and relationships. Nature here in California made people think beyond America itself. It made them have larger thoughts about human frailty and the fragility of human institutions in relation to the whole.

This may well be deeply relevant to the future. The future, philosophers tell us, will never resemble the past. The future is indeed much larger than the past. If one takes man's age for about twenty million years and puts it into a twenty-four hour scale, six thousand years of recorded history do not amount to half a minute. Who is entitled, on the basis of what we already know about the age of man, to set limits on the future? When people set limits on the future, history is finished for them, but not for others. There are many people today who are willing to cooperate with the future, who are not threatened by the universal extension of the logic of the American Dream to the whole of humanity, and who are also willing, despite past mistakes, to persist and to continue to make experiments in the use of space and time and energy. One day, maybe even in our lifetime, perhaps around the year 2000, there might well be those who, remembering these trying times of subtle pioneering in the surrounding gloom, could say without smugness:

> We dreamers, we derided
> We mad, blind men who see
> We bear ye witness ere ye come
> That ye shall be.

Lobero Theatre, Santa Barbara
October 20, 1975
Hermes, July 1976

UNIVERSALITY AND SECTARIANISM

Universality and sectarianism are of fundamental significance to all of us. They are interlinked with an intractable problem in relation to nature, in relation to knowledge, and in relation to what we call *Theosophia* – the Wisdom of the Ages. They are also reflected in the enigmatic relationships between past, present and future, between all three and the Eternal, between the abstract and the concrete, the manifest and the unmanifest. In the Vedic hymns we have a supreme statement of affirmation combined simultaneously with a note of agnosticism. We find this tradition in all the great Teachers of Wisdom who truly came to formulate and also to intimate, knowing that formulation could become the enemy of the unformulated. They knew that, while in a Platonic sense Time is the moving image of Eternity, there is another sense in which there is an unavoidable war between the dreams, the ideas, the potentialities that lie within Eternity and the cycles that work themselves out with highs and lows, ups and downs, through all the vicissitudes of historical time.

The problem is cosmological and metaphysical. Philosophically it becomes a problem of epistemology, of the relation between the knower and the known. Ethically it becomes a problem of action, of the relation between the individual as an actor or agent and the world that is external to him, a problem of inner and outer. And, of course, if the Theosophical Movement in time is an integral part of a vaster history that extends far beyond the recorded annals of time, then the Theosophical Movement, in our historical sense, will participate in the age-old problem. This was a distinction that H.P. Blavatsky was extremely concerned to make.

She made it in the very first article that she wrote, stating what Theosophy is, and she maintained this distinction till the end. Mystically, it is present in *The Voice of the Silence*, sometimes illuminated in the footnotes that she prepared. She was asked by the Brotherhood to hint at the distinction between the *psyche* and the *nous*, the psychic and the noetic in man and in nature. At the very end of her life she wrote her article on psychic and noetic action. All of this is deeply worth pondering upon, but it is something that each of us must do for himself, something on which there can be no formulated consensus among those who call themselves either Theosophists or students of Theosophy, least of all among formal organizations.

In a way the problem is acutely present on the political scene. It arises in the relation of world order to its materialization on the visible plane – the connection between the *cosmopolis* which is metaphysical and mystic, existing already for some though utterly irrelevant for others, and some kind of megalopolis which we would like to see emerge in the realm of political institutions. It is bound up with the problem of identity for individuals in all cultures and nations, of all races, of both sexes, of different age groups. It is involved in all the feuds of our time – those tensions which cannot be resolved merely by words, by gestures or symbols, and which cannot be resolved vicariously for the many by a few, however gifted or generous they may be as leaders of thought and opinion. It cannot be resolved for the laity by popes or bishops, swamis or lamas, self-styled or otherwise. It is a problem that is at the very core of every human being. We face the problem collectively, in all walks of life, as a problem of organizations.

Historically, it is the problem of why, at the very times and in the very places where the most ardent movements emerged in the name of the very greatest ideals, we find in those very places and springing therefrom in a subsequent period the most hideous nightmares – long shadows cast by large causes. We find this in all the syncretist movements in the nineteenth century, often succeeded by the most terrible forms of separatism. It is almost as if to speak of unity and universality, and to speak more often than one means it or more than it is possible to mean it, is to tempt the satan or the devil in every man and in collective humanity, and to invite more disorder, more division. This is an age-old story. This may well be the reason why some of the greatest students of even the recorded and over-written history of the West came to dismal, grim and pessimistic conclusions. This could be the reason why Gibbon said that history is a story of crimes, follies and misfortunes. This could be why Hegel, among philosophers, could assert that the only lesson men seem to learn from history is that they learn nothing from it.

In this larger context students of Theosophy cannot but be truly humble. There never was a suggestion, and there never could be, that by any act of association with any Theosophical organization, even by long years of study and involvement with Theosophical texts, even by long years of ethical and mystical training along Theosophical lines, that a person somehow has a privileged access to the Wisdom-Religion. No man can speak as its sole custodian or its ultimate authority. No man can claim that he is any different from other men. The very thought of separation becomes for him a wall, a barrier that will divide him both from other men and also, alas, sometimes unknown to him but often painfully so, separate him from the Great Custodians of the Wisdom-Religion. It is only appropriate, recognizing these limitations and the immensity of the fundamental problem of unravelling and using *Theosophia* in our lives, that we should turn beyond the nineteenth century, beyond the centenary cycle that began in 1875, to the Mahatmas of whom H.P. Blavatsky spoke and to the wider vision we can discern in the scriptures and the teachers of world history.

Five thousand years ago Krishna, the enigmatic and mysterious Teacher who came at the beginning of Kali Yuga, both ended a cycle and struck a keynote for the long Dark Age into which humanity would be plunged. On the battlefield of Duty, *Kurukshetra*, which was *Dharmakshetra*, he made a beautiful and puzzling statement to Arjuna – who went through all the many vagaries and ambivalences of friendship and discipleship, and indeed at the end proved himself to have been a worthy friend and pupil of Krishna though not ready for initiation. After giving Arjuna the universal vision of "the Divine Eye," Krishna said to Arjuna: "But what, 0 Arjuna, hast thou to do with so much knowledge as this? I established this whole universe with a single portion of myself, and remain separate." This statement partakes of that deeply puzzling relation between the transcendent and the immanent in all subsequent theologies and concepts of the Godhead. It is dramatically put forward here in a manner that seems to be personified and yet has the curious obscurity of an impersonal cosmic enigma. There is a world and yet there is no world. The world has a mind and a Logos, and yet it does not. There is meaning to the world and yet there is absurdity to it. There is a supreme concern and compassion in the world flowing from whatever preceded it, whatever sustains and nourishes it, whatever destroys and recreates it. At the same time there is a supreme detachment that may sound to us almost like cold indifference.

While it is a classical stance, the importance of the statement is not merely what it says about Krishna. Like everything else that a great Teacher does, it is meant to release in Arjuna authentic representations of an archetypal stance. Whatever part he chose or course of action he took, it was possible for Arjuna to have unconditional help from Krishna. It was also possible for him – in relation to his world – both to be involved and to stand outside it. This central message of that Great Teacher became a clue for ancient Brahmins who were torn between deploring the end of what looked like a Golden Age in comparison to what was emerging, and a deep concern to preserve and maintain something in the new age. It became a keynote pointing to a new modulus of growth, a principle of self-reliance not merely grounded in individual human nature but also serving as a basic pattern for social structures.

It was a very difficult lesson, hardly capable of being absorbed and assimilated by those who conservatively became attached to the existing and subsequent representations of an ideal, classical social order. At the same time, there was an awareness that the lesson could be grasped in principle by any man, especially when he had really got into a series of messes, when he had been betrayed on the basis of the trust he had put in fathers and teachers who failed him, when he was involved in all those acts of betrayal that are a part of the human inheritance. It would still be possible for him to say, "I am not abandoned," or "I do not have to insult the integrity of the universe, because if there is meaning, divinity and dignity to the world and in my life, it is always possible for me to claim it. This is my privilege. In order to be a man by self-assertion in the deepest sense, by self-definition, I shall declare my destiny as one who is proud to inhabit a human form." Hence in art, in literature and in traditions of mystical training, the celebration of the privilege of birth in a human form. It became part of the recognition that every man is given in trust that which he did not make – a potential temple in which there is an indwelling god – where Krishna is closer to each one of us than anyone else outside.

The way to that Krishna within requires a transformation and a humbling of the insecure, weak and personal self, representative of all the conflicting doubts of Arjuna. This self that wants to be loved, that wants guarantees of salvation, has got to be abandoned, to yield. Arjuna is ready for the universal vision only when he reaches that point where he ceases fault-finding and Krishna is able to say to him: "Unto thee who findeth no fault, I shall now make known this most mysterious knowledge." In all human relationships there must be a certain magical quality of trust – between mother and child, between teacher and pupil – though this is more easily seen in areas that appear mystically or morally neutral, like music, than in our ordinary encounters in society and the system. Unless there is that spontaneous ceasing of a sense of difference there will not be the possibility of the magic, the magic of pregnancy which will be fruitful, which would culminate in the birth of something meaningful and joyous – the birth of Wisdom.

We have, then, five thousand years ago, an archetypal statement of the relation between the whole and the part, the unmanifest and the manifest, the transcendent and the immanent. Krishna is both. He is the cosmic Krishna – more a force than a person, not to be understood in ordinary terms – and he is also a historical personage. The same tradition, but in another mode, is enunciated again two thousand five hundred years ago, in the coming of the Buddha. While he ridiculed the claims of any men to be the exclusive heirs, to be the custodians, the trustees in Time, of the eternal revelation, the *Sanatana Dharma*, he at the same time redefined the very notion of the Eternal Religion. The *Sanatana Dharma*, he said, is the religion which teaches that hatred ceaseth not by hatred, but by love. It is only the person exercising the extraordinarily and increasingly elusive skill of being able to draw the larger circle, of resolving and reconciling by going beyond, without getting caught in confrontations and dichotomies, who can speak authentically about the Eternal Religion.

There is an Eternal Religion written in the very hearts of men that is reinforced by the most natural modes of transmission from the old to young, from teacher to pupil, from mother to child. There are these intimations in the hearts of all human beings. There are certain things that no one can be told or need be told, because if he does not know them already, telling will never be able to instruct. These fundamental truths are not merely felt. They can also be known, but this involves conceptions of knowing and of knowledge that are remote from our time because they presuppose the dissolution of the very separation between the knower and the known. You can truly know these fundamental truths only when they cease to be external and become the very breath of your life and basis of your being. Then they set the context or perspective in which everything else may be known and identified in a more specific sense. Unless we could know something – and this would require a particular kind of meditation – about abstract, absolute, unmanifest Space, all statements that are spatial in context would have a disproportionate significance. In affirming they would also be denying. In the truth they tell they would also be lying. As with Space, so too with Time. Unless we could recover a sense of an unconditioned reality reflected in an eternal and perpetual process that far transcends all limited conceptions of times that have a beginning and an end, there would be no way by which we could emancipate ourselves from the tyranny of beginnings and endings, no way by which immortality could become not merely a right or an ideal but a fact for human beings.

Similarly with Consciousness and Motion. Unless we could visualize unconditioned consciousness we would always be liable to be caught in the conditionalities of manifested consciousness. We would be involved in illusions. How would we know this? Because every time we were involved in that which is conditioned, we would pretend that it is not and exaggerate its value. This becomes the root of what we call the problem of the ego – the problem of the shadowy self that pretends to be that which it can never be. Growing from childhood like a spoilt child, it becomes a terrible tyrant who displaces from the central throne the inner ruler, the unknown god, the Krishna within, and actually becomes the enemy, the satan. Until a person could recognize this within himself, there would be no solution to the human problem. But metaphysically he could never recognize it unless there were in that shadow a vulnerable point, a connection between that lower self and the unconditioned.

Hence the enormous significance of the assertion by the Buddha:

> Ho! ye who suffer! know
> Ye suffer from yourselves. None else compels,
> None other holds you that ye live and die,
> And whirl upon the wheel, and hug and kiss
> Its spokes of agony,
> Its tire of tears, its nave of nothingness.

You are free, but you can only assert that freedom by exercising it, and you could only exercise that freedom authentically by becoming and behaving like a man who is in awe of no one, afraid of nothing. Any other conception of human dignity or of human equality has a compensatory value. It strikes a false note. It cannot carry the certification of the absolute assurance with which Krishna speaks of immortality in the second chapter of the *Gita*, the absolute assurance with which Buddha speaks of the possibility for every man of becoming a Buddha, or the like assurance he displays at the end of his life in making light of all distinctions – between Buddhas, Bodhisattvas and hierarchies – that people try to impose upon One Universal Life.

We find the same principle in subsequent teachings. We find it in the elusive magic of the relationship of Pythagoras to his own School. He insisted upon a certain kind of acceptance by all, of their individual unimportance in relation to the collective, while at the same time he found the need for taking upon himself responsibility. In his life this meant his assumption of all ascriptions of credit. This was done to disallow anyone from corrupting the common core. He also tried to make men see it mathematically, to make men understand the supreme sovereign importance of limit, which they would better understand in the architecture of the world and of all creativity when they already had some sense of the unlimited, the illimitable. Zero must be seen and understood before we can appreciate the number series and the distinction between odd and even numbers.

Similarly, it is found in the life of Jesus, the most dramatic and tragic of incarnations in the recorded history that we have so over-celebrated and are now trying to get away from in what we call the Christian era. This extraordinary Initiate, in his own direct relations with those around him, was able to carry conviction about the indwelling Christos in every man. He made each feel much better and, indeed, a participant in the glorification of the Kingdom of God on earth. At the same time he made each one aware that nobody, not even himself, could be any more than merely a pointer to That which does not come into the world, which is not in the realm of appearances, That which will come again but which in one sense never began and never can be seen or shown in time. Understanding of this enigma underwent a complex subsequent development, which came to a certain culmination crucial to history in St. Augustine, concerning the relation between the unmanifest and the manifest, the tension between the Platonic element in Christianity and the more narrowly materialistic aspects of both Hellenic and Hebraic thought, for various reasons known only to a few who were the custodians of the other and unspoken side of both.

It is a very complex story, but knowing its subtle details is not relevant here. We do know it writ large in history in the name of the Prince of Peace. Untold bloodshed and violence have been dropped upon the human sea in the name of the meekest of men, that paradigm of saintly Initiates and Teachers who went to preach the gospel of universal love and goodwill. There emerged the most monstrously narrow and shallow claims to a historic and physical uniqueness, which people are now trying somehow to rationalize. There is something in the human mind that is insulted, the subtler the apologetics. There is also something which makes one feel "I've been that way before." Is there, then, a sense in which all of us – from wherever we come, whatever tradition we inherit in this life, whatever memories we bear from our possible previous lives – come into the Theosophical Movement in the hope of a transubstantiation that will make us free? But only as we grow older do we see the scars and the wounds in our *psyche*. We can see in each other, and more painfully in ourselves, mirror images of the fundamentalist, of the latitudinarian, of every kind of heretical denomination to be found in the Christian tradition or in all of the religious schools.

We find them even in that most crucial of arenas, the very relationship of a man, who calls himself a student of Theosophy, to Theosophy itself; the relationship of the seeker to the wisdom he seeks; the relationship of a man, who is a potential disciple of a Brotherhood of Bodhisattvas, to that Brotherhood itself. Perhaps more caricature, more ridicule, more martyrdom was psychologically experienced in the modern age by the great Teachers of Theosophy than in past ages, even though endured at a level of humorous compassion. Those Beings took the extraordinarily bold and unprecedented decision to make known publicly what was always guarded secretly – their very existence and accessibility in time to any man. Yet They themselves came to be appropriated both by individuals who tried to claim special relationships and treated Them like personal gods or household idols, and by those who transcendentalized Them out of existence.

We are dealing with a fact of human consciousness. In love, in family life, in scholarship, in the quest for truth, in the pursuit of skills in music or art – anyone may understand the profound importance of continuity of consciousness, of being true to an ideal despite one's forgetfulness and one's limitations. Surely in this realm too, it is evident that the world of the future which Theosophists wish to frame will be determined by what dominates their consciousness twenty-four hours a day and seven days of the week, as much as by the wisdom and the compassion, the energy and the ideation of Adepts. Now, when all earlier judgments which at first appeared so Olympian have subsequently proven absurd in regard to great Teachers – small men trying to size up greater Beings and put them in a Pantheon – are we going to try to have a true assessment, a correct scholarly estimate of H.P. Blavatsky? We are liable to the same error on which a whole tragic novel was written by Hermann Hesse – *The Journey to the East*. Is it not like asking, "How do I know that the Fraternity exists?" when in the very asking of that question one is defining oneself: "Because my life is meaningless, I may think the universe is meaningless. Scriptures are empty and do not speak, but let me be careful." We may fall into the trap but how long do we stay in it? Do we give ourselves a chance to come out of it? Or do we box the compass and become unwitting partners in our own self-destruction? This is a fateful question bound up with the problem of survival – psychological survival for men and women today at all levels of the contemporary revolution.

The only persons who can psychologically accommodate themselves to the kind of world we live in and which is emerging are those who can authentically inherit the whole of human history, even though most of it is unknown to us. Which of us can say: "Everything human is deeply relevant and meaningful to me, and where I cannot know, at least I will not condemn. Even if I cannot understand the myths of particular peoples, the scriptures of other times, the languages, the cultures, the folkways of other men which may be strange to me, let me not mock, let me not make a great thing of my pathetic ignorance. Let me be silent. Let me be open. Let me in some way that is natural to me show that I too can acclimatize myself to the more rarefied altitudes of world citizenship that are authentic, that are more than mere assertions of goodwill, but are filled with a positive enjoyment and exaltation at every kind of human endeavour, every form of excellence as well as positive appreciation for every kind of struggle and compassion for every kind of failure."

Unless a man can do this, can he even survive into the future? There are those who are afraid they cannot, who therefore want to write about the end of history, but only find themselves unable to communicate with others who, though young, weak-willed, lazy, lonely, spoilt and everything else, still know something else – that they are not going to play that game. They do not want sophistication at that price. They do not want a packaged Great Books from whichever university. They can see through that. They at least want to be able to feel that inwardly they can extend a hand to the wretched of the earth, that they can understand what it means to take one's place in the great galaxy of mankind's history. Minimally, they are willing to stand in the backstage of the theatre on which world history is being played.

This is a crucial question. For some it may seem that the world "outside" has very little relevance to the Theosophical Movement as it was constituted in 1875. To others it might seem exactly the opposite. It may well be that in the world outside more has been gained and more is at stake that involves Theosophical issues than we shall ever be able to recognize within the narrower groups and organizations that are called Theosophical. Stranger things have happened in the history of man. Today there are men outside the countries where Krishna taught and the Buddha preached to whom Krishna and the Buddha are more meaningful than they are to those who might claim a kind of inherited relationship to them purely because of race or pride of birth, but who cannot sustain that relationship or be credible in it. Equally, there may be those who do not call themselves Theosophists but who may better understand what is at the core, what is at stake, in the great drama of coming events.

H.P. Blavatsky, of course, wrote about this. In her letter to the Archbishop of Canterbury she pointed out that there were many people calling themselves Christian who simply did not find it convenient or possible to speak frankly but who knew more than the subtlest and even seemingly generous liberal flights of the theologians. Something more was at stake which has now increasingly come to the fore. The man in the pew might for many reasons have gone along with what came from the pulpit, but inwardly he was asking himself questions and making distinctions. There are people all over the world, of whatever race or religion, or totally uprooted in every feasible cultural and social sense, who understand intuitively authentic affirmations of universal needs, of universal propositions that are fundamental, of universal compassion and charity. A Yevtushenko could understand and celebrate a Martin Luther King more than his own compatriots. It is possible for men in far places to identify with those forerunners, few and far between, of the authentic language of the human race. To take a magnificent phrase of Stringfellow Barr, "Let us join the human race." Anyone can join the human race. There are many young people who are afraid to be joiners, no doubt for a variety of reasons, some of whom are seekers, and seekers who perhaps need more help than they know. But there is also a sense in which whatever one joins that is universal will not limit one's capacity to communicate with or reach out to anything outside.

These are curious, inchoate, compelling and sometimes contradictory demands upon the human sea. Does Theosophy, in its primordial statement by H.P. Blavatsky, show an awareness of all of this? Surely the only way to know is by reading what she said. In her articles she gave many definitions, and that was always typical of her. She constantly varied, like an Indian musician, the manner in which she expressed herself. She was a dialectician. She did not want people to get fixated on particular formulations, and she varied them so much that only years of commitment allow one to recognize the immense inner consistency of her work, the pointing to That which is beyond, to which all forms of music point – That which is the Soundless, the music of the spheres. We find this in her writings, archetypally, again and again. One has to read every word carefully, which is difficult, because most of us have lost that habit, and some of us have never learnt it. But if we are going to value the privilege of reading her, then surely we should assume she meant the words that she used. It takes years before one comes to see, given the limitations of language, the multi-dimensional nature of what she is saying.

In the article "What is Theosophy?" she declares: "With every man that is earnestly searching in his own way after a knowledge of the Divine Principle, of man's relation to it" – not his own, but man's relation to it "and Nature's manifestation of it, Theosophy is allied." If Theosophy is allied with this, then it is less so with any man who is not earnestly searching but merely claiming second-hand knowledge of that symbol or token of the Divine Principle to which he wishes to pay allegiance or by which he wishes to be saved. It is less allied with those men who are more concerned with being left out, or with their own relationship to the universe than they are with the relationship of all men or of man as a species to the universe. It is less allied to those men who think that Theosophy is only to be found in the written word or in so-called great examples of art and music, but who cannot read it in the heavens every night, read it in their dawn meditation – in that which is so profound and yet so unmanifest – who cannot read it in what can be seen in every aspect of nature's infinite library – superb and supreme teaching where everything is covered and hidden, but everything is expressed. Everything is a veil upon that which is yet to be found.

Growth is invisible. It is under the soil. Yet the visible is an immense representation of the diversity and the variety sustained by a central unity in growth, the one in the many. The relation between the abstract and the concrete can be seen and shown in any child or in any tree. People refuse to recognize, however, that there is any connection between all of that and themselves, and are more concerned to come to a correct judgment in regard to which book will help them or how they should regard H.P. Blavatsky. They are fortunate whose innocence and ignorance protect them from childhood and make them feel that with Teachers of Wisdom, whoever they be, there is no such thing as half-hearted commitment. You either commit yourself a hundred percent, or you do not bother about it.

This is built into the Indian tradition. If an Indian boy wants to go and make claims on behalf of religious teachers, a wise mother may often tell him, "No, choose another profession." Religion does not have to do with making claims or with reconciling them, but with transcending everything that divides men. All of us must come to know for ourselves – and each one can only speak for himself – that if we are going to be serious about committing ourselves to the study, the practice and above all, the service, of the wisdom in *The Secret Doctrine* and *The Voice of the Silence*, then that commitment must be complete at some level. It must be unconditional at the very core, even though we may participate as fallible and personal beings in ups and downs, the vagaries of the implications of that commitment. Each must choose a particular way, and each one must choose his own, but let there be no doubt that we can ever come any closer to the Wisdom without an immense gratitude, a profound unqualified reverence for the Teachers.

"From the Teachings to the Teacher" can have meaning as a motto only if we understand that with the Teachers there is no dilly-dallying, no game-playing. This is as old as the wisdom of mankind, as old as all the Orders and goes beyond the Orders in the East. Whenever H.P. Blavatsky speaks of her Teachers, it is with a reverence that exalts her with a beauty, a feeling, an *eros* that is magical. When she spoke at the end of her life about herself, the only claim she made, and was rightfully insistent upon making, was that "Never for one moment have I denied or doubted Him, my Teacher." She invoked – and there is a lot of complicated paradox and irony in that – the servant in *As You Like It*, to illustrate her point. She quoted the statement: "Master, go on; and I will follow thee to the last gasp, with truth and loyalty." Anyone reading this should know that it is real, that it is a hallmark of the true Teacher. You can tell it at any time. But he should also know that he is in no position to make any assessments of her, but simply to desire to learn at her feet, and to look where she pointed to Those beyond her, to the Path of which she spoke. Whoever is able to take such a decision with a natural simplicity will find that it makes all the difference to their own particular life. What some few do as naturally as breathing they will also find, in their lives, has been possible for other rare individuals in every part of the world. These men do not happen, like Topsy. They are not *lusus naturae* or accidents. These men can never be explained empirically. They are souls, incarnating the vested wisdom of the maturity of the past in the context of the present, pointing to the future. They are the true Theosophists of whom H.P. Blavatsky spoke – Theosophists who are the friends of all living beings.

This is not to deny that any one of us can self-consciously recover an authentic universality, remain within and yet refuse to be enclosed within the sectarianism of every single person, whether on the religious, the political, the social or even the Theosophical plane. Of course *something* can be done about it. That was why H.P. Blavatsky came. To do *everything* about it is to prepare oneself for the Path, for discipleship, for initiation. She pointed out that it was the Buddha who decided – for no one else could take that decision – that in a humanity that was old in the Dark Ages, the rules could not be relaxed, but the access to the Mysteries could be increased for all. Hence many new and subtle guises of the age-old relationship most connected with the sacred – that between the esoteric and the exoteric – will be available. Anyone may wish to become a companion of the Brotherhood of Initiates. Everyone in life may go through many initiations on many planes in many forms. But if he is sensitive and delicate, and in this is authentic and concerned with the sacred, he is going to be suspicious of people who talk about it out of season, people who call attention to it. He is going to be as embarrassed as any man would be in speaking too openly about parents he loves or about those closest to him, to those for whom it may mean nothing. He knows better than that. Of course this has been done in the name of religion. It is the standard compensatory device offered, but it never worked. It did not work for the Brahmins, nor did it work in any single religion, whether for the Jews, the Egyptians, or Christians; and it is not going to work for Theosophists today. But that does not mean that men should be caught in the dichotomy between saying, "Oh, the sacred doesn't exist," and on the other hand, becoming insanely anxious about it.

There is always a middle way. It is always possible for a person to gain access into the most exalted chambers of initiation, to take his place in various sanctuaries, even in this day and age, anywhere in this world. But whoever he be, he can only do that by taking vows, assuming trials with a certain courage, with a certain detachment, with an authentic compassion to do it only for the sake of the whole, and with a deliberate decision to be utterly uninvolved in worry, let alone waste of energy, on behalf of his own salvation. This requires a break with the salvationism that may have been part and parcel of the Piscean Age, but will have no place in the future. W.Q. Judge wrote of that future moment "when powers will be needed and pretensions will go for naught." That was perhaps true even in his own day for a few. Today it is true at all levels. Above all, no one can make or unmake the invisible degrees to which souls belong, nor can they easily be known because those who know will never tell, and those who tell, by definition, do not know. In regard to the invisible, spiritual stature of any human being, those who truly know are pledged to eternal secrecy, and those who are outside can never know by definition. This is analogous to the Wittgensteinian affirmation in regard to immortality, as well as to the

Shavian aphorism comparing marriage and freemasonry.

There is a sense in which self-definition or self-validation becomes an authentic key towards a great universality. It opens doors and we can test it in terms of our capacity to come closer to, communicate with, and become credible to more and more human beings wherever they be, whatever their language, their upbringing, their external labours. It does not happen automatically with a Constitution, even where that Constitution had behind it the blessing and the benediction and the deliberation of Adepts, such as that of the United States of America. Canada may be fortunate to know that while America aimed higher than any historical society, it failed so greatly too, that now the aim and the failure have both to be reckoned with. The time may yet come when *Theosophia* alone, in the broad and the deep sense, could provide the only metaphysical basis for the U.S.A., for Canada, or for any vast experiment that is, like the Greek *polis*, a microcosm of mankind. There is enough in Theosophy to be relevant by translation and application to every single problem.

When H.P. Blavatsky speaks of the universal solvent of *Akasa* and the true philosopher's stone, if one is very serious one is either going to find out something about them or one is going to say, "Well, there is something I don't know." Alas, there will be many who will never even notice the deadly earnestness with which such profound matters were spoken of in *The Secret Doctrine*. Many of the greatest minds of the age are looking for the equivalent to $E = mc^2$ which will apply to a variety of fields. They seek a philosopher's stone. Leading men in various fields of thought know enough now to realize that there is something more that could not be known by the existing methodologies and presuppositions. They are not concerned with which book you find it in. They seek to know individuals, multi-lingual in a conceptual sense, who can help. They also sense that someone who really knew would not help them unless they deserved it, unless there is a reasonable likelihood that they will not misuse the help. The universal solvent and the elixir of life are realities and not metaphorical expressions. Why, then, do we who inherit so much tend to narrow the universe and put it in a little box, instead of mirroring the universe in a grain of sand and seeing it there mirrored? Instead of doing that of which the poets and the mystics speak, why do we try to behave like those individuals who, when the Bodhisattva in the guise of an elephant came striding majestically, simply clung to their particular metaphorical planks of salvation which the compassionate elephant swept aside on its way.

Adepts, Mahatmas, and Universal Beings are not here to consolidate anyone's pet ideas, pet likes and dislikes, but watch over those who can appreciate and enjoy what is involved in the gait of a noble elephant, who will accept it like children, who will cling to nothing. Yet many people, because of fears that are understandable enough, want to save something and therefore there is sectarianism. Coleridge put the problem very well in regard to Christianity, but it is true equally in regard to Theosophy. He who loves Christianity more than every other religion will love his own sect more than every other sect, and in the end love himself best of all. There is a logical and psychological connection between egocentricity and claims on behalf of the uniqueness of institutions or of formulations. This much is by now clear in relation to each other's orthodoxies and isms, and every man is desperately wanting to get out of the problem within himself in some way. But there is no technique. Authentic solutions involve a redefinition of self, a breakthrough – from the realm of *kama manas*, the psychic self, with its elaborate and boring history of likes and dislikes, fears and personal memories – to the sphere of the noetic, with its golden moments of freedom of awareness, which every human soul has and which may be threaded together on a single strand.

So the problem again becomes one of sifting and of recovering continuity of consciousness. When a person is able to do these things, he can rise to those planes of consciousness where the great universal archetypal ideas are ever-present. He will also have a due wisdom in rendering them into the language and the form that is best suited to meet human need and to serve the circumstances of people's space and time. Since he would see every human being as a mirror of the whole of humanity, he would not think statistically about humanity, but know that each individual is infinitely important. He would, in other words, become an apprentice in the art of the dialectic so magnificently exemplified by the Buddha, who said different things to different individuals because he knew that the Teaching was multi-dimensional. Something of what he did under trees and on the great dusty pathways of a vast, teeming, and torrid country, of which we have images in fables, myths and legends that as much conceal as reveal what really happened, could well be true now in another form. In the old days wisdom was veiled by various devices – cryptic devices, codes, cyphers, glyphs, symbols – but also by saying too little. In our time wisdom is veiled by seeming to say too much. There is a luminous nature in *The Secret Doctrine* enabling an incredible concealment which the Intuitive student can gradually learn to enjoy. The most ineluctable forms of priceless magic and incantatory mantramic teaching reside within the foliage of references that connect at many points with the complicated and many-sided story of the soul of man.

That, then, is our heritage. It is universal not merely in an abstract sense. It has amazing diversity, and the variety is infinite, as is the wonderment of the Theosophical enterprise. But the point is not whether a person goes this far or adopts that way, but whether at any level he is able to develop the fruit of his study and meditation into an authentic capacity to draw the larger circle. We should truly try to put ourselves in a proper mental relationship – for some of us this may come naturally, for others this may be a strain, but every man could attempt it – to the Brotherhood, to the Mahatmas, to Beings like H.P. Blavatsky. We should see her in a long lineage of Teachers and do the same in regard to one or all the Teachers. We may choose any as our particular *Ishtaguru*. If we could really do this, then it would truly be possible to become capable of negating those thought-forms that become divisive sources of human suspicion. It would become possible to make that extraordinarily elusive linkage between the eternal and the momentary but timely, the appropriate and the relevant, the abstract and the concrete – the dynamic relationship implicit in the divine dialectic.

This is challenging because synonymous with living. But when a person does it with the help of the knowledge that he gains from Theosophical Teachers, it is living dangerously. It is living with a new self-consciousness, living with increased pain and anguish on behalf of human beings, living with great heightening of joy that may make one manic at times with regard to the Divine Dance of the whole of life and of history. That is why people today and in the future are really going to make *Theosophia* important in their lives, especially the young, the lost and the rootless. It is a whole way of life. It is too late for the equivalent of going to churches on Sundays, synagogues on Saturdays, mosques on Fridays, temples on Mondays, and so on. It is too late to find the equivalent of all the elaborate complexities of human attitudes towards the Vedas or the Bible in our attitudes towards Theosophical texts. It is the all or nothing attitude that could be dangerous on the plane of the mind but is, for many, part of the historical compulsion of our time.

Therefore, as the Maha Chohan stated in his letter, unless Theosophy can be shown to be relevant to the most crucial problems that affect mankind as a whole, and involve ultimate questions in regard to the very struggle for existence and the meaning of life, Theosophy will not be relevant. The Fraternity will have nothing to do with it. Perish the thought, says He, rather than that They should have anything to do with anything that evades the crucial issue – the full demands of universal brotherhood in thought, feeling, word and deed. So They have spoken. They have spoken in terms of the immensity of the challenge. The Theosophical Movement of the nineteenth century, like the Constitution of the United States, is an educational phenomenon where the invisible Founding Fathers knew that it might take a hundred years for people both to see that it is not easy and that while it looks irrelevant, it had better be made relevant. This may take the coming hundred years for those individuals who really are alive to the problems of our time and worthy of the enormous privilege of the inheritance that they have as students of Theosophy. They must at the same time have the proper posture in regard to the Fraternity of Teachers who are invisible, but who could become more real than anything else, according to a person's degree of development. Anyone could come to see in the future a new relevance, a new magic, a new significance to the work of H.P. Blavatsky and her predecessors.

Therefore, as the 1975 cycle unfolds, we must become less apologetic in every sense on behalf of, or about, any aspect of the Teachings, and we need be less concerned with claims. But at the same time we have to be immensely and actively concerned with the effective embodiment and translation of Theosophical ideas and principles that can be seeds for meditation, because the pioneers of the future want to learn about meditation. If they cannot learn it under a banyan tree, they are willing to learn it in a cafe. But they seriously want to learn about it. Of course, there are many mistakes that they could make. How could we be of any help unless we ourselves have attempted it enough to be humble about ourselves, while at the same time remaining proud about the undertaking. One might say that the Theosophist of the coming cycle will be the kind of person who will show himself not merely by his acts, but by the whole of his mental attitude to other beings, from the most exalted to the most wretched. He will show that it is more important to travel than to arrive; that there is a difference between perfection and perfectibility; that it is true, as Samuel Butler wrote, that everything matters more than we think it does, and at the same time nothing matters so much as we think. It is true that to become a Buddha is impossibly difficult, but it is equally true that it could be said of every man "Look inward: thou art Buddha."

Theosophy must be both as elusive as the empyrean of the most universal kinds of space, time, motion and matter, and as close to home and as real as our daily breathing. It must be relevant to our every problem. This will be eternally enigmatic. In a Platonic sense this could never be taught, could never be learned, but could only be developed by a series of intimations – efforts at living by these ideas – so that the whole world becomes for every one of us, as it became for Arjuna, a *Kurukshetra*, a theatre of trial, a tremendous drama in which the stakes are high. But the stakes are not high for us as separate beings who are going to be individually saved or damned. They are high for us all collectively, even at a time in which there is a great deal of absurdity. We must learn to become the psychological equivalents of those who can ascend and descend into the depths like divers, adapting ourselves to different altitudes and perspectives, becoming flexible and multi-dimensional. And we must do this with a certain panache, but in every case as the result of honest striving, and with compassion, with laughter and love. This is existentially to show what it means in our time to be a true Theosophist, and anyone who wishes to do this might well reflect upon the timeless injunction of Mahatma K.H.: "If you wish to know us, study our philosophy. If you wish to serve us, serve our Humanity."

Presidential Address
North American Theosophical Convention
Toronto, October 8, 1971

Hermes, June 1976

THE GOSPEL ACCORDING TO ST. JOHN

> *Let us beware of creating a darkness at noonday for ourselves by gazing, so to say, direct at the sun ... , as though we could hope to attain adequate vision and perception of Wisdom with mortal eyes. It will be the safer course to turn our gaze on an image of the object of our quest.*
>
> – The Athenian Stranger
> Plato

Every year more than three hundred and fifty Catholic and Protestant sects observe Easter Sunday, celebrating the Resurrection of Jesus, the Son of God who called himself the Son of Man. So too do the Russian and Greek Orthodox churches, but on a separate calendar. Such is the schism between East and West within Christendom regarding this day, which always falls on the ancient Sabbath, once consecrated to the Invisible Sun, the sole source of all life, light and energy. If we wish to understand the permanent possibility of spiritual resurrection taught by the Man of Sorrows, we must come to see both the man and his teaching from the pristine perspective of Brahma Vach, the timeless oral utterance behind and beyond all religions, philosophies and sciences throughout the long history of mankind.

The Gospel According to St. John is the only canonical gospel with a metaphysical instead of an historical preamble. We are referred to that which was in the beginning. In the New English Bible, the recent revision of the authorized version produced for the court of King James, we are told: Before all things were made was the Word. In the immemorial, majestic and poetic English of the King James version, *In the beginning was the Word and the Word was with God, and the Word was God*. This is a *bija sutra*, a seminal maxim, marking the inception of the first of twenty-one chapters of the gospel, and conveying the sum and substance of the message of Jesus. John, according to Josephus, was at one time an Essene and his account accords closely with the *Qumran Manual of Discipline*. The gospel attributed to John derives from the same oral tradition as the Synoptics, but it shows strong connections with the Pauline epistles as well as with the Jewish apocalyptic tradition. It is much more a mystical treatise than a biographical narrative.

Theosophically, there is no point or possibility for any man to anthropomorphize the Godhead, even though this may be very touching in terms of filial devotion to one's own physical father. The Godhead is *unthinkable* and *unspeakable*, extending boundlessly beyond the range and reach of thought. There is no supreme father figure in the universe. In the beginning was the Word, the *Verbum*, the *Shabdabrahman*, the eternal radiance that is like a veil upon the attributeless Absolute. If all things derive, as St. John explains, from that One Source, then all beings and all the sons of men are forever included. Metaphysically, every human being has more than one father, but on the physical plane each has only one. Over a thousand years or thirty generations, everyone has more ancestors than there are souls presently incarnated on earth. Each one participates in the ancestry of all mankind. While always true, this is more evident in a nation with mixed ancestries. Therefore it is appropriate here that we think of him who preached before Jesus, the Buddha, who taught that we ask not of a man's descent but of his conduct. *By their fruits they shall be known*, say the gospels.

There is another meaning of the 'Father' which is relevant to the opportunity open to every human being to take a decision to devote his or her entire life to the service of the entire human family. The ancient Jews held that from the illimitable *Ain-Soph* there came a reflection, which could never be more than a partial participation in that illimitable light which transcends manifestation. This reflection exists in the world as archetypal humanity – Adam Kadmon. Every human being belongs to one single humanity, and that collectivity stands in relation to the *Ain-Soph* as any one human being to his or her own father. It is no wonder that Pythagoras – *Pitar Guru*, "father and teacher," as he was known among the ancient Hindus – came to Krotona to sound the keynote of a long cycle now being reaffirmed for an equally long period in the future. He taught his disciples to honour their father and their mother, and to take a sacred oath to the Holy Fathers of the human race, the "Ancestors of the Arhats."

We are told in the fourth Stanza of *Dzyan* that the Fathers are the Sons of Fire, descended from a primordial host of *Logoi*. They are self-existing rays streaming forth from a single, central, universal Mahatic fire which is within the cosmic egg, just as differentiated matter is outside and around it. There are seven sub-divisions within *Mahat* – the cosmic mind, as it was called by the Greeks – as well as seven dimensions of matter outside the egg, giving a total of fourteen planes, fourteen worlds. Where we are told by John that Jesus said, *In my Father's house are many mansions*, H.P. Blavatsky states that this refers to the seven mansions of the central Logos, supremely revered in all religions as the Solar Creative Fire. Any human being who has a true wakefulness and thereby a sincere spirit of obeisance to the divine demiurgic intelligence in the universe, of which he is a trustee even while encased within the lethargic carcass of matter, can show that he is a man to the extent to which he exhibits divine manliness through profound gratitude, a constant recognition and continual awareness of the One Source. All the great Teachers of humanity point to a single source beyond themselves. Many are called but few are chosen by self-election. Spiritual Teachers always point upwards for each and every man and woman alive, not for just a few. They work not only in the visible realm for those immediately before them, but, as John reminds us, they come from above and work for all. They continually think of and love every being that lives and breathes, mirroring "the One that breathes breathless" in ceaseless contemplation, overbrooding the Golden Egg of the universe, the *Hiranyagarbha*.

Such beautiful ideas enshrined in magnificent myths are provocative to the ratiocinative mind and suggestive to the latent divine discernment of Buddhic intuition. The only way anyone can come closer to the Father in Heaven – let alone come closer to Him on earth Who is as He is in Heaven – is by that light to which John refers in the first chapter of the *Gospel*. It is the light that lighteth every man who cometh into the world, which the darkness comprehendeth not. Human beings are involved in the darkness of illusion, of self-forgetfulness, and forgetfulness of their divine ancestry. The whole of humanity may be regarded as a garden of gods but all men and women are fallen angels or gods tarnished by forgetfulness of their true eternal and universal mission. Every man or woman is born for a purpose. Every person has a divine destiny. Every individual has a unique contribution to make, to enrich the lives of others, but no one can say what this is for anyone else. Each one has to find it, first by arousing and kindling and then by sustaining and nourishing the little lamp within the heart. There alone may be lit the true Akashic fire upon the altar in the hidden temple of the God which lives and breathes within. This is the sacred fire of true awareness which enables a man to come closer to the one universal divine consciousness which, in its very brooding upon manifestation, is the father-spirit. In the realm of matter it may be compared to the wind that bloweth where it listeth. Any human being could become a self-conscious and living instrument of that universal divine consciousness of which he, as much as every other man or woman, is an effulgent ray.

This view of man is totally different from that which has, alas, been preached in the name of Jesus. Origen spoke of the constant crucifixion of Jesus, declaring that there is not a day on earth when he is not reviled. But equally there is not a time when others do not speak of him with awe. He came with a divine protection provided by a secret bond which he never revealed except by indirect intonation. Whenever the Logos becomes flesh, there is sacred testimony to the Great Sacrifice and the Great Renunciation – of all Avatars, all Divine Incarnations. This Brotherhood of Blessed Teachers is ever behind every attempt to enlighten human minds, to summon the latent love in human hearts for all humanity, to fan the sparks of true compassion in human beings into the fires of Initiation. The mark of the Avatar is that in him the Paraclete, the Spirit of Eternal Truth, manifests so that even the blind may see, the deaf may hear, the lame may walk, the unregenerate may gain confidence in the possibility and the promise of Self-redemption.

In one of the most beautiful passages penned on this subject, the profound essay entitled "*The Roots of Ritualism in Church and Masonry,*" published in 1889, H.P. Blavatsky declared:

> Most of us believe in the survival of the Spiritual Ego, in Planetary Spirits and *Nirmanakayas*, those great Adepts of the past ages, who, renouncing their right to Nirvana, remain in our spheres of being, not as 'spirits' but as complete spiritual human Beings. Save their

corporeal, visible envelope, which they leave behind, they remain as they were, in order to help poor humanity, as far as can he done without sinning against Karmic Law. This is the 'Great Renunciation,' indeed; an incessant, conscious self-sacrifice throughout aeons and ages till that day when the eyes of blind mankind will open and, instead of the few, *all* will see the universal truth. These Beings may well be regarded as God and Gods – if they would but allow the fire in our hearts, at the thought of that purest of all sacrifices, to be fanned into the flame of adoration, or the smallest altar in their honour. But they will not. Verily, 'the secret heart is fair Devotion's (only) temple,' and any other, in this case, would be no better than profane ostentation.

Let a man be without external show such as the Pharisees favoured, without inscriptions such as the Scribes specialized in, and without arrogant and ignorant self-destructive denial such as that of the Sadducees. Such a man, whether he be of any religion or none, of whatever race or nation or creed, once he recognizes the existence of a Fraternity of Divine Beings, a Brotherhood of Buddhas, Bodhisattvas and Christs, an Invisible Church (in St. Augustine's phrase) of living human beings ever ready to help any honest and sincere seeker, he will thereafter cherish the discovery within himself. He will guard it with great reticence and grateful reverence, scarcely speaking of his feeling to strangers or even to friends. When he can do this and maintain it, and above all, as John says in the *Gospel*, be true to it and live by it, then he may make it for himself, as Jesus taught, the way, the truth and the light. While he may not be self-manifested as the Logos came to be through Jesus – the Son of God become the Son of Man – he could still sustain and protect himself in times of trial. No man dare ask for more. No man could do with less.

Jesus knew that his own time of trial had come – the time for the consummation of his vision – on the Day of Passover. Philo Judaeus, who was an Aquarian in the Age of Pisces, gave an intellectual interpretation to what other men saw literally, pointing out that the spiritual passover had to do with passing over earthly passions. Jesus, when he knew the hour had come for the completion of his work and the glorification of his father to whom he ever clung, withdrew with the few into the Garden of Gethsemane. He did not choose them, he said. They chose him. He withdrew with them and there they all used the time for true prayer to the God within. Jesus had taught, *Go into thy closet and pray to thy father who is in secret,* and that, *The Kingdom of God is within you.* This was the mode of prayer which he revealed and exemplified to those who were ready for initiation into the Mysteries. Many tried but only few stayed with it. Even among those few there was a Peter, who would thrice deny Jesus. There was the traitor, Judas, who had already left the last supper that evening, having been told, *That thou doest, do quickly.* Some among the faithful spent their time in purification. Were they, at that point, engaged in self-purification for their own benefit? What had Jesus taught them? Could one man separate himself from any other? He had told those who wanted to stone the adulteress, *Let him who is without sin cast the first stone.* He had told them not to judge anyone else, but to wait for true judgment. Because they had received a sublime privilege, about which other men subsequently argued for centuries and produced myriad heresies and sects, in their case the judgment involved their compassionate concern to do the sacred Work of the Father for the sake of all. The Garden of Gethsemane is always here. It is a place very different from the Wailing Wall where people gnash their teeth and weep for themselves or their tribal ancestors. The Garden of Gethsemane is wherever on earth men and women want to cleanse themselves for the sake of being more humane in their relations with others.

Nor was the crucifixion only true of Jesus and those two thieves, one of whom wanted to have a miracle on his behalf while the other accepted the justice of the law of the day, receiving punishment for offences that he acknowledged openly. Every man participates in that crucifixion. This much may be learnt from the great mystics and inspired poets across two thousand years. Christos is being daily, hourly, every moment crucified within the cross of every human being. There are too few on earth who are living up to the highest possibility of human god-like wisdom, love and compassion, let alone who can say that in them the spirit of Truth, the Paraclete, manifests. Who has the courage to chase the money-changers of petty thoughts and paltry desires from the Temple of the universal Spirit, not through hatred of the money-changers, but through a love in his heart for the Restoration of the Temple? Who has the courage to say openly what all men recognize inwardly when convenient, or when drunk, or when among friends whom they think they trust? Who is truly a man? How many men are there heroically suffering? Not only do we know that God is not mocked and that as we sow, so shall we reap, but we also realize that the Garden of Gethsemane is difficult to reach. Nonetheless, it may be sought by any and every person who wants to avoid the dire tragedy of self-annihilation. Indeed, there are many such people all around who barely survive from day to day because of their own self-hatred, self-contempt and despair, and who tremble on the brink of moral death. We live in terribly tragic times, and therefore there is no one who cannot afford to take a little pause for the sake of making the burden of one's presence easier for one's wife or husband, for one's children, or for one's neighbours. Each needs a time of re-examination, a time for true repentance, a time for Christ-like resolve. The Garden of Gethsemane is present wherever there is genuineness, determination and honesty. Above all, it is where there is the joyous recognition that, quite apart from yesterday and tomorrow, right now a person can create so strong a current of thought that it radically affects the future. He could begin now, and acquire in time a self-sustaining momentum. But this cannot be done without overcoming the karmic gravity of all the self-destructive murders of human beings that he has participated in on the plane of thought, on the plane of feeling, especially on the plane of words, and also, indirectly, on the plane of outward action.

If the Garden of Gethsemane did not exist, no persecuting Saul could ever become a Paul. Such is the great hope and the glad tiding. As Origen said, Saul had to be killed before Paul could be born. The Francis who was a simple crusader had to die before the Saint of Assisi could be born. Because all men have free will, no man can transform himself without honest and sincere effort. Hence, after setting out the nature of the Gods, the Fathers of the human race, H.P. Blavatsky, in the same article quoted, spoke of the conditions of probation of incarnated souls seeking resurrection:

> . . . every true Theosophist holds that the divine HIGHER SELF of every mortal man is of the same essence as the essence of these Gods. Being, moreover, endowed with free-will, hence having, more than

they, responsibility, we regard the incarnated EGO as far superior to, if not more divine than, any spiritual INTELLIGENCE *still awaiting incarnation*. Philosophically, the reason for this is obvious, and every metaphysician of the Eastern school will understand it. The incarnated EGO has odds against it which do not exist in the case of a pure divine Essence unconnected with matter; the latter has no personal merit, whereas the former is on his way to final perfection through the trials of existence, of pain and suffering.

It is up to each one to decide whether to make this suffering constructive, these trials meaningful, these tribulations a golden opportunity for self-transformation and spiritual resurrection.

If this decision is not made voluntarily during life, it is thrust upon each ego at death. Every human being has to pass at the moment of death, according to the wisdom of the ancients, to a purgatorial condition in which there is a separation of the immortal individuality. It is like a light which is imprisoned during waking life, a life which is a form of sleep within the serpent coils of matter. This god within is clouded over by the fog of fear, superstition and confusion, and all but the pure in heart obscure the inner light by their demonic deceits and their ignorant denial of the true heart. Every human being needs to cast out this shadow, just as he would throw away an old garment, says Krishna, or just as he would dump into a junkyard an utterly unredeemable vehicle. Any and every human being has to do the same on the psychological plane. Each is in the same position. He has to discard the remnants, but the period for this varies according to each person. This involves what is called "the mathematics of the soul." Figures are given to those with ears to hear, and there is a great deal of detailed application to be made.

Was Jesus exempt from this? He wanted no exception. He had taken the cross. He had become one with other men, constantly taking on their limitations, exchanging his finer life-atoms for their gross life-atoms – the concealed thoughts, the unconscious hostilities, the chaotic feelings, the ambivalences, the ambiguities, the limitations of all. He once said, *My virtue has gone out of me*, when the hem of his garment was touched by a woman seeking help, but does this mean that he was exposed only when he physically encountered other human beings?

The Gospel according to John makes it crisply clear, since it is the most mystical and today the most meaningful of the four gospels, that this was taking place all the time. It not only applies to Jesus. It takes place all the time for every person, often unknown to oneself. But when it is fully self-conscious, the pain is greater, such as when a magnanimous Adept makes a direct descent from his true divine estate, leaving behind his finest elements, like Surya the sun in the myth who cuts off his lustre for the sake of entering into a marriage with Sanjna, coming into the world, and taking on the limitations of all. The Initiator needs the three days in the tomb, but these three days are metaphorical. They refer to what is known in the East as a necessary gestation state when the transformation could be made more smoothly from the discarded vehicle which had been crucified.

People tend to fasten upon the wounds and the blood, even though, as Titian's painting portrays clearly, the tragedy of Jesus was not in the bleeding wounds but in the ignorance and self-limitation of the disciples. He had promised redemption to anyone and everyone who was true to him, which meant, he said, to love each other. He had washed the feet of the disciples, drawn them together, given them every opportunity so that they would do the same for each other. He told them that they need only follow this one commandment. We know how difficult it is for most people today to love one another, to work together, to pull together, to cooperate and not compete, to add and not subtract, to multiply and serve, not divide and rule. This seems very difficult especially in a hypocritical society filled with deceit and lies. What are children to say when their parents ask them to tell the truth and they find themselves surrounded by so many lies? In the current cycle the challenge is most pointed and poignant. More honesty is needed, more courage, more toughness – this time for the sake of all mankind. One cannot leave it to a future moment for some pundits in theological apologetics and theosophical hermeneutics to say this cycle was only for some chosen people. Every single part of the world has to be included and involved.

The teaching of Jesus was a hallowed communication of insights, a series of sacred glimpses, rather than a codification of doctrine. He presented not a *summa theologica* or *ethica*, but the seminal basis from which an endless series of *summae* could be conceived. He initiated a spiritual current of sacred dialogue, individual exploration and communal experiment in the quest for divine wisdom. He taught the beauty of acquiescence and the dignity of acceptance of suffering – a mode appropriate to the Piscean Age. He showed salvation – through love, sacrifice and faith – of the regenerated *psyche* that cleaves to the light of *nous*. He excelled in being all things to all men while remaining utterly true to himself and to his "Father in Heaven." He showed a higher respect for the Temple than its own custodians. At the same time he came to found a new kind of kingdom and to bring a message of joy and hope. He came to bear witness to the Kingdom of Heaven during life's probationary ordeal on earth. He vivified by his own luminous sacrifice the universal human possibility of divine self-consecration, the beauty of beatific devotion to the Transcendental Source of Divine Wisdom – the Word Made Flesh celebrating the Verbum In the Beginning.

Above all, there was the central paradox that his mission had to be vindicated by its failure, causing bewilderment among many of his disciples, while intuitively understood only by the very few who were pure in heart and strong in devotion, blessed by the vision of the Ascension. After three days in the tomb, Jesus, in the guise of a gardener, said to a poor, disconsolate Mary Magdalene, *Mary*! At once she looked back because she recognized the voice, and she said, *Rabboni* – "My Master" – and fell at his feet. Then he said, *Touch me not*. Here is a clue to his three days in the tomb. The work of permanent transmutation of life-atoms, of transfiguration of vehicles, was virtually complete. He then said, *Go to my brethren, and say unto them, I ascend unto my Father and your Father; and to my God and your God*. Subsequently he appeared three times to his disciples.

Jesus gave the greatest possible confidence to all his disciples by ever paying them the most sacred compliment, telling them that they were children of God. But, still, if a person thinks that he is nothing, or thinks that he is the greatest sinner on earth, how can the compassion and praise of Jesus have meaning for him? Each person has to begin to see himself undramatically as one of many sinners and say, "My sins are no different from those of anyone else." The flesh is weak but *pneuma*, the spirit, is willing. And *pneuma* has to do with breath. The whole of the Gospel according to John is saturated with the elixir of the breathing-in and breathing-out by Jesus of the life-infusing current that gives every man a credible faith in his promise and possibility, and, above all, a living awareness of his immortality, which he can self-consciously realize when freed from mis-identification with his mortal frame.

The possibility of resurrection has to do with identification and mis-identification. This is the issue not for just a few but for all human beings who, in forgetfulness, tend to think that they are what their enemies think, or that they are what their friends want them to be. At one time men talked of the *imago Christi*. We now live in a society that constantly deals in diabolical images and the cynical corruption of image-making, a nefarious practice unfamiliar in simpler societies which still enjoy innocent psychic health. Even more, people now engage in image-crippling – the most heinous of crimes. At one time men did it openly, with misguided courage. They pulled down statues and defaced idols. They paid for it and are still paying. Perhaps those people were reborn in this society. That is sad because they are condemning themselves to something worse than hell – not only the hell of loneliness and despair – but much worse. The light is going out for many a human being. The Mahatmas have always been with us. They have always abundantly sent forth benedictory vibrations. They are here on earth where they have always had their asylums and their ashrams. Under cyclic law they are able to use precisely prepared forums and opportunities to re-erect or resurrect the mystery temples of the future. Thus, at this time, everybody is stirred up by the crucial issue of identity – which involves the choice between the living and the dead, between entelechy and self-destruction.

The central problem in the Gospel according to John, which Paul had to confront in giving his sermon on the resurrection, has to do with life and with death. What is life for one man is not life to another. Every man or woman today has to raise the question, "What does it mean for me to be alive, to breathe, to live for the sake of others, to live within the law which protects all but no one in particular?" Whoever truly identifies with the limitless and unconditional love of Jesus and with the secret work of Jesus which he veiled in wordless silence, is lit up. Being lit up, one is able to see the divine Buddha-nature, the light vesture of the Buddha. The disciples in the days of the Buddha, and so again in the days of Jesus, were able to see the divine raiment made of the most homogeneous pure essence of universal Buddhi. Immaculately conceived and unbegotten, it is *Daiviprakriti*, the light of the Logos. Every man at all times has such a garment, but it is covered over. Therefore, each must sift and select the gold from the dross. The more a person does this truly and honestly, the more the events of what we call life can add up before the moment of death. They can have a beneficent impact upon the mood and the state of mind in which one departs. A person who is wise in this generation will so prepare his meditation that at the moment of death he may read or have read out those passages in the *Bhagavad Gita, The Voice of the Silence,* or *The Gospel According to St. John,* that are exactly relevant to what is needed. Then he will be able to intone the Word, which involves the whole of one's being and breathing, at the moment when he may joyously discard his mortal garment. It has been done, and it is being done. It can be done, and it will be done. Anyone can do it, but in these matters there is no room for chance or deception, for we live in a universe of law. Religion can be supported now by science, and to bring the two together in the psychology of self-transformation one needs true philosophy, the unconditional love of wisdom.

The crucifixion of Jesus and his subsequent resurrection had little reference to himself, any more than any breath he took during his life. Thus, in the Gospel, we read that Jesus promises that when he will be gone from the world, he will send the Paraclete. This archaic concept has exercised the pens of many scholars. What is the Paraclete? What does it mean? "Comforter"? "The Spirit of Truth"? Scholars still do not claim to know. The progress made in this century is in the honest recognition that they do not know, whereas in the nineteenth century they quarrelled, hurled epithets at each other out of arrogance, with a false confidence that did not impress anyone for long. The times have changed, and this is no moment for going back to the pseudo-complacency of scholasticism, because today it would be false, though at one time it might have had some understandable basis. Once it might have seemed a sign of health and could have been a pardonable and protective illusion. Today it would be a sign of sickness because it would involve insulting the intelligence of many young people, men and women, Christian, Jewish, Protestant, Catholic, but also Buddhist, Hindu, Moslem, Sikh, and every other kind of denomination. No one wants to settle for the absurdities of the past, but all nonetheless want a hope by which they may live and inherit the future, not only for themselves or their descendants, but for all living beings.

This, then, is a moment when people must ask what would comfort the whole of mankind. What did Jesus think would be a way of comforting all? Archetypally, *The Gospel According to St. John* is speaking in this connection of the mystery temple, where later all the sad failures of Christianity took place. This is the light and the fire that must be kept alive for the sake of all. Who, we may ask, will joyously and silently maintain it intact? Who will be able to say, as the dying Latimer said in Oxford in 1555, "We shall this day light such a candle . . . as I trust shall never be put out." Jesus was confident that among his disciples there were those who had been set afire by the flames that streamed through him. He was the *Hotri*, "the indispensable agent" for the universal alkahest, the elixir of life and immortality. He was the fig tree that would bear fruit, but he predicted that there would be fig trees that would bear no fruit. He was referring to the churches that have nothing to say, nothing real to offer, and above all, do not care that much for the lost Word or the world's proletariat, or the predicament and destiny of the majority of mankind.

His confidence was that which came to him, like everything in his life, from the Father, the *Paraguru*, the Lord of Libations, who, with boundless love for all, sustains in secret the eternal contemplation, together with the two Bodhisattvas – one whose eye sweeps over slumbering earth, and the other whose hand is extended in protecting love over the heads of his ascetics. Jesus spoke in the name of the Great Sacrifice. He spoke of the joy in the knowledge that there were a few who had become potentially like the leaven that could lift the whole lump, who had become true Guardians of the Eternal Fires. These are the vestal fires of the mystery temple which had disappeared in Egypt, from which the exodus took place. They had disappeared from Greece, though periodically there were attempts to revive them, such as those by Pythagoras at Krotona. They were then being poured into a new city called Jerusalem. In a sense, the new Comforter was the New Jerusalem, but it was not just a single city nor was it merely for people of one tribe or race.

Exoterically, the temple of Jerusalem was destroyed in 63 B.C. by Pompey and was rebuilt. Later it was razed to the ground again in 70 A.D. Since the thirteenth century no temple has been in existence there at all because that city has been for these past seven hundred years entirely in the hands of those who razed the old buildings and erected minarets and mosques. Now, people wonder if there really ever was a true Jerusalem, for everywhere is found the Babylon of confusion. Today it is not Origen who speaks to us, but Celsus, on behalf of all Epicureans. Everyone is tempted, like Lot's wife, to be turned into salt by fixing their attention upon the relics and memories of the past long after they have vanished into the limbo of dissolution and decay.

Anyone, however, who has an authentic soul-vision is El Mirador. Jesus knew that the vision, entrusted to the safekeeping of a few, would inspire them to lay the basis of what would continue, because of what they did, despite all the corruption and the ceaseless crucifixion. Even today, two thousand years later, when we hear of the miracle of the limitless love of Jesus, when we hear the words he spoke, when we read about and find comfort in what he did, we are deeply stirred. We are abundantly grateful because in us is lit the chela-light of true reverential devotion to the Christos within. This helps us to see all the Christs of history, unknown as well as renowned, as embodiments of the One and Only – *the One without a Second*, in the cryptic language of the *Upanishads*. When this revelation takes place and is enjoyed inwardly, there are glad tidings, because it is on the invisible plane that the real work is done. Most people are fixated on the visible and want to wait for fruits from trees planted by other men. There are a few, however, who have realized the comfort to be derived in the true fellowship of those who seek the kingdom of God within themselves, who wish to become the better able to help and teach others, and who will be true in their faith from now until the twenty-first century. Some already have been using a forty-year calendar.

There have been such persons before us. Pythagoras called them Heroes. The Buddha called them *Shravakas*, true listeners, and *Shramanas*, true learners. Then there were some who became *Srotapattis*, "those who enter the stream," and among them were a few *Anagamin*, "those who need never return on earth again involuntarily." There were also those who were *Arhans* of boundless vision, Perfected Men, Bodhisattvas, endlessly willing to re-enter the cave, having taken the pledge of Kwan-Yin to redeem every human being and all sentient life.

Nothing less than such a vow can resurrect the world today. These times are very different from the world at the time of John because in this age outward forms are going to give no clues in relation to the work of the formless. Mankind has to grow up. We find Origen saying this in the early part of the third century and Philo saying the same even in the first century. Philo, who was a Jewish scholar and a student of Plato, was an intuitive intellectual, while Origen, who had studied the Gnostics and considered various philosophical standpoints, was perhaps more of a mystic or even an ecstatic. Both knew that the Christos could only be seen by the eye of the mind. *If therefore thine eye be single, Jesus said, thy whole body shall be full of Light.* Those responding with the eyes of the body could never believe anything because, as Heraclitus said, "Eyes are bad witnesses to the soul." The eyes of the body must be tutored by the eye of the mind. *Gupta Vidya* also speaks of the eye of the heart and the eye in the forehead – the eye of Wisdom-Compassion. Through it, by one's own love, one will know the greater love. By one's own compassion one will know the greater compassion. By one's own ignorance one will recognize the ignorance around and seek the privilege of recognition of the Paraclete. Then, when the eye becomes single in its concentration upon the welfare of all, the body will become full of the light of the Christos. Once unveiled at the fundamental level of causality, it makes a man or woman an eternal witness to the true resurrection of the Son of Man into the highest mansions of the Father.

Hermes, April 1977

PURITY AND POLLUTION

> *Every 'Round'* (on the descending scale) *is but a repetition in a more concrete form of the Round which preceded it, as every globe – down to our fourth sphere* (the actual earth) *– is a grosser and more material copy of the more shadowy sphere which precedes it in their successive order, on the three higher planes. On its way upwards on the ascending arc, Evolution spiritualises and etherealises, so to speak, the general nature of all, bringing it on to a level with the plane on which the twin globe on the opposite side is placed; the result being, that when the seventh globe is reached (in whatever Round) the nature of everything that is evolving returns to the condition it was in at its starting point — plus, every time, a new and superior degree in the states of consciousness.*
>
> The Secret Doctrine, i 232

The archetypal image of man as the sacred seven-leaved *Saptaparna* plant suggests the sublime integrity of human development, encompassing the spiritual, mental, moral and astro-physical spheres of existence. The heart of the Man-Plant is the *sutratman*, the thread-soul spun from the distilled essence of the diverse experiences of the threefold *Atma-Buddhi-Manas* in its repeated incarnations in the lower quaternary. The triadic heart of hebdomadic humanity mirrors the complex differentiation of the triple Logoi which takes place at the dawn of cosmic manifestation. But to comprehend the correlation between the ONE, the twofold and the threefold in the cosmos, between *Atma*, *Atma-Buddhi* and *Atma-Buddhi-Manas* in man, one must understand the cyclic processes of evolution throughout the hierarchies and kingdoms of Nature. In particular, one must appreciate, morally and spiritually, the immense scope and vital significance of human self-consciousness. Unless and until human beings overcome their unnaturally protracted fascination with the lunar aspects of their evolutionary ancestry, they will be unable to discern their present predicament or discover their true status as conscious participants in the cosmic process.

The complex ills of contemporary humanity result from a long history of abdication of responsibility in consciousness. Many souls have assuredly utilized the prerogative of self-consciousness to move closer to enlightenment, whilst others have already irreversibly fallen off the human path during this epoch of manifestation. The great bulk of humanity has failed to meet its fundamental obligations to the rest of Nature. In order to understand this collective karma, it is necessary to see human existence within the broader context of cyclic evolution. The earth, as the common theatre of evolution, is comprised of a circle of seven stages or globes, around which the evolutionary life-impulse passes seven times, each immense circling of the seven globes constituting one of the seven Rounds. Each stage of activity in each of the successive Rounds provides for the development of certain states of consciousness which correspond to the plane of matter correlative with that stage. As the *Atma-Buddhic* Monads engaged in this process are themselves divisible into seven kingdoms falling under seven hierarchies of being, owing to their attained development in earlier periods of evolution, their internal and external relations to each other vary enormously in the different cycles of terrestrial activity.

Whilst all the elements of this vast and variegated process are ontologically reducible to one absolute substance-principle, no mere assertion of this metaphysical reduction will generate a sense of ethical responsibility. Instead, what is needed is a shrewd comprehension of the intimate relationship between the partially awakened self-conscious human Monad and the hosts of unself-conscious Monads which constitute the vestures of man and the deceptive veils of external nature. In regard to the laws that apply to the elemental kingdoms, H.P. Blavatsky cited the work of Henry Pratt, who sketched the Kabbalistic teaching:

> They held that, functionally, Spirit and Matter of corresponding opacity and density tended to coalesce; and that the resultant created Spirits, in the disembodied state, were constituted on a scale in which the differing opacities and transparencies of Elemental or uncreated Spirit were reproduced. And that these Spirits in the disembodied state attracted, appropriated, digested and assimilated Elemental

Spirit and Elemental Matter whose condition was conformed to their own.

The Secret Doctrine, i 234

The greater the purity and ethereality of a human being's vestures, the greater will be the transparency of the Buddhic light of the *Atman*. When the vestures are composed of a very fine set of filtering elementals, light will shine through them without obscuration. The capacity to focus the light of universal awareness resides in *Manas*. When acting naturally, *Manas* chooses universal themes for focussing the noumenal light of *Atma-Buddhi*. This means that *Manas* tends to levitate, to rise upwards higher and higher, towards ever-expanding perspectives upon consciousness, matter and energy. At the same time, as is all too evident, *Manas* can, through its projected ray, get locked within the lower sensorium, the mundane class of promiscuous perceptions connected with name and form, comparison and contrast, status and security, novelty and curiosity, all that is evanescent and illusive. This in itself is a result of the impure quality and leaky texture of the lower vestures, especially of the astral form. Through recurrent patterns of temporizing thought, strong associations are forged between a human being and vampirizing sub-classes of the elemental kingdoms. Through these profane alliances, the embodied human consciousness is drawn into sterile fields of suffocating material existence, following the destructive lines of its carnal attractions. These conditions vary tremendously, as Pratt suggested:

> ... there is a wide difference in the condition of created Spirits; and in the intimate association between the Spirit-world and the world of Matter, the more opaque Spirits in the disembodied state were drawn towards the more dense parts of the material world, and therefore tended towards the centre of the Earth, where they found the conditions most suited to their state; while the more transparent Spirits passed into the surrounding aura of the planet, the more rarefied finding their home in its satellite.

The Secret Doctrine, i 234

This clearly connotes that not all human beings live in the same dimension of space-time. They may be grouped according to divergent states of consciousness; hence there could be within a single family, within a community, certainly within a nation, people representing differences of consciousness so vast that they constitute a virtual subspecies of humanity. In the most propitious cases these beings, having achieved a certain level of personal invulnerability, would always be universalizing and elevating themselves. But others, despite the best will in the world, have consolidated or inherited extremely tenacious tendencies that push them constantly towards the shadow-play of the physical senses. They are, therefore, blinded to the joyous possibilities of what would otherwise be the natural upward arc of the metaphysical imagination. Human beings of all sorts may be characterized in terms of these marked divergences in consciousness which invariably reflect the closeness or looseness of the relation between the immortal triad and the mutable quaternary, between spiritual will and material ossification. *What might be called a human being's basic level of self-consciousness is directly proportional to that Monad's evolution as an independent centre of primordial formless intelligence.* In any particular case, the degree of this noetic individuation is a direct function of how that ray of self-consciousness has, over a period of eighteen million years, used life-atoms and the vestures, either universalizing itself or failing to do so. This, then, is the secret history of every human soul.

Looked at in the aggregate, all immortal souls presently experiencing the complexities of this earth chain in the Fourth Round are themselves the inheritors of an evolution that goes back to prior Rounds and earlier periods of evolution. In the first three Rounds, before reaching the stage of nascent self-consciousness, every Monad would have acquired a wealth of spiritual experiences in ethereal vestures, all of which is part of the universal memory of mankind. Each unfolding Round of evolution is like a day of *Brahma*, composed of one revolution of the wheel of the planetary chain or one circling of the Monadic Hosts around the seven globes. In the Fourth Round, human evolution reaches the high point of physical development, crowning its work with the development of the perfect physical vesture. This point of maximum involution of spirit into matter represents the fullest development of physical consciousness. After attaining this threshold, evolution begins its return movement towards spirit. In this vast perspective of human evolution, humanity has already passed that point of intense involvement in differentiation at the atomic and molecular level. This is evident in the subtlety and refinement of the human cellular structure, nervous system and specialized organs. There is an immeasurable gap between, for example, the human hand and an animal's paw. Each human being carries in his hands and other organs instruments that are the product of an extraordinary specialization of natural intelligence. But this privilege – having a hand with a firm thumb, five fingers and all its mounds corresponding to the different planets – is too little considered and too often taken for granted.

Even those fortunate enough to have had access to the arcane teachings regarding Rounds and globes, the correspondences and analogies between Nature and Man, have neglected this meditation. Though supposedly liberated from both theistic and materialistic conceptions of evolution, they have succumbed to superficial views of spirituality. Few, if any, have thought to connect the ten virtues with the twice-five fingers of the two hands. However many have reflected upon the phrase "constitutionally incapable of deviating from the right path", few have tried to understand irreversibility even on the physical plane, to recognize that it might apply to leading a little child by the hand across precipitous terrain. There is no point in being *more or less* reliable when guiding a child along the edge of an abyss; one needs nothing less than absolute irreversible stability. Gandhi understood this well and tirelessly attempted to impress it upon his followers. Even disregarding so extreme a case, one can remind oneself that such a firm stability is the indispensable basis of industrial civilization. People must be prompt and reliable in going about their work. No matter how much they may be driven by lesser or distracting motives, they either turn up at work at a certain time or accept, and expect, the inevitable consequences. This works all the way through Nature and society, so much so that it is taken to be common sense. The difficulty, then, is for people to bring to bear this stringent sense of reliability upon the inner life, with its whirling thoughts, chaotic feelings and everyday moral choices.

Put another way, the fundamental problem is to generate a sufficient sense of reality for the inner pilgrimage when it is freely chosen and when it is neither baited by external rewards nor buffeted by internal fears. Not all human beings are the same in this regard. Some need the stimulus of fear more than others. This is due to the aggregate character of all the impressions they have made upon the life-atoms in their vestures during their incarnations over the past eighteen million years. At any given time, through one's predominant state of consciousness, one establishes a link with elementals, which on different planes belong by affinity to quite different classes. They themselves function in groups and are connected with the five visible and two invisible elements of nature. They are also therefore connected, by analogy, with other globes of the earth chain, and are consubstantial with matter, either in a rarefied form corresponding to the first three Rounds or in an extremely dense state connected with the point of maximum differentiation in the Fourth Round.

Viewed in a larger time scale than is ordinarily accessible to human beings, the entire process of nature is circular; every Round on the descending scale is but a more concrete repetition of the one preceding it. Similarly, every globe within a Round on the descending arc is a materialized copy of a more ethereal sphere which preceded it in the successive descents of consciousness through the three higher planes of the earth chain. On the fourth globe in the Fourth Round, humanity has completed the involutionary arc of this process and is now engaged in the difficult push upwards and inwards towards the source of all life-energy. The immense suffering of present humanity comes from the lapses of irresponsible beings who lost touch with the great evolutionary thrust. Regardless of the exact nature of these collective failures of prior civilizations, and regardless of the particular burdens that these failures have placed on present humanity, it is now necessary for all human beings to learn to move upwards self-consciously in the ascending arc.

In practice, this means that human beings must acquire greater control over their conscious energies, a much greater capacity to withdraw from external stimuli and deformed images. This internal refinement of consciousness is the method of evolution itself, which acts to spiritualize and etherealize the complex nature of all beings, bringing them successively on to the levels of the globes in the descending arc of evolution. Thus, on the ascending arc the fifth globe corresponds to the third globe of the descending arc, the sixth to the second and the seventh to the first. A corresponding relationship exists between the Rounds themselves. This upward process is essentially the sublimation of matter and its impressibility by intelligence, which is the constructive function of thinking beings in the creative use of matter. The general sum-total of impulse given by thought to matter includes the laser-sharp contributions of legions of Adepts as well as the more haphazard effusions of millions of laggard souls. Without being an Adept, it is impossible to assess the awesome nature of this sum-total. Most human beings are, by definition, active at a middle level of consciousness and therefore are unable to understand the enormous range of alchemy that arises in human experience. They touch only a minute segment of meaningful experience in any given lifetime. Whilst the humanity of a particular Race and Round will act under a general limiting curve of consciousness, present humanity falls far short in optimizing its opportunities under the curves that apply to it, and this is largely through compulsive identification with lower classes of elementals negatively impressed in the past.

For the *Manasa*, the pure self-conscious intelligence burning brightly in the divine sphere of every human Monad, there is no inherent difficulty in understanding the nature of embodied experience. Yet for the incarnated ray, the personality, merely to talk of *SAT*, to talk of the eternal bliss experienced by the higher Triad, does nothing to bring about the progress of the Monad as a sevenfold being. On the contrary, idle and egotistic speech about spirituality precipitates the terrible dead weight of religious orthodoxy which stultifies human aspiration. The selfish desire for liberation, the warped assumptions of self-righteous judgementalism and the delusion that human souls can somehow opt out of the cosmic programme have never been a part of the true esoteric Teaching. What is true, however, and comprehensible is that any human being can by deep meditation, by noble association and by good fellowship learn to apply the sacred Teachings at some level, gaining brief though nourishing glimpses of spiritual realities. When through moral perseverance such moments are threaded together, they may become the basis of lines of noetic ideation which will have a definite bearing upon the quality of astral vesture and the degree of refinement one will possess in the next life. Given the great sum-total of thoughts and choices made over eighteen million years, no human being can make an abrupt or marked difference to these factors in one brief incarnation. Half of life is spent in sleep, childhood and old age; there is hardly sufficient time and continuity of effort to make a radical difference to one's vestures in the next life. But there is time enough to change the direction of one's consciousness, the type of impression one is continually making upon elementals, and the pattern which one can extend and refine in future incarnations. After successive lifetimes of such endeavour, it is possible to create a refined and pellucid brain-mind, exquisitely tuned centres in the astral form, immediately responsive to the highest aspirations, to the most impersonal ideation.

As so few have grasped the logic and the mathematics of the Teachings of the Brotherhood of Mahatmas, many have, alas, grossly oversimplified the doctrine of Adeptship and cheapened the notion of chelaship. They never asked themselves how, if over eighteen million years they had made themselves what they were, they could expect in one short lifetime to become so different from all others. Perhaps they thought of elementals as nothing more than a convenient category of explanation for unusual phenomena, with no application to the most intimate details of mundane experience. Nonetheless, the fact remains that every human being has an inheritance of karma extending back over eighteen million years, and Nature is not about to exchange its integrity for the wishful thinking of would-be neophytes. Every human being needs to realize the texture of the sevenfold vestures and to refine them to a degree that is coordinate with the entire Fourth Round and to the Races within that Round. In the far distant future, in the Fifth Round, will come the decisive moment of choice after which no one can go any farther who has not already become benevolent and altruistic, not just in intention or on one plane, but at the primary level of root consciousness, at the level of polarity of life-atoms. A human being who has not done this will not be able to go beyond the Fifth Round at a certain threshold.

This is the crucial juncture which is being anticipated by analogy in the Fifth Race of the Fourth Round right now. Owing to the enormous retardation in evolution in the past, it became absolutely necessary for the original vibration of the Planetary Spirit, the Avataric vibration of eighteen million years ago, of a million years ago in the time of Rama, of five thousand years ago in the time of Krishna, to be resoundingly struck again so that the resultant karma would force a widespread quickening of choice. In this way, those who cannot really keep pace may be eased out of the human form, and what would otherwise be resolved in the Fifth Round through a titanic struggle between benevolent and malevolent magic may be facilitated at this point in the Fifth Race.

This compelling necessity makes the compassionate programme of the Bodhisattvas crucial and indeed indispensable. Selfish dreams of salvation have no place in our philanthropic work for the humanity of the future. It is altogether inadequate to entertain some vague intellectual awareness that there is *SAT*. To live *SAT*, to impress every life-atom with *SAT*, is to become a Magus. As Gandhi understood from the ancient Indian texts, to be able to exemplify one great act of *saccakriya*, with the potent energy of pure altruistic truth, is to release so powerful a force that it can radically transform the consciousness of a myriad souls and minds over great spans of space and time. This is the perpetual theurgy enacted by the Brotherhood of Bodhisattvas. Even to apprentice oneself in this benevolent art requires lifetimes of rigorous mental and moral training. Knowing at one level that there is *SAT* in no way dispenses with the immensity and complexity of this programme. Whosoever hopes or tries to circumvent this necessarily arduous course has simply not begun to understand the profound Teaching concerning cosmic hierarchies.

The psychic complement of selfish salvationism and shallow spirituality is the equally destructive view that there is something inescapably evil about the physical body. There is very little to choose between orthodox religion, which condemns the physical body, and empirical pseudo-science, which refuses to really respect the human form. From the standpoint of the Wisdom Religion the physical body is a temple. Materialist and religious creedalists alike, whether prating of original sin or taking pride in mechanistic innovation, degrade the most divine form on earth. If children learnt to revere their bodies before the age of puberty, there would result a cultural revolution of fundamental proportions. As one of the Mahatmas explained in the last century:

> Man (physically) is a compound of all the kingdoms, and spiritually – his individuality is no worse for being shut up within the casing of an ant than it is for being inside a king. It is not the outward or physical shape that dishonours and pollutes the five principles – but the mental perversity. Then it is but at his fourth round, when arrived at the full possession of his *Kama*-energy and completely matured, that man becomes *fully responsible*, as at the sixth he may become a *Buddha* and at the seventh before the Pralaya – a 'Dhyan Chohan'.
>
> Mahatma M.

The root of all retardation is the persistent refusal to learn, to revere elders and to keep still. If children do not learn silence and respect, they have learnt nothing. Reverence must be instilled so firmly that it prevails in adolescence against that cowardly minority which is endemically perverse owing to its protracted inability to use its creative faculties. This perversity is a kind of demoniac defiance, often a desperate desire for inordinate attention; but it is also sometimes the influence emanating from the astral light of the soulless beings who are increasingly converging with the decay of the old order. Congregating in the so-called centres of urban civilizations and of global tourism, they have nothing but a total contempt for everything that lives and breathes. Individuals must learn to shield themselves against these appalling and polluting influences.

In his solemn warning Mahatma M. was hinting that this mental perversity is rooted over the last five million years in Atlantis. In the Fifth Root Race it is wholly abnormal, because by the end of the Fourth Race it was largely eradicated. There was a tremendous victory and as a result of the tragedy of what transpired in those closing million years of the Atlantean race, the wise deliberately sought to lay down the great norms and patterns of human life at the foundation of the Fifth Root Race. The complex codes of *Manu* spring from this era over a million years ago. The archetypal injunctions regarding monogamous family life, reverence for elders, mutual responsibility between social orders, and the correct participation through gratitude and devotion in the Guru-chela relation were all exemplified and set down by the divine law-givers at the inception of the present Race. Everything in present humanity that is truly ethical and based upon divine wisdom goes back to that origin, though obscured in its inner meaning through the course of time and through the hypocritical misuse of sacred Teachings by people enthralled by external forms. So great has been the recrudescence of Atlantean pride and wilfulness that the mighty victory of light over darkness at the inception of the Fifth Root Race has been eclipsed in the consciousness of many human beings. Many have wavered and wandered under the karmic pressure of atavistic tendencies, so that they are now altogether too suggestible to the forces of superstition, materialism and self-destruction.

One must clearly delineate the moral lines within the fivefold field of the middle human principles. Eschewing idle claims about the *Atman* and a preoccupation with the physical form, mature human beings must, in full possession of fohatic energy, nurture a sense of full responsibility for themselves. The only authentic mental standpoint to take is that of total responsibility for oneself, never descending to transfer blame to anything outside oneself. The right discipline for the present and coming age is that of "the mango principle" enunciated in *The Voice of the Silence*. One must learn to be as soft as that fruit's pulp to the woes and limitations of others, and as hard as its stone to one's own weaknesses and limitations. Only by doing this can one gain the inner firmness and moral strength needed to withdraw consciously from the astral form, and eventually to dissipate that form at will. This in itself is a high stage of development, and it cannot be attained until one has paid one's debts to other human beings. Even where one is still carrying debts to others both mentally and morally, it should still be possible to be profoundly grateful and responsible in relation to one's opportunities as a self-conscious Monad. Nothing less is being aimed at than the fullest possible recovery of the true meaning of the word 'man'. Derived from *manu* and *manushya*, "the thinker", it is man alone in Nature who is capable of keeping his head erect, capable of standing firm, capable of having a straight spine and above all capable of consciously directing benevolence towards all beings. But before one can gain full control over, or some comprehension of, the ultimate destination, one must set one's inward course in the right direction. Every human being is intuitively capable of knowing whether one is going in the right direction or not.

The forward march of human evolution has nothing to do with cowardliness or evasion, with pseudo-chelaship or nefarious manipulations. These belong to the murderers of souls, whether they parade themselves in the garb of science or sexology, psychology or religion. Every decent human being will have a natural distaste towards these grotesque mockeries of human life which only serve to weaken human responsibility. But those who consult their own consciences will discover a natural sympathy with that essential tendency in nature which evinces a progressive march towards self-mastery. They will learn to discern a design and compassion in the activity of the apparently blind forces in the vastitude of visible and hidden Nature. They will learn to appreciate the intimate adaptations of natural form to intelligent purpose; through their joyous meditations, they will learn how to assist evolution onwards from within. Rejecting all irrational conceptions of evolution based upon truncated categories, they will begin to cherish the beauty and integrity of the continual process of sifting that is spiritual evolution.

Though sharp in their immediate results and distressing to the inflated personal shadow, the tests of karma are entirely moral. In the long run they can only serve to instruct humanity in the dual law of universal justice and unconditional compassion. Those who willingly submit themselves to these ethical tests and who become freely capable of breathing for the sake of others will earn an entitlement to share in the resplendently noetic civilization of the future. Those who do not will be spewed forth by Nature. Under the ancient though eternally young Avataric impulse of the Aquarian Age, there is challenge, guidance and protection for every human being who aspires to work truly on behalf of the humanity of the future. The choice belongs to each and all.

Hermes, August 1983

THE HEALING OF SOULS

> *The whole essence of truth cannot be transmitted from mouth to ear. Nor can any pen describe it, not even that of the recording Angel, unless man finds the answer in the sanctuary of his own heart, in the innermost depths of his divine intuitions. It is the great SEVENTH MYSTERY of Creation, the first and the last; and those who read St. John's Apocalypse may find its shadow lurking under the seventh seal.*
>
> The Secret Doctrine, ii 516

Self-exiled from the spiritual sanctuary at its core and perversely deaf to the divine promptings of intuition, mankind in our time has enacted a protracted melodrama which has become tedious to participants and spectators alike. For a painstaking but utilitarian chronicler like Gibbon, history seemed to be nothing but a record of crimes, follies and misfortunes. Somewhat more perceptive, though shackled by a rationalist framework of truncated idealism, Hegel at least identified the central issue in his laconic observation that if men learn anything from history, it is that they learn nothing at all. Clearly, there is something about human beings that is mulish and proud, that mutilates inner aspirations and divine hopes. When the innate power of learning is obscured, human beings fall prey to an unrelenting succession of misshapen thoughts, distorted emotions and self-negating actions. This intimate if inverse connection between the spiritual anatomy of man and the outward play of events was sensed by Gandhi in his conclusion that history, as ordinarily conceived, is merely a grandiose record of the interruptions of soul-force.

From a diagnostic standpoint, it is as if a heavy stone lodged in the spine were to block the inflow of Divine Light from the top of the head. The baby's fontanelle, connected with the *Brahmarandhra chakra*, is soft in the first months of life, but, owing to the karma of past misuse of powers, astral calcification of that vital aperture reaches to an unprecedented degree in modern man. Thus the "shades of the prison-house begin to close upon the growing boy", and the essential *nadis* become listless in the absence of the divine efflux. This morbid condition cannot be corrected from below or from without; it is only a radical realignment of one's inner mental and devotional posture that will restore the free flow of the currents in the spiritual spinal cord. One has to learn before teaching. One must be still and listen before speaking. One must meditate before attempting to conceive and create or engage in outward action.

If human beings are to be more than animals, if they are to reclaim their descent from the Divine, there can be no fakery and foolery, no pretence or deception. They must take their stand as fallible learners, growing and acknowledging errors through candour and self-correction, clearly and cleanly admitting their ignorance but firmly and fearlessly strengthening their own willingness to learn. Regardless of all exoteric and external tokens of class and caste, of culture and social station, each individual must become a humble, though self-accredited, ambassador of goodwill in a global society of learning. If in future lives such honest seekers are to approach the true Mystery temples, they must begin now by laying aside any false sense of superiority and inferiority, all unctuousness and hypocrisy, and learn to greet each other as souls with pride in the beauty and bounty of all lands and in the nobility of common folk and the ancestors of the earth, thereby acknowledging their mutual membership in mankind.

Along with its ancient gurus and preceptors, the human race – most of whose mature graduates are not incarnated at any given time – is waiting to see how many true learners may emerge in our epoch. How many are willing to acknowledge in daily practice what they really know about playing a musical instrument? It is only through years of discipline that one may learn any true art, whether it be meditation or the practice of political diplomacy, the therapeutics of self-transcendence or authentic friendship for one's comrades in humane endeavours. As Cicero taught, divine nature has no interest in perpetually underwriting human folly. Twentieth century America with its celluloid media is neither the first, nor will it be the last, society to be disabused of its self-perpetuated delusions. Even Americans can wisely use their magnificent resources in libraries, the finest available on earth, and really begin to learn. The moment one truly begins to learn, one starts to speak from knowledge, with the accents of genuine confidence that naturally combine with a sense of proportion, without adolescent exaggerations and extravagances. Mature men and women honour their sacred obligations to their children and their moral debts to their fathers and mothers; authentic learners are proud of their illiterate grandparents and rustic ancestors who helped in their own way to make possible the opportunities of the present. The emergence of a widely diffused sense of individual integrity in the common cause of human learning is a mighty undertaking, rooted in a spiritual reformation of the human psyche. It requires saying adieu to the homogenization and humbug of modern mass education, and courageously choosing the elevating ideal of lifelong learning based upon spiritual self-education through ethical self-renewal in the altruistic service of others.

Many more people in the world are ready for this today than in any previous epoch. Yet some who desperately want to learn do not know how because they imagine that they cannot start until everyone else does. This is the peasant mentality at its timidest, but it is not the true state of mind of pastoral exemplars of the *grihastha ashrama*, who have nurtured and sustained humanity over a myriad centuries. Whilst every village and town has its share of those who substitute pretension and crudity for learning and life, there are always a scattered few who are willing to be Promethean. These are the humble pioneers who husband the new seeds and who plan ahead for the coming year's crop. In villages results count, but they are essentially those supported by nature's rhythms. Without the ingenuity and inventiveness of farmers in responding to nature, the subsidies of kings and courts are of no avail, and if in contemporary capitals people have become insensitive to the rhythms of nature and thereby cut off from their sense of the need to learn, so much the worse for them. To the extent that any group of people imagines itself divorced from the natural necessity of learning, its culture is a sham and its society a fabric of deceit built on ignorance. Puzzled and frightened by the raucousness and violence caused by its own unacknowledged delusions, it moves through a succession of misunderstood non-crises to utilitarian non-solutions, unable to learn because unwilling to listen either to its own inner voice or to the wisdom of others.

Who, for example, could tell the facts of life to Americans in this century? How many know anything about what is going on in the world or even in the U.S.A.? As Robert Hutchins warned so poignantly in the thirties, America was facing, and has now realized, the prospect of being a nation of illiterates, who do not know how to read, how to write, how to do arithmetic. What is worse, as an inevitable consequence of this indolence and as a compensation for self-induced inferiority, some hawkers have become the most strident pseudo-enthusiasts of spiritual mountain climbing – a subject about which they know nothing. This is a contagious fever amongst the hucksters and charlatans of the world, many of whom have come to America's shores seeking their fortunes. As H.P. Blavatsky noted in the last century, wherever spiritual truth is dishonoured and elementary discrimination is lacking, the mysteries of nature cannot be divulged. One must begin by honouring the humblest truths by honest application and through some philosophical comprehension before one may raise one's hand to the latch which guards the gate of the Greater Mysteries. Initially, one must be willing to honour the Delphic injunction "Know thyself" on the planes of relative learning, and thereby restore the power of inner perception before one may apprehend any absolute truth.

> Absolute truth is *the symbol of Eternity*, and no *finite* mind can ever grasp the eternal, hence, no truth in its fulness can ever dawn upon it. To reach the state during which man sees and senses it, we have to paralyze the senses of the external man of clay. This is a difficult task, we may be told, and most people will, at this rate, prefer to remain satisfied with relative truths, no doubt. But to approach even terrestrial truths requires, first of all, *love of truth for its own sake*, for otherwise no recognition of it will follow.
>
> H.P. Blavatsky

The Victorian age, with all its cant and hypocrisy as well as its latent sense of human dignity and integrity preserved through the recollection of the Enlightenment, is gone. It is now obvious to many that there was neither irony nor polemic, but only compassion, in the stern warnings that H.P. Blavatsky delivered on behalf of the Mahatmas to Theosophists and non-Theosophists alike. The collapse of the acquisitive and parochial civilizations of the past two millennia is approaching completion, and on behalf of the Aquarian dawn of the global civilization of the future, it was essential since 1963 to encourage rebels and victims alike to come out of the old and decaying order. This anarchic rebellion entailed the risk that the weak would become like Trishanku in the Indian myth, who was suspended between heaven and earth, neither able to land on his feet in the world nor capable of scaling celestial heights. This was a great but well-calculated risk, because large numbers of pilgrim-souls have awakened to a sense of their common humanity, both in the old world and the new. For example, prior to the spiritual upheavals that were initiated in 1963, the depths of self-obsessive messianic delusion were so great in America that scarcely any of her citizens could feel any real kinship with the rest of humanity, whilst outside observers could only wonder whether Americans were becoming *en masse* a race of megalomaniacs or restless demons. Throughout the world honourable statesmen, scientists, businessmen and even inveterate travellers refused to set foot in America, not because of any ideological or economic considerations, but out of intense moral revulsion.

Whilst the wisest statesmen and most perceptive peoples of the globe did not think that the Second World War had drained all the sources of discord on the earth, they were nonetheless willing to move towards the establishment of a juridical basis of enduring peace. What they did not foresee was that their endeavours on behalf of a new era of security and welfare for the whole of humanity would be flouted by the flagrant jingoists of the so-called American century, backed by sectarian bigotry and pervasive racism. Like Lisa in Dostoevsky's *Notes From The Underground*, they may not have comprehended the details of what America claimed to know, but they soon understood that their smug benefactor was so self-deluded as to be incapable of offering timely help. Perhaps now a growing core of Americans has realized that the decent peoples of the world dislike self-righteous bullies. They do not like the bombing of defenceless people, nor do they wish to see what happened to Dresden recur *ad nauseam* after the war. Rather, they expect true courage and ethical sensitivity from the proud champions of freedom and human solidarity. No one capable of resonating to the authentic meaning behind the American experiment could be but saddened to see it turning into a vulgar display of chauvinistic rhetoric and moral cowardice, an unholy alliance of Mammon, Moloch and Beelzebub.

It was the strange karma of the modern Theosophical Movement to attract many souls who were able neither to stand up in the world nor to renounce it for the sake of the spiritual welfare of humanity, and so in the nineteenth century it largely failed in America. Although it quickly travelled to England and Europe and also found receptive soil abroad, from India to Japan, in North America it engendered a crop of delusions, despite the sacrifices of a few pioneers. People actually thought that simply because they were middle-class salvationists they could pretend to be the chosen race of forerunners of future humanity. These pathetic delusions do not belong to the past, but have persisted like poison amongst pseudo-spiritual coteries and the crowded ranks of those who have not yet learnt that they cannot get something for nothing, or purchase wisdom for a price. Whilst America welcomed the wretched of the earth with a noble promise of liberty and justice for all, it also pampered the shallow autodidacts and plausible hypocrites who treated America as a land where anything goes and all is permitted. Many of these and their descendants eventually congregated in California and in the environs of the city of the angels (which its original Indian inhabitants had prophetically associated with demons). Blind greed, the perverse refusal to learn and the profanation of the sacred are so widespread today that the anger of humanity is sufficiently aroused to call for a halt to the further spread of the diseases of the psyche. The time for fascination with the pathology of the soul is past.

America must now take a firm stand and foster human beings who can marry, bring up children, and can love without merely demanding to be loved. They must learn to show true and direct personal charity to the deserving, and not just presume on some evangelical committee to plan out other lives. They must learn to esteem the ethical dignity of their neighbours every day of the year, regardless of race, creed, sect or ideology. What is required is nothing superhuman, but merely the reduction of subhuman activity through the exemplification of true values, and by a cool recognition of the enormous difference between delusive posturing and the real world in which diverse human beings are born, grow old and die, burdened by the sorrows caused by their own ignorance. Though they suffer, they may learn by acknowledging their errors, and paralysing their pride rather than their spiritual faculties. Relinquishing both conceit and guilt, they can learn to say that they are sorry when they hurt others, and they may begin to learn the manners of the common man and the authentic accents of the voice of mankind. Then they may take their place once again in the community of man by refusing to live like tawdry traducers, cheats and fakes. Each and all must learn to live lives built upon intrinsic value and reality, not upon appearances and noisy self-assertion. The heavenly maiden of Truth can descend only in a context congenial to her, the soil of an impartial, unprejudiced mind, receptive to pure spiritual consciousness.

Whilst it is true that the mad rush of material civilization leaves one little time for reflection, thus increasing the irksomeness of a life of empty custom and barren conventionality, this alienation from humanity and nature is the inescapable karma of past lives. The real danger in the present is that the simulation and deceit of conventional existence will be mistaken for the true substance of fellow-feeling and concern for others. Whatever its varied masks, selfishness remains the same, and its inflammation through "double ignorance" is the primary disease of the soul.

> SELFISHNESS, the first-born of Ignorance, and the fruit of the teaching which asserts that for every newly-born infant a new soul, *separate and distinct* from the Universal Soul, is 'created' – this Selfishness is the impassable wall between the *personal* Self and Truth. It is the prolific mother of all human vices, *Lie* being born out of the necessity for dissembling, and *Hypocrisy* out of the desire to mask *Lie*. It is the fungus growing and strengthening with age in every human heart in which it has devoured all better feelings. Selfishness kills every noble impulse in our natures, and is the one deity, fearing no faithlessness or desertion from its votaries. Hence, we see it reign supreme in the world and in so-called fashionable society. As a result, we live, and

move, and have our being in this god of darkness under his trinitarian aspect of Sham, Humbug and Falsehood, called RESPECTABILITY.

H.P. Blavatsky

There is nothing more cleansing than the truth, for, as Jesus taught, it is by learning and knowing the truth that one becomes free. Wherever the truth is obscured, whether by individuals or governments, responsibility is weakened, and with it the connection between the higher Triad and the lower principles. Hence, it is a form of needless self-destruction to be continually speaking of the so-called predicament of the age, and never facing one's own failings. The critical question is not what is wrong with the world, but what is one's own individual responsibility for particular choices and acts. There is need for less talk of nihilism and Nietzsche and more attention to one's individual responsibility to parents, to spouse and children, and to those nobler human souls with whom one has the privilege of associating in the pilgrimage of life. Vast numbers of people in America and all over the globe are pleased with the prospect of the termination of a tired old cycle of cowardly irresponsibility, and the burgeoning promise of a saner and more cooperative way of life. Many young people are aware that what Lenin called the bourgeoisification of the proletariat is doomed. The time has come for perceptive Americans of all ages to cherish their common ancestry with the rest of mankind, neither from gorilla nor Jehovah, but from the solar Fathers of the human race, the *Agnishwatha Pitris*, the mythic Lords of Light, who long ago breathed life into those who were human in form but devoid of self-consciousness. Through the controlled power of mystic ideation, they lit up the divine spark in the soul which makes possible both learning and choice, and thereby all spiritual, moral and mental growth.

The authentic learner will seek to rekindle and strengthen that light, the Akashic lustre in the saddened eyes of every human being. Witnessing the world with eyes of maturity, of honesty and truth, one must learn to be on the side of germinal goodness, not debasement, of inner beauty, not crudity, of light itself, not shadow, and above all, the needs of the many rather than the cravings of a few. One must make a decisive break with the endless chain of personal self-pity, and affirm pure "I am I" consciousness in order to prepare to take one's true place, stand confidently in the Light of the Spiritual Sun, and ardently follow the Way of Wisdom-Compassion. That way is as high as the stars. It is also as near as the next step, for it is the way of humanity. It is the way of humility and true affirmation, and the way of the inmost camaraderie of spirit which is more profound and potent than outward speech can convey.

When people are lost in silent thought, like Rodin's statue, asking not who they are or what is their tribe and pedigree, but thinking of the nature of man and the future of all mankind, that is the sign of growth. When people learn to forget themselves and their petty concerns, and to think instead of the stars and of all the souls on earth and of the resources of the globe and of world peace and government, then they will discern the great challenge of our time. They will see that they must come out of the multitude and out of the forests of delusion and exemplify through their endeavours the true meaning of human existence. They will live richly yet humbly and without guarantees or scapegoats, but purely for the joy of breathing benevolently and working quietly. Guided by a calm and secure intuition of the possibilities of the academies, ashrams and monasteries of the future, the initiation chambers, mystic rites, and sacred sanctuaries to be spread all over the globe, those who courageously seek the privilege of inclusion without any glory other than in the joy of participation may stand up and be counted. Though they make their mistakes and are put through many trials, they will still govern themselves and crucify the pride of self rather than the *imago* of Christos, spurning the *Kamsa* within the mind rather than the life-giving gift of Krishna.

Present in every human heart, and hidden by the veil of the mystery of the *Atman*, the life-giving power and spirit of eternal Truth finds its voice in the languages of love, of truth, and of purity of intention, purpose and will that is awakened when one gains the priceless privilege of being in the presence of the self-luminous Mahatmas and their Avatar on earth. Like the central sun and the sacred planets, they are ever present in their invisible forms. Having nothing to prove to human beings of any age or clime, they are simply *yogins* who love mankind. Masters of themselves, they are the illustrious servants of the human race and the inimitable embodiments of the unmanifest universe of divine obeisance and sacred learning. In the mystical language of the *Anugita*:

> Glory, brilliance and greatness, enlightenment, victory, perfection and power – these seven rays follow after this same Sun (Kshetragna, the Higher Self).... Those whose wishes are reduced (unselfish)...whose sins (passions) are burnt up by restraint, merging the Self in the Self, devote themselves to Brahman.
>
> The Secret Doctrine, ii 639

If the highest *jnanis* are also the purest *bhaktas*, responding in magical sympathy to the cosmic will of Krishna, entering the stream of incarnation or abiding in the regions of invisible space only for the sake of service, can souls on earth who aspire to learn take any other standard? In the present period of human transformation, the opportunities for growth are great although the law of retrogression claims its toll amongst the weak. It may help to recall Longfellow's reminder that "Dust thou art, to dust returnest, was not spoken of the soul." One need not be like a dumb driven creature; but through unassuming heroism one may live a real life of earnest striving after the good. In a time of profanation one must refine the potent energy of thought through the living idea of the sacred, and though one might have humour and humanity, this need never be at the expense of another human being. One should recognize that *ahimsa* sweetens the breath, that non-violence dignifies the human being and straightens the spine, and that prostration adds inches to one's stature and health to one's frame. Integrity resides in the ability to recognize the difference between what one knows and what one does not know, coupled with a commitment to make good use of the divine gift of the power of learning right until the moment of death, so that one may arrive at the farther shore of earthly life with a sense of having contributed to that which was vaster and more profound than anything that could be contained in the compass of one lifetime.

To recover one's own inheritance as a Manasic being, and to resonate to the vibration of the Avatar which reverberates throughout the invisible world, one must raise one's horizons of thought. One must renounce the confined chronologies and parsimonious ontologies of Western thought. Almost by definition, a Westerner is an individual who believes in only one life. Yet there are many both in America and throughout the world who take rebirth for granted, integrating it into their way of life. Whilst there is a risk that one may speak in terms of many lives but act in terms of one life (which is cheating), once the mind and heart are firmly fixed upon the idea of karma, there is a spontaneous recovery of the capacity to learn and to show reverence and kinship to other human souls. Like the majority of mankind and the ancient inhabitants of the New World, the early Americans, including the Founding Fathers, believed in reincarnation. What, then, is the point of cowardice? Reincarnation is not merely a fashionable topic of conversation for actors and prostitutes sharing autobiographies, nor is it only designed for behind-the-scenes discussions. It should be brought out into the open, as the great sages have always done. If one has doubts, one must ask oneself if there is any reason to affirm another alternative. If so, then freely adopt the philosophy of the behaviourists and nihilists who openly expect to end their existence at death. As Jesus taught, either blow hot or blow cold, for the lukewarm are spewed forth.

If you choose the language of karma and the logic of reincarnation, universal unity and causation, and human solidarity, then you must also accept that theory is only as good as its practice. On this clarified and purified basis it becomes possible to make some small difference by one's life to the lives of others through showing true reverence and humility and an authentic agnosticism because of the ineffability of the One, the universality of the Law of Karma, the intricacy and exactitude of philosophical astrology, and the mysterious mathematics of sum-totals pertaining to the series of reincarnations. Thus one may learn to take an accurate account of the heavy toll exacted by the blockage of the Divine Light in the interior principles. A strenuous effort is required to learn the *ABC*'s of occultism, and it would be folly to expect to discover the origins of consciousness through the self-restricted evidence of only one of its states. The ontological depths of *Prajna* can only be approached after there is a thorough mastery of the psychological and moral planes of human existence. Through firm detachment and unwavering attention, one must make oneself invulnerable to the siren calls of the past and cloying fantasies about the future, for the *narjol* is not safe until after having crossed beyond the regions of illusion, in which, as the *Anugita* teaches,

> ... fancies are the gadflies and mosquitoes, in which grief and joy are cold and heat, in which delusion is the blinding darkness, avarice, the beasts of prey and reptiles, and desire and anger are the obstructors.
>
> The Secret Doctrine, ii 637

Above all, if one would seek freedom from the forests of delusion, from the enslavement of *Manas* to the senses, one must turn to the one and only source which can give protection and refuge, the *Kshetragna* within the sun. This is not to be understood in terms of any of the foolish salvation myths built up by failed disciples, but rather because of the logic and the law of the reflection of supernal light. Try to see the world not from below above but from above below. Try to see the world through the eyes of all those *yogins*, Mahatmas, who live both in the Himalayan crests of consciousness and in the lowliest heart of every sincere and aspiring human being. They can pass through any metal or substance named by man, and be simultaneously in many places. Established in the transcendental freedom of *Mahat*, they travel at will throughout the planes of the globe, though this has nothing to do with pseudo-occult notions of astral travel. They are masters; their life-atoms are so pure that they can never hurt a single being. Supremely chaste, men of truth who never know what it is to foster a lie, they are perfected in the practice of *Karma Yoga*, using many guises, playing jokes, veiling themselves constantly and thereby always guarding and protecting each and every human being without exception. They are what they are before they ever take illusory birth in the races of man, and they do not become anything different. Taking on illusory bodies of form from time to time for the instruction of mankind, Avatars create before mortal eyes a re-enactment of the path towards supreme enlightenment, but it is only a foolish fancy that supposes, for example, that Christ was not Christ, that Buddha was not Buddha, aeons before taking birth in a mortal frame. It was only for the sake of instruction that Jesus the Chrestos became Christos seemingly in three years, or that Gautama the Prince became the Enlightened Buddha through his travail in the forest on behalf of mankind.

The Buddha taught that the entire world is like a lake of lotuses, each representing beings in different stages of *maya*. He explained that his life was not for the sake of those few who had already approached the Light of the Spiritual Sun, nor for those so deeply plunged in the mud of *maya* and *moha* that they could make no significant progress in their present incarnation, but rather for those in the middle, struggling to come out, those who need the assurance and the confidence that they too can move further up through the swirling currents of earth life and reach the surface of the waters and open to the sun. All such births of spiritual Teachers of Mankind are conscious incarnations of beings who knew millions of years ago who they were, and who, in enacting their self-knowledge that spells out as self-conquest, assume a compassionate veil.

In the *Bhagavad Gita*, Lord Krishna explains that there are seven classes of human beings. There are those who are wicked, those who are deluded, and those who are totally drunk with passion. These three classes neither know nor recognize Krishna. Then there are the four classes of true and good beings who have some degree of recognition: the sufferers and afflicted, who, in their pain, desperately want to find peace and give their lives meaning; those who seek truth and spiritual knowledge which could be used for self-transformation, knowledge that by use they could convert into wisdom which, through suffering, becomes compassion; and then there are those who are wise and yet seek further wisdom, understanding that the basis of all wisdom is the knowledge of Krishna. Finally, there are those who already know Krishna because they are already a part of Krishna. These beings are the dearest unto Krishna; eternally united to him, they are never apart from him. They are the Mahatmas difficult to find. They became Mahatmas in the only way that any human being ever can, out of many lives of struggle and search, of honest striving and pure devotion. They are the custodians of the Seventh Mystery, that most secret Wisdom, which ever lives in the heart of every being and from which ultimately none is excluded.

Krishna explains that when he comes into the world, any beings who recognize him at any level and truly place their hearts on him – in their thoughts and dreams, their hopes and aspirations – and who truly think of him in times of trouble will be helped. Those who truly love him for his own sake and not for their own will certainly find the grace that comes with such honest love. Those whose minds are still enthralled within the forest of illusions, and who seek therein their good, will under karma find there the sad fruits of their misguided search. But as Bhagavan revealed in the *Anugita*, for those who have learnt to subdue their senses and for whom the light of *Buddhi-Manas* has begun to dawn,

> . . . another forest shines forth, in which *intelligence is the tree*, and emancipation the fruit, and which possesses shade (*in the form of*) tranquillity, which depends on Knowledge, which has contentment for its water, and the KSHETRAGNA (*the 'Supreme SELF,'* says Krishna, in the Bhagavad Gita) within for the Sun.... Those people who understand the forest of Knowledge (Brahman, or SELF) praise tranquillity. And aspiring to that forest, they are (re-) born so as not to lose courage. Such indeed, is this holy forest...and understanding it, they (the Sages) act accordingly, being directed by the KSHETRAGNA.
>
> *The Secret Doctrine*, ii 638–640

Those who seek for nothing in the world but only wish to serve humanity and Krishna in the heart of every being are fortune's favoured soldiers. They alone come to Krishna, realizing that they are already in him though he is not contained in them, for he is everywhere and cannot be only in a few. This is the supreme mystery of the *Adhyatman*, the comprehension of which dispels all darkness. It is the mystery of immortality veiled by the appearances of the life and death of beings. It is the supreme glory and light of the Divine made visible by the Divine, and it is beyond all light and darkness, beyond all the wondrous and myriad forms and shapes of the celestial and terrestrial worlds which are only the veil upon itself. It is the very Self of Wisdom and Compassion, and the secure refuge of truth sought by all beings in the vast vale of soul-making called the world. It is the deathless core of fearlessness in all the prisoners in all the dungeons of the world, in the hearts of all the children who hope against hope that there will be a tomorrow, hope that despite the errors of generals, the follies of politicians, the ignorance of pseudo-spiritual leaders, there will be peace and goodwill amongst men, and there will be some rare breeze over the Himalayas which comes to bless all beings.

Hermes, January 1982

THE GANDHIAN BRIDGE BETWEEN HEAVEN AND EARTH

The Angels keep thou ancient places; –
Turn but a stone, and start a wing!
'Tis ye, 'tis your estrangèd faces,
That miss the many-splendoured thing.
But (when so sad thou canst not sadder)
Cry; – and upon thy so sore loss
Shall shine the traffic of Jacob's ladder
Pitched betwixt Heaven and Charing Cross.

Francis Thompson

My heart has become capable of every form;
It is a pasture for gazelles and a convent for Christian monks,
And a temple for idols and the pilgrim's Ka'ba
And the tables for the Torah and the book of the Quran.
I follow the religion of Love: whatever way
Love's camels take, that is my religion and my faith.

Ibn al-'Arabi

Selfless service is the secret of life.

Mahatma Gandhi

Mahatma Gandhi held that all human beings are always responsible to themselves, the entire Family of Man and to God, or Truth (*SAT*) for their continual use of all the goods, gifts and talents that fall within their domain. This is necessarily true because of his basic assumption that Nature and Man are alike upheld, suffused and regenerated by the Divine. There is a luminous spark of divine intelligence in the action of each atom and in the eyes of every man, woman and child upon this earth. This is the enduring basis of effective self-regeneration at all levels – individual, social, national and global. We fully incarnate our latent divinity when we deliberately and joyously put our abilities and assets to practical use for the sake of the good of all. In this tangible sense, the finest exemplars of global trusteeship are those who treat all possessions as though they are sacred or priceless, beyond any worldly or monetary scale of valuation.

Thus, it is only through daily moral choices and the meritorious and sagacious employment of our limited resources that we sustain our inherited or acquired entitlements. For this very reason, the divisive notion and dangerous illusion of exclusive ownership is systematically misleading and, at worst, a specious and subtle form of violence. It connotes assertive rights or claims, and even privileged access, that far exceed the legitimate bounds of actual human need – even though protected by statutory law or social custom. It also obscures the generous bounty of Nature and the potential fecundity of human resourcefulness and innovation, which together can readily provide enough for all denizens of the earth, if only each person would hold in trust whatever he has to meet his essential needs, without profligate excess or any form of exploitation. This is the basic presupposition behind *sarvodaya*, non-violent socialism at its best, which is as old as the spiritual communism taught by Buddha and Christ.

Ancient Indian thought viewed the entire cosmos and all human souls as continually sustained by the principle of harmony (*rita*), the principle of sacrifice (*yajna*), and the principle of universal interdependence, solidarity and concord. This is enshrined in the Golden Rule, which is found in all the major religions of mankind and is mirrored in the codes and norms of all cultures at different stages of development. The Vedic chants portrayed heaven and earth as indissolubly linked through the mighty sacrificial ladder of being, which is found in the Pythagorean philosophy and memorably conveyed in Shakespeare's *Troilus and Cressida*. Similarly, Jacob's celestial ladder of angels between heaven and earth signifies the indispensable linkage or Leibnizian continuity between the universal and the particular, the unconditional and the contextually concrete, the divine and the human, the Logos and the cosmos, the macrocosm and the microcosm. Jacob sensed, in his celebrated dream, that this vital connection provides a shining thread of hope for souls in distress. He also saw that it provides a helpful clue to action by binding together profound contemplation and the apt choice of available means, not because he claimed any supernatural wisdom or superhuman power, but only because he was content to remain an ardent seeker and a constant learner.

Philo Judaeus saw in Jacob a transparently good man who had gained the talismanic insight that everyone learns best by emulating noble exemplars instead of merely repeating the words of the wise without even trying to enact what they teach. Philo, who also saw the true statesman as a disguised soothsayer in the sense that he could interpret the deepest dreams of ordinary men and women, their irrepressible longings for the greater good, stated in his *De Congressu Eruditionis Gratia*:

> It is characteristic of the learner that he listens to a voice and to words, for by these alone is he taught, but he who acquires the good through practice and not through teaching pays attention not to what is said but to those who say it, and imitates their life in its succession of blameless actions. Thus it is said in the case of Jacob, when he is sent to marry one of his kin, 'Jacob hearkened to his father and mother, and journeyed to Mesopotamia' (*Genesis* 28:7), not to their voice or words, for the practicer must be the imitator of a life, not the hearer of words, since the latter is characteristic of one who is being instructed, the former of one who struggles through to the end.[1]

Jacob was perhaps a *karma yogin* (or its rabbinical equivalent), who conscientiously sought to translate what he knew into the concrete discipline of moral conduct. He deeply cherished his vision of the celestial bridge between *theoria* and *praxis*, the invisible arch (or ark of salvation) linking the rarefied empyrean of scriptural ethics and the actual pathway each human being must trace and tread in his life on earth. To Jacob it was given to discern the divine ladder upon which the angels tread (depicted like a spinal column in the Kabbalistic Tree of Life), and to salute the old men who dream dreams as well as the young men who see visions (Joel 2:28). This is poignantly suggestive of the profound statement of Herzen, which contemporary detractors of *perestroika* and *glasnost* ignore at their peril, that political leaders do not change events in the world by rational demonstrations or by

---

1 Philo of Alexandria (Philo Judaeus), *The Contemplative Life, The Giants and Selections*, David Winston, trans., Paulist Press (New York, 1981), p. 215.

syllogisms, but rather by "dreaming the dreams of men". No doubt, this is easier said than done, but it would be an elitist form of defeatism to abandon the attempt in a world bedevilled by obsolete isms and irrational ideologies, yet trembling on the brink of nuclear annihilation and global chaos. As Mikhail Gorbachev frankly admitted:

> The restructuring doesn't come easily for us. We critically assess each step we are making, test ourselves by practical results, and keenly realize that what looks acceptable and sufficient today may be obsolete tomorrow. . . .
> There is a great thirst for mutual understanding and mutual communication in the world. It is felt among politicians, it is gaining momentum among the intelligentsia, representatives of culture, and the public at large. . . .
> The restructuring is a must for a world overflowing with nuclear weapons; for a world ridden with serious economic and ecological problems; for a world laden with poverty, backwardness and disease; for a human race now facing the urgent need of ensuring its own survival.
> We are all students, and our teacher is life and time. . . . We want people of every country to enjoy prosperity, welfare and happiness. The road to this lies through proceeding to a nuclear-free, non-violent world.

Whilst Gandhi was doubtless closer in spirit to Jacob and Philo than to Herzen and Lenin, he would have concurred in the sentiments behind *perestroika* and *glasnost*.[2]

Mohandas Karamchand Gandhi saw himself essentially as a *karma yogin*, who, without claiming any special or supernatural wisdom, was unusually receptive in his readiness to honour remarkable men such as Naoroji, Gokhale and Rajchandra as rare models of probity worthy of emulation. He showed consistent fidelity to the paradigm of the self-governed Sage[3] portrayed in eighteen *shlokas* which were daily chanted at his *ashram*. He took this classical model as the basis for assiduous self-study, ever seeking to correct himself whenever he

---

2 Mikhail Gorbachev, *Perestroika*, Harper and Row (New York, 1987), pp. 253–54.
3 *The Bhagavad Gita*, Raghavan Iyer, ed., Concord Grove Press (Santa Barbara, 1985), pp. 84–90.

saw that he had erred, especially when he made what he called, with playful hyperbole, "Himalayan blunders". He strenuously maintained the hard-won awareness that sensitive leaders must always share the trials and travails of the human condition, that ubiquitous suffering is the common predicament of humanity, whilst all earthly pleasures and intellectual joys are ephemeral and deceptive.

Gandhi, like Gautama, did not try to escape the evident truth of human suffering through seeking mindless oblivion or neurotic distractions, nor did he choose to come to terms with it through compensatory spiritual ambition or conventional religious piety. Rejecting the route of cloistered monasticism, he pondered deeply and agonizingly upon the human condition, and sought to find the redemptive function and therapeutic meaning of human misery. Translating his painful insights into daily acts of *tapas* – self-chosen spiritual exercises and the repeated re-enactments of lifelong meditation in the midst of fervent social activity – he came to see the need for a continual rediscovery of the purpose of living by all those who reject the hypnosis of bourgeois society, with its sanctimonious hypocrisy and notorious "double standards" for individual and public life.

Gautama Buddha had taught his disciples in the *Sangha* that *bodhichitta*, the seed of enlightenment, may be found in the cleansed heart and controlled mind, and that it may be quickened by diligent practice of meditative altruism and honest self-examination of one's unconscious tendencies and hidden motives. As stressed in the later *Mahayana* schools of India, China and Tibet, *bodhichitta* can serve, like the Upanishadic *antaskarana* or mediating principle of intellection, as a reliable bridge between fleeting sense-experience and enduring spiritual aspiration, as an aid and stimulus to the ascent of consciousness to its highest possible elevation and even to the plane of *svasamvedana*, universal self-consciousness in the midst of *shunyata*, the voidness released through persistent philosophical negation.

Spiritual striving towards enlightenment can help to raise a ladder of contemplation along which the seeker may ascend and descend, participating in the worlds of eternity and time, perfecting one's sense of timing in the sphere of action. In most people, alas, the seed is not allowed to sprout or grow owing to chaotic and contradictory aims and desires, tinged by vain longings and delusive expectations, fantasies and fears, blocking any vibrant encounter with the realities of this world as well as any possibility of envisioning Jacob's ladder, "pitched betwixt Heaven and Charing Cross". Gandhi's own spiritual conviction grew, with the ripening of age, that social reformers and non-violent revolutionaries must repeatedly cleanse their sight and remove all self-serving illusions by placing themselves squarely within the concrete context of mass suffering.

Gandhi knew that his ideas and ideals were difficult to instantiate precisely because of their inherent simplicity. He recognized, therefore, that he could only clarify and illustrate them to all who sought his counsel. Those others would, through *tapas*, have to assimilate and apply them for themselves. But the hero and villain jostle in every soul. Morally sensitive individuals must learn to detect self-deception with firmness and forbearance, mellowness and maturity. They must come to know the obscuration of light within before they can ferret out evil at its roots. Eventually, "a man with intense spirituality may without speech or gesture touch the hearts of millions who have never seen him and whom he has never seen".[4] Through meditation, man can attain a noetic plane on which thought becomes the primary and most potent mode of action. Gandhi unwaveringly affirmed that living this conviction would bring sacrificial suffering, as well as an inner joy which cannot be conveyed in words.

On his seventy-eighth birthday in 1947, when well-wishers showered him with lavish and affectionate greetings, Gandhi thought only of the violence and suffering of his recently independent and hastily partitioned motherland:

> I am not vain enough to think that the divine purpose can only be fulfilled through me. It is as likely as not that a fitter instrument will be used to carry it out and that I was good enough to represent a weak nation, not a strong one. May it not be that a man purer, more courageous, more far-seeing, is wanted for the final purpose? Mine must be a state of complete resignation to the Divine Will.... If I had

---

4 M.K. Gandhi in Young India, Mar. 22, 1928.

the impertinence openly to declare my wish to live 125 years, I must have the humility, under changed circumstances, openly to shed that wish.... In that state, I invoke the aid of the all-embracing Power to take me away from this 'vale of tears' rather than make me a helpless witness of the butchery by man become savage, whether he dares to call himself a Mussalman or Hindu or what not. Yet I cry, 'Not my will but Thine alone shall prevail.'[5]

Gandhi was sometimes apt to speak of God in the language of Christian mystics, despite his explicit commitment to a more philosophical view of Deity, as given in the most advanced Hindu schools of thought and practice. He wavered at times between the standpoints and terminologies of contemplative monists and ecstatic dualists, but he never abandoned his early axiom that Truth is God, which he preferred to the statement that God is Truth, and he also held that Truth is the root of pure love and unconditional compassion.[6] His lifelong faith in God as Truth (*SAT*) implied a concrete, if inviolable, confidence in the spiritual and ethical potential of all humanity, far surpassing the historicist and immanentist beliefs of reductionist sociological doctrines and rival political ideologies. He could, he felt, honestly call himself a socialist or a communist, although he explicitly repudiated their materialistic assumptions, violent methods, utilitarian programmes and totalistic claims. He spoke of socialism of the heart and invoked the Ishopanishadic injunction to renounce and enjoy the world, which nourished his own reformist aspirations, revolutionary zeal, and Tolstoyan conviction that the Kingdom of God is attainable on earth and is, in any event, a feasible, life-sustaining ideal. He knew, especially in his last decade, moods of pessimism and even moments of despair, when his inner voice would not speak, which lent a poignant and heroic quality to his life reminiscent of the passion of Jesus Christ, the psychological martyrdom of saints, and the early strivings of the wandering monk, Siddhartha Kapilavastu, who became the

---

5   M.K. Gandhi in D.G. Tendulkar, *Mahatma: Life of Mohandas Karamchand Gandhi*, V.K. Jhaveri and D.G. Tendulkar (Bombay, 1951-1954), vol. 8, p. 144; reprinted in *The Moral and Political Writings of Mahatma Gandhi*, Raghavan Iyer, ed., Clarendon (Oxford, 1986–1987), vol. 1, pp. 10–11 (hereafter cited as *MPWMG*).

6   M.K. Gandhi, "Speech at Meeting in Lausanne", Mahadev Desai's Diary (MSS); *MPWMG*, vol. 2, pp. 164–66.

enlightened Buddha. But he returned always to the conviction that it is presumptuous to deny human perfectibility or the possibility of human progress, let alone to take refuge in the fashionable armchair doctrine that *Ramarajya* irrelevant to *Kali Yuga*, that the Kingdom of God is wholly unattainable in the world of time.

He held firmly to the view which Vinoba Bhave, his leading disciple, made his life-motto, that the social reformer and spiritual anchorite must be committed to the gospel of the *Gita* and to a life of ceaseless, selfless service of the weak and the wretched of the earth. He must choose to become a *satyayugakari*, an exemplar and witness of *Ramarajya* even in the midst of *Kali Yuga*, the Age of Iron. He could thus serve as a heroic pioneer and a patient builder, contributing bricks to the invisible, ideational endeavour to rebuild Solomon's Temple, to re-establish the reign of Truth and Love even in the small circles of human fellowship. As a *karma yogin*, he could yoke a microcosmic approach to social experimentation with a macro-cosmic vision of universal peace, human solidarity and a global "civilization of the heart". This requires a staunch refusal to think in terms of nations, tribes, castes and classes, or the tedious distinctions made by the insecure in terms of race and creed, sex and status. What is needed at all times is a purgation of the psyche, a restoration of purity of the heart, and a release of the spiritual will in simple acts consecrated to the good of all. This was strongly stressed by Soren Kierkegaard and Simone Weil. It was powerfully exemplified by many a legendary hero and heroine of the Indian epics and *Puranas*, extolled in song and story to this day among millions of impoverished but indefatigable peasants in thousands of Indian villages, and also known to the homeless and the dispossessed exiles and tramps in crowded cities and decaying townships.

Towards the close of his extraordinarily eventful life, so crowded with petitioners and visitors of every sort from all over the globe and from the farthest corners of rural India as well as from the towering Himalayas, he reaffirmed his inward vision of the "Himalayas of the plains" and the inextinguishable integrity of socialist *sannyasa* and Bodhisattvic compassion. He ever recalled the formative early influences in his life – the *Vaishnava* ideal of Narasinh Mehta, *The Key to Theosophy* of Helena Petrovna Blavatsky, and the telling instructions of Bishop Butler, William Salter and Henry Drummond. He evidently knew the vivid encomiums of Drummond to Jesus as the Man of Sorrows, though he never explicitly cited the most memorable of such statements:

> Christ sets His followers no tasks. He appoints no hours. He allots no sphere. He Himself simply went about and did good. He did not stop life to do some special thing which should be called religious. His life was His religion. Each day as it came brought round in the ordinary course its natural ministry. Each village along the highway had someone waiting to be helped. His pulpit was the hillside, His congregation a woman at a well. The poor, wherever He met them, were His clients; the sick, as often as He found them, His opportunity. His work was everywhere; His workshop was the world.[7]

In his *ashrams* and during the periods of abstention from politics, which were longer and more frequent than many imagined, Gandhi was fortunate to experience the secret joy of living in the *atman*, which he early saw in Rajchandra, the jeweller and *theodidact*. Gandhi's demanding conception of his *svadharma*, his self-chosen obligations, repeatedly thrust him back into the arenas of political conflict and conciliation, as well as into the wider forums of the Constructive Programme, social reform and nation-wide rural reconstruction. Even here his quintessential philosophy of *anasakti yoga*, the gospel of selfless, disinterested action taught by Krishna in the *Gita*, came to his aid in distilling non-violent socialism to its irreducible core, as construed by Henry Drummond:

> The most obvious lesson in Christ's teaching is that there is no happiness in having and getting anything, but only in giving.... And half the world is on the wrong scent in the pursuit of happiness. They think it consists in having and getting, and in being served by others. It consists in giving and serving others. He that would be great among you, said Christ, let him serve. He that would be happy, let him remember that there is but one way – it is more blessed, it is more happy, to give than to receive.[8]

---

7   Henry Drummond, "The Ministry of Christ", in *The Jewel in the Lotus*, Raghavan Iyer, ed., Concord Grove Press (Santa Barbara, 1983), p. 201.
8   Henry Drummond, "Happiness", *Ibid.*, p. 71.

This is the secret of *sarvodaya*, the doctrine of non-violent socialism which Gandhi fused with his alkahest of global trusteeship and his lifelong experience of the reality and continual relevance of radical self-regeneration through selfless service. Krishna's sovereign remedy of *Buddhi Yoga*, the *yoga* of divine discernment, points to the crucial connection between *viveka*, discrimination, and *vairagya*, detachment, between self-chosen duty and voluntary sacrifice, *dharma* and *yajna*, individual self-conquest and the welfare of the world, *lokasangraha*. Even a little of this practice, as taught in the *Gita* and as realized by Gandhi, is invaluable:

> In this path of yoga no effort is ever lost, and no harm is ever done.
> Even a little of this discipline delivers one from great danger.[9]

In the words of Dnyaneshwar, the foremost saint and poet of Maharashtra, "just as the flame of a lamp, though it looks small, affords extensive light, so this higher wisdom, even in small measure, is deeply precious".

This is the ideal of the suffering servant of Isaiah, the means of entry into the wider human family as shown by Ibn al-'Arabi in his haunting poems, the evocative vision of the monkish revolutionaries known to the Russian Populists, the basis of inspiration of many a Christian socialist and even the Christian Communists of the thirties, the demanding conception of Philo, who concluded from his observation of the Therapeutae and other small communes that "every day is a festival",[10] let alone the ancient Hindu ideal of the true Mahatma or self-governed Sage, the *jivanmukta* or spiritually free man, for whom each day is like unto a new incarnation, and each incarnation like unto a *manvantara*, the vast epoch of cosmic manifestation.

Gandhi prophesied that for thirty years after his death, his ideas would be largely forgotten, but that, generations later, the *tapas* of millions would bear fruit, and that out of his ashes "a thousand Gandhis will arise".[11] Even though this is still an elusive hope, it is enormously

---

9 *The Bhagavad Gita*, Raghavan Iyer, ed., p. 79.
10 Philo of Alexandria, *The Contemplative Life*, p. 200.
11 M.K. Gandhi, "Message to Students", *Harijan*, Jan. 16, 1937; *MPWMG*, vol. 1, p. 35.

encouraging that courageous pioneers have emerged from the host of the disillusioned who find the world of today too ghastly to contemplate, a world of mindless mass consumerism induced by the rising curve of shallow expectations, a world in which there is a widespread alienation of lonely individuals from disintegrating societies, of conscience from the intellect, of angry rebels from the agonies of the compassionate heart, of impotent politicians from the global imperatives of radical change and genuine coexistence among all nations and peoples, creeds and ideologies. Ragnarok, the end of the gods and of the world, is the sole alternative in Nordic mythology to the rainbow bridge between heaven and earth, Bifrost, at which crossing many may camp at the boundary of a new land, a new frontier, a new settlement. Whether or not a New Jerusalem is attainable on earth in the lifetime of the humanity of the present, there is much wisdom in Gandhi's own well-tested message in times of trial.

In "*One Step Enough for Me*" he said:

> When, thousands of years ago, the battle of Kurukshetra was fought, the doubts which occurred to Arjuna were answered by Shri Krishna in the *Gita*; but that battle of Kurukshetra is going on, will go on, forever within us; the Prince of Yogis, Lord Krishna, the universal *Atman* dwelling in the hearts of us all, will always be there to guide Arjuna, the human soul, and our Godward impulses represented by the Pandavas will always triumph over the demoniac impulses represented by the Kauravas. Till, however, victory is won, we should have faith and let the battle go on, and be patient meanwhile.[12]

Those who cannot share this testament of faith, rooted in the spiritual convictions of antiquity concerning the periodic descent of Avatars or Divine Redeemers, the immortality of the soul and the inexorable law of Karma, the law of ethical causation and moral retribution, may yet actively respond to "the still, sad music of humanity". After all, even agnostics and atheists, socialists, humanists and communists, may share a living faith in the future of civilization and hold a truly open view of human nature, social solidarity and global progress. All alike

---

12 M.K. Gandhi, "*One Step Enough for Me*", Speech at Wardham Ashram, Navajivan, Dec. 27, 1925; *MPWMG*, vol. 1, p. 21.

may well ponder upon Mahatma Gandhi's life-message. Towards the end of his pilgrimage on earth he delivered a deeply moving and testable challenge to theophilanthropists everywhere:

> I will give you a talisman. Whenever you are in doubt, or when the self becomes too much with you, apply the following test. Recall the face of the poorest and weakest man whom you may have seen, and ask yourself if the step you contemplate is going to be of any use to him. Will he gain anything by it? Will it restore him to a control over his own life and destiny? In other words, will it lead to *swaraj* [self-rule] for the hungry and spiritually starving millions? Then you will find your doubts and yourself melting away.[13]

Hermes, January 1988

---

13 M.K. Gandhi in D.G. Tendulkar, *Mahatma*, vol. 8, p. 89; *MPWMG*, vol. 3, p. 609.

BUDDHI YOGA AND SVADHARMA

> Whosoever knoweth me to be the mighty Ruler of the universe and without birth or beginning, he among men, undeluded, shall be liberated from all his sins. Subtle perception, spiritual knowledge, right judgement, patience, truth, self-mastery; pleasure and pain, prosperity and adversity; birth and death, danger and security, fear and equanimity, satisfaction, restraint of body and mind, alms-giving, inoffensiveness, zeal and glory and ignominy, all these the various dispositions of creatures come from me. So in former days the seven great Sages and the four Manus who are of my nature were born of my mind, and from them sprang this world. He who knoweth perfectly this permanence and mystic faculty of mine becometh without doubt possessed of unshaken faith. I am the origin of all; all things proceed from me; believing me to be thus, the wise gifted with spiritual wisdom worship me; their very hearts and minds are in me; enlightening one another and constantly speaking of me, they are full of enjoyment and satisfaction. To them thus always devoted to me, who worship me with love, I give that mental devotion [Buddhi Yoga] by which they come to me. For them do I out of my compassion, standing within their hearts, destroy the darkness which springs from ignorance by the brilliant lamp of spiritual discernment.
>
> *Bhagavad Gita*, X

Lord Krishna represents the universality and versatility of boundless joy (*ananda*) and the unconditional love at the core of cosmic and human evolution. Wherever thought has struggled to be free, wherever the human heart has opened itself to the invisible Spiritual Sun, and wherever even a drop of wisdom has been awakened through suffering and pain, courage and persistence, there you will find the immortal Spirit, the sovereign power of the omnipresent *Purusha*. All the Rishis and Mahatmas reside within the universal form (*brahmanda*) of Vishnu-Narayana-Krishna. In saluting them, one experiences a sense of the timeless, a transcendence that reaches beyond all limits, frontiers and boundaries of manifestation. One may greet the Supreme in the midnight sun, in the dawn of Venus, at midday or in the gathering dusk – the time of memory or the time of reverie. And one must always reach out towards that Divine Darkness which is prior to all worlds and beyond all forms. Myriads upon myriads of worlds of billions of beings arise from that Divine Darkness and reside in the unmanifest light of the invisible form of Vishnu-Narayana.

That light neither rises nor sets, neither waxes nor wanes. It is the same light which, in the words of the Gospel according to John, irradiates every soul that comes into this world. It is the light to be found in the sound of the AUM, uttered, however imperfectly, by every baby at birth. It is the light that descends upon every human being at the moment of death, when he or she stands ready to cast off the external garments of this world and return to the inmost vesture, the *karana sharira*, and come closer to the *Atman*. It is also the light-vibration of the ever-present *Brahma Vach* that pulsates throughout the cosmos, maintained in motion by mighty men of meditation, Dhyanis, Rishis, Mahatmas, Buddhas and Bodhisattvas. All human beings can return, again and again, to sit at the feet of Lord Krishna and so learn how to brighten their lives and awaken compassion in their hearts.

Every pilgrim soul who seeks to increase skill in action for the sake of increasing his or her capacity to add even a little to the sum of human good can benefit from the Teachings of Lord Krishna in the *Bhagavad Gita*. Taken as a whole, the *Gita* is a treatise on *yoga*, the kingly science, of the individual soul's union with the universal Self. That union is, ontologically, ever existent. But because of the *maya* of manifestation and the descent of consciousness through vestures which seem to create a world of many selves and many forms, the human mind becomes alienated from the true inmost Self in which *Ishvara* resides. It becomes confined within time and space, within past, present and future, and it must struggle to overcome these illusions. Thus the whole of the *Gita* is a summons and challenge to engage in that righteous warfare which every human soul must undertake. In the eighteenth chapter of the *Gita*, Lord Krishna declares that if one will not voluntarily choose to engage in this righteous war, karmic necessity will compel one to do so. The wise are those who cooperate with cosmic necessity, with their own divine destiny, with their own sacrosanct duty or *svadharma*. The wisest are those who choose as firmly and as early as possible, making an irreversible and unconditional commitment, in the gracious manner and generous spirit of Lord Krishna. Without doubt or hesitation, they choose His path, His teaching and His prescribed mode of skill in action.

In the second chapter of the *Gita*, Krishna begins by affirming to Arjuna the eternal existence of one indivisible, inconsumable, inexhaustible Source of all life, light and energy. Having dispelled the danger that Arjuna would abandon through fear the righteous battle and his *svadharma*, Krishna presents before Arjuna the talismanic teaching of *Buddhi Yoga*:

> Yet the performance of works is by far inferior to mental devotion [*Buddhi Yoga*], O despiser of wealth. Seek an asylum, then, in this mental devotion, which is knowledge; for the miserable and unhappy are those whose impulse to action is found in its reward. But he who by means of *yoga* is mentally devoted dismisses alike successful and unsuccessful results, being beyond them; *yoga* is skill in the performance of actions: therefore do thou aspire to this devotion. For those who are thus united to knowledge and devoted, who have renounced all reward for their actions, meet no rebirth in this life, and go to that eternal blissful abode which is free from all disease and untouched by troubles.
>
> *Bhagavad Gita*, II

Buddhi Yoga requires a fixity and steadfastness in intuitive intelligent determination which is superior to *Karma Yoga*, the yoga of works, as a means of gaining enlightenment. It involves an eye capable of recognizing essentials, which, once awakened, will give a decisiveness without wavering or wandering. Through this resolute intellect, one's actions may become shadowless – *nischaya*. Even though one may be obscured, as a member of the human family participating in the world's pain, ignorance and turbulence, nonetheless one inwardly preserves the dignity of the power of choice. It is, therefore, possible to touch within oneself that level of absolute resolve which ensures that something essential will never be abandoned, or diluted or doubted, never weakened by careless speech nor lost in the chaos of compulsive acts, but always protected from discursive and dissecting Manasic reasoning. Every human being enjoys such moments of assurance. Otherwise it would not be possible to survive. Even fools and knaves have a few moments of *sushupti* at night inspiring them to awaken in the morning to greet another day. Were it not for this abiding sense of assurance about one's minimum dignity within the core of one's being, one could not go on.

This sense of one's distinct place in the total scheme of things is what Spinoza called the *conatus*, the urge or will to sustain rational and spiritual self-preservation. This is not merely an intellectual notion, but a biological fact. When a person begins to approach death, the *anahata* vibration in the spiritual heart ceases to sound in the *linga sharira*. The Sage or Seer can recognize this cessation of sound and a subtle alteration in the rate of breathing several months before the time of physical death. Throughout this period, the human being is engaged in a protracted review of the whole of his or her life, a review which is too often chaotic and confused, a jumble of recent memories and childhood events. Only at the time of separation from the physical body is the soul enabled to view in an orderly and rapid manner the entire film of an entire life. In the final preparation for this there is an ebbing of the connection between the sound vibration in the spiritual heart and the *karana sharira* and the vibration in the *linga sharira*, and therefore also in the *sthula sharira*. Once this ebbing begins, the person has begun to withdraw or die.

The sense of resolve and human dignity is so weak in human beings today that vast numbers, in the phrase of T.S. Eliot, are only "living and partly living". They have become so disgusted with the world, so confused about the events of our times and the precipitous decline of humane values throughout the globe, that they are hardly incarnated. They are mostly asleep or sleep-walking, drowsy or passive, or they mechanically go about their duties. They maintain none of that minimal wakefulness that is found in many a humble villager who, through desperation and poverty, maintains intact the light in the eyes, the light of *Manas* and human self-awareness. Paradoxically, one can sometimes sense the ray and radiance of pure consciousness in the most desperate and despised of human beings, whilst others have, alas, been educated beyond their capacity to make use of their knowledge. Between the head and the heart there is a terrible chasm, or even a battle. Many tend to be lost and therefore they live and partly live. It is as if the will to live, the *conatus*, has weakened; nothing remains but an automatism of habit and the power of cohesion in the *skandhas*. This is the pitiable condition referred to by Lord Krishna when he speaks of those who are wedded to the fruits of action. The plight of those who have conditioned themselves only to act for the sake of results is an indictment of modern education in *Kali Yuga*. The Iron Age arms too many people to live only in terms of what is perceptible, measurable and tangible. Having reduced all to the terms of a utilitarian consciousness, they come to view their fellow human beings in a crude Lockean fashion: "Every human being is a threat to you, unless you can join interests with him." If a person is neither a threat nor an accomplice in some selfish interest, he is a stranger. Today vast numbers of human beings live in cities of strangers. They live alone amidst humanity, unloved, with no sense of warmth. Such is the tragic condition of "modern man".

Over five thousand years ago Lord Krishna anticipated this condition of *varnashankar*, the confusion of castes. Although it will increase and proceed throughout the entirety of *Kali Yuga*, it will also provide an opportunity for those who engage consciously and voluntarily in a discipline of intuitive determination, *Buddhi Yoga*. Human beings who are yoked to *Buddhi* are lifelong exemplars of *Buddhi Yoga*. Preferably before the age of seven, and in rare cases even before the age of three, they have permanently married themselves to the Light of the Logos within the secret spiritual heart. Having so early betrothed themselves and permanently married themselves to the Lord within, they go through the obligations of life with ease, without much expectation, but with a certain lightness and skillfulness in the performance of duty. They do what is needed for their parents and grandparents. They do not despise those who claim to be their rivals or enemies. They do not become too attached to their own siblings, and see themselves as essentially no different from the other children they encounter from poorer families, from humbler circumstances, or even from rich and unhappy families. All of them they recognize as a part of one sacred family.

Between the ages of seven and fourteen, having already secretly betrothed themselves to this inner core of the *Ishvara* within, they become quite ready to engage in the duties of the *grihastha ashrama*. At the same time, they have cultivated that skill in self-education which will last all through the *grihastha ashrama* and take them into the third *ashrama*. Even if they cannot retreat into the solitude of forests, mountains or caves, but remain in the midst of society, they will be like wanderers or *parivrajakas*, preparing themselves for the fourth *ashrama*. They will always be one step ahead of the stages of life. By the age of twenty-one they will have sharpened their powers of reason and by the age of twenty-eight they will have developed sufficient Buddhic insight to be able to synthesize and select. So they are able to let go of what is irrelevant and inessential. They can follow the teaching of Buddha: "O Bhiksu, lighten the boat if you will cross to the other shore." While others who are less wise are engaged in amassing and accumulating, they learn to lighten their claims upon the world and their demands upon others. By lightening their expectations from institutions, their hopes and fantasies in relation either to the opposite sex or in relation to children or parents, they become capable of looking with eyes of wonder each day for what is unexpected. They begin to perceive the unwritten poetry of human life and the silent drama of human existence. Thus they become witnesses to the divine dialectic ceaselessly at work.

Such souls are fortunate, for they have chosen to become yoked to *Buddhi*. Having established true continuity of consciousness in youth, by the age of thirty-five they have already started withdrawing. At the moment of death, whether it come early or late, they are able to engage in a conscious process of withdrawal, maintaining intact the potency of the AUM. In life they have not merely learnt to meditate upon the AUM, but also to enact it. They have learnt the art of will-prayer and gained the ability to act in any and every situation for the good of others, without expectation of reward. They have learnt to cast their actions, like offerings, into the ocean of universal sacrifice in the spirit of the AUM. Thus they are able to experience the AUM, whether in the silence that precedes the dawn or in the noisy rush and din of cities. Even in the cacophony and cries of human pain they hear the AUM. It cries out to them in all of Nature's voices. So they maintain continually an awareness of the AUM, and well before the moment of death they are able to receive the help that will enable them to follow a life of *svadharma* and *Buddhi Yoga* in their future incarnations.

Having given Arjuna preliminary instruction in *Buddhi Yoga* in chapter two of the *Gita*, Krishna conveys in chapter four the correct mental posture of the disciple. He depicts that divine *bhakti* which is the prerequisite for *jnana* and also the true spirit of *Karma Yoga*, because they all fuse into a sacred current of consciousness.

> Seek this wisdom by doing service, by strong search, by questions, and by humility; the wise who see the truth will communicate it unto thee, and knowing which thou shalt never again fall into error, O son of Bharata. By this knowledge thou shalt see all things and creatures whatsoever in thyself and then in me.
>
> *Bhagavad Gita*, IV

In this depiction of the perfect posture of the *chela*, Krishna stresses the humility of the wise and the silence of the strong, virtues of the Sage whose portrait was given in the second chapter of the *Gita*. Having conveyed this ideal posture, Krishna proceeds in the seventh chapter to present *Buddhi* as an element in cosmic manifestation. Here he goes beyond the teachings of the Sankhya School, which holds that *Buddhi* is a kind of radiant matter or substance present throughout all Nature. Krishna affirms *Buddhi* as wisdom itself and inseparable from himself, something that no human being can develop except by the grace of the Lord.

> In all creatures I am the life, and the power of concentration in those whose minds are on the spirit. Know me, O son of Pritha, as the eternal seed of all creatures. I am the wisdom [*Buddhi*] of the wise and the strength [*tejas*] of the strong.
>
> *Bhagavad Gita*, VII

To understand this a human being must be able to insert himself or herself into the whole of humanity, recognizing that there is a cosmic force working in human evolution. This is *Mahabuddhi*, connected with *Mahat* and *Akasha*, the alkahest of the hierophants and magicians.

It is the universal solvent and the elixir of life. It is the basis of self-conscious immortality and self-conscious transmutation of the *linga sharira* and the *sthula sharira*. It is the Light of the Logos. All expressions of intelligence – whether latent, partial or highly specialized, whether precise, diffused or merely potential, whether in a dog or an Adept – are drops in one universal shoreless ocean of cosmic *Buddhi*. Therefore, no human being can develop *Buddhi Yoga* on the basis of individualistic conceptions of progress. One cannot simply say to oneself that because one has seen through one's illusions, one is now going to become an apprentice in *Buddhi Yoga*. To say that is to misapprehend the nature of the quest. All forms of yoga require, at some level, what M.K. Gandhi called *anashakti*, egolessness; this is supremely true in *Buddhi Yoga*.

In the practice of spiritual archery one must forget oneself. One can do this meaningfully only if, at the same time, one remains spiritually awake. One must become intensely conscious of one's kinship with all of creation, capable of enjoying its beauty and intelligence without any sense of "mine" or "thine". Wherever there is a display of wisdom, one must salute it. Wherever one finds an exhibition of that true common sense which is helpful in the speech of any human being, one must acknowledge and greet it. This does not mean merely saying "*Namaste*" outwardly, but inwardly bowing down, prostrating oneself before others. At night, before falling asleep, one must count all the benefactors and teachers that one met during the day. No matter how they are disguised, you must be so taken up in rejoicing that you have learnt from other human beings that you have no time to complain of injustice or to become discontented, let alone contentious and cantankerous. In the *Uttara Gita*, long after the Mahabharata War had ended, Krishna told Arjuna that every time one speaks unnecessarily or falsely, one's astral shadow lengthens. If one speaks unwisely, harshly or without thought and deliberation, one expands and fattens the *linga sharira*. So one creates a smoky obscuration of the power of *tejas*, the light within the spiritual heart. The true yogin does the opposite, becoming very conscious and deliberate in the exercise of mental and therefore uttered speech. He learns the art of what D.K. Mavalankar calls self-attenuation. Through this stripping away of inessentials, one becomes capable of maximizing one's every use of life-energy.

Paradoxically, one cannot acquire this self-mastery without recognizing that one cannot do it on one's own. Therefore, Krishna teaches that the power of universal *Buddhi* is an omnipresent essence. Krishna is the radiance in all that is radiant and the intelligence in all the intelligences in the universe. Thus it is only by Krishna's gift that one can arouse that power of devotion which brings the disciple to him. This ultimate paradox, which can be understood in relation to music and love, is vital to spiritual life. It is not only that one must strive and try; a moment comes when one is so absorbed in the object of the quest that one feels the magnetic attraction of that which one seeks. Therefore, the more one enjoys being drawn towards the Lord, the more one can recognize and receive His gift of *Buddhi Yoga*. To prepare oneself to use the gift of the Lord, one must, as the second chapter of the *Gita* teaches, become a spiritual archer, skilled in the art of action. One must become perfected in the precise performance of one's self-chosen duty or *svadharma*. Initially, when Krishna uses the term *svadharma* in the second chapter of the *Gita*, he uses it in relation to the duties of birth, of calling and of caste. He chides Arjuna for forsaking the *svadharma* of a *Kshatriya*. He suggests that if one does not fulfil one's own obligations, chosen and accepted over lifetimes, and if one does not come to terms with the limits, possibilities and opportunities of one's birth, one is moving in the wrong direction and will accrue much evil. Even this initial definition of *svadharma* in terms of one's starting-point in life is much more than a reference to mere occupation and caste.

In the early years of life, most human beings have so little meaningful choice with regard to circumstances that it is difficult to talk credibly of freedom at an early age. Nonetheless, there is for every human being a clear opportunity to accept or not accept that which one cannot alter. In that context, one may be said to choose one's *svadharma*. The concept of choosing that which one cannot change is not fatalism. Rather, it is a critical assessment in consciousness of those elements in one's life which are innate. In the very act of understanding and in the attempt to give meaning to these initial parameters, one must develop and apply some understanding of the karmic field. Moreover, by understanding the karmic tendencies in one's own constitution and confronting one's likes and dislikes, one may come to sense something about one's lower nature and gain some understanding of one's possible behaviour in other lives. Thus, one will recognize that in one's family, for all its obvious limitations, there may be many opportunities for enjoyment and for learning. All true soul-education is an unfoldment through worship and affection, and it is open to every human being to make all life a celebration of learning.

If one really wishes, through the power of worship coupled with affection, to become skilled in the performance of duties, one must recognize that there are those who have gone beyond the initial stages of *Buddhi Yoga*. They have become constant in the power of *Jnana Yoga*, men and women of ceaseless meditation and contemplation. They are the Buddhas and Bodhisattvas of ceaseless contemplation, constantly ideating and thereby sustaining the possibility of human aspiration. They are able to do this through their conscious choice of mental solitude and their freedom from attraction and repulsion. Above all, they exemplify perfection of mental devotion. They have become supremely steadfast, like the immovable Himalayas. They are rock-like in their strength of *tapas*, *bhakti* and *dhyana*. Krishna repeatedly gives encouragement to all beginners making their first tentative steps on the path by urging them to discern in themselves something in common with the highest beings who have ever existed. He offers to Arjuna a living portrait, in potent words, of the true Sage. Whilst it is difficult for modern man to understand, there are in fact many more sages, *munis* and *yogins* than guessed by human beings incarnated on earth. Whilst there are billions upon billions of human beings, there are also galaxies of adepts and Bodhisattvas. Whilst they are invisible to the physical senses, they nonetheless exist and they all have their roles in the task of cosmic and human evolution.

To become capable of recognizing them and saluting them means that it is possible to gain some light with regard to one's own *svadharma*. Hence, Krishna affirms that it is even better to die in one's own *svadharma* than to be concerned with the duty of another. Even if little is going to change significantly in one's life, the acquisition of wisdom always remains possible and worthwhile. It is a useful mental exercise just to imagine that one is going to die in exactly one's present situation.

Then, without giving any room to fantasy and expectation, one must understand how, through this acceptance of immediate *svadharma*, one may strengthen the power of mental devotion or *Buddhi Yoga*. Growth in the power of sacrifice or *Jnana Yajna* is always possible in every circumstance. But that growth requires a turning away from the region of separative consciousness towards the realm of the united hosts of perfected performers of *yoga* who reside within the universal form of Krishna.

To begin to apprehend this is to begin to prepare for the opening of the Wisdom-Eye, a process that is beatified by the realization of the universal vision given to Arjuna by Krishna in the eleventh chapter of the *Gita*. At the end of that vision Krishna makes a statement which is the foundation of all self-conscious transcendence: "I established this whole universe with a single portion of myself, and remain separate." Here Krishna is the paradigm of the Pythagorean spectator, the *Kutashtha*, he who is aloof and apart from all manifestation. He is the fount of those great *Dhyanis* who descend in the dawn of manifestation, knowing its limits and uninvolved while performing their tasks in manifestation. Maintaining their continuity of consciousness and self-transcendence in the Logos, they remain free from the hypnotic spell of *Mahamaya*. What is exemplified by *Dhyanis* in the dawn of manifestation is repeatedly re-enacted in the course of human evolution when human beings, by the power of *vairagya* – true dispassion established by the power of a vow of fixed determination – are able to generate a continuous current of Buddhic insight. Establishing and maintaining this current, testing it in action and correcting themselves by it, individuals may become constant witnesses to the truth. After a while, their minds become so firmly yoked to Buddhic discrimination that it becomes as natural as breathing. In many Buddhist schools and sanctuaries, particularly in the *Hinayana* tradition, neophytes are taught to observe their breathing. When coupled with the *Mahayana* refinement of motive, this can serve as the enduring basis of bare mindfulness and pure attention.

Vinoba Bhave sums up the whole teaching of *svadharma* in the *Gita* in terms of the concept of *chittashuddhi* – purity of consciousness. All human beings, even in *Kali Yuga*, and even surrounded by pollutions, are capable of mental purification. All are capable of maintaining unbroken and intact a stream of pure consciousness, but this requires spiritual food. One must learn to devise one s own rituals and sacrifices, to treat one's body as a temple in which one will greet and bathe in the Light of the Logos. One must learn to consecrate one's own vesture, becoming wholehearted, uncalculating and without expectation in one's relationship with Krishna. When through self-consecration *bhakti* and *Buddhi* come together, *jnana* is released. From *jnana* one may eventually rise to *dhyana*, ceaseless contemplation. Then it is possible to return to *svadharma* and understand it in the salvific sense expressed by Krishna in the eighteenth chapter of the *Gita*. There Krishna puts *svadharma* in terms of a universal formula, independent of birth, of early circumstances, of vocation and calling. It is the art of discovering one's true nature, and therefore becoming creative in one's capacity for self-expression.

Each human being is an original, and each act is unique. Out of enjoyment of the cosmic *lila* and out of veneration for the universal form and omnipresent light of Krishna, a human being can become unrestricted and spontaneous in enacting and delivering *svadharma*. There is a great joy in this and such *ananda* is so all-absorbing that there is no time to interfere with other people or to criticize them. There is no distraction in relation to the demands of *dharma*. Instead, there is full concentration on becoming a servant and instrument of the universal Logos in the cosmos, the God in man, Krishna in the heart.

> With thy heart place all thy works on me, prefer me to all else, exercise mental devotion [*Buddhi Yoga*] continually, and think constantly of me. By so doing thou shalt by my divine favour surmount every difficulty which surroundeth thee; but if from pride thou wilt not listen to my words, thou shalt undoubtedly be lost. And if, indulging self-confidence, thou sayest 'I will not fight', such a determination will prove itself vain, for the principles of thy nature will impel thee to engage. Being bound by all past karma to thy natural duties, thou, O son of Kunti, wilt involuntarily do from necessity that which in thy folly thou wouldst not do. There dwelleth in the heart of every creature, O Arjuna, the Master – Ishvara – who by his magic power causeth all things and creatures to revolve mounted upon the universal wheel of time. Take sanctuary with him alone, O son of Bharata, with all thy

soul; by his grace thou shalt obtain supreme happiness, the eternal place.

Bhagavad Gita, XVIII

To become a true votary of *Buddhi Yoga* through the performance of *svadharma* is to become ready to serve the divine will of the *Atman*, the workings of the Logos and the Avatar behind all the turbulent sifting and chaos of the historical process. The *Buddhi Yogin* recognizes the intimations of the divine dialectic in maturing human beings, mellowing minds and hearts, broadening and expanding their quintessential humanity. Cooperating with the Light of the Logos within, they are able to rediscover the germ of purity of consciousness and thereby enter the family of the wise, the fraternity who know all of this and exemplify it ceaselessly. The true hallmark of these Rishis and Mahatmas is the power of devotion and adoration. They are constant in adoration of Krishna, His *lila*, His wisdom, the joy of His dance, the beauty of His unconditionality. They understand from within themselves the way in which Krishna may be seen in Arjuna, in Arjuna's aspiration to reach up to Krishna, and also in Krishna's enjoyment of the seeming separation of himself from himself in Arjuna. This is the mysterious art of the universal diffusion of the one Light, the problem of the One and the many, and the participation of the many in the One. Through *Buddhi Yoga, bhakti* and *svadharma* there can be a self-conscious return to the One, but only on behalf of the many. This is the sacred Teaching of Lord Krishna in the *Bhagavad Gita*, given to sustain humanity throughout *Kali Yuga*. All may benefit from the Teaching, returning to it again and again, using it in individual ways, enjoying and appreciating its beauty. Those who are perceptive and appreciate this great gift will make resolute vows to be steadfast in maintaining unbroken a sacred relationship with the Teaching and its great Giver.

Hermes, January 1985

BUDDHA AND THE PATH TO ENLIGHTENMENT

I. Renunciation and Enlightenment

From sky to earth he looked, from earth to sky,
As if his spirit sought in lonely flight
Some far-off vision, linking this and that,
Lost, past, but searchable, but seen, but known.

The Light of ASIA
SIR EDWIN ARNOLD

The *Dhammapada* is the laser-like quintessence of Buddha's luminous message to all humanity. Bridging eternity and time, the unmanifest and the manifest, thought and action, *theoria* and *praxis*, it is a highly potent *therapeia*, a catalytic agent of self-transformation, rooted in the realization of that essential unity which enshrines the meaning of events and relations in an ever-changing cosmos. Although the Pali, the Chinese and Tibetan Buddhist canons contain thousands of treatises which reveal myriad facets of Buddha's "Diamond Soul", the *Dhammapada* is a preamble to all of them. It is a direct mode of transmission, succinct in style and fundamental in its content. Transparent and shimmering like the calm surface of the shining sea in contrast to the variegated contours of the diverse lands whose shores it touches, it has awesome oceanic depths, sheltering vast kingdoms of obscure species, in which every form of life finds its place, rhythm and balance, in which everything is inexplicably interconnected in a complex whole that teases and taunts the untapped potentials of human cognition. Its immense cleansing and restorative power conceals a hidden alchemy.

It teaches receptive seekers to free themselves without external props, without vicarious atonement or adventitious aids, through a self-chosen mode of purification which eludes the categories of behavioural psychology, utilitarian ethics and salvationist theology. It points to a radical rebirth, a programme of progressive self-initiation, becoming more than human, yet being in accord with all humanity, even in the most basic acts of daily life – rising in the dawn, rejoicing in bathing the body, in simple food, in sitting, thinking, meditating, speaking and working, and in preparing for sleep and death. The *Dhammapada* stands in relation to Gautama Buddha as the Gospels of John and Thomas stand in relation to Jesus Christ, for Ananda is like the beloved apostle John as well as the intuitive Thomas. Ananda walked with Buddha for twenty-five years and could recall the Master's words after his passing.

Although Buddha told his disciples that they should not blindly follow him or assume that they understood him, he so lived his life that it could serve as the paradigm and proof of the Path to Enlightenment. His life and his teaching were a seamless whole, the pristine expression of *Sanatana Dharma*, the Eternal Doctrine, the Ancient Way of the Noble Predecessors, the Tathagatas who have gone before. Whilst modern scholarship[1] has focussed on the details of Buddha's life, viewing recorded history as an accurate chronicle and providing a firm chronology of events, Buddhists have been sceptical of modern claims to explain the true significance of events by reference to their temporal order rather than to the mature thoughts and feelings of those who meaningfully participated in them. They have been even more concerned with Buddha's life as what the Tibetans call a *namtar*, the story of an exemplary Sage, which can help the intuitive to pursue the timeless track to illumination and emancipation. These traditional accounts, fusing fact with myth, do not reduce fidelity to truth to emasculated literalism.

Born early in the sixth century B.C., Siddhartha Gautama (Gotama) was the handsome and gifted son of King Shuddhodana, who ruled Kapilavastu, the small, prosperous kingdom of the Shakyas in northern India. According to tradition, Siddhartha's birth was heralded in a strange dream which came to his mother, Queen Maya. In it a snowy

---

1 A rare exception is A. Foucher's perceptive life of Buddha. "My task has been to sketch as close a likeness of Buddha as possible, but I have been careful not to neglect reflections from the Doctrine that have highlighted the face of its Founder."

white elephant with six tusks approached the mother and pressed a lovely lotus to her side. The lotus entered her womb and became the embryo of the Buddha to be. When the time for birth drew near, Queen Maya followed the custom of her ancestors and set out on the short journey to her father's home. The pains of labour came upon her while she rested in an exquisite grove midway between her husband's and her father's abodes, and she delivered Siddhartha beneath a great sala tree. Though the baby was born easily and in good health, Queen Maya died seven days later. Her sister, Mahaprajapati, brought up the baby.

Since *maya* means "illusion", the essential characteristic of the seven *prakritis* or planes of manifest existence, it is held to be hardly surprising that Queen Maya died seven days after Siddhartha's birth. The lotus symbolizes the architectonic paradigm of the cosmos, and the six tusks are its six primary powers or *shaktis*. The elephant itself is an emblem both of divine wisdom and its timely application in this world. Siddhartha was born between two homes, in the homeless state which is the mental perspective, and often the physical condition, of ordained monks or *bhikkhus*. Born away from his father's house and losing his mother shortly after birth, Buddha was indeed *anupadaka*, parentless. Thus his entire life as a homeless wanderer was prefigured in his birth. There is no reason to doubt the broad outlines of the traditional story, even if some of its symbolic elements were embellishments after the event. The legendary lives of Great Teachers are inimitably rich with allegorical significance that is readily enshrined in myth and sacred symbolism. About two centuries after Buddha's *Parinirvana*, the emperor Ashoka raised an inscribed stone pillar to mark Buddha's actual birthplace, and the striking pillar stands even today.

The court astrologers found Prince Siddhartha's horoscope enigmatic. Some thought it indicated that he would become a *Chakravartin*, an emperor who justly rules over many lands, but others, including Kaundinya, saw in it the cryptic lineaments of a consecrated life of renunciation and spiritual teaching. The *Sutta Nipata* tells of the Rishi Asita, who divined Buddha's birth and hastened to the palace to see him. Upon seeing the baby he wept, because he would not live long enough to hear Buddha's teaching. Siddhartha's father, King Shuddhodana, took due note of these discordant responses and sought to guide his son gently towards statesmanship. He initiated a plan of systematic study and royal training that provided Siddhartha with all the arts and sciences appropriate to a Kshatriya ruler, whilst screening him from those tragic experiences in life which turn the mind to profound and radical thoughts. So Prince Siddhartha grew up, blest in myriad ways, shielded from the unsettling facts of human misery which plunge so many into a state of utter helplessness. The prince's education was by no means easy, for he was subjected to a demanding intellectual discipline, mastering arts and letters, astronomy and mathematics; he was schooled in the kingly arts of diplomacy and warfare, learning to drive chariots, to handle deftly the spear and the bow, and gaining that combination of courage, stamina and magnanimity essential to statecraft; and he learnt the intricate etiquette which enables a man of high authority to set others at ease, to treat all with courtesy and correctness and to wield his gifts with grace and propriety.

While still rather young, Prince Siddhartha married his beautiful cousin Yashodhara, who gave him a son, Rahula. Established in a lavish court appropriate to a compliant Crown prince within the royal compound, Siddhartha took up the cloistered life of a future monarch. Traditional accounts of Buddha's life depict this formative period as a time of enjoyment, and even dalliance, perhaps to contrast it sharply with the rigorous and austere life to follow. Nonetheless, the allegorical *Jataka* stories seek to show that Buddha did not attain his astounding insight in a single life. He had spent many lifetimes learning to render the highest wisdom accessible to the awakened soul into skilful, compassionate action that could aid others without violating the subtle, interconnected balances of karma. Queen Maya's dream of the white elephant suggests that Buddha, like Krishna Avatar, chose to take up incarnate existence at a specific time for a specific purpose. The persisting discontent that hampered his princely life culminated in four critical events. Tradition testifies that Prince Siddhartha insisted upon investigating the world beyond the palace grounds and asked his faithful charioteer, Channa, to drive him through the city and into the countryside. On successive occasions he saw decrepitude, sickness, death and, finally, a homeless ascetic. Several chronicles show

Siddhartha as wholly unprepared for these disturbing sights, for he had none of the defensive indifference that preserves the average person from collapsing under their cumulative impact.

Allegorically, they point to the receptive nature of a noble soul who combines *prajna* and *karuna*, insight and compassion, for whom the inexplicable, immense suffering of others became more urgent than his own concerns. He felt that the very core of cyclic existence is *duhkha* – suffering, pain and dissatisfaction – for all that lives must decay and die. Even if one could hide the inevitable end of each incarnate existence under a glittering veil of hedonistic distractions, ceaseless and chaotic change marks the filigree of the intricate veil itself and so reveals starkly that all things fade and vanish every moment. Since life and death are necessarily interrelated terms in a complex series of events, the prime fact of suffering is a powerful stimulus for altering and even transforming radically one's own consciousness. Siddhartha sensed that the only solution to omnipresent *duhkha* lay in that timeless realm beyond the vicissitudes of change, a realm so far beyond the familiar plane of the senses that only a fundamental metamorphosis of fragmented consciousness could experience it, a realm in which there could be no " I " and "you", "mine" and "thine". If any such solution were at all possible, it must apply to all sentient beings and not to oneself alone.

Prince Siddhartha's Great Renunciation is poignantly depicted in his stealthily leaving his palace, exchanging his embroidered robes for the rags of a mendicant, turning his back with pained resolve on his regal destiny, family and wealth, friends and enjoyments. Yet his renunciation was deeper and more drastic than this, for he had dared to challenge the very basis of temporal existence, of all that the mortal mind craves in its desperate search for satisfaction, of all the heart's longings for lasting fulfilment. He was ready to face death in life, to confront the root cause of human misery and its permanent cure and emerge victorious in his uncharted quest, or lose everything in forsaking those closest to him. Tradition vindicates his sudden departure into a new life as motivated by a magnanimous resolve, an uncompromising sacrifice of everything for one single goal – the assured deliverance of humanity from the

Buddha and the Path to Enlightenment   275

agonizing thraldom of a hypnotic spell which entices, enslaves, mocks and mutilates all human existence. Not once did he imagine he alone could save all others, but if he could chart the way, even as a trailblazer marks a jungle track, some others might choose to pursue it courageously to its ultimate end. In pointing out the way by treading it, he would at least provide fresh choices for humanity, and thus testify to the possibility of redemption from bondage to worldly delusion.

Having renounced his life of luxury and even his princely name, Gautama crossed the Anoma River and made his way as a wandering ascetic to Rajagriha (now Rajgir), the capital of Magadha. His poise and charm attracted the attention of King Bimbisara, who was so captivated by his nobility of demeanour that, when he discovered his regal descent, he offered to share his kingdom with him. Gautama declined to take up the very trappings he had renounced, saying that he had no use for them in his quest for truth. He readily assented, however, to Bimbisara's wish that, should he be successful, he would return to Rajagriha and freely share his findings. He then journeyed across Magadha in search of any teachers who might guide him in his self-study. Though the generous responses of each one he met fell short of the goal he sought, he never reviled or ridiculed them, but rather gratefully accepted what they could give and then moved on. After his hard-won Enlightenment, he spoke of two of these teachers in discourses to his disciples. Arada Kalama, an esteemed thinker, had accepted him and freely taught him all he could. Gautama had not only mastered Arada Kalama's recondite philosophy, but also attained the high states of meditation fathomed by his teacher. The highest of these states was *akincannayatana*, the sphere of nothingness, which is called the third *arupa dhyana*, the stage in which consciousness is lifted beyond the realm of physical and mental forms. Despite the deep mystic state such a meditation induces, Gautama had pressed on. While staying with Udraka Ramaputra, he had entered the fourth *arupa dhyana*, called *nevasanna nasannayatana*, the sphere of neither perception nor non-perception.

Although Gautama had tasted the joys of exalted states of consciousness, he discerned a subtle temptation. To reach that level of meditative absorption, wherein even perception and its negation were swallowed up in pure consciousness, was still not to get to the root of noumenal reality. Whilst such sublime states can neither be articulated in ordinary language nor apprehended by ordinary consciousness, they are somewhat analogous to mistaking the manifest First Cause for the Ultimate Ground of All, or to mistaking the prime number 1 which initiates the number series for the primordial 0 presupposed by the entire system. Gautama, having gone as far in his fearless search for truth as he could with the willing assistance of others, now set out wholly on his own. Near the peaceful village of Senanigama, not far from Uruvela, Gautama joined five ascetics, including Kaundinya, one of those present at his birth who had seen in him a future Sage and Teacher. Together they attempted stringent forms of asceticism, as if one could so dominate and deny the body that it would be forced to yield up the hidden truth. One day, towards the end of the sixth year of these severe austerities, Gautama collapsed and came close to death. When he regained consciousness, he saw clearly that pitiless self-torment could no more release spiritual insight than thoughtless self-indulgence. A well-bred peasant girl, Sujata, noticed his emaciated condition and brought him a bowl of rice with milk. He ate with relish, restored his health and began to elucidate the Middle Way. Mistaking his fresh confidence for furtive abdication, the five ascetics who had hitherto followed his lead in asceticism were now shocked and hastily withdrew from his presence, leaving him alone to pursue his path.

Even though Buddha gave scattered hints about his solitary vigil in his subsequent discourses, it would be difficult to discern what actually transpired, for he had begun the steep ascent to summits of contemplation wherein the familiar contours and contents of consciousness are so radically altered that our conventional categories of thought and speech cannot possibly convey the ineffable experiences of inward Enlightenment. He had sat below an Ashwattha tree, now called a *bodhi* tree or *ficus religiosa*, and was totally resolved not to move until he had found the object of his single-minded quest. Apart from his unwavering resolve, his whole-hearted determination sprang from an inmost conviction that he had, at last, found the Way. As he persisted in his deepest meditation, Mara, the personification of severe impediments on the narrow pathway to truth, sought to distract him with his vast hordes of demonic tempters, ranging from hideous emblems of terror and torment to ethereal purveyors of ecstasy and enchanting reminiscence. Buddha calmly confronted and renounced all alike, calling upon *bhumi*, the earth, as his sole witness. According to the *Padhana Sutta*, Buddha once depicted Mara's array of distractions thus:

> Lust is your first army, and dislike for the higher life the second; the third is hunger and thirst, and the fourth craving; the fifth army consists of torpor and sloth, and the sixth is fear; the seventh is doubt, the eighth hypocrisy and obduracy; the ninth includes gain, praise, honour and glory; and the tenth is looking down on others whilst exalting self. Such are your armies, Mara, and none who are weak can resist them. Yet only by conquering them is bliss attained.

Buddha held that human suffering is so deeply rooted in spiritual ignorance that the two concepts are essentially psychological correlates. His graphic account of Mara's hosts suggests that *duhkha* and *avidya* may be seen as delusions on the mental plane, false expectations at the psychic level, physically painful and ethically pernicious. Summoning the six and ten *paramitas* or virtues as invaluable aids on the Path, Buddha's approach to Enlightenment instantiated the immense truth of the ancient axioms that clarity is therapeutic, cupidity is ignorance and virtue is knowledge.

In his climactic meditation, Buddha cut through the myriad veils of mental rationalization to release the pristine light of universal, unconditional awareness beyond form, colour and limitation. This supreme transformation of consciousness, which shatters worlds, is sometimes conveyed through the recurrent temptations of Mara, vividly portrayed as magnetic personifications of the ten chief fetters which bind the unwary victim to the inexorable wheel of involuntary cyclic existence, the spell of *Samsara*. The first is *attavada*, which *The Voice of the Silence* calls "the great dire heresy of separateness" and which Sir Edwin Arnold depicted in *The Light of Asia* as

> The Sin of Self, who in the Universe
> As in a mirror sees her fond face shown,
> And, crying ' I ', would have the world say ' I ',
> And all things perish so if she endure.

The familiar egocentricity which deludes the personal self into seeing itself as the fixed centre around which the whole world revolves, and dramatizes reality in inverse proportion to the seeming distance from that imagined centre, can become on the spiritual Path the subterfuge that one is so much more perceptive than all others that one is no longer compatible with any of them. Even the goal of spiritual emancipation can be invoked on behalf of an expanded egoity which absorbs all around itself and thereby distorts everything in its sphere of awareness.

The second fetter is doubt, *vichikichcha*, which can become so deeply embedded in the psyche that one not merely mocks the very possibility of attaining Enlightenment but even the point of doing so, for if all is delusion, might not even the quest for freedom be delusive? In such a state of chronic doubt, the conception of partial knowledge can itself be subsumed under the category of abject ignorance by a sleight of hand which conceals the fact that ignorance and knowledge are relative terms, and even absolute knowledge is construed by the unenlightened chiefly through analogy. *Silabbataparamasa*, the third fetter, commonly assumes the cloak of faith in conventional religion, which restricts the sacred to a specific set of rituals based upon dogmatic beliefs. Even one's loftiest conceptions can hinder growth by excluding the hazards of progressive self-exploration. Furthermore, even when renouncing the lesser anchor for a plunge into the greater abyss, one may encounter new forms of *kamaraga*, sensory attraction which, together with buried memories, may suddenly pull against the upward path by stirring up forgotten fears and unsuspected longings. Even if one could set these aside, the force of craving can invert itself and focus upon the highest goal, becoming obsessional, ruthless, vampirical and strangely amoral.

If one managed to elude the deadly coils of *kamaraga*, the fetter of hostility and hate, *patigha*, may be harder to remove. Though one may seem to have moved beyond the polarity of attraction and repulsion which ensnares the unenlightened, one may experience intense disgust at the depravities of others and thus succumb to the familiar opposition that one had seemingly transcended. Then there is *ruparaga*, the craving for form, the longing for embodied life, sometimes assuming the unrealizable wish for physical immortality, and more often seeking its analogue in an imaginary paradise of endless enjoyment. A subtler temptation is *aruparaga*, the desire for formless goods, such as fame and glory or other alluring states of mind focussed upon immaterial ends. When the aspirant has freed himself from all these, then conceit (*mana*) and restlessness (*uddhachcha*) will manifest their most insidious aspects – the one turning inward to extol secondary accomplishments which hinder Enlightenment, and the other turning outward in shallow judgementalism towards other seekers. Thus the ten fetters comprise a tenacious chain which reinforces the common source, *avidya*, root ignorance. Only when all its aspects are dispelled is ignorance itself confronted in its naked hollowness, "the voidness of the seeming full", and when the entire chain is calmly analysed and stripped of its deceptive allure, it collapses utterly and pure awareness alone remains.

Hermes, May 1986[2]

---

2. NOTE: The other 3 essays in this series – II, The Message of Buddha; III, The Dharma and the Sangha; IV, The Dhammapada and the Udanavarga – are available at http://www.theosophytrust.org/rni_articles.php..

CHOOSING THE TAO

Look, it cannot be seen – it is beyond form.
Listen, it cannot be heard – it is beyond sound.
Grasp, it cannot be held – it is intangible.
These three are indefinable;
Therefore they are joined in one.
                                                    Lao Tzu

Inflexibility of modes cripples our contemporary institutions. Inertia of thought dulls our mental faculties, whilst insensitivity of moral perception weakens the will power to realize good resolutions. It is conspicuously difficult for the brain-mind, faintly mirroring the chaotic flux of sense-impressions, to sift essential meaning from the monotonous succession of trivia. The *Tao Teh Ching* invites us to withdraw the mind from the cacophony of the world, to liberate the heart from the jungle fever of the passions. Above all, it counsels us to renounce our constricting conceptions of ourselves. These merely echo fleeting externalities extolled by the fickle opinions of the epimethean crowd, which is sadly captive to crude conceptions of success and failure, status and reward. All such shallow distinctions are entrenched in the feudal shibboleths and the *petit-bourgeois* vocabulary of a commercial culture. They are entangling weeds of pain, sprouting in the parched soil of cavernous delusion, choking the living germs of human encounter. Flexibility is elusive without some degree of detachment. Until a person attains to a mature indifference to the illusory objects of desire and the volatile pairs of opposites, he cannot be truly practical. He cannot become sufficiently plastic in mind, resilient in imagination, creative in sentiment and speech, to enjoy the divine estate to which every human being is heir. To become constructively flexible requires a preliminary purification of the passions, a thorough cleansing of the mind, a deliberate sorting out of the chaos that bewilders one's shadowy self. In seeking to do this, one may initially be restless, anxious and devoid of calm.

One must face the perilous paradox set forth in the ancient mystical texts – the beginning foreshadows the end, the end inheres in the beginning. Without a valiant attempt to negate the world and to void one's very conception of oneself, it is not feasible to take the first critical step on the Path to Enlightenment. Many are called, but few constitute themselves as truly chosen to become sincere and credible servants of the whole of mankind. Nevertheless, many thinking beings have already reached a point of maturation from which they can see through the negative, contradictory and melodramatic valuations of the necropolis. This is a moment in history when Time itself seems to have stopped. Most people know too well that behind the futile exaggerations and false claims of external institutions and structures, there is an emptiness and hollowness, an unfathomable void. At a time of poignant and ever-increasing distance between human beings, there is a danger that aggression and desperation will enter even into the spiritual quest, thereby closing the door to spiritual awakening for myriad lives. This awful if unintended tragedy can be remedied only by courage and toughness in braving mental agony. Divine manliness consists in becoming heroic when it counts and where it hurts, in sacrificing every puny conception of selfhood. Everyone not only glimpses the fundamental truths known to poets, philosophers and sages, but hears them now on the lips of millions of messengers on earth.

The present historical moment offers a golden opportunity to learn from the wisdom of the *Tao*. For many centuries, men contemplated the *Tao*, though no one in China would have claimed to comprehend it. The first commentary was written in the middle of the second century before Christ, perhaps about four centuries and a half after the appearance of the great Master, Lao Tzu. From birth Lao Tzu was greeted as an old man because he began by showing a mellow awareness of the teaching, and was apparently known by more than one name. Among his closest disciples the most influential was Confucius, in whose memory elaborate rituals emerged over millennia which eventually became frozen into stylized play-acting, with massive pride masked by self-mockery, a tradition of hypocrisy which terminated in a total disruption of the old order. A fearless Mandarin hinted fifty years ago that what China needed then was not more people but more prisons for its corrupt politicians. The anger of the masses was directed against endless game-playing in the name of the Confucian Analects. This is a predictable part of the recurring story of mankind.

The Tao can only be attained by the human being who approaches the Tao through the Tao. One must become the Tao. One must meditate ceaselessly upon the Tao while seeming to be engrossed in the daily round and common task. One must find the secret sanctuary of inner peace and repose within it from dawn through dusk to midnight, while retaining calm continuity of contemplation in the soul's shrine through the sleep of the night and even amidst dislocating dreams. The process of self-surrender takes time because it can only become continuous and constant when it flows from within without, from above below. The Tao is the motionless centre of all the wheels of cyclic change. It is the centre which is everywhere, in every point of space, in every moment of time. Yet no boundaries can ever be drawn to contain it. Everything participates in the illusion of birth and in the inertia of systems that hide the simultaneous disintegration and decay known among men and women as sickness, error, suffering and death. The Tao teaches that in no single thing will be found any freedom or exemption from the eternal process of ceaseless change behind the shadow-play of colours, forms and events. Everything that has a beginning in time and space must have a limit in space and an end in time.

Everyone must necessarily seek the Tao within oneself. Each must seek that which is consubstantial with the Tao that is before all things. Words like 'before' and 'behind', 'below' and 'above', can only be relevant to the seeming reflections of the Tao. The Tao is formless form, the primordial pure substance prior to all differentiation, and it is accessible to all human beings as the one and only Source of eternal energy streaming forth in limitless light from the Invisible Sun. It is hidden within what seems to be darkness but is in truth absolute light. It is ever bestowing nourishment and sustenance, shedding light and yielding the vital power of hidden growth. The causal principle of true growth is necessarily invisible to the naked eye. If one is to come to understand how the transcendent Tao is in oneself, or how one can come closer to the Tao within, one must calmly ask how one's false mind and fictitious harriers – self-created, self-maintained, self-imposed limitations – may be pierced by the light of pure awareness. One may become the Tao more and more consciously yet effortlessly, starting from small beginnings, and patiently allowing for gradual, silent growth.

All growth is invisible. No one can see or measure the growth of a baby or a little child from moment to moment. No one can mark by visible and external tokens the point of transition from childhood to youth. No one can put a date on the boundary between youth and manhood. These divisions are arbitrary and relative. When a person remains constant in his cool awareness of the utter relativity of all of these false and over-valued distinctions, he comes to understand that there is nothing dead and nothing alive. He is no less and no more than the Tao, and so is everyone else. The divisions and distinctions in consciousness arising from sense-objects, through words and by images, are a smokescreen that obscures, limits and distorts reality. The supreme, carefree joy of non-striving that flows from the omnipresent light can no more be conveyed by one to another than the taste of water can be described to someone who has never drunk a drop. No truly meaningful experience can be communicated to another except in terms of his own modes of living.

The wisest disciples, teachers and sages learn from the Tao all the time. The Tao is not a book. The Tao is not a scripture. The Tao was not given by any one person for the first time to other people. It is everywhere and nowhere. It is what some call God, what others designate as the One Reality, and what still others salute merely by saying "I do not know." To the extent to which men do not understand the Tao, instead of their choosing the Tao, the Tao seems to use them. A great deal of what is often called choosing is an illusion. No one chooses except by the power of the Tao. No one chooses thoughts except by a self-conscious comprehension of what is behind the energy of the Tao. No one can be a knower of the Tao, a true Taoist, without becoming a skilled craftsman of *Akasa*, a silent magician of the Alkahest, a self-conscious channel for the universal divine flame which, in its boundless, colourless, intangible, soundless and inexhaustible energy, may be used only for the sake of all. Only these universal, deathless, eternal verities may become living germs in the emerging matrix of the awakening mind of the age of Aquarius, a current of consciousness that flows into the future.

Following the ever-young example of the Ancient of Days, each and every person today may focus his mind upon the eternal relevance of the ever-flexible and never-caring Tao:

> Under heaven all can see beauty as beauty only because there is ugliness. All can know good as good only because there is evil.
>
> *Tao Teh Ching*, 2

How can one be flexible if one is fiercely attached to any external forms of good and of evil? *There is the same mutual relation between existence and non-existence in respect to creation as there is between striving and spontaneity, effort and ease, in respect to accomplishment.* What is easy for one person is hard for another; what is easy for the same person at any time was hard once; and what is difficult now might become easy in the future. Fumbling with the strings of a musical instrument may be rather painful in the long period of apprenticeship, yet all can find supreme enjoyment in listening at any time to a great master of music who plays his enchanted instrument with lightness and versatile adeptship. The seeker who is patient and persistent, like the good gardener who plants the seed but does not examine it daily to gauge its growth, does no more than is needed, giving Nature time to do its own alchemical work.

How, then, can one contrive a hard-and-fast distinction between effort and ease in the many modes of human striving? Furthermore, is there any reason for preference between one person and another in human excellence? Not from the serene standpoint of the Sage. Those who enjoy good music do not feel threatened every time they listen to a great musician, but merge their selves into the motion of the music. There is that which every human being knows and yet forgets, though if one chooses one may remind oneself. A person always knows that what helped one to walk as a child may also help one to maintain oneself in a world of turmoil. Through the archetypal logic of non-action in activity, he can move away from the *turba* and the tumult of the crowd, and discover an inner peace through deliberate but casual control in the midst of spontaneous activity. *The same mutual relation exists between long and short in respect to form, as between high and low in respect to pitch.* What seem to be precipitous mountains in one country might be seen as hilly ranges in a distant land. The Alps are unquestionably beautiful, but, as Byron suggested, there are beauties in Derbyshire which are no less enjoyable than the Alps. The Sierras may be more inviting than the forbidding Himalayas. Each can make the most of what he finds where he can find it, between treble and bass on the scale of musical pitch, between before and after in the contest of priorities. There are no seniors and juniors among human souls – all alike are pilgrims on multitudinous pathways to enlightenment. All souls have participated variously in the immense pilgrimage extending through and beyond successive millennia. *The Voice of the Silence* teaches: "Such are the falls and rises of the Karmic Law in nature." He who was a prince is a beggar now, the Buddha taught, and he who is exalted today may tomorrow "wander earth in rags."

In the eyes of the Sage, all temporal distinctions are absurd not only because they are foreshortened in time but also because they pretend to an ultimacy which cannot be upheld except by coercion. No one who has not conquered the will to coerce could freely practise the art of Wu-Wei even in everyday encounters. The Tao is the ontological basis of the archetypal teaching of non-violence, non-retaliation and true benevolence. Nature is not partial, partisan or sentimentally benevolent. This is known to the Sage, who fuses wisdom in action with compassion.

> Heaven and earth are ruthless;
> They see the ten thousand things as dummies.
> The wise are ruthless;
> They see the people as dummies.
>
> *Tao Teh Ching*, 5

From a superficial standpoint, it looks as if God is the chief conspirator, but there is no arbitrary theism in the vision of Tao. The inscrutable mathematics of cosmic balance needs nothing like what Hegel called the cunning of history to upset the best-laid plans of mice and men. From a broader perspective, it seems as if what appears bad in the beginning turns out in time for the better, even for the best. The Good Law ever moves inexorably towards righteousness. The Sage is not benevolent to personal claims. He treats all with a light inexorability. From an external locus in the realm of changing appearances, nothing that is true could ever be said or could even be found. It is only by the inner light that a person becomes a disciple of the Tao, and in the progress of time may even become a friend of the Tao with the help of those who are the Masters of the Tao.

In China reverence for the primordial Divine Instructors of mankind eventually degenerated into empty rituals of ancestor worship. As with ancient Chinese civilization, so also with classical Indian culture there was a progressive diffusion and inward loss of meaning. In ancient India there was a solemn kindling of the sacrificial fire, and every sacred word and ritual act were offered at the altar of the *Prajapatis*, the *Kumaras*, the *Rishis*, the *Agnishwatha Pitris* or Solar Fathers. In time such practices were reduced to ritual propitiation of the dead for fear of consequences. The weaker souls who participated in that ritualization in China and India are no different from those who incarnated in European and American bodies. Immigrants came in succeeding waves from different parts of the world to the American continent not only for the sake of their own future, but also, under Karma, as pathfinders of the future of mankind. That which caused violence and deception in the past must return, but cyclical justice will also bring back gentleness and truth and beauty in the nobler ancestors. No human being is without ancestors of whom one could be proud. Over a thousand years every man and woman has had a million ancestors. Nothing that was accomplished by a million people over a thousand years is irrelevant to any person. Everyone has a lineage that ultimately traces one back to the Divine Instructors of the human family. Everyone has kinship to those who are the Friends of all beings and who forever abide as Silent Watchers in the night, guarding orphan humanity.

There is not a person who could not at any time enter his inmost sanctuary and so come closer to the Krishna-Christos within. "Where two or three are gathered in my name, there I am present." Those potent words of promise, uttered as a benediction by the Avatars, were not meant only for a chosen few or for any particular tribe. It is possible at any time for any human being to invoke and invite the sacred presences of any of the divine Teachers. They are not in any one place or epoch – they are always here, there and everywhere. One cannot say of enlightened beings that physical proximity in space and time determines the nearness or closeness or their sphere of divine radiance. By the strength of mind and the spiritual will released through true sacrifice, one may consecrate the altar within the secret heart and kindle the sacrificial fire, thereby becoming worthy of the living benediction of those who are ancestral in a spiritual sense, who are ageless and parentless, *Anupadaka*. Enlightened Sages are eternally in unison with the supernal light of *Shekinah*, the perennial wisdom of *Svabhavat*, the ceaseless ideation of *Svayambhu* or Self-Existent, the absoluteness of the Tao.

The Tao antecedes all ancestors by reaching out to that which was before everything and yet which has no beginning, which ever exists and embraces every moment and the myriad beings who are sustained by its inexhaustible strength. It reaches beyond name and utterance, colour and form. It is the Soundless Sound, the divine intonation, the *Svabhavat* which cannot be aroused except by those who enter the light and become one with its unending compassion. Its potency is limitless. It can heal the sick and raise the dead. It is that light which never shone on land or sea, yet lighteth every man that cometh into the world. If any sincere seeker wishes to invoke that primordial light which is parentless, *Anupadaka*, he must create an oasis of calm within the mind, a haven of peace within the heart, a diffused quiescence in the whole of his being. He cannot do this all at once, but must, as Krishna teaches, adopt the strategy of recurrent exercise (*abhyasa*) in a spirit of disinterestedness (*viraga*). In the course of time he will build his bridge, his mental pathway to the light of *Atman* in the lamp of *Buddhi*. For any human being there is nothing more beneficent than, by concentrating upon that which corresponds to the throat, opening up the devotional channel within his wandering mind between his heart-light and the star overhead.

All Avatars are apparent manifestations of *Mahapurusha*, while every Enlightened Being is an eternal branch of the ever-living Banyan, the Tree of Immortals. By invoking in consciousness with a proper reverence taught by the Tao, every true devotee may enter the radiant sphere of the spiritually wise and transmit to others the sweetness and light of the Tao. Every child experimenting with a palette of colours discovers rapidly that there are not only the seven prismatic hues but also many shades, tones and blends, that unforeseen combinations are possible by an adroit mixing of colours. It also learns through fumbling beginnings at mixing pigments for the sake of painting a landscape that mistakes and false starts must be endured. There is not a child that starts to paint who does not take many distracting bypaths, and sometimes fiercely assumes the posture of Shiva, destroying its own work. Sometimes it adopts the posture of Vishnu, thinking, "I am pleased." At other times it assumes the posture of Brahmâ and attempts something new and original. All human beings as creative agents participate in the myriad scatterings and subtle hues of the prismatic seven.

Every human being in some life chooses the Tao, the pristine light which is colourless and beyond the differentiation of hues. Each of the great religions – originally a pure ray pointing to the One Light – in time produces tints that anathematize other people, thus resulting in walls of separation. This repeatedly arises because, as people no longer have access to the colourless light, they fall off the line of direction along the ray of their immortal individuality pointing towards the One that transcends all and yet is immanent in all. Sectarians thus speciously identify the pristine light with the *namarupa* of its reflected ray. They proclaim that all is contained in this particular book or that special scroll. But All is in every sacred book, is in the book of Nature. It is inscribed in every atom, and is in the pinpoint of light within every human eye. Men and women limit the inexhaustible richness of the All through fear, which kills the will and stays all progress. This is sad, and it arises because they become unbalanced. Either they have aggressively sought a selfish end or – when this went wrong – they retreated into some inversion and christened it by profane names such as cynicism, liberalism, this or that ism, protecting an insupportable illusion.

The harmony of the Tao is ever alive because it allows for endless change while at the same time ceaselessly balancing out. This is graphically represented in the familiar symbol of *yin* and *yang* within the invisible circle of Tao. When a person watches a slowly revolving wheel, studying the spokes, he will begin to understand the great wheel on which all beings revolve and in which all are involved. Those who cling to the circumference feel most the motion of the wheel. Those who cling to the spokes, the colours and the tints, find they do not have any sense of the subtler rhythm. The cyclic spin of the smaller wheel moves faster, so rapidly that it seems to be motionless. It has a centre which is an invisible, mathematical point. This may seem to be a mental abstraction and logical construction, but it is known on a subtler plane of homogeneous matter in a serene mental state of purified consciousness. Such centres could be consciously activated, thereby becoming gyroscopic in their power to awaken potential energies lying everywhere.

Every person may consciously choose to return to the central source, the pure light-energy of the motionless Tao without a name. This does not mean one should cease breathing. That would be a hasty reading of the Tao because one cannot live without breathing in and breathing out, and in this rhythmic activity one participates in the Tao, the Mother of Ten Thousand Things. When people are running or rushing they do not breathe rhythmically, but needlessly distort the rhythm. It is always possible to balance the chaotic breathing and the disorderly motions of daily life by providing spaces within the passage of time for a self-conscious return to the inner stillness, the serenity of meditation whereby one may renew oneself. Nature provides priceless opportunities for daily regeneration, and the Tao is experienced each night by every human being in deep, dreamless sleep. The Tao could also be known during waking life by the vigilant and contented person who practises deliberate mental withdrawal, self-surrender and non-violent action. The true seeker may heed the talismanic counsel of the Sage:

> In meditation, go deep in the heart.
> In dealing with others, be gentle and kind.

> In work, be diligent.
> In action, watch the timing.

Hermes, November 1978

THE ZERO PRINCIPLE

> *Laya is what Science may call the Zero-point or line, the realm of absolute negativeness, or the one real absolute Force, the NOUMENON of the Seventh State of that which we ignorantly call and recognize as 'Force'; or again the Noumenon of Undifferentiated Cosmic Substance which is itself an unreachable and unknowable object to finite perception; the root and basis of all states of objectivity and subjectivity too; the neutral axis, not one of the many aspects, but its centre.*
>
> The Secret Doctrine, i 148

The arcane conception of *laya* and the modern notion of a neutral axis are applications of what might be called the "zero principle". According to the *Stanzas of Dzyan*, the formation of a cosmos proceeds through a primordial set of seven *laya* centres, noumenal points in metaphysical space that mediate between the unmanifest and the manifest. From an "objective" standpoint, a *laya* centre is a point of rarefied matter wherein all differentiation has ceased. Given the cosmogonic distinction between undifferentiated matter and differentiated matter, theoretically there must be a point at which differentiation commences and also a point at which differentiation ceases. This is sometimes called the "zero point". Zero as a general concept originated among the Hindus and was transmitted through the Arabs into Europe in the fourth century. It is a natural accompaniment of the decimal system, also an invention of Hindu thinkers, since the one and the zero are metaphysical correlates of each other.

These fundamental conceptions exist within a broader philosophical framework which is metaphysical and postulates that the whole universe progressively emanates from a Divine Ground. This Ground is empty of all form, prior to all differentiation and is often designated by the term *shunyata*, meaning "Voidness" or "Emptiness". Thus, in its first and foremost philosophic meaning, the zero principle refers to that No-Thing which is equally the maximal and universal potential of the cosmos. This is the primary paradox of the zero, which, as a glyph, portrays the maximum potential that can be confined within an irreducible minimum space. Ultimately, when speaking of zero one is speaking of a point. That is, the zero contracts to an invisible minute zero, which is no other than a metaphysical or mathematical point. Such a point, representing the limit of an abstract capacity to contain potentiality within minimal space, is a depiction on the conceptual plane of the realm of absolute negation. The crucial significance of these abstruse ideas is that space is more real than anything it contains. Invisible metaphysical space is more real than anything perceivable by any human being.

A second major aspect of the zero is that it encompasses everything. It represents that which is complete while at the same time it represents that which is No-Thing. This feature of completeness is also present in the idea of a sphere, a kind of three-dimensional zero, metaphorically represented in all those ancient myths that speak of the womb of space and the cosmic egg. All of these allude to the principle of plenitude, the *plenum* within the voidness of the egg or a sphere. Thus, in addition to the idea of maximal containment within a minimum of space, the zero also signifies the idea of self-sufficiency and all-completeness. A third significant aspect of the zero is that it abides in itself without any external reinforcement. It is without a source, *anupadaka*, parentless. It represents the anti-entropic principle; it is inherently indestructible and incapable of running down. As the zero is intrinsically capable of self-maintenance, it signifies that principle in Nature which is the basis of all paradigms of perpetual motion and also of instantaneous, telepathic communication throughout space.

Such intuitive ideas are very much in the air in our time – if not yet within the acknowledged sciences, at least within that penumbra of imaginative conceptions called science fiction. Nonetheless, they are no more than a dim foreshadowing of those facts of Nature which are fully known, at every moment, to enlightened beings. Buddhas and Bodhisattvas continually experience metaphysical truths as tangible facts, whilst these same truths serve as tantalizing conceptions and imaginative ideals to ordinary human beings. The profound truths inherent in the zero principle will, for some time, stand as inaccessible ideals for modern science, primarily because they cannot be conclusively established by any known empirical methods, nor can they be comprehended in terms of any conventional framework of ideas which imposes arbitrary limitations upon the untapped capacities of human beings. Nevertheless, if one approaches the subject philosophically, one may discern that throughout Nature, in all material manifestation and in all differentiated forms of consciousness and energy, there must be points joining and separating distinct phases of differentiation. In a remarkable passage linking together conceptions crucial to the process of cosmic manifestation and the idea of *Nirvana* so central to the path towards enlightenment, H.P. Blavatsky declared:

> No world, as no heavenly body, could be constructed on the objective plane, had not the Elements been sufficiently differentiated already from their primeval *Ilus*, resting in *Laya*. The latter term is a synonym of Nirvana. It is, in fact, the Nirvanic dissociation of all substances, merged after a life-cycle into the latency of their primary conditions. It is the luminous but bodiless shadow of the matter *that was*, the realm of negativeness – wherein lie latent during their period of rest the active Forces of the Universe.
>
> *The Secret Doctrine*, i 140

The close connection between the familiar notion of a neutral centre or neutral axis and the recondite conception of *Nirvana* has many ramifications. It contains the seed of an explanation of why the attainment of *Nirvana* is relative to a particular *manvantara*, a fact crucial to the distinction between the paths of renunciation and liberation. It also parallels the proposition that *manvantara* and *pralaya* are equivalent to the three *gunas* existing in alternating states of equilibrium and disequilibrium. This, as Patanjali taught, is connected with the cognitive basis of the appearance or non-appearance of the illusion of a differentiated world and sequential time before the eye of the soul. *Laya* and *Nirvana* have to do with the noumenon of undifferentiated substance, which is also the noumenon of force, both inaccessible to finite perception. The zero principle points to that which is the root and basis of all states of objectivity and subjectivity. Thus, the zero is inseparable from the mysteries of *nitya pralaya* and *nitya swarga*, ceaseless dissolution and ceaseless instantaneous creation.

To apprehend the zero principle fully, to plumb its depths completely, is to realize the degree to which anything and everything is possible, and simultaneously to understand that nothing actual has any real bearing upon that sublime state. The system of spiritual self-discipline and ethical training leading towards such a realization requires rare virtues like *uparati* and *titiksha*. The aspirant must wholly renounce all external means and adventitious aids and must simultaneously perfect the power of contemplation and abjure all desires. No disciple can realize the zero principle unless he or she is ready to part with everything in the world. They must be prepared to cancel all the noise that arises out of the endless oscillations of the manifested pairs of opposites and so bring the mind to a supreme state of stillness. The realization of the zero means the transcendence of all opposites. This, in turn, means the attaining of a plane of consciousness which is prior to all pairs of opposites. Thus, the disciple may reach a plane of reality wherein all the subjective and objective existences created through the interplay of opposites are held in pure potential.

In this realm of metaphysical negation, the realm of the zero, there is, in the words of Nicholas of Cusa, a *coincidentia oppositorum* – a reconciliation of opposites. Life and death, the real and the unreal, all pairs of opposites, become one. This can be put in terms of the standpoint of the sage, for whom there is no difference between light and darkness, night and day, birth and death. He himself is like the sacred *lingam*, a pillar of light, endlessly and dynamically linking up the formless *arupa* worlds to the worlds of form, the hidden archetypal and noumenal realms of causation to the phenomenal regions of effects. Such an enlightened being can traverse the limits of consciousness from the most ethereal empyrean of pure potential to the most limiting sphere of reference within physical space and time. He can do this at will because he has already created the equivalent of the zero principle within his body, and this can only be done in the body because it had been done in the astral, and this in turn is possible only if it has been done in the subtler bodies ultimately reaching back to the *karana sharira*, even to the *augoeides*. The sage, in other words, has mastered the principle of untrammelled mobility and instantaneous transmission.

What is realized by the highest beings is inherent in the universe as a whole, and therefore has a vital reference to what all human beings may glimpse or touch at certain moments. It is possible to understand the zero principle in a simpler way as a neutral centre or a limiting point in relation to a given set of senses.

> Thus, imagine two consecutive planes of matter as already formed; each of these corresponding to an appropriate set of perceptive organs. We are forced to admit that between these two planes of matter an incessant circulation takes place; and if we follow the atoms and molecules of (say) the lower in their transformation upwards, these will come to a point where they pass altogether beyond the range of the faculties we are using on the lower plane. In fact, to us the matter of the lower plane there vanishes from our perception into nothing – or rather it passes on to the higher plane, and the state of matter corresponding to such a point of transition must certainly possess special and not readily discoverable properties.
>
> *The Secret Doctrine*, i 148

If one wants to see, one should see until one can no longer see. If one wants to hear, one should hear until one can no longer hear. And, similarly, with touch and taste and smell. A point comes, often recognized by people who are blind or handicapped in one or other of the senses, at which one actually goes beyond the known limit of the common sensory range. To learn to do this consciously is to learn to move from plane to plane. If neutral centres did not exist, there could be no possible connection or communication between two consecutive planes. They would remain separated by unfathomable abysses. Yet it is possible to move from plane to plane and to alter one's responsiveness to the limits that pertain to sensory fields. So too, one can alter limits that pertain to cognitive and conceptual fields. It is no wonder, then, that the range of mentality is so vast; the plane of mentality must contain the set of all possibilities that are made manifest on the more gross sensory planes. This plane is so immense that few human beings could even begin to think of the virtually infinite range of possibilities for human ideation and imagination, cognition and thought, consciousness and self-consciousness.

Before one can begin to understand the possibilities of universal self-consciousness, one must grasp in principle and at a simpler level what is logically involved in the transcendence of any pair of opposites. Take, for example, any two points and draw intersecting lines through them that meet at an apex. Then draw a third line horizontally connecting the two original points. In relation to these two points on the base line – which is analogous to substance – the apex represents that which enables one to transcend a particular field, which is represented by the enclosed triangle formed by the three points. This is a simple enough idea but it must be applied to those five pairs of opposites, cited by the Maha Chohan, which are so perplexing to human beings. To take the simplest, consider pain and pleasure. Most human beings are stuck in the basement of human evolution, wrestling with the pain-pleasure principle. Yet it is possible to overcome the oscillation of the two opposites and to move to a point of balance, indifference or neutralization between them. If one is really willing to think it out, one will be amazed to discover the degree to which one can neutralize one's propensity towards pleasurable sensations and thereby one's corresponding aversion to painful sensations.

Moving to the moral plane, the neutralization and transcendence of egotism and altruism is the toughest challenge for those high souls truly struggling in spiritual mountain climbing. As soon as these souls take birth, they are burdened with the obligation and the temptation of taking on the karma of others, the problem of wise non-interference. They are also stuck with the principle of self-assertion for the sake of self-preservation. Though a difficult dichotomy, this is, in principle, no different from any other pair of opposites. Ethical dichotomy, having to do with right and wrong, must be understood in terms of metaphysical distinctions between good and evil. These, in turn, have their application in all relationships, social, political and otherwise, which give rise to the dichotomy of liberty and despotism. It is possible, with each of these dichotomies, to find a mode of neutralization. One may take as a starting point the simplest mode of neutralization, which is to find the mid-point between the extremes. In Buddhist terms one should seek out the Middle Way. If one can discover a moderating principle within oneself, one may begin to moderate one's preoccupation with right or wrong, good or evil, pleasure or pain, one's tendency to dominate or to be submissive. By continually engaging in self-correction, guided by the principle of the Middle Way, one may avoid both pitfalls and extremes.

This teaching of Buddha is accessible to all human beings. It is always possible for anyone to slow down, to cut down, to moderate. But in doing so one must avoid any tendencies to become passive, escapist or vague. To fall into these traps is not to follow the Middle Way but merely to flee reality. Thus, while remaining fully engaged in the field of *dharma*, one must also learn to moderate. One should begin with an appreciation of the principle of the Middle Way – lying between the extremes of unedifying self-indulgence and equally unedifying self-mortification. Then through meditation one must go beyond this initial point of departure, taking advantage of the teaching of the Aryan eightfold path as a bridge between metaphysics and ethics. One must, in practice, come to experience through meditation neutral states. The entire cycle of the eightfold path, beginning in right views and concluding in right meditation, requires a continual process of formation and dissolution of perspectives and assumptions. Whatever one's present mode of perception of the *Dharma*, whatever one's present practice of the *Dharma*, one must be prepared both to affirm and negate this framework. Only so can one pass through a neutral condition to a renewed and regenerated understanding of the *Dharma*. Whilst this will be understood at first in terms of one's solemn perspective and strenuous actions, owing to the salvationist tendency to project the idea of a path outside oneself, in time there will dawn a sobering realization that in fact this process of formation and neutralization is occurring within one's faculties of perception, within the substance of one's vestures.

It is not easy to master this mature understanding of the path, wherein there is no external travelling and the aspirant becomes one with the path itself. There is no room for haste or pretense. Rather, one should approach the task a day at a time. Those who attempt to jump ahead at the start, because they know nothing better, will quickly despair and abandon the path. That opens up the even worse risk of making judgements about the path and about those who authentically are attempting to follow it. Anyone finding himself or herself in this self-begotten predicament should immediately stop engaging in such self-destructive behaviour and try to make a fresh beginning. They should get back to the basics, find a different rhythm, follow it out each day and each week, learn to act incrementally as Nature does. Then they may discover that though the process of enlightenment and self-transcendence is slow, it is authentic. There will be moments of exhilaration and joy, moments of freedom and beautiful insight, as well as moments of pure love and true compassion. Above all, there will be moments of true selflessness when, in thinking of other beings, one reduces oneself to a zero. One's eventual goal must be to thread one's life together out of such moments, learning how, through daily meditation and right mental posture, one can be of service to humanity.

If this is the immediate and existential meaning of the teaching regarding transcendence as well as the significance of the zero principle, the ultimate metaphysical meaning of the idea lies in the unfathomable bosom of the unmanifest. The mysterious neutral axis within the cosmos and within man, around which coil the diverse powers of dual manifestation, is also a luminous thread leading to the core of the mystery of the individuality. By discovering the more and more abstract aspects of the zero within Nature and Man, one may draw closer and closer to the universal basis of spiritual immortality. All the hosts of spiritual monads on all the many planes of existence in the manifested cosmos derive from a single hebdomadic Logoic source. Preceding the differentiations of consciousness and form in the solar and terrestrial worlds, that fount of immortality radiates through seven centres from one eternity to another.

> The seven *Laya* centres are the seven Zero points, using the term Zero in the same sense that Chemists do, to indicate a point at which, in Esotericism, the scale of reckoning of differentiation begins. From the Centres – beyond which Esoteric philosophy allows us to perceive the dim metaphysical outlines of the 'Seven Sons' of Life and Light,

the Seven Logoi of the Hermetic and all other philosophers – begins the differentiation of the elements which enter into the constitution of our Solar System.

The Secret Doctrine, i 138–139

At this level the degrees of plenitude, self-sufficiency and self-regeneration connected with the *laya* principle are so profound that they have no comprehensible analogue within human life. This is the realm of Initiates. Nevertheless, every human being, as an immortal ray of the Central Spiritual Sun, has the opportunity and privilege of meditating upon the idea of *Fohat*, which is an emanation of the Seven Sons of Light. Whatever plane of self-consciousness a being inhabits, it is always helpful to a group of monads held together by an irresistible ideal and an overarching transcendental vision of the good to come together and strengthen their collective capacity to reduce themselves to zeros in the service of their common ideal. Training in this magical power of transmission is the essential meaning of the *Sangha*. When people come together, truly forgetting themselves and united by the magnetic attraction of the good, they emulate and serve in some small measure the Teachers of Humanity, the great galaxy of Buddhas and Bodhisattvas.

The highest beings learn to do this ceaselessly, invoking the Fohatic principle which is present potentially at every point in space. Even at the level of ordinary, unenlightened human beings, it is possible to take advantage of the zero principle at some elementary level. The integrity of human nature itself assures that every human being can mirror the transcendental beneficence of the highest beings. Ultimately, all the potentiality of the zero, of *shunyata* or the void, is present throughout the *plenum*. The void is the *plenum*. All of Nature stands as an open invitation to every group of human beings to take conscious advantage of the Fohatic potential that exists everywhere throughout the body of Nature, but which is most powerful in the realm of ideation, the realm of *Mahat*, universal mind or *Aether-Akasha*. This is an invaluable lesson for any group of pilgrim souls to learn if they would constitute themselves true helpers of the servants of humanity in the coming decades and in the dawn of the Aquarian Age. In all relationships – in one's household, at work and in the greater society – one may participate in the unfoldment of the ascending cycle that will stretch right into the next century.

To ally oneself truly with other human beings on behalf of the cause of humanity is to touch upon a much greater richness in human nature than can ever be experienced otherwise. Apart from the activation of the germ of spiritual self-consciousness, human beings are mostly semi-conscious, unconscious in relation to themselves and the potential in humanity. Once one learns to neutralize the lower self to some degree, thus transcending the opposites at a preliminary level, one will immediately discover what a fruitful diversity there is within oneself, between any two human beings, much less amongst larger groups. One will begin to see the profound importance of the plane of mentality – the plane of intellection – which is broader in its scope than any other plane. One will also begin to grasp the grandeur and magnitude of the vast inheritance of all human beings over eighteen million years.

Access to the plane of *Chit* – the vast and inexhaustible realm of boundless possibilities – inevitably depends upon self-conscious assimilation of the Law of Sacrifice. Within the planes of manifest existence there is a continual giving and receiving between all atoms, monads and beings. One may view all of this in terms of a calculus that seeks to measure how much one is getting in relation to how much one is giving. But the arithmetic of the marketplace is not easily applied to human affairs; moral calculus is tricky. It would be most unwise to perform this moral arithmetic inefficiently and on behalf of one's ego. When human beings edit, forget and fall prey to ingratitude, they generate a tragic inversion of the principles of karma and justice. They think that whatever good they experience is self-generated, whilst whatever is bad comes from outside. In the end, this amounts to a denial of the compassion at the core of the cosmos. In effect, by becoming obsessed with personal ratios of giving and receiving, one cuts oneself off entirely from the well-spring of one's own true being. Instead of succumbing to such a tragic fate, it is far healthier and much more human to learn to enjoy giving generously and wisely at all times. By stepping outside the realm of petty calculation, one becomes a creative participant in the universal wisdom-sacrifice, the *jnana yajna*, of the cosmos.

Each breath is a sign of involvement in the Great Sacrifice. Each thought is itself a part of that sacrifice. How, then, can human beings impose some narrow view, whether egotistic or bilateral, upon the boundless stream of universal sacrifice? Instead of ensnaring oneself in the unnecessary tensions of a pseudo-sense of justice, which is merely a noisy mass of humbug that will leave, at death, an ugly *rupa*, one should reduce oneself to a zero. No amount of self-inflation and fearful grasping, no adherence to concretized images of oneself and one's possessions – physical, mental or even spiritual – can contribute one iota to one's well being as a soul. It is not prudence but folly that leads human beings to store up treasures in the realm of manifestation. From instant to instant, the entire cosmos passes through a neutral point, a metaphysical zero point, and instantly and effortlessly it is regenerated in all its vastness. If the universe itself continually depends upon the mystery of All and Nothing within the Zero, there can be no greater wisdom for human beings than to cooperate self-consciously with the zero principle. Living from day to day and moment to moment in calm assurance of the ontologically boundless plenty of the Great Sacrifice, the neophyte can learn to rest upon the bosom of the infinite waters of Truth.

Hermes, February 1986

DRAWING THE LARGER CIRCLE

> *'Great Sifter' is the name of the 'Heart Doctrine', O Disciple. The wheel of the Good Law moves swiftly on. It grinds by night and day. The worthless husks it drives from out the golden grain, the refuse from the flour. The hand of Karma guides the wheel; the revolutions mark the beatings of the karmic heart.*
>
> The Voice of the Silence

The 1975 cycle will continue to precipitate momentous choices for individuals and societies. What are the vital elements in this decisive choosing, and what will be the chief consequences? There is in the life of every human being a series of minor choices which add up to a crucial choice, but often it is made with incomplete knowledge of its critical nature. To grow and to age is to recognize with increasing clarity that all events in the past have had their irreversible consequences. Therefore, within any shallow philosophy centred essentially on the physical body and premised upon a single incarnation, a personal sense of futility and fatalism looms large as one comes closer to the moment of death. As with individuals, so with civilizations. Civilizations are apt to conduct the deepest reflection upon their storied past in times of depression, either out of self-indulgent nostalgia or sheer bewilderment at their bygone glory. This has shadowed every great civilization in its hour of decline, and today we are witnessing this in Western Europe and in the nostalgic mood which is intermittent in the United States. Civilizations seek to cling to something of the past, and perceptive chroniclers like Toynbee in England or Jaspers in Switzerland sense that something went wrong as early as before 1914, that the seeds of today's malaise lay far back in the past. When we look back to that past, we surmise that a lot could have been avoided, that there were viable alternatives and missed opportunities. This is the sad state of societies as well as individuals who, because of narrowness of perspective and myopia in relation to the future, impose upon their lives a delusive dependence upon their own edited versions of a truncated past. But whenever human beings are willing to rethink their basic assumptions about themselves, about their shrouded past and about their cloudy future, then they do not need to edit. They do not have to limit unduly the horizon of their gaze.

This is difficult to understand initially. One might think in terms of the extreme example of a person with Promethean foresight who can discern in the cycles of this century long-term factors that go back a thousand years into the past and will go forward a thousand years into the future. In the Victorian Age, T. H. Huxley observed that in the myriad worlds around us there is no reason why there cannot be beings with an intelligence as far beyond our present level as ours is beyond that of the black beetle, and with a control over nature as far beyond our own as ours is beyond that of the snail. He also suggested that even ordinary human beings can look back and forward over a millennium and make broad projections. It is, in principle, possible for there to be beings in the universe who can see all pasts and all futures. The power of choice is partly a function of the scope of perspective. With wider perspectives our choices become more intelligent, but as they become more informed, we readily recognize that there are many factors that are constant. One cannot wish away causes generated over a long cycle. The more clearly a person sees what he cannot alter right now in this incarnation, the more effectively he can use his energies to alter what he can. All this requires a measure of balance, but most human beings are unable to choose wisely by clearly facing the alternatives before them. All too often they vainly hope that by proceeding in one direction, everything else will automatically come to them. Energy cannot move in all directions at once, and though there are many planes of matter, it is always the case that everything adds up in a mathematical universe. One's capacity to choose is a function of one's knowledge, not merely of particular causal chains but also of what is at the very core of the phenomenal process of becoming: breathing in and breathing out. Ideally, if one could comprehend the meaning of a single day, one would by analogy be able to understand what is enacted over a lifetime.

It has been taught that for the truly wise, each day is like a new incarnation. In small space they see the subtle motions of unbounded space. In a single moment they can grasp quintessentially the infinite possibilities that are spread out in eternal duration. They can retain in consciousness the freedom that belongs to those who are not rushing to manifest, while displaying a shrewd awareness of what it is possible to manifest with a due respect for the feelings of others, for collective strengths and weaknesses, for the limits and possibilities of the current cycle. Theosophical teaching offers the vast perspective of eighteen million years of human history and also of the sixth sub-race which will emerge far in the future but which must clearly have some relationship to the fifth sub-race – now visibly on the decline – that flowered forth in Europe and partly in America. At this point of time there is, by analogy and correspondence, a critical moment of choice bearing upon the alternatives that confront our intelligence. The ratiocinative mind has become adept, because of modern upbringing and so-called education, because of so much dichotomous thinking since Aristotle, at rationalizing its wants, desires and limitations. Now we find at a global level the logical limit of this rationalizing mind, which insists there is not enough room or food on earth for all human beings on our globe. This no-exit barrier in thinking arises because of assumptions that were too limited from the start. It hinges upon a view of the universe which is incompatible with the vast resources of the creative imagination, with the inventiveness displayed in the last three centuries in building up the structures of applied science and sophisticated civilization. Even this is merely a recent example of the immense resourcefulness of the human race over many millennia. The type of thinking which is inductive, inferential and dichotomous, functioning within the perspective of a closed universe or of a one-life system, has become sterile and has no real answers to the awesome problems of our time.

Today, we face a decisive moment of choice. Human beings cannot by mere repudiation of an obsolete mode of thinking efface it entirely from their minds. Many people are muddled and fearful victims of the collective psychosis, and seem to be constantly in need of psychological reinforcement. The more they look back, like Lot's wife, the more they are in danger of being immobilized. The threshold of awakening is touched when mature souls search for spiritual wisdom and sense the reality of Mahatmas and their boundless compassion for the whole of humanity. When a person is profoundly affected by a preliminary vision of the quest for enlightenment, it is impossible to go back – the moment of choice has come. Initiates alone know what is the critical threshold for any individual or civilization. In recent years many souls have been confronted with a collective bewilderment that is a prelude to fateful choices. For some it is already too late. Others, unknown to themselves, when they least expect it, will find their way into the civilization of the future. All such choices involve complex chains of causation that are shrouded in the arcane mathematics of Karma. All acts have their exact consequences and all thinking generates appropriate results. The degree of intensity is a function of the level of awareness, motivation and concentration. To think on universal lines is to initiate stronger currents than those generated from a sectarian or separative standpoint.

H.P. Blavatsky said:

> The co-disciples must be tuned by the guru as the strings of a lute (*vina*) each different from the others, yet each emitting sounds in harmony with all, Collectively they must form a keyboard answering in all its parts to thy lightest touch (the touch of the Master). Thus their minds shall open for the harmonies of Wisdom, to vibrate as knowledge through each and all, resulting in effects pleasing to the presiding gods (tutelary or patron-angels) and useful to the Lanoo. So shall Wisdom be impressed forever on their hearts and the harmony of the law shall never be broken. . . . The mind must remain blunt to all but the universal truths in nature, lest the 'Doctrine of the Heart' should become only the 'Doctrine of the Eye'.

The true chela is one who has no taste for the small talk of the world, not owing to disinterest in individuals but because of caring so deeply for all souls. Deaf to deceptive formulations of the complexities of human existence, the chela can hold his strength within, instead of being ceaselessly concerned to reform everyone else. The prime concern is to secure a firm anchor within the divine sphere of one's being, to stay aloof from turbulent currents, so as to remain continually attuned to the sacred music of the flute of Krishna, to the *filia vocis* within, the promptings of the higher Self, the dictates of one's *Ishtaguru*. There are varying levels of intensity to diverse modes of thinking. If the disciple is to achieve the quantum jump to a totally new and initially painful way of thinking, which is abstract and universal but wholly free, this requires continuity of concentration to be established as a stream of ideation and untrammelled awareness. Then it will be possible to initiate far more potent consequences in a short span of time than could be generated through muddled kama-manasic thinking over a long period of time. This change of polarity and scope of ideation is connected with the intensity and continuity of the energy level of radiant matter. At higher levels there is an increasing fusion of thought, feeling and volition. The deeper one draws from the central source of noumenal energies in the universe, the greater the potency of thought, feeling and will – provided one protects this current by the power of silence and true reticence. At one level this is sheer good taste; at another level it demands absolute fidelity to the highest and most sacred. If one can master this mode, one may work as nature works, in silence and secrecy, from the depths of the soil wherein germinates the seed within the seed, slowly unfolding the humble acorn and the mighty oak.

Spiritual life involves taking a risk far greater than any other. One is risking the collapse of one's personal identity, not merely worldly conceptions of success and failure, but also the rooted identification with name and form and physical existence, with likes and dislikes, delusions and fears. To take that risk and plunge into the void requires real courage. This cannot come without a preliminary purificatory process of asking why one is afraid. One has to look at one's attachments and see them without illusion as far as possible. One has to grasp why yesterday's attachments, which seemed to be all-absorbing, are utterly meaningless today. An unfortunate soul gets trapped in the cycle of involvement for a lifetime, experiencing one disillusionment after another. A wiser soul soon sees to the core of the delusive process of externalizing the self. Herein lies the great enigma of the noetic variation among human beings, in terms not only of environment and heredity, but even more in the appreciation of the karma brought into this life, the karma shared with others and the karma engendered by oneself. To become capable of moral and spiritual courage, to see everything from the standpoint of the Ishwara within, means in practice that one is willing to work patiently, like a private in the army, without any access to the well-guarded plans of the Chief of Staff. What matters is doing the best one can and knows how. To master this mental posture is to come closer to the sacred orbit of the Brotherhood of Bodhisattvas. They can see every stumbling mountain climber, every little lamp, from the terrace of enlightenment. They instantaneously see what they call "the Tathagata light", the spirit of true devotion, abstention from fault-finding, and altruism in thought, word and deed.

A person so preoccupied with learning that he entertains no expectations for self, may suddenly receive the privilege of sharing glimpses of a universal vision, such as that which Krishna conferred upon Arjuna. Soul-wisdom cannot be construed in terms of any known symbols or visible tokens. True disciples are fortunate to live in an epoch when so many people have reached the terminus of an entire way of thinking, the salvationist mentality of looking for instant results and vicarious atonement. Over two thousand years this spiritual materialism sullied the pure teaching of Jesus Christ. In the last decade a lot has happened fast. Those who frantically sought quick results have been rapidly disillusioned. The great sifting of souls has enormously facilitated the emergence of the truly courageous, the self-selected pioneers who seek the good of the whole, and are willing to train as "fortune's favoured soldiers" in the ancient Army of the Voice. The key note of universal brotherhood was already struck in the nineteenth century in the message of the Maha Chohan, who calmly declared: "He who does not feel competent to grasp the noble idea sufficiently to work for it, need not undertake a task too heavy for him." There need be no chastising of those who are not ready for the larger task, and it is too late in history to coax the weak to simulate the language of the strong. One of the paradoxes of our time is that those who cannot maintain continuity of consciousness even for a week preach spiritual tenets for their own psychological survival. But out of such will not come the forerunners of the coming civilization, the alchemical agents for the radical transformation of modes of thought and action. These rare souls define themselves in an unmistakable manner, by unconditionality of commitment, magnanimity of mind and reverence for all the spiritual teachers of humanity.

The idea of unconditionality lies at the core of the perennial philosophy of the great sages at all times, in all conditions and in all cultures. This is the identifying hallmark of the authenticity of every true intimation of *Theosophia*. *The Secret Doctrine* points to the unthinkable and the unspeakable in the accents of the *Mandukya Upanishad*. H.P. Blavatsky prefaced *The Secret Doctrine* by the Rig Vedic Hymn to Creation, wherein the highest beings suggest that they perchance know not the ultimate purpose of creation, showing the authentic agnosticism of the enlightened. When men have attained to gnosis, their profound agnosticism diffuses a peerless fragrance that touches the hearts of the humblest people. If one tries to move from any concept of the immense to a sense of infinity, it may seem as if one is coming closer to the unconditional, but no concept of immensity or infinity can capture the boundlessness of invisible space, eternal duration, perpetual motion or unmodified consciousness. One cannot ever bring to the level of expression, symbolization or conceptualization that which one can apprehend and experience at a deeper level, wherein the whole of one's being is alive and awake. When the deep calls to the deep, the ineffable awareness of the boundless cannot be intimated except through silence and stillness. This is profoundly fundamental to the entire universe and all consciousness, to God, law and man. It entails unending reverence for the unknown in every being, not just as a mode but as the central truth in all relationships. It alone gives one true freedom and complete openness in relation to the inexhaustible possibilities of the future. Those who vainly seek to limit the future to their impressionistic scenarios and linear projections will be supplanted by the tidal wave of feeling that arises from the abundant fullness of human hearts, the untrammelled ideation of human minds and the creative wills of immortal souls.

As the structures of the past atrophy and crumble, only that could replace them which would existentially reflect the inner truth of soul-evolution, the insights of monads that pierce the veil of forms. The inversions of the insecure, allowing moral pygmies to speculate upon spiritual giants, will have no sway in the civilization of the future. There will be a pervasive recognition of the logical impossibility for the lesser to judge the greater, and the sure sign of littleness is the tendency to convert beliefs into verdicts. The Aquarian Age will foster that openness in relation to the larger circle which will be a natural extension of the open texture of our primary relationships – with parents, teachers, siblings, so-called enemies and friends. There will be a more widespread acknowledgement that as veil upon veil may lift, there must remain veil upon veil behind. When the human race as a whole can afford to live with such mature awareness, it will be hospitable to the sort of spiritual and moral toughness that can cope fully with the accelerated pace of karmic precipitation. Many will readily grasp the elementary axiom of the mathematics of the soul that in order to comprehend an Adept or Mahatma, one must first devote a lifetime to true discipleship. This is an immensely liberating prospect, when compared with the stifling spiritual limitations of the last century. H.P. Blavatsky had to undergo the pain of risking profanation in testifying to the existence of Mahatmas in the heyday of Victorian prejudice and conceit. The spoilt victims of centuries of sectarian stupidity, more skilled in image-crippling than in true devotion, were almost constitutionally incapable of understanding Mahatmas. Speaking of them was then a great sacrifice. This is fortunately no longer necessary, because those who need to participate in the clamour of pseudo-claims and shallow judgements are now confronted with an abundant supply of readily available gurus. This offers a considerable protection to the real work in the world of the Brotherhood of Bodhisattvas. During the 1975 cycle there is no more need to make any concessions to the weak in the West that were unknown in the East. This augurs well for the future of humanity.

All over the globe, the paramount problem is one of renewing and maintaining the minimal standards of being truly human. Only those souls who already have a profound grasp of *sunyata* and *karuna*, the voidness of all and the fullness of compassion, will undergo the lifelong training of discipleship and awaken the *Bodhichitta*, the seed of the Bodhisattva. There is thus the immense gain that the mixing of incompatible vibrations may be mitigated in this century. At the widest level, universal good – *Agathon* – is the keynote of the epoch. The religion of humanity is the central emphasis of the 1975 cycle. Those who are self-elected by their own meditations, by their generous natures, and by their cooperative acts, who are willing to become true disciples of the Mahatmas, will readily undergo the rigorous discipline and share the rich resources of the divine dialectic, *Buddhi Yoga*, mirroring the divine wisdom of Brahma Vach or *Theosophia*. They will ceaselessly attempt to draw the larger circle. There is no reason why breadth should be at the expense of depth. A new balancing between a much broader diffusion of the fundamental truths of "the golden links" and a much deeper penetration into the visible is now possible and will come to a full flowering by the end of the century. In the climactic rush of the closing years, there will be an unprecedented outpouring of creative energies and spiritual resources, as well as the closing of many doors, plunging into obscurity many protracted illusions of the past. The religion of humanity is the religion of the future, fusing the philosophy of perfectibility, the science of spirituality and the ethics of growth in global responsibility.

Hermes, August 1978

THEOSOPHICAL GLOSSARY IN BRIEF

Adept (*Lat.*). *Adeptus*, "He who has obtained." In Occultism one who has reached the stage of Initiation, and become a Master in the science of Esoteric philosophy.

Agathon (*Gr.*). Plato's Supreme Deity. Lit., "The Good", our ALAYA, or "Universal Soul".

Agnishwattas (*Sk.*). A class of Pitris, the creators of the first ethereal race of men. Our solar ancestors as contrasted with the *Barhishads,* the "lunar" Pitris or ancestors, though otherwise explained in the *Purânas.*

Akâsa (*Sk.*). The subtle, supersensuous spiritual essence which pervades all space; the primordial substance erroneously identified with Ether. But it is to Ether what Spirit is to Matter, or *Âtmâ* to *Kâma-rûpa*. It is, in fact, the Universal Space in which lies inherent the eternal Ideation of the Universe in its ever-changing aspects on the planes of matter and objectivity, and from which radiates the *First Logos*, or expressed thought. This is why it is stated in the *Purânas* that Âkâsa has but one attribute, namely sound, for sound is but the translated symbol of Logos—"Speech" in its mystic sense. In the same sacrifice (*the Jyotishtoma Agnishtoma*) it is called the "God Âkâsa". In these sacrificial mysteries Âkâsa is the all-directing 'and omnipotent Deva who plays the part of Sadasya, the superintendent over the magical effects of the religious performance, and it had its own appointed Hotri (priest) in days of old, who took its name. The Âkâsa is the indispensable agent of every *Krityâ* (magical performance) religious or profane. The expression "to stir up the Brahmâ", means to stir up the power which lies latent at the bottom of every magical operation, Vedic sacrifices being in fact nothing if not ceremonial magic. This power is the Âkâsa in another aspect, *Kundalini*—occult electricity, the alkahest of the alchemists in one sense, or the universal solvent, the same *anima mundi* on the higher plane as the *astral light* is on the lower. "At the moment of the sacrifice the priest becomes imbued with the spirit of Brahmâ, is, for the time being, Brahmâ himself". (*Isis Unveiled*).

Alaya (*Sk.*). The Universal Soul (See *Secret Doctrine* Vol. I. pp. 47 *et seq.*). The name belongs to the Tibetan system of the contemplative *Mahâyâna* School. Identical with *Âkâsa* in its mystic sense, and with *Mulâprâkriti,* in its essence, as it is the basis or root of all things.

Antaskarana (*Sk.*)., or Antahkarana. The term has various meanings, which differ with every school of philosophy and sect. Thus Sankârachârya renders the word as "understanding"; others, as "the internal instrument, the Soul, formed by the thinking principle and egoism"; whereas the Occultists explain it as the *path* or bridge between the Higher and the Lower Manas, the divine *Ego*, and the *personal* Soul of man. It serves as a medium of communication between the two, and conveys from the Lower to the Higher Ego all those personal impressions and thoughts of men which can, by their nature, be assimilated and stored by the undying Entity, and be thus made immortal with it, these being the only elements of the evanescent *Personality* that survive death and time. It thus stands to reason that only that which is noble, spiritual and divine in man can testify in Eternity to his having lived.

Anupâdaka (*Sk.*). Anupapâdaka, also Aupapâduka; means parentless", "self-existing", born without any parents or progenitors. A term applied to certain self-created gods, and the Dhyâni Buddhas.

Arûpa (*Sk.*). "Bodiless", formless, as opposed to *rûpa*, "body", or form.

Atmâ (or **Atman**) (*Sk.*). The Universal Spirit, the divine Monad, the 7th Principle, so-called, in the septenary constitution of man. The Supreme Soul.

Avidyâ (*Sk.*). Opposed to *Vidyâ*, Knowledge. Ignorance which proceeds from, and is produced by the illusion of the Senses or *Viparyaya*.

Barhishad (*Sk.*). A class of the "lunar" Pitris or "Ancestors", Fathers, who are believed in popular superstition to have kept up in their past incarnations the household sacred flame and made fire-offerings. Esoterically the Pitris who evolved their shadows or *chhayas* to make there-with the first man. (See *Secret Doctrine*, Vol. II.)

Bodhi or *Sambodhi* (*Sk.*). Receptive intelligence, in contradistinction to *Buddhi*, which is the potentiality of intelligence.

Bodhisattva (*Sk).* Lit., "he, whose essence (*sattva*) has become intelligence (*bodhi*)"; those who need but one more incarnation to become perfect Buddhas, i.e., to be entitled to Nirvâna. This, as applied to *Manushi* (terrestrial) Buddhas. In the metaphysical sense, *Bodhisattva* is a title given to the sons of the celestial *Dhyâni* Buddhas.

Brahma (*Sk.*). The student must distinguish between Brahma the neuter, and Brahmâ, the male creator of the Indian Pantheon. The former, Brahma or Brahman, is the impersonal, supreme and uncognizable Principle of the Universe from the essence of which all emanates, and into which all returns, which is incorporeal, immaterial, unborn, eternal, beginningless and endless. It is all-pervading, animating the highest god as well as the smallest mineral atom. Brahmâ on the other hand, the male and the alleged Creator, exists periodically in his manifestation only, and then again goes into pralaya, i.e., disappears and is annihilated.

Brahmâ Vâch (*Sk.*). Male and female Brahmâ. Vâch is also some-times called the female logos; for Vâch means Speech, literally. (See *Manu* Book I., and *Vishnu Purâna*.)

Buddha (*Sk.*). Lit., "The Enlightened". The highest degree of knowledge. To become a Buddha one has to break through the bondage of sense and personality; to acquire a complete perception of the REAL SELF and learn not to separate it from all otherselves; to learn by experience the utter unreality of all phenomena of the visible Kosmos foremost of all; to reach a complete detachment from all that is evanescent and finite, and live while yet on Earth in the immortal and the everlasting alone, in a supreme state of holiness.

Buddhi (*Sk.*). Universal Soul or Mind. *Mahâbuddhi* is a name of Mahat (see "Alaya"); also the spiritual Soul in man (the sixth principle), the vehicle of Atmâ exoterically the seventh.

Chelâ (*Sk.*). A disciple, the pupil of a Guru or Sage, the follower of some adept of a school of philosophy *(lit.,* child).

Chréstos (*Gr.*). The early Gnostic form of Christ. It was used in the fifth century B.C. by Æschylus, Herodotus, and others. The *Manteumata pythochresta*, or the "oracles delivered by a Pythian god" "through a pythoness, are mentioned by the former (*Choeph*.901). *Chréstian* is not only "the seat of an oracle", but an offering to, or for, the oracle.

Chréstés is one who explains oracles, "a prophet and soothsayer", and Chrésterios one who serves an oracle or a god. The earliest Christian writer, Justin Martyr, in his first *Apology* calls his co-religionists Chréstians. It is only through ignorance that men call themselves Christians instead of Chréstians," says Lactantius (lib. iv., cap. vii.). The terms Christ and Christians, spelt originally Chrést and Chréstians, were borrowed from the Temple vocabulary of the Pagans. Chréstos meant in that vocabulary a disciple on probation, a candidate for hierophantship. When he had attained to this through initiation, long trials, and suffering, and had been *"anointed"* (i.e., "rubbed with oil", as were Initiates and even idols of the gods, as the last touch of ritualistic observance), his name was changed into Christos, the "purified", in esoteric or mystery language. In mystic symbology, indeed, *Christés*, or *Christos,* meant that the "Way", the Path, was already trodden and the goal reached ; when the fruits of the arduous labour, uniting the personality of evanescent clay with the indestructible INDIVIDUALITY, transformed it thereby into the immortal EGO. "At the end of the Way stands the *Chréstes"*, the *Purifier,* and the union once accomplished, the *Chrestos,* the "man of sorrow", became *Christos* himself. Paul, the Initiate, knew this, and meant this precisely, when he is made to say, in bad translation : "I travail in birth again until Christ be formed in you" (Gal. iv.19), the true rendering of which is . . . "until ye form the Christos within yourselves" But the profane who knew only that Chréstés was in some way connected with priest and prophet, and knew nothing about the hidden meaning of Christos, insisted, as did Lactantius and Justin Martyr, on being called *Chréstians* instead of Christians. Every good individual, therefore, may find Christ in his "inner man" as Paul expresses it (Ephes. iii. 16,17), whether he be Jew, Mussulman, Hindu, or Christian. Kenneth Mackenzie seemed to think that the word *Chréstos* was a synonym of Soter, "an appellation assigned to deities, great kings and heroes," indicating "Saviour,"—and he was right. For, as he adds:"It has been applied redundantly to Jesus Christ, whose name Jesus or Joshua bears the same interpretation. The name Jesus, in fact, is rather a title of honour than a name— the true name of the Soter of Christianity being Emmanuel, or God with us (*Matt.*i, 23).Great divinities among all nations, who are represented as expiatory or self-sacrificing, have been designated by the same title." (*R. M. Cyclop.*) The Asklepios (or Æsculapius) of the Greeks had the title of *Soter*.

Daiviprakriti (*Sk.*). Primordial, homogeneous light, called by some Indian Occultists "the Light of the Logos" (see *Notes on the Bhagavat Gita*, by T. Subba Row, B.A., L.L.B.); when differentiated this light becomes FOHAT.

Devachan (*Sk.*). The "dwelling of the gods". A state intermediate between two earth-lives, into which the EGO (Atmâ-Buddhi-Manas, or the Trinity made One) enters, after its separation from Kâma Rupa, and the disintegration of the lower principles on earth.

Dhyan Chohans (*Sk*). Lit., "The Lords of Light". The highest gods, answering to the Roman Catholic Archangels. The divine Intelligences charged with the supervision of Kosmos.

Dhyâna (*Sk.*). In Buddhism one of the six Paramitas of perfection, a state of abstraction which carries the ascetic practising it far above this plane of sensuous perception and out of the world of matter. Lit., "contemplation". The six stages of Dhyan differ only in the degrees of abstraction of the personal Ego from sensuous life.

Fohat (*Tib.*). A term used to represent the active (male) potency of the Sakti (female reproductive power) in nature. The essence of cosmic electricity. An occult Tibetan term for *Daiviprakriti* primordial light: and in the universe of manifestation the ever-present electrical energy and ceaseless destructive and formative power. Esoterically, it is the same, Fohat being the universal propelling Vital Force, at once the propeller and the resultant.

Grihastha (*Sk.*). Lit., "a householder", "one who lives in a house with his family". A Brahman " family priest" in popular rendering, and the sarcerdotal hierarchy of the Hindus.

Gunas (*Sk*). Qualities, attributes (See" Triguna") ; a thread, also a cord.

Guru (*Sk.*). Spiritual Teacher; a master in metaphysical and ethical doctrines; used also for a teacher of any science.

Jnâna (*Sk.*). or *Jhana*. Knowledge; Occult Wisdom.

Kamarupa (*Sk.*). Metaphysically, and in our esoteric philosophy, it is the subjective form created through the mental and physical desires and thoughts in connection with things of matter, by all sentient beings, a form which survives the death of their bodies. After that death three of the seven "principles"—or let us say planes of senses and consciousness on which the human instincts and ideation act in turn—viz., the body, its astral prototype and physical vitality,—being of no further use, remain on earth; the three higher principles, grouped into one, merge into the state of Devachan (*q.v.*), in which state the Higher Ego will remain until the hour for a new reincarnation arrives; and the *eidolon* of the ex-Personality is left alone in its new abode. Here, the pale copy of the man that was, vegetates for a period of time, the duration of which is variable and according to the element of materiality which is left in it, and which is determined by the past life of the defunct. Bereft as it is of its higher mind, spirit and physical senses, if left alone to its own senseless devices, it will gradually fade out and disintegrate. But, if forcibly drawn back into the terrestrial sphere whether by the passionate desires and appeals of the surviving friends or by regular necromantic practices—one of the most pernicious of which is mediumship—the "spook" may prevail for a period greatly exceeding the span of the natural life of its body. Once the Kamarupa has learnt the way back to living human bodies, it becomes a vampire, feeding on the vitality of those who are so anxious for its company. In India these *eidolons* are called *Pisâchas*, and are much dreaded, as already explained elsewhere.

Kshatriya (*Sk.*). The second of the four castes into which the Hindus were originally divided.

Kshetrajna or *Kshetrajneswara* (*Sk.*). Embodied spirit, the Conscious Ego in its highest manifestations; the reincarnating Principle; the "Lord" in us.

Kumâra (*Sk.*). A virgin boy, or young celibate. The first Kumâras are the seven sons of Brahmâ born out of the limbs of the god, in the so-called ninth creation. It is stated that the name was given to them owing to their formal refusal to "procreate their species", and so they "remained Yogis", as the legend says.

Lanoo (*Sk.*). A disciple, the same as "chela".

Laya or *Layam* (*Sk.*). From the root *Li* "to dissolve, to disintegrate" a point of equilibrium (*zero-point*) in physics and chemistry. In occultism, that point where substance becomes homogeneous and is unable to act or differentiate.

Logos (*Gr.*). The manifested deity with every nation and people; the outward expression, or the effect of the cause which is ever concealed. Thus, speech is the Logos of thought; hence it is aptly translated by the "Verbum" and "Word" in its metaphysical sense.

Mahat (*Sk.*). Lit., "The great one". The first principle of Universal Intelligence and Consciousness. In the Purânic philosophy the first product of root-nature or *Pradhâna* (the same as Mulaprakriti); the producer of *Manas* the thinking principle, and of *Ahankâra*, egotism or the feeling of "I am I" (in the lower Manas).

Mahâtma (*Sk.*). Lit., "great soul". An adept of the highest order. Exalted beings who, having attained to the mastery over their lower principles are thus living unimpeded by the "man of flesh", and are in possession of knowledge and power commensurate with the stage they have reached in their spiritual evolution. Called in Pali Rahats and Arhats.

Manas (*Sk.*). Lit., "the mind", the mental faculty which makes of man an intelligent and moral being, and distinguishes him from the mere animal; a synonym of *Mahat*. *Esoterically,* however, it means, when unqualified, the Higher EGO, or the sentient reincarnating Principle in man. When qualified it is called by Theosophists *Buddhi-Manas* or the Spiritual Soul in contradistinction to its human reflection—*Kâma-Manas.*

Mânasa or *Manaswin* (*Sk.*). "The efflux of the *divine* mind," and explained as meaning that this efflux signifies the *manasa* or divine sons of Brahmâ-Virâj. Nilakantha who is the authority for this statement, further explains the term "manasa" by *manomâtrasarira*. These Manasa are the *Arupa* or incorporeal sons of the Prajâpati Virâj, in another version. But as Arjuna Misra identifies Virâj with Brahmâ, and as Brahmâ is Mahat, the universal mind, the exoteric blind becomes plain. The Pitris are identical with the Kumâra, the Vairaja, the Manasa-Putra (mind sons), and are finally identified with the human "Egos".

Manvantara (*Sk.*). A period of manifestation, as opposed to Pralaya (dissolution, or rest), applied to various cycles, especially to a Day of Brahmâ, 4,320,000,000 Solar years—and to the reign of one Manu— 308,448,000. (See Vol. II. of the *Secret Doctrine*, p. 68 *et. seq.*) Lit., *Manuantara*—between Manus.

Mâyâ (*Sk.*). Illusion ; the cosmic power which renders phenomenal existence and the perceptions thereof possible. In Hindu philosophy that alone which is changeless and eternal is called *reality* ; all that which is subject to change through decay and differentiation and which has therefore a beginning and an end is regarded as *mâyâ*—illusion.

Nirmânakâya (*Sk.*). Something entirely different in esoteric philosophy from the popular meaning attached to it, and from the fancies of the Orientalists. Some call the *Nirmânakâya* body "Nirvana with remains" (Schlagintweit, etc.) on the supposition, probably, that it is a kind of Nirvânic condition during which consciousness and form are retained. Others say that it is one of the *Trikâya* (three bodies), with the "power of assuming any form of appearance in order to propagate Buddhism" (Eitel's idea); again, that "it is the incarnate avatâra of a deity" (*ibid.*), and so on. Occultism, on the other hand, says that Nirmânakâya, although meaning literally a transformed "body", is a state. The form is that of the adept or yogi who enters, or chooses, that *post mortem* condition in preference to the Dharmakâya or *absolute* Nirvânic state. He does this because the latter *kâya* separates him for ever from the world of form, conferring upon him a state of *selfish* bliss, in which no other living being can participate, the adept being thus precluded from the possibility of helping humanity, or even *devas*. As a Nirmânakâya, however, the man leaves behind him only his physical body, and retains every other "principle" save the Kamic—for he has crushed this out for ever from his nature, during life, and it can never resurrect in his post mortem state. Thus, instead of going into selfish bliss, he chooses a life of self-sacrifice, an existence which ends only with the life-cycle, in order to be enabled to help mankind in an invisible yet most effective manner. (See *The Voice of the Silence*, third treatise, "The Seven Portals".) Thus a Nirmânakâya is not, as popularly believed, the body "in which a Buddha or a Bodhisattva appears on earth", but verily one, who whether a *Chutuktu* or a *Khubilkhan,* an adept or a yogi during life, has since become a member of that invisible Host which ever protects and watches over Humanity within Karmic limits. Mistaken often for a "Spirit", a Deva, God himself, &c., a Nirmânakâya is ever a protecting, compassionate, verily a *guardian* angel, to him who becomes worthy of his help. Whatever objection may be brought forward against this doctrine; however much it is denied, because, forsooth, it has never been hitherto made public in Europe and therefore since it is unknown to Orientalists, it must needs be "a myth of modern invention"—no one will be bold enough to say that this idea of helping suffering mankind at the price of one's own almost interminable self-sacrifice, is not one of the grandest and noblest that was ever evolved from human brain.

Pitris (*Sk.*). The ancestors, or creators of mankind. They are of seven classes, three of which are incorporeal, *arupa,* and four corporeal. In popular theology they are said to be created from Brahmâ's side. They are variously genealogized, but in esoteric philosophy they are as given in the *Secret Doctrine*. In *Isis Unveiled* it is said of them "It is generally believed that the Hindu term means the spirits of our ancestors, of disembodied people, hence the argument of some Spiritualists that fakirs (and yogis) and other Eastern wonder-workers, are *mediums*. This is in more than one sense erroneous. The Pitris are not the ancestors of the present living men, but those of the human kind, or Adamic races; the spirits of human races, which on the great scale of descending evolution *preceded our races* of men, and they *were physically, as well as spiritually, far superior* to our modern pigmies. In *Mânava Dharma Shâstra* they are called the *Lunar Ancestors*." The *Secret Doctrine* has now explained that which was cautiously put forward in the earlier Theosophical volumes.

Pragna (*Sk.*). or *Prajna*. A synonym of *Mahat* the Universal Mind. The capacity for perception. (*S. D.*, I. 139) Consciousness.

Pralaya (*Sk.*). A period of obscuration or repose—planetary, cosmic or universal—the opposite of Manvantara *(S. D.*, I. 370.).

Rishis (*Sk.*). Adepts; the inspired ones. In Vedic literature the term is employed to denote those persons through whom the various Mantras were revealed.

Rûpa (*Sk.*). Body; any form, applied even to the forms of the gods, which are subjective to us.

Samâdhi (*Sk.*). A state of ecstatic and complete trance. The term comes from the words *Sam-âdha*, "self-possession". He who possesses this power is able to exercise an absolute control over all his faculties, physical or mental; it is the highest state of Yoga.

Samsâra (*Sk.*). Lit., "rotation"; the ocean of births and deaths. Human rebirths represented as a continuous circle, a wheel ever in motion.

Sarîra or *sharira* (*Sk.*). Envelope or body.

Sattva or *Satwa*, (*Sk.*). Goodness; the same as Sattva, or purity, one of the trigunas or three divisions of nature.

Skandha or *Skhanda* (*Sk.*). Lit., "bundles", or groups of attributes; everything finite, inapplicable to the eternal and the absolute. There are five—esoterically, *seven*—attributes in every human living being, which are known as the *Pancha Shandhas*. These are (1) form, *rûpa*; (2) perception, *vidâna*; (3) consciousness, *sanjnâ*; (4) action, *sanskâra*; (5) knowledge, *vidyâna*. These unite at the birth of man and constitute his personality. After the maturity of these Skandhas, they begin to separate and weaken, and this is followed by *jarâmarana*, or decrepitude and death.

Sushupti Avasthâ (*Sk.*). Deep sleep; one of the four aspects of Prânava.

Sûtrâtman (*Sk.*). Lit., "the thread of spirit"; the immortal Ego, the Individuality which incarnates in men one life after the other, and upon which are strung, like beads on a string, his countless Personalities. The universal life-supporting air, *Samashti prau*; universal energy.

Svabhâvat (*Sk.*). Explained by the Orientalists as "plastic substance", which is an inadequate definition. Svabhâvat is the world-substance and stuff, or rather that which is behind it—the spirit and essence of substance. The name comes from *Subhâva* and is composed of three words—**su**, good, perfect, fair, handsome; **sva**, self; and **bkâva**, being, or *state of being*. From it all nature proceeds and into it all returns at the end of the life-cycles. In Esotericism it is called "Father-Mother". It is the plastic essence of matter.

Svasam Vedanâ (*Sk.*). Lit., "the reflection which analyses itself"; a synonym of Paramârtha.

Svapna (*Sk*). A trance or dreamy condition. Clairvoyance.

Tamas (*Sk.*). The quality of darkness, "foulness" and inertia; also of ignorance, as matter is blind. A term used in metaphysical philosophy. It is the lowest of the three *gunas* or fundamental qualities.

Tapas (*Sk.*). "Abstraction", "meditation". "To perform *tapas*" is to sit for *contemplation*. Therefore ascetics are often called Tâpasas.

Theosophia (*Gr.*). Wisdom-religion, or "Divine Wisdom". The substratum and basis of all the world-religions and philosophies, taught and practised by a few elect ever since man became a thinking being. In its practical bearing, Theosophy is purely divine ethics; the definitions in dictionaries are pure nonsense, based on religious prejudice and ignorance of the true spirit of the early Rosicrucians and mediæval philosophers who called themselves Theosophists.

Turîya (*Sk.*). A state of the deepest trance—the fourth state of the Târaka Râja Yoga, one that corresponds with Âtmâ, and on this earth with *dreamless sleep*—a causal condition.

Upâdhi (*Sk.*). Basis; the vehicle, carrier or bearer of something less material than itself: as the human body is the *upâdhi* of its spirit, ether the *upâdhi* of light, etc., etc.; a mould; a defining or limiting substance.

Vâch (Sk.). To call Vâch "speech" simply, is deficient in clearness. Vâch is the mystic personification of speech, and the female *Logos,* being one with Brahmâ, who created her out of one-half of his body, which he divided into two portions; she is also one with Virâj (called the "female" Virâj) who was created in her by Brahmâ. In one sense Vâch is "speech" by which knowledge was taught to man; in another she is the "mystic, secret speech" which descends upon and enters into the primeval Rishis, as the "tongues of fire" are said to have "sat upon" the apostles. For, she is called "the female creator", the "mother of the Vedas", etc., etc. Esoterically, she is the subjective Creative Force which, emanating from the Creative Deity (the subjective Universe, its "privation", or *ideation*) becomes the manifested "world of speech", i.e., the *concrete expression of ideation*, hence the "Word" or Logos. Vâch is "the male and female" Adam of the first chapter of *Genesis*, and thus called "Vâch-Virâj" by the sages. (See *Atharva Veda*.) She is also "the celestial Saraswatî produced from the heavens", a "voice derived from *speechless* Brahmâ" *(Mahâbhârata);* the goddess of wisdom and eloquence. She is called *Sata-rûpa*, the goddess of *a hundred forms*.

Vidyâ (*Sk.*). Knowledge, Occult Science.

Yajna (*Sk.*). "Sacrifice", whose symbol or representation is now the constellation Mriga-shiras (deer-head), and also a form of Vishnu. "The Yajna", say the Brahmans, "exists from eternity, for it proceeded from the Supreme, in whom it lay dormant from *no beginning"*. It is the key to the *Trai-Vidyâ* , the thrice sacred science contained in the *Rig Veda* verses, which teaches the Yajna or sacrificial mysteries. As Haug states in his *Introduction* to the *Aitareya*

Brâhmana—the Yajna exists as an invisible presence at all times, extending from the *Âhavanîya* or sacrificial fire to the heavens, forming a bridge or ladder by means of which the sacrificer can communicate with the world of devas, "and even ascend when alive to their abodes". It is one of the forms of Akâsa, within which the mystic WORD (or its underlying " Sound") calls it into existence. Pronounced by the Priest-Initiate or Yogi, this WORD receives creative powers, and is communicated as an impulse on the terrestrial plane through a trained *Will-power*.

Yogi (*Sk.*). (1) Not "a state of six-fold bodily and mental happiness as the result, of ecstatic meditation" (Eitel) but a state which, when reached, makes the practitioner thereof absolute master of his six principles", *he now being merged in the seventh*. It gives him full control, owing to his knowledge of SELF and Self, over his bodily, intellectual and mental states, which, unable any longer to interfere with, or act upon, his Higher Ego, leave it free to exist in its original, pure, and divine state. (2) Also the name of the devotee who practises Yoga.

Know, Conqueror of Sins, once that a Sowanee hath cross'd the seventh Path, all Nature thrills with joyous awe and feels subdued.

The silver star now twinkles out the news to the night-blossoms, the streamlet to the pebbles ripples out the tale; dark ocean-waves will roar it to the rocks surf-bound, scent-laden breezes sing it to the vales, and stately pines mysteriously whisper: "A Master has arisen, a MASTER OF THE DAY".

He standeth now like a white pillar to the west, upon whose face the rising Sun of thought eternal poureth forth its first most glorious waves. His mind, like a becalmed and boundless ocean, spreadeth out in shoreless space. He holdeth life and death in his strong hand.

Yea, He is mighty. The living power made free in him, that power which is HIMSELF, can raise the tabernacle of illusion high above the gods, above great Brahm and Indra. *Now* he shall surely reach his great reward!

Shall he not use the gifts which it confers for his own rest and bliss, his well-earn'd weal and glory—he, the subduer of the great Delusion?

Nay, O thou candidate for Nature's hidden lore! If one would follow in the steps of holy Tathagata, those gifts and powers are not for Self.

Would'st thou thus dam the waters born on Sumeru? Shalt thou divert the stream for thine own sake, or send it back to its prime source along the crests of cycles?

If thou would'st have that stream of hard-earn'd knowledge, of Wisdom heaven-born, remain sweet running waters, thou should'st not leave it to become a stagnant pond.

Know, if of Amitabha, the "Boundless Age," thou would'st become co-worker, then must thou shed the light acquired, like to the Bodhisattvas twain, upon the span of all three worlds.

Know that the stream of superhuman knowledge and the Deva-Wisdom thou hast won, must, from thyself, the channel of Alaya, be poured forth into another bed.

Know, O Narjol, thou of the Secret Path, its pure fresh waters must be used to sweeter make the Ocean's bitter waves—that mighty sea of sorrow formed of the tears of men.

Alas! when once thou hast become like the fix'd star in highest heaven, that bright celestial orb must shine from out the spatial depths for all—save for itself; give light to all, but take from none.

The Voice of the Silence, 70–73

978-0-979-3205-0-7
0-979-3205-0-X